Other Kaplan Books of Interest to Business School Applicamts

GMAT CAT
GMAT CAT with CD-ROM
GRE/GMAT Math Workbook
Guide to Distance Learning
Yale Daily News Guide to Fellowships and Grants

Business School Admissions Adviser 2000

SELECTION · ADMISSIONS · FINANCIAL AID

by Shari Holmer Lewis and Alice Murphey
and a nationwide team
of business school admissions advisers

Simon & Schuster

Kaplan Books
Published by
Kaplan Educational Centers and Simon & Schuster
1230 Avenue of the Americas
New York, NY 10020

For bulk sales to schools, colleges, and universities, please contact Vice President of Special Markets, Simon & Schuster Special Markets, 1633 Broadway, 8th Floor, New York, NY 10019.

Kaplan® is a registered trademark of Kaplan Educational Centers.

GMAT is a registered trademark of the Graduate Management Admission Council, which is not affiliated with this book.

Contributing Editor: Trent Anderson
Project Editor: Julie Schmidt
Cover Design: Cheung Tai
Interior Page Design: Jobim Rose
Database Administrator: Enid Burns
Production Editor: Maude Spekes
Desktop Publishing Manager: Michael Shevlin
Managing Editor: David Chipps
Executive Editor: Del Franz

Special thanks to Rebecca Argyle, Doreen Beauregard, Jude Bond, Alison May, Kiernan McGuire, Joyce Smith, and Linda Volpano.

Manufactured in the United States of America
Published simultaneously in Canada

July 1999
10 9 8 7 6 5 4 3 2 1

ISBN 0-684-85957-2
ISSN 1097-5381

CONTENTS

AUTHORS

Shari Holmer Lewis is assistant dean for graduate business programs at the University of Illinois—Chicago, where she has also served as director of the M.B.A. program. Prior to coming to UIC, she administered admission, financial aid, and student affairs functions at Northwestern University Medical School. She holds a Ph.D. in German language and literature from Northwestern University and an M.B.A. in finance and public and not-for-profit management from the University of Chicago.

Holmer-Lewis's professional activities include service as primary representative to the Graduate Management Admission Council (GMAC), six years as coordinator of the Chicago M.B.A. Forum, and numerous presentations at the M.B.A. Forums and professional workshops. She was one of the editors of *The Official Guide to Financing Your M.B.A.* A former chair of the Graduate and Professional Financial Aid Council, she now sits on the steering committee of the National Committee on Graduate and Professional Financial Aid.

Alice Murphey is the former director of financial aid at the New York University Stern School of Business/Graduate Division. While at Stern, she worked closely with admissions office personnel in the integration of the admission and financial aid process for entering students. Prior to her tenure at NYU, she held financial aid positions at the University of Southern California and Fordham University. She is currently the assistant director of financial aid for systems management at the City University of New York. She holds an M.Ed. in counselor education from Penn State University.

Murphey has served as an annual presenter for the Graduate Management Admission Council (GMAC) at the M.B.A. Forums for the last six years, and was one of the editors of *The Official Guide to Financing Your M.B.A.*, published by GMAC in 1992, revised 1994. She has also been very active in graduate financial aid organizations. Currently, she is a member of the steering committee for the National Committee for Graduate and Professional Financial Aid.

Chris Rosa, who wrote chapter 16, is director of the Office of Services for Students with Disabilities at Queens College, where he coordinates the provision of support services to more than 450 students with disabilities. A member of the Muscular Dystrophy Association's National Task Force on Public Awareness, Rosa has written several articles published in scholarly journals on the sociology of disability, and is a recipient of the Muscular Dystrophy Association's National Personal Achievement Award. He is currently enrolled in a doctoral program in sociology at the City University of New York Graduate Center.

James W. Schmotter, the author of chapter 1, is dean of the Haworth College of Business at Western Michigan University. Previously, he was dean and professor of management at the College of Business and Economics at Lehigh University, and associate dean and assistant dean for admissions and student affairs at Cornell University's Johnson Graduate School of Management.

James Stevens wrote chapter 17. He is senior associate director of admissions and chairperson of the admissions committee at New York University's Stern School of Business. With over one-third of Stern's applicant pool coming from outside the U.S., he has had extensive experience working with international admissions. Stevens has also held positions in admissions and student services at the University of Michigan and in financial aid at American University. He holds a B.A. in international relations and French from American University and an M.B.A. in marketing and management from the University of Michigan—Ann Arbor.

CONTRIBUTORS

Alex Duke has been involved in M.B.A. admissions since 1987. He is currently associate director of M.B.A. admissions at the John Anderson Graduate School of Management, University of California—Los Angeles. He has also held positions at the University of Illinois—Chicago and Indiana University.

Ben Baron is currently Mid-Atlantic regional director for Kaplan Educational Centers. He received his M.B.A. from Harvard Business School, where he subsequently worked as assistant director of admissions for the school's M.B.A. program.

Nike Irvin is executive director of the Riordan Programs, a career-based outreach program that helps minorities and individuals with little exposure to graduate education to prepare their applications to the nation's top business schools. Irvin is a graduate of Yale University, where she earned a B.A. in economics and political science, and University of California—Los Angeles, where she earned an M.B.A. in marketing. Prior to serving with the Riordan Programs, she worked in brand management for Pepsi-Cola™ and Nestle™.

Dorothy J. Umans is currently the director of graduate admissions at the George Washington University School of Business and Public Management, and has 24 years of admissions experience. She holds an M.B.A., a master's, and an educational specialist degree in counseling and personnel services, and is currently working on her comprehensive exams and dissertation for a Ph.D. in higher education policy. In addition to management consulting and conducting workshops on strategic marketing, Umans has conducted research on doctoral student attrition and retention.

PART ONE

Down to Business

CHAPTER 1

New Directions in Business Schools

by James W. Schmotter

Over the past three decades, the M.B.A. has become the most visible and popular of graduate degrees. More than 90,000 M.B.A. degrees are awarded annually in the United States alone, and the numbers of programs and graduates are proliferating all around the world. In both the business press and more popular media, the behavior and career prospects of M.B.A.'s are repeatedly described, analyzed, and stereotyped. The global selection process for admission to the M.B.A. programs has developed a life of its own, producing hundreds of thousands of GMAT examinations every year, numerous guides and publications, a worldwide recruiting network of admissions forums, and sophisticated ranking systems designed to provide information to prospective consumers of M.B.A. education.

Yet all this media hype has also produced negative publicity. As far back as 1980, a cover story in *Time*, "The Golden Ticket," described in unflattering terms "what M.B.A.'s have done to us." This theme continued throughout the decade of the 1980s, when soaring Wall Street salaries, greed, and M.B.A.'s became synonymous. And more recently, M.B.A.'s—with their command of quantitative financial analysis and the latest management theories—are often held responsible for corporate downsizing, shifting of manufacturing overseas, and other scary aspects of 1990s capitalism. They come in for almost as many jibes in Scott Adams's popular *Dilbert* cartoons as do engineers and bosses. In 1992, a cover article in *Forbes* announced the "M.B.A. Glut" and suggested the degree's value was fading.

So what's the truth? And more importantly, what does all this mean for you, someone who's considering whether or not an M.B.A. is worth the time, effort, and money it will require?

First of all, it's necessary to cut through the marketing and media hype to understand a few things about the multifaceted, evolving phenomenon we call M.B.A. education. The fact is that the M.B.A. remains a very good investment for most business careers. For some careers—for example, investment banking or management consulting—it is virtually a prerequisite. Business schools strive to meet the practical needs of business leaders, and it is certainly still the case that those who wish to attain the highest positions in the world of business would do well to get their M.B.A.'s.

The obvious fact about M.B.A. programs is that—like anything else worthwhile—one gets out of them what one puts into them. Usually the enthusiasm and dedication of the student will be more important to his or her eventual success than the "reputation" or "ranking" of any one program. Woody Allen's famous comment that "80 percent of success is showing up" doesn't pertain to M.B.A. education. Quality programs require effort and commitment from students.

Segments of the M.B.A. Market

M.B.A. programs differ in terms of their histories, the reputations of their missions, and financial resources. It's important that the prospective M.B.A. applicant realize this as he or she considers to which schools to apply. Increasingly, the M.B.A. landscape has become stratified and differentiated, with individual schools seeking to identify and exploit particular niches in the market. Indeed, the mission-based accreditation standards of AACSB, the International Association for Management Education, encourage such differentiation. There are currently at least five broad segments of this market, each encompassing many variations.

Full-Time Programs Aspiring to National or International Reputations

These schools are generally highly selective, feature carefully cultivated corporate relationships, and charge premium tuition. Such programs are the marquee players in the industry; they are the names that most frequently appear in national rankings as well as the wannabes who aspire to play in the big leagues. They influence the entire field of M.B.A. education through the research of their faculties and, often, through innovations that their substantial financial resources permit. Examples of such programs are the Harvard Business School, the Amos Tuck School at Dartmouth College, Stanford University, the

University of Chicago, and the Fuqua School at Duke University. Internationally, INSEAD in France, the London Business School, and Hong Kong University of Science and Technology fall into this category.

Regionally Oriented Programs that Successfully Meet the Needs of Local Employers

Such programs, both full and part time, usually focus on local industries and economic needs, and often do not provide the breadth of curriculum that the national programs do. Such programs often partner closely with corporate constituents to ensure that their academic programs address business needs in the region. Examples of such programs are the University of Santa Clara in California's Silicon Valley and Baruch College of the City University of New York.

Large, Part-Time Programs Designed to Meet the Needs of Working Professionals

This is perhaps the largest sector of M.B.A. education, and nearly every region of the nation contains such programs. The best of these understand their mission and develop programs and schedules specifically designed to meet the needs of evening or weekend students. It is also in this category that the most innovative advances in new learning delivery methods, such as distance learning and Internet instruction, are taking place. Examples of such programs include New York University, DePaul University in Chicago, and Georgia State University in Atlanta.

Executive M.B.A. Programs

Executive M.B.A. programs are a particular category that has developed, especially in major metropolitan areas, to meet the special educational needs of executives more experienced than the usual M.B.A. student. Executive M.B.A. programs are usually intense experiences scheduled on weekends. Their performance expectations and costs are high, and most participants are sponsored by their companies.

Smaller, Unaccredited Programs

Often found at private colleges and universities, these programs have arisen in the past twenty years to take advantage of the growth of M.B.A. education. While some of these programs do an excellent job at serving local markets with high-quality education, many are simply revenue-generating devices with low standards that offer minimal educational or career value to their graduates. If an M.B.A. program looks too convenient or easy, it probably is, and the applicant should carefully assess the faculty backgrounds and student experiences of such programs.

Reforms and Innovations

M.B.A. education has undergone rapid and significant change over the past decade. In response to criticism from the corporate world and thanks to the creative thinking of professors and deans on many campuses, business schools have engaged in an exciting array of reforms and innovations. Some of the most important of these changes include:

Integration of Subject Material from a Variety of Academic Areas into the Required Core Curriculum

Some M.B.A. programs have eliminated traditional required courses in areas such as accounting, finance, economics, and organizational behavior. Instead, they have combined this material into academic experiences that demonstrate how these intellectual areas fit together in the real world of business practice. Often such experiences are delivered by teams of faculty members from different academic disciplines, with the active involvement of business practitioners.

Self-Assessment Exercises and Personal Skills Development for Students

Increasingly, business schools are developing orientation programs that encourage students to engage in honest self-assessment not only of academic abilities, but also of personal communication and teamwork styles, career interests, and individual strengths and weaknesses. Often, such programs are followed by required or optional personal skills training outside the required curriculum.

Increased Use of Student Projects

Nearly all M.B.A. programs now feature extensive opportunities for students to gain direct experience in the group project work so common in today's business environment. This takes place in individual courses everywhere, but at some schools, larger project assignments for outside constituents are required. The University of Michigan's Management Assistance Program or Wharton's Field Application Project are especially good examples of such project assignments.

Attention to the Global Dimension of Business

The majority of M.B.A. programs now affirm their commitment to preparing students for the interconnected global economy of the 21st century. Some do this through changes in individual courses; others through the expansion of exchange opportunities with business schools overseas or through teaching their own courses abroad, usually in a concentrated format. A few specialized programs, such as the

---

The International Angle

Graduate training and work experience in international business have become the quickest way up the ladder in many corporations. "Most people who rise to the top have worked overseas," says Joel Davis, a Gillette senior vice president, "and the majority have had multiple foreign postings." Any business school that hopes to survive offers its students at least brief exposure to foreign countries, as well as studies in international management.

—adapted from Newsweek/Kaplan's
How to Choose a Career and Graduate School, 1999

University of South Carolina's Master in International Business, the Thunderbird Graduate School of International Management near Phoenix, and the Wharton School's Lauder Institute at the University of Pennsylvania require foreign language competency.

Greater and More Innovative Use of Information Technology

While most business schools are endeavoring to keep apace with rapid changes in technology in their management information systems courses, some are creatively employing concepts such as groupware and the World Wide Web to facilitate new kinds of learning experiences. Duke's Fuqua School, for example, coordinates its worldwide Executive M.B.A. Program through a sophisticated software package that permits participants to stay in touch on a regular basis across time zones and continents.

Greater Attention to Entrepreneurship and Small Business Management

Historically, M.B.A. programs have built academic programs to meet the needs of the large companies that were the largest hirers of their graduates. In recent years, however, they have understood that exciting opportunities await their students in the smaller and medium-sized businesses that provide most U.S. job creation. The result has been the development of very successful programs for small businesses and entrepreneurship. Stanford, UCLA, and the Wharton School are only three examples of the exciting work going on in this area.

> ### *Catering to Entrepreneurs*
>
> With failure rates of 40 to 80 percent for companies in their first five years, more and more young entrepreneurs are clamoring for classes that will put them ahead of the pack. The result: in the last few years, dozens of top M.B.A. programs across the country have begun offering classes in entrepreneurial studies.
>
> —adapted from Newsweek/Kaplan's *Careers 2000*

Growth in New Ways to Deliver M.B.A. Education

One of the largest changes in part-time M.B.A. education in the 1990s has been the development of opportunities for students to tailor their studies to their personal schedules through distance learning. Delivered by satellite relay, compressed video, the Internet, or videos, M.B.A. education is reaching audiences in many new ways. While none can argue with the convenience implicit in these new delivery modes, debate continues on campuses about the quality of the experience. But it is clear that these new approaches are here to stay.

Attention to the Realities of Human Diversity in the Workplace of the 21st Century

M.B.A. schools are working to change curricula to take into account the implications of the changing demographics of the American market and workforce as well as the ramifications of global competition. In recognition of the fact that certain groups are underrepresented in boardrooms, sincere efforts toward affirmative action continue.

Responsiveness to Students

The growing importance of media rankings as well as faculty members' own work on areas such as Game Theory and Continuous Improvement have made business schools increasingly responsive to the concerns and priorities of their students. Students are now routinely surveyed on a variety of academic and professional issues, and occasionally play active and equal roles with faculty members in areas such as curriculum development and admissions decision making. This tendency to view M.B.A. students as customers has played an important role in recent changes in academic programs on many campuses.

Business schools are among the most vibrant and successful components of universities all around the world. By practicing what they preach, they have continued to adjust to economic and market changes and continue to provide arguably the best preparation for the challenging careers of business in the 21st century.

Is an M.B.A. a necessary prerequisite to a successful business career? Of course not. Just ask Bill Gates, Richard Branson, or Mary Kay Ash. But, putting aside the unusual genius of people like those listed above, can an M.B.A. help you achieve more success and satisfaction in your career? Absolutely. If, that is, you're willing to approach it with the seriousness and dedication that any important venture in life requires. And that starts with a careful and systematic examination of what individual schools offer and a candid self-assessment of your priorities. You'll find help in both regards in the pages ahead. Good luck!

CHAPTER 2

Should You Get an M.B.A.?

The simple fact that you are reading this book indicates that you have already given the question above some thought and are considering pursuing an M.B.A. degree. But since this question is so basic and will arise in various forms throughout the process of selecting and completing an M.B.A. program, it is useful to review it again.

The M.B.A. as an Investment

The M.B.A. degree is a major personal investment of time and money. Although the degree has become widely popular in recent years, it may not be the appropriate choice for meeting your career goals. You need to consider whether you can do what you want to do in your career without the M.B.A., or whether another degree or non-degree study would serve you just as well or better, perhaps for a smaller investment of time and money.

Your education may be the second largest investment you make in your life, after the purchase of a house. It is such a major investment because it demands so much of your time and can be expensive. Although there are a growing number of exceptions, the typical full-time M.B.A. program still requires two academic years of study, usually with an internship between the first and second years of the program. Part-time students often spend four or more years of evenings and weekends finishing a program. As for the financial side of the calculation, if you plan to study full time, you need to consider the foregone earnings from the months you are not working, as well as direct educational costs, such as tuition, fees, and books. The potential financial return on this investment is, of course, your future earning potential, which, on an annual basis, could be significantly enhanced by the degree.

Most people would agree that the purchase of a home typically should not be made on the spur of the moment. Rather, the decision should be preceded by an examination of the financial aspects of the purchase, the house's location, projected resale value, and quality. The same is true of your investment in an M.B.A. education. The value of your degree will be greatly enhanced if you approach this decision with as much care as the decision to buy a house, and perhaps even more—many people will own more than one house over the course of a lifetime, but no one earns more than one M.B.A. degree.

What Do You Want from the Degree?

For many purposes, the M.B.A. degree is the straightest road between where you are now and where you want to go. Career advancement, management expertise, and increased earnings are some of the common reasons given for pursuing an M.B.A. You are the best judge of the suitability of the M.B.A. to help you achieve your goals.

Career Advancement

Your primary consideration in obtaining an M.B.A. may be a desire to enhance your ability to gain a position of greater responsibility in your current field. The additional responsibility may come as a result of managing others, and/or of making a direct personal contribution to the organization for which you work.

Career Change

It is not at all unusual for someone to use the M.B.A. degree as a means of switching career focus. This change may be from one area of business to another—e.g., from marketing or sales to human resources or finance—or to obtain a business or management position after working as a practitioner in a field such as nursing, teaching, music performance, or free-lance writing. It is also not uncommon for individuals who have expertise in engineering, medicine, education, social work, and the arts to seek an M.B.A. degree to allow them to move from the practitioner side of the field to a management or administrative position that capitalizes on both their management training and their field experience.

Some individuals who pursue an M.B.A. are particularly interested in starting their own business or acquiring the skills that will allow them to develop a business they currently operate. In addition to formal knowledge, the degree may provide a higher level of credibility in working with clients and customers and in communicating business plans and goals with bankers and other business partners.

You may have a specific career goal in mind and aspire to a position that "requires" an M.B.A. It is often helpful to consider why this requirement exists. Is it because of the knowledge and training that is needed in the position and that is gained in an M.B.A. program, or is it because the employer uses the M.B.A. degree as a screening device for prospective employees? If it is solely the latter, you may be able to attain the specific job you want by demonstrating capabilities through job performance or other means.

However, since M.B.A. programs can be very demanding, completion of such a program can demonstrate to a prospective employer that you have the persistence, energy, and even time management skills to succeed in a demanding job, as well as specific knowledge and skills. And successfully completing such a program may give you a boost of self-confidence that will manifest itself in your future business dealings.

> ### Confidence Booster
>
> "My M.B.A. has given me a better framework for understanding business and for appreciating the language and realities of business. It also gave me confidence to know that my 'gut' on things was usually right. An M.B.A. can be a real confidence booster."
>
> —M.B.A., Harvard Business School

Specific Management Training

The acquisition of specific management training and expertise is another common reason for pursuing an M.B.A. Although the M.B.A. is, by definition, a general management degree, most programs provide opportunities to study one or more areas in greater depth. However, if you have a single focus and need in-depth work in one field only, you may want to consider a specialized master's program, a set of courses in the area that you complete as a nondegree student or student-at-large, or even nonuniversity based courses, seminars, and workshops. You need to decide whether you want the combination of the general master's degree with some specialized work in the field, the greater depth of a specialized degree program, or training outside a graduate or professional degree program. If you are looking for knowledge of a few specific topics, executive education programs, typically workshops or seminars lasting from a few hours to several days, may provide the training you need.

Earn More Money

Many M.B.A. graduates realize more than marginal income enhancement upon completion of their degrees. Individuals with M.B.A.'s, in general, have higher average salaries than most individuals with a comparable amount of work experience, but with only a bachelor's degree. The most immediate way to measure the incremental financial value of an M.B.A. is to compare the salary a person received prior to starting full-time study in an M.B.A. program and the starting salary the same person received upon graduation. Although a similar approach can be taken in evaluating the benefits of part-time M.B.A. study, the number of career events that can occur during the course of study make a comparison more difficult. Part-time students usually do not suffer the same loss of income while they are in school, but may also not reap any benefits as quickly, since it takes longer to finish. Hence the financial rewards of finishing a part-time program may not be tied as closely to actual degree completion as those of a full-time program.

The M.B.A. degree does not guarantee a fabulous job at a fabulous salary. When you look at placement and salary reports from schools or in the media, remember that half of the salaries listed fall below the average, and that salaries are influenced by local conditions. But even if the financial rewards are not all you hoped for, don't lose sight of the fact that the M.B.A. degree may give you greater job mobility, access to positions that offer greatly enhanced job satisfaction, a network of contacts, or other nonfinancial advantages.

Full Time or Part Time?

If you do decide to get an M.B.A., you will have to decide whether to study full time or part time. Both types of programs offer advantages and disadvantages. You should make yourself aware of the implications of both forms of study before you commit to any M.B.A. program.

Pros and Cons of Full-Time Study

Full-time M.B.A. study traditionally means that you leave your job and go back to school full time. Typically, it also means that you are free of geographic ties and can consider a program anywhere in the country, indeed anywhere in the world. You have greater flexibility in choosing an M.B.A. program and the advantage of devoting your full attention to your course of study and your job search at the end of your program.

Course Work

M.B.A. programs can be very demanding and may require long hours of study and group work. It is not unusual for each course to require 12 or more hours of study each week, in addition to class time and group meetings. As a full-time student, you can focus your attention solely on the program and gain the maximum benefit from the academic work. Since you will get the degree only once, you don't have the chance to go back and redo it if you didn't devote enough time to your studies the first time around.

Networking

Course work is not the only area on which you will spend time. Many full-time programs offer a broad range of extracurricular or social activities that aid your professional growth and strengthen your personal network. Discipline-based clubs, in such areas as marketing, information systems, or health care, may sponsor speakers from corporations or professional organizations that provide insight into current developments in business and access to information about careers. Active participation, particularly in a leadership role, can help develop management skills and demonstrate them to a future employer.

The network that you build among your classmates during the months of studying, working, and, sometimes, living together in a full-time M.B.A. program is one of the greatest advantages of following this route. Personal and professional networks provide immediate access to a set of individuals whom you know and trust, whether you are looking for a lead on a supplier for a company project, a possible solution to a problem, the name of a prospective new employee, or a referral of a position for yourself. The phrase *It's not what you know, but who you know* may not capture the full reality of today's management environment, but it does express the true power of networks.

Job Opportunities and Internships

The opportunity to gain professional experience during the program, either through a summer job or a professional internship, is another advantage of full-time study. Whatever your professional background, this work experience can be valuable in testing out your interest in a specific functional area or in providing you with credentials in an area in which you do not yet have experience.

Study Abroad

Another benefit of full-time study is the chance to participate in an international study program. Although some schools offer short sessions that may be meshed with the obligations of a full-time job, most study-abroad opportunities entail full-time involvement over an extended period of time. It is often not practical or possible to participate in these programs if you are not a full-time student.

Making Connections

"I attended B-school full time. I am still 'connected' to many of my classmates and I believe that over the course of my career, I will come into important business contact with them."

—M.B.A., Harvard Business School

"Going full time is the best way to make strong connections with a large number of your classmates. Business school can be all-consuming academically and socially. My colleagues were the best part about business school, and I wouldn't have done it any other way."

—M.B.A., Stanford Graduate School of Business

Placement

Placement opportunities may be the most visible of the advantages of full-time study. Placement services at many schools are geared primarily toward assisting graduating full-time students with their job search.

Looking for a job is a job in and of itself. Some placement directors consider the time demands of a job search equivalent to that of a heavy course. You need to factor the job search time and stresses into your planning not only of your coursework, but also of your family and personal life.

Family Ties

Many M.B.A. students return to school after several years in the work force and may already be married, perhaps even the parent of one or more children. Spouses and children may be left out of program activities, forcing a choice between participation in career-enhancing activities and family obligations. And if your choice of program causes you to relocate, your spouse and children will of course be affected.

Some students try to avoid relocation issues by assuming long commutes from home to a full-time program. This tactic eliminates the problems of moving family and finding new jobs and schools, but can also consume vast quantities of the student's time. This may preclude participation in worthwhile professional and social activities at school, which form one of the primary advantages of full-time over part-time study.

Financial Cost

Perhaps the greatest disadvantage of full-time study is its financial cost. In addition to the expense of tuition, fees, books, and related items, students who leave a full-time job to return to school experience a loss of the income that had paid living expenses and provided savings. You cannot assume that you will be able to find and hold even a part-time job while you are a full-time M.B.A. student, especially during your first year of study. If you relocate with your working spouse, there is no guarantee that the job your spouse finds will offer equivalent pay or satisfaction to the one left behind. Other relocation issues, such as a house and even moving expenses, can add to the financial burden. Although financial aid is available, and is discussed later in this book, financial issues are often one of the key factors in tipping the balance toward part-time study.

Pros and Cons of Part-Time Study

Although most articles that appear in the media are written about full-time M.B.A. programs, there are more students in part-time programs in the United States than in full-time programs. Part-time study, however, has its own set of pros and cons.

The Long Haul

Unlike full-time programs, which can usually be completed in two years or less, the minimum time to degree for part-time studies is rarely less than two and a half years and often three to four years. The maximum time to degree typically falls in the range of five to seven years. When you think about the time commitment you will need to make in completing your M.B.A., you need to think about how this commitment will fit with your professional obligations and family responsibilities over the entire course of study.

Flexibility

On the other hand, the flexibility of being able to choose terms of enrollment and to not have to commit yourself to a block of 21 or more months is one of the advantages of part-time study in many programs. Additionally, there may be multiple times during the year that you can start a part-time program, whereas many full-time programs restrict your entry to the fall term.

As a part-time student, you may have the option of not registering for courses in a given term. If your job pressures are seasonal, if you experience a major family change, or if you simply need a break in the demands of your schedule, the chance to take classes out of your schedule for a few months can make program completion possible when it otherwise might not be. On occasion, a part-time student may take a leave of absence from a program for a year or two to accept an assignment elsewhere in the country or overseas.

Such program breaks add up, however, and can soon push you to the limit of time to degree. If you run up against the time limit, you may be able to petition for an extension of the time to degree, but you cannot assume that it will be approved. You may need to become a full-time student for one or more terms to finish your course work. In the worst case scenario, difficulties in managing your time to degree may lead to a dead end. You may need to start over, perhaps at another institution, or be satisfied with an incomplete degree.

In most part-time programs, you will be able to decide your individual course load each term. There are several strategies that you can employ in making the work load of the program more manageable. Since M.B.A. programs typically require a mix of quantitative and nonquantitative courses, the combination of courses you choose to take in any given term can make the program more or less manageable for you. If you have an engineering background, for example, you may find it very easy to handle two quantitative courses in one term and possible to manage one quantitative and one nonquantitative course in the same term, whereas two nonquantitative courses with extensive reading lists may be difficult. A social science or English major may plot a different strategy. If your job demands are seasonally heavy, you may be able to complete one carefully selected course during that period instead of taking the term off.

> ## Costs of Flexibility
>
> The very flexibility of part-time study is also one of its disadvantages. Your classmates are unlikely to follow the same pattern of course enrollment as you. It is usually more difficult to form the close relationships facilitated by the full-time experience. Part-time students spend limited time on campus and are less likely to be involved in school-related activities outside the classroom.

The extended period of study in a part-time program allows you to spread your cost over a greater span of time and may make it possible to finance your education out of your current income, if you do not receive tuition assistance from your employer. Tuition reimbursement plans can greatly reduce the out-of-pocket costs to you.

Financial Cost

There is, however, a financial cost to the extended time to degree in a part-time program. Tuition levels tend to rise each year; the more years you spend in a program, the more tuition increases you are likely to experience. You also need to consider how the decision to take more or fewer courses at a time may impact your final cost, given the tuition and fee structure of the program. In some programs, every student pays the same amount of fees, regardless of hours on enrollment. In this case, a full-time student may pay these fees only four times, whereas a part-time student may pay them eight or more times. Similarly, the flat tuition rate offered by many schools to full-time students allows students to take 18 credit hours for the same price as 12; part-time students may not have an equivalent opportunity for a "quantity discount."

Employment Issues

Although graduate management education can contribute to your career advancement, whether you attend full time or part time, the story for part-time students is far more complicated than it is for full-time students who seek a new job, degree in hand, upon graduation. Employers who hire graduates of full-time M.B.A. programs know they are getting an M.B.A. Some companies have programs in which they hire holders of a baccalaureate degree with the requirement that they earn an M.B.A. while in training, but most part-time students are in positions in which there is no expectation that they will pursue advanced study. This difference makes it important for you to investigate your company's policy and culture regarding the value of an M.B.A.

Balancing Act

Your success in completing an advanced management degree while remaining employed full time may depend in part on your company's willingness to provide support in terms of both time and job flexibility. The more demanding your job, the more likely that such is the case. Academic terms and cycles of papers and exams will inevitably conflict with business cycles, business travel, and other professional obligations.

If you have substantial control over your schedule, work predictable hours with few exceptions, or have a supportive employer who will grant you flexibility in your hours and responsibilities and in scheduling business travel, there should be few problems. However, if your job is all-consuming during certain periods of time, you may find that you need to interrupt your studies and not enroll for courses during the terms that coincide with these business cycles. These interruptions will lengthen the time to degree. Some part-time programs are essentially lock step; that is, the students move through the program together following a set registration pattern. Lock step programs do not readily accommodate breaks in enrollment.

Strong Bargaining Position

"[. . .]Though the chances of landing a solid job offer right after graduation are somewhat higher for [students at full-time programs], if you've been going to school part time, you still have your day job and can probably bargain for a deserved raise or take your time looking around."

—"The Postgraduate," *GQ*, February 1996

Company Attitudes Toward Education

Whereas some companies strongly encourage their employees to obtain graduate management education, others are not as supportive. Often, nonsupportive companies are concerned about the job mobility employees attain along with their degrees. In part, they may be worried that current employees will form expectations about their future with the company as a result of the M.B.A., and, if these expectations are not met, will depart for greener fields elsewhere. This climate makes degree completion more difficult. Under these circumstances, leaving your job for full-time study may be a preferable alternative.

Some companies clearly recognize the value of further education for their employees, but have turned away from support of full degree programs toward in-house training programs or shorter certificate programs. These companies prefer the direct connection they see between focused, just-in-time learning and the company's bottom line to the more tenuous connection between this bottom line and lengthy M.B.A. studies.

Tuition Reimbursement

Many companies provide educational benefits that subsidize tuition expenses for employees who pursue additional study. The various kinds of benefits companies may offer are discussed in more detail in chapter 13. In general, large companies are more likely to support additional education for employees, particularly through reimbursement of tuition costs, than are small and medium-sized enterprises (SMEs). In part, this difference can be attributed simply to the greater financial resources available in a large firm. However, it is also possible that owners of some small companies may feel threatened by overeducated employees. Here again, full-time study may be the preferable route, especially given the placement support for graduates of many full-time programs.

Job Transfer

What if you anticipate receiving a transfer to another job location? Should you start an M.B.A.? M.B.A. programs, unlike many undergraduate programs, often have strict limits on the amount of course work and number of credit hours you can transfer into a degree program. Most recognize, however, that part-time students may face relocation issues, and allow transferred students to complete credits at the end of their program at an approved institution.

Executive M.B.A. Programs

If you have a significant amount of experience, such as 10–15 years in middle management or in charge of a small business, and you plan to continue with your current employer, you may wish to investigate the possibility of attending an executive M.B.A. program. These programs, a growing area for many business schools, essentially bring together individuals with similar educational needs and provide a focused, intensive learning experience, and can be described as "mini-M.B.A.'s". Most often, classes meet on weekends or alternating Fridays and Saturdays.

The E.M.B.A. Advantage

"If you are looking for training in very specific areas, perhaps much of a typical M.B.A. program's curriculum would not be of interest to you. Executive education would probably make more sense for you to pursue, particularly if you aren't concerned with getting the formal M.B.A. degree credential."

—Former admissions official, Harvard Business School

One advantage of the executive M.B.A. model is that the program may often be completed in two years while maintaining full-time employment, in contrast to the length of most part-time programs. Admission may be limited to students who have been nominated by a sponsoring corporation. Since the cohort of students who start the program together usually complete the entire program together, all taking exactly the same set of courses, you usually cannot choose an area of interest for advanced study.

If no executive M.B.A. program is available in your area and you are able to "commute" to an appropriate program in another city, you may wish to explore having your company pay your way to attend a full-time program. Under this type of arrangement, you would typically be obligated to return to your sponsoring employer for a minimum period of time or to repay the cost of your education. On occasion, an employer will sponsor someone to attend a full-time program even if an executive M.B.A. program is available locally. Firms may be particularly inclined to choose the full-time route if the employee needs to master a specific field, is targeted for advancement, does not have the work experience required for executive M.B.A. study, or meets other special criteria.

With the information provided in this chapter, you should be in a position to answer the three big questions: Should I get an M.B.A.? What do I want to get out of the degree? Should I attend full time or part time? The next step is to start looking for a program that matches your needs.

PART TWO

Selecting a Program

CHAPTER 3

Starting Your Search

There are nearly 800 M.B.A. programs in the United States alone (281 of which are accredited by the AACSB), and the number abroad is growing rapidly. It's a daunting task to sort through all the information available to identify the programs that are right for you.

Researching M.B.A. Programs

M.B.A. programs make academic, admissions, and other general information available to prospective students, and the simplest way to get this information is to write or call the office of programs that interest you or to visit school Web sites. Other sources of information include media reports highlighting selected programs or developments, alumni, current students, and recruiters.

M.B.A. Forums

The series of M.B.A. school fairs known as M.B.A. Forums that are sponsored by the Graduate Management Admission Council (GMAC) each year are a great source of information and an excellent way to browse among programs. Representatives of more than 75 graduate management schools from the U.S. and abroad are available at each Forum to answer questions about their programs.

> ### Go to the Forum
>
> "I attended an M.B.A. Forum that gave me an opportunity to meet alumnae and talk to current students. For me, meeting the students and alumnae was the major reason that I picked my program. The Forum allowed me to make the right choice."
>
> —M.B.A., Yale University

These events can be helpful in the following ways:

- They are a source of general information about M.B.A. programs that will help you identify the attributes of a program that will meet your needs

- Once you have decided what characteristics of a graduate management program are most important to you, they can help you find schools that meet that profile

- If you have identified a group of programs to which you plan to apply; it may be possible for you to arrange an individual meeting with a school representative before or after an M.B.A. Forum to talk at greater length about the program and your qualifications

The schedule of M.B.A. Forums typically includes eight cities in the U.S., and sites in Asia, Europe and Canada. Six U.S. Forum sites are permanent, with events every year; these are Boston, New York, Chicago, Los Angeles, San Francisco, and Washington, DC. Two additional U.S. Forums rotate among cities in various regions of the country. The exact calendar of sites and dates is determined annually.

Information about the GMAC M.B.A. Forums is available on the M.B.A. Explorer Web site, http://www.gmat.org, or by calling (800) 537-7982 (or (609) 683-2230 from outside the U.S. or Canada). You may also send an inquiry by fax to (609) 279-9149.

The M.B.A. Forums also include "Destination M.B.A.," a series of half-day workshops designed to acquaint underrepresented minorities with graduate management education and career possibilities. Scheduled in cities around the United States., the Destination M.B.A. programs are often held in conjunction with the M.B.A. Forums, allowing attendance at both on the same day. In those cities in which no M.B.A. Forum is scheduled, the Destination M.B.A. workshop is often complemented by a school fair or other activity.

Kaplan M.B.A. Forums

Kaplan M.B.A. Forums will be held in October, 1999 in several cities. Visit www.kaplan.com, the Kaplan Web site (AOL keyword: Kaplan), or call 1-800 KAP-TEST to get information about these forums and additional events.

Kaplan Educational Centers holds several events and seminars throughout the year on the secrets of the GMAT, how to get into business school, women and M.B.A.'s, and several other topics. At these forums, attendees will meet representatives from individual business schools, learn about the application process, and listen to panelists discuss how an M.B.A. has enhanced their career.

Graduate Management Admission Search Service

The Graduate Management Admission Search Service (GMASS℠) is a free service that makes your name available to schools whose specifications for applicants match the profile you furnish when you register for the Graduate Management Admission Test (GMAT). This automatic service will bring you mailings from many schools about their M.B.A. programs, admission procedures, and financial aid.

Program Brochures and Materials

M.B.A. programs prepare a wide variety of materials to assist prospective students in learning about them. When you request information from a school, ask them to send you both a brochure and a course catalog, so you can review both the overall structure and philosophy of the program as well the specific courses that will be available to you. If possible, obtain a list of courses taught in the past and current years as well as projected course offerings for the coming year. If you have an interest in a particular course or field, make sure that there will be adequate coverage of your interest when you reach that part of the program.

Most B-schools have Web sites offering the most recent data available about their programs. Since some of these sites are also used to post materials of interest to current students, they can be an excellent source of information about clubs, activities, corporate recruitment visits, and course schedules that is not included in the program's general brochure or that may not be mentioned as extensively in the printed materials.

Increasingly, programs also have CD-ROMs that contain information about the school, students, curriculum, and surrounding geographic area. In addition to giving you the profile of the latest class admitted to the program, program materials provide an insight into the culture of the program. Many programs send copies of recent newspaper or magazine articles about the program.

Visit the School

In addition to the materials you can obtain from M.B.A. programs themselves, there are a variety of ways to get information and a feel for the programs that interest you. Attend open houses and receptions hosted by the school; many schools schedule these both on their campus and in cities around the country, often to coincide with the M.B.A. Forums. These functions usually provide a less crowded, hectic atmosphere than you will encounter at the M.B.A. Forums, and will allow you to speak with a school representative, alumni, or current students at much greater length.

For all the reasons you are unlikely to buy a house sight unseen or a car without taking a test drive, it is important to visit the program you are seriously considering. Seeing the campus will help you visualize what it would be like to study there. You will certainly spend some time meeting with individuals in the admissions office, but make sure you have an opportunity to speak with students who are not involved in the admissions and recruitment effort. M.B.A. students tend

Try Out a Course

If you plan to study part time, some schools allow you to take a course as a nondegree student before applying to the degree program. If the program requires certain prerequisites that you do not have, consider taking them at the school at which you are planning to study for your M.B.A. This will give you the opportunity to personally experience conditions in the program before committing yourself to it.

to spend a lot of time in the building where they have class, and you should be able to find a few in the hall between classes, in the student lounge or cafeteria, or in the placement office.

Ask students how they feel about the environment in which they are studying. Do you like the current students you have met? Do they seem like the kind of people you would enjoy knowing and working with? The best predictor of the personality of your future classmates is the personality of the current group of students. Sit in on a class session. Is the material challenging? Does it excite you? Is the class-room atmosphere one that matches your learning style?

Guidebooks

A wide variety of guidebooks have appeared on the shelves of bookstores in recent years. Although many are oriented primarily toward dispensing advice, they often include pieces of both objective and subjec-tive information about M.B.A. programs. However, most books cover only a very small subset of the programs you can consider. It is important that you do not limit your search to these few profiled pro-grams, since none of them may be appropriate for your goals and aspirations.

Nonetheless, the different perspectives of the various guides may suggest questions to you that you did not previously have. Or they may contain a quote or piece of data that will shed light on a specific area of interest. In using these sources, you need to remember that admissions officers providing informa-tion to any guide are doing so in the hopes of expanding their marketing reach to qualified and attractive candidates, however the particular program in question may define those qualities.

Web Sites

An excellent source of general information about M.B.A. programs and admissions is the M.B.A. Explorer Web site (http://www.gmat.org). This site is maintained by the Graduate Management Admission Council (GMAC), an international organization of 121 graduate schools of management with the mission to create awareness of management education and to extend access to it. It provides information about types of programs, M.B.A. admission requirements, the Graduate Management Admission Test (GMAT), and M.B.A. careers. It also contains a database of individual school programs that allows you to search for program in a particular state in the United States or in other countries, or to seek out a program with specific features.

Check out This Site

The comprehensive site www.mbainfo.com provides details on more than 1,800 M.B.A. programs around the world.

The individual school profile form for each school included in the M.B.A. Explorer database covers such areas as enroll-ment, tuition, and projected living expenses, types of mas-ter's and joint degree programs offered, minimum time to degree, entrance dates, characteristics of the student body, types of financial assistance available, and average starting salaries. Not all schools with program entries supply information about all these elements. When reviewing the information that is provided, it is important that you scroll to the very end of each profile to check the date on which the information was last updated. You will gain a false impression of the differences between schools if you compare older data from one school to more recent data from another.

You will also find contact information for each program at this site. Most Internet locations listed here are linked to the M.B.A. Explorer, providing quick and easy access to the individual school Web pages. Individual school Web sites are often the most timely source of information about the program, since they can be updated quickly and without the major expense of printing a new brochure.

Alumni, Business Persons, and Recruiters

The objective data about a program will provide numbers and facts, but may tell you very little about the actual experience you will have at a particular school. Conversations with alumni, members of the business community, and corporate recruiters can supply valuable clues about the program's culture, general reputation, and specific placement strengths. Remember, however, that the program may have changed since alumni attended and that subsequent experience may have colored their perceptions.

The most important question to ask alumni may be whether or not, knowing what they now know about their alma mater, they would choose to attend it again for an M.B.A., or would recommend the program to a close friend or relative. Whether the answer is "yes" or "no," find out why, so you can determine if your reaction would be the same. Someone may have liked a program because it was not academically challenging and he did not want to spend much time studying. Similarly, someone might say she did not like her program, because it did not offer the advanced area she needed for her chosen career path.

There are a number of other questions you should pose to alumni:

- How has your M.B.A. affected your career?

- How much of your M.B.A. course material is helpful in your job?

- Would you hire other graduates of the program?

- Were the faculty members well prepared and accessible?

- Were you able to get the courses you wanted?

- Did the school provide academic advising? financial support? placement assistance?

- Did you like and respect your classmates?

- Was the program academically challenging?

- Do students in the program compete with each other or cooperate?

- Which non-curricular aspects of the program were most valuable?

- Was the program enjoyable?

The general perceptions of a program held by most members of the business community may be most readily pinpointed by corporate recruiters. Companies may target certain programs as a source of good people in a particular functional area or with specific skills. These categorizations typically highlight areas of strength in a program, but may hide other opportunities. It is important to scratch beneath the surface of generalizations. Also, if a particular firm does not recruit at a certain school, this does not necessarily mean that it does not hire that program's graduates or would not consider them for hire. A radical difference between your interests and personality and the perception that the business community holds of a program you are considering should trigger a closer look on your part, however. It may signal that you may not fit into the program as well as you should, or that you may be forced to fight negative perceptions of your program when you start to look for a job.

Rankings

Each year seems to bring a new avalanche of surveys and rankings of M.B.A. programs. It is easy to allow yourself to be swayed by this mass of information. It is important, however, that you not limit your search to those schools that are favorably portrayed in rankings. Although rankings provide a general guide to reputation and quality, they are far from exact. If you take the time to examine the various survey results closely, you will find that no two rankings agree with each other. In a scientific sense, these results are invalid because they are not reproduced by an independent assessment.

If you look not at precise rankings, but at broad categories of schools, however, you will find greater correlation among the survey results. These broad bands of school groupings can provide you with an overall sense of how the market perceives the reputation and relative quality of the institution. People in graduate management education often talk about the "50 schools in the top 20"—and with good reason. There is a continuum of quality, and very few, if any, schools excel along all lines and in all areas. The best program can be defined in any number of ways, and many schools will fit these criteria. Moreover, what one person defines as "best" might not satisfy another person's definition. Given these differing expectations and the difficulties in measuring these attributes, one might go beyond speaking of the "50 in the top 20" to speak of the "100 schools in the top 50."

It is also important to realize that rankings and surveys cover only a limited number of institutions. Because many surveys weigh opinions from around the country, rankings typically only include national schools. Fine regional programs are often not mentioned, since their excellent reputation in one region does not outweigh their low profile elsewhere. Surveys often imply a correlation between current reputation and current quality, even though reputation typically lags behind quality, both going up and going down. If you are thinking of attending a program outside the United States, meanwhile, you need to be aware that international programs are usually not considered in assembling rankings, although the

Financial Times did publish a survey in January 1999 ranking programs in North America and Europe. In addition, note that rankings typically look only at AACSB-accredited programs, which make up no more than one-third of U.S. M.B.A. programs.

The two best known rankings of U.S. business schools are compiled and published by *Business Week* and *U.S. News & World Report*. Each uses its own methodology to derive its results.

The *Business Week* ranking, which is published in October of every even-numbered year, relies on surveys of M.B.A. graduates of the programs and corporate recruiters. The rating of each school is based on the combined measure of satisfaction these two groups have with the program. This approach takes consumer satisfaction as the ultimate measure of quality and looks at the two major consumers of the school's product and services—the students who consume the education offered, and the employers who "buy" or do not buy the school's primary product (M.B.A. graduates).

Despite the appeal of asking the "consumer" about the quality of the product, there are potential biases in the methodology. Students who know that their schools' rankings and their future salaries may depend in part on positive survey results may be inclined to rate the program more highly to boost their own standing. On the other hand, students may express dissatisfaction because of a matter not related to general quality, such as a tuition increase, departure of a popular professor, or disagreement about a student club. The employer survey may be influenced by regional recruiting patterns, differing expectations of graduates from different programs, and sample bias, due to nonresponse or lack of representation of smaller firms.

The *U.S. News & World Report* methodology incorporates a number of objective factors, such as admissions selectivity and placement data, as well as reputation. Although the use of multiple quantifiable factors suggests a more scientific approach, there are pitfall and potential biases here as well.

Forty percent of the final score is based on the school's reputation, as measured by two surveys, one of business school deans and directors of AACSB-accredited M.B.A. programs and one of corporate recruiters. The survey of deans and M.B.A. program directors asks them to rank each program along a five-point scale; these results account for 25 percent of the total in the overall rankings. The remaining 15 percent of the reputational portion of the rankings score is based on responses of corporate recruiters, who were asked to select the top 25 business schools in the country based on their reputation for academic excellence and ability to program outstanding managers and business leaders.

Even someone who works daily in the graduate management field is unlikely to have a sufficiently solid knowledge of all these schools to rate them with any accuracy or consistency. With opinions formed more on the basis of public information than on close scrutiny, the results of reputational ratings may

> ## "Objective" Statistics
>
> Many of the seemingly objective statistics upon which rankings rely, such as average undergraduate GPA, percentage of applicants admitted, and average starting salaries, are actually rife with potential biases and problems of interpretation. Use them with caution.

be more reflective of the effectiveness of the program's public relations efforts than of the quality of the program itself.

Thirty-five percent of the score comes from placement data, including average starting salaries, the percentages of graduates placed at graduation and within three months of graduation, and the number of on-campus recruiters compared to the number of graduates. These figures also pose problems, despite their seeming objectivity and comparability. Average starting salaries, which are the most heavily weighted component of this measure, are lower in manufacturing than in investment banking, and both salaries and costs are less in Kansas City than in New York City. The lower salary in a lower cost area may actually yield greater buying power and a higher standard of living.

Faculty Figures

Another dicey statistic is that of the number of full-time faculty members. One program may have a smaller number of professors, but these professors may be dedicated solely to the M.B.A. program. Another may have more faculty members, but it may also have an undergraduate program, a doctoral program, and/or other master's programs. Which is better?

Another problem arises from the salaries of graduates who accept positions overseas. Is a salary in India reported on the basis of dollar exchange equivalent, buying power, or multiple of some average worker's wage, or is it not reported at all? How does one deal with compensation packages abroad that contain housing and social benefits not included in U.S. salaries? Because schools may use different approaches to answer these questions, the answers are not always comparable, even if each school tries to be absolutely honest and forthcoming.

Admissions selectivity accounts for 25 percent of the score, based on average GMAT score of entering students, undergraduate grade point average (GPA), and percentage of applicants admitted. These numbers are individually subject to interpretation, however, and the picture becomes more cloudy when they are considered in combination. For example, a 40 percent rate of acceptance at one school may make that school appear more competitive than a 50 percent rate at a second school. But the second school may have had a pool of applications in which nearly everyone was competitive, whereas the first school may have had a significant number of applications that did not meet even minimum criteria for consideration.

International students, meanwhile, typically do not have a GPA equivalent to that of American applicants. Are the international marks somehow converted, or are they omitted? Has the school discouraged receipt of applications from individuals not likely to be considered for admission, driving the percentage of admitted applicants up, or has the school encouraged anyone and everyone to submit an application, knowing that the swollen applicant pool will yield a small percentage of applicants who are offered admission?

If you do decide to consider rankings in assembling your list of possible schools, you should keep the following points in mind. Don't just look at one ranking list; look at as many as possible and then form an opinion about what programs belong in a grouping of top schools. Familiarize yourself with what the rankings do and don't tell you about a program. Don't apply to a program simply because it appears on someone else's "top" list or even because it is on the "top" list you compiled from other ranking lists. The most important consideration in selecting a program is the fit of the program with your interests and goals. It is of little use to attend a highly ranked program, if you are miserable while you are there and don't get the education you need.

Issues to Consider

We've discussed the wide variety of sources of information about M.B.A. programs. As you use these resources to embark upon your M.B.A. program search, there are a number of issues you'll want to keep in mind.

Logistics of Full-Time versus Part-Time Study

We've already looked at the question of part-time versus full-time study from your perspective as a student. It is also important to examine the question from the standpoint of the institution. Does the school offer study on both a full-time and part-time basis or only one of these? If both full-time and part-time study are available, what is the relationship between the programs? Are they integrated? Are all courses and areas of study equally available to both part-time and full-time students, or only a subset? Although it is sometimes possible to transfer freely between full-time and part-time status at a school, you should not assume that such is the case. Sometimes full-time and part-time programs have different degree requirements, though occasionally the curricula may be entirely separate. If transfer is possible, may it be done at any point in the program or only at set intervals?

If you have decided to study on a part-time basis, do you have constraints on when you can attend courses? It is important to look at specifics of class times and locations. Some schools that offer courses at multiple sites do not offer the entire program at each site and may require that you take some courses at the main campus to finish your degree. Class schedules may be different at each site, a factor you may need to consider as you are planning your commute to and from the program. If there are multiple programs, schedules, or sites, do you have equal access to all

Full Time versus Part Time

In comparing full-time and part-time programs at different schools, you should research the following:

- Is there one admissions committee and one set of admissions standards for part-time and full-time programs?

- Do the same faculty members teach both full time and part time?

- Is the curriculum the same? If it is not the same, is it still appropriate for your goals?

- Do full-time and part-time students have access to the same services?

of them? Even if a school offers both a full-time day program and a part-time evening program at the same site with the same curriculum and degree requirements, you cannot assume that you will be able to finish your degree by taking day courses on a part-time basis.

There is no rule of thumb that will let you distinguish between full-time and part-time admissions criteria. For example, in some cases, admissions officers feel that full-time employment compensates for less competitive prior academic work, whereas in other cases, the sentiment is that a student with a full-time job needs to have a stronger prior academic record to balance the demands of a professional position. Making specific inquiries at the admissions offices of the schools to which you plan to apply will help you gauge your competitiveness and address any likely issues of concern in your application.

Major Program Distinctions

At this juncture it would be useful to explore more fully the differences between the broad categories of programs that were touched upon in the introduction, and to determine exactly how these differences will impact you as a student. This is also the time to decide whether you want to stay in the United States for your graduate management education or whether you want to include internationally based programs among your M.B.A. options.

Regional versus National

Some full-time M.B.A. programs recruit the majority of their students from one region of the country, whereas others draw their students from around the country and around the world. The pattern of placement following graduation is often very similar. Programs based outside the United States may also be categorized as regional or national/international, depending on whether the majority of their students come from the country or region of the country where the program is located or from a much broader geographic area.

The visibility of national programs gives their graduates name recognition virtually everywhere. National programs tend to be the programs that are ranked by the various business publications as "top-tier" programs. These schools usually have students from around the United States and around the world in their classes and recruiters from all over the country vying for their graduates. You will find graduates of these programs working in every region of the country and throughout the world.

If you want the flexibility to seek a position anywhere, national programs may provide you with the broadest range of contacts. The national pool of applicants, however, may make program admission more competitive.

If you want to work in a certain area of the country, you may be better served by a regional school that has developed strong ties to companies in that area. These firms may view the regional graduates as potential long-term employees, who will not jump ship at the first offer from outside the area. You may, then, have a better chance of being hired and promoted. And despite the name recognition factor, regional schools may be a preferred provider in their own areas.

Traditional versus Two-Tier Programs

The traditional model for a two-year M.B.A. program is for students to spend the first year of the program studying the basic functional areas of business. In some cases, students who have completed prior course work in the business disciplines can be exempted from some of these classes; in other cases, all students, whatever their educational background, are required to take the entire "core," as it is known. Teaching methodology, integration of subject matter, and program culture may all be factors that the school considers when deciding to offer course waivers or substitutions.

Course waivers do not always allow you to reduce the length of your program. Often, if you don't have to take the required course, you must substitute another course in its place. This substitute course may or may not have to be in the same subject area.

The second year of the traditional model allows you to take a selection of elective courses, often allowing you to complete a concentration or specialization, the M.B.A. version of a major course of study. Typically, students choose a concentration in the functional area in which they intend to seek employment after completion of the degree. Very often, special program opportunities, such as study abroad or project courses, are also included in the second year of study in a traditional two-year program.

Another common model, the two-tier program, divides the curriculum into two portions: 1) the core, all of which can be waived, and 2) advanced courses, some of which may be required. Here, students with an undergraduate degree in business typically enter directly into the second half of the program, which can be completed in 9 to 12 months of full-time study.

The shortened program length for students who have an undergraduate degree in business relieves some of the financial burden of full-time study under the two-tier system. The entrance of students at various levels in the program, however, may lessen program cohesion among students and decrease the long-term value of the full-time student network. It can make integration of the program from start to finish much more difficult and may eliminate the possibility of a summer internship in a new functional area or industry.

> ### *Two-Tier Programs*
>
> Examples of two-tier programs include:
>
> - Thunderbird Graduate School of International Management offers a Master of International Management in which noncredit "Common Body of Knowledge" courses are separated from courses beyond the CBK level. Graduates of AACSB-accredited programs (with language ability) can complete the degree in two semesters.
>
> - The Johnson School at Cornell University offers a Twelve-Month Option for scientists and engineers already holding graduate degrees.

Within this framework, students have also have fewer opportunities to choose advanced courses on the basis of their interests.

One-Year versus Two-Year Programs

An increasing number of full-time programs have designed curricula that allow you to finish your M.B.A. in less than two years. These programs typically last 12 to 18 months, with all students following the same program. The obvious advantage of a shorter program is the decreased financial cost: You may pay less in tuition, and you will spend less time out of the full-time work force. These one-year programs, however, may not accommodate specialized advanced course work or a summer job or internship while in the program. The inability to complete an internship may present a special problem when you want to change careers. You will find that this professional experience is essential to show a future employer your aptitude in the new area. If you are interested in gaining international experience, perhaps from study abroad, you may find that you can accommodate it only by lengthening your course of study beyond the 12 or 18 months usually needed to complete the degree.

The longer two-year program, which typically lasts approximately 21 months from orientation to graduation, usually provides a chance to gain professional work experience while in the program. It may also offer you greater opportunities for advanced study or other professional growth activities. Even on the financial side, the benefits of the shorter program need to be weighed carefully, considering not only the salary you can earn in a summer job or internship, but also the effect of that summer experience on the salary offers you receive post-M.B.A.

Not surprisingly, it is generally not possible to pack as many courses and experiences into a shorter period of time as into a longer program. As with the other factors you will consider in choosing a program, however, there is nothing inherently superior about a program that is shorter or one that is longer. The question you need to answer is whether or not a particular program allows you to obtain the course work and experiences you want.

Domestic versus International

The increasingly international environment of business has led to increased emphasis on international business in M.B.A. programs and increased opportunities for studying business in a variety of geographic settings. Many U.S. programs offer opportunities to spend a term abroad, either during the regular academic year or in a summer program, or to participate in international projects. It is also possible to earn your M.B.A. from a foreign institution.

Should you look outside the United States for graduate management education if you are interested in an international career? Not necessarily. If you have limited fluency in a language other than English, you plan to base your career in the United States or in an American company, or you are as likely to focus on South America as on Africa, Asia, or Europe, there may be no advantage to studying outside the United States. Indeed, there may be drawbacks. On the other hand, if you have a strong interest in one region of the world and have both the language and cultural background necessary to thrive in that setting, an M.B.A. program located in that part of the world may give you both the functional knowledge you want and the cultural context you can get only by immersing yourself in an internationally based program. Refer to chapter 5 for a more extensive discussion of the pros and cons of various study-abroad options.

Accreditation

Another issue that will impact your program search is that of accreditation. There are two basic levels of M.B.A. program accreditation: institutional and professional. This first level of accreditation is granted by an officially recognized regional accrediting body that examines the institution as a whole and certifies the general quality of education in accordance with set standards. An example of such an accrediting body is the North Central Association of Schools and Colleges. Professional accreditation looks solely at the quality within the particular discipline under the jurisdiction of that body. The accrediting body for business schools is the AACSB, the International Association for Management Education. Programs such as the Master of Public Administration do not come under the accrediting jurisdiction of the AACSB, even though they have a management component.

AACSB standards for accreditation look at the areas of faculty quality, student quality, curriculum, and program resources, including support staff, library holdings, and computer facilities. It is granted at the baccalaureate and masters levels, indicating that the school has achieved certain standards in each of these areas. However, although regional accreditation is necessary for an institution to participate in the federal student aid programs and thus may be very important for you, professional accreditation may not be. More specialized programs may not even be able to obtain such accreditation because of the unorthodoxy of their curricula, even if they are of a very high quality.

> ### How Important Is Accreditation?
>
> Only one-third of the M.B.A. programs in the U.S. are professionally accredited by the AACSB. Don't cross a school off your list just because it is not accredited. There is no way for you to know if the school lacks accreditation because the program is not eligible for accreditation, because the school did not seek it, or because the program did not fulfill the required standards.

Now that you know what kinds of programs are available and what you are looking for, how do you choose the specific programs to which you want to apply? The next chapter will deal with the specifics of choosing a program.

CHAPTER 4

Narrowing the Field

When you sit back and imagine your ideal M.B.A. program, you may see yourself rubbing shoulders with industry barons between intense class discussions, running out to the beach to relax, or living minutes away from the ski slope. But the critical issue in selecting an M.B.A. program is finding the right academic program, the program that will allow you to take as much advantage as you can of this unique opportunity to learn.

You will need to take a number of factors into account when assessing which M.B.A. programs fit your wants and needs, ranging from curriculum to quality of life issues.

Curriculum

M.B.A. curricula are typically divided into two distinct segments: the common core (Common Body of Knowledge), which consists of business fundamentals, and advanced elective courses. To maximize the value of your business school experience, you need to be sure that a school's curriculum matches your needs and interests. If your primary interest is general management, then seek out those programs whose strengths include general management. Some fields, such as marketing and finance, are taught in virtually every school, whereas others, such as insurance and real estate, are available at relatively few programs.

Basics

You will find the fundamentals of business in every M.B.A. program. Accounting, economics, finance, organizational behavior, marketing, statistics, and operations are primary business disciplines and are expected repertoire for any M.B.A. How and when this learning is accomplished varies, however. In most programs, these subjects will be taught in a group of core courses required of every student; they often consume most or all of the first year of study in a two-year, full-time program.

Some programs regard some of these areas as background knowledge and expect you to have learned the material before you start your program. Statistics, economics, and accounting often fall into this group. When you are comparing the length of programs and time to degree, be sure you remember to consider any program prerequisites. Calculus and computer skills are other common prerequisites for M.B.A. programs.

Other programs take another approach, offering the core courses within the structure of the program but requiring this course work only of those students who have not mastered it previously. If your program has two tiers, with two entrance points, one for students with undergraduate degrees in business and one for others with degrees in nonbusiness areas, you may be exempted from the entire first year of the program if you are an undergraduate business major.

If you have been exempted from one of the core course requirements because you have done prior course work in that core area, you may be able to waive the course entirely. Alternatively, you may be able to substitute another course in the program for it. If you are allowed to waive the course entirely, you have effectively shortened your program and will be able to graduate with one fewer course than your classmates who do not have a waiver. If you are allowed to substitute another course for the exempted core course, your program length remains the same, but you have the opportunity to take an additional advanced or elective course in the program.

Advanced Study

In spite of the importance of the business fundamentals, most M.B.A. programs are marked by the advanced areas of study that they offer. Although some programs consider themselves to be general management programs only, the majority of schools offer defined areas of advanced study, termed concentrations and specializations or majors.

In the brief span of an M.B.A. program, it is not possible to accommodate the equivalent of an undergraduate major. The typical concentration area within an M.B.A. program consists of a group of three related courses, some of which may be required for that concentration. A specialization or major, typically five courses in the area, provides greater depth of training in the field.

The most highly regarded programs tend to be strong in all areas, but even these programs are viewed as having particular specialties. For example, Kellogg is known for marketing; Wharton and Chicago for finance; and Harvard for general management. Of course, many Harvard M.B.A.'s pursue finance careers; Wharton grads, marketing; and Chicago and Kellogg grads, general management. You should, nevertheless, familiarize yourself with general marketplace perceptions about the programs you are considering. It will help you think more clearly about the selection process.

Beyond ensuring that you will receive the functional training that you desire, you should seek out the programs offering the courses that interest you the most. Schools differ dramatically in course offerings and areas of concentration. Whether you are interested primarily in international business, health care, entrepreneurship, or any other aspect of business, be sure to select schools that will enable you to meet your educational goals.

> ### Plan Your Career Direction
>
> "Potential M.B.A.'s should have a pretty good idea of what career direction they're looking to take before starting the application process. Unlike with undergraduate programs, you tend to start taking classes within your focused area and specialty by your first or second semester."
>
> —M.B.A., Stern School of Business, New York University

Computer and Quantitative Skills

Whatever the precise set of degree requirements in your program, you may be sure that you will be expected to have computer and quantitative skills. Some programs offer math and computer "camps" in the summer before the first full M.B.A. term begins. Many, however, simply assume that you will arrive on campus with the required background.

In an ongoing effort to adapt to technological change, most business schools have integrated personal computers into their programs. Many schools will require you to have your own computer. The degree to which you will be expected to use the computer will vary by program, but you should make an effort to have at least a minimum comfort level with computers and the most common application programs—involving word processing, spreadsheets, and databases—before starting school. You may want to check with the schools in which you are interested to find out both computer specifications and preferred software for the program.

It has been said that mathematics is the language of business. Many M.B.A. programs are moving away from the analytical approaches that predominated several years ago and giving increased emphasis to the "soft" areas of communication and interpersonal skills, but the mathematical elements of business studies have not gone away. The level of mathematical knowledge that you will need varies widely from program to program. Some schools expect you to have studied statistics before entering the program, and some will expect you to use calculus on a regular basis. You should certainly feel comfortable with college algebra and brush up on your skills if they are rusty.

Degree Programs

In examining the curriculum at a school, you should pay attention to the number of elective courses that you will be able to take within the degree program. You should also find out how many sections of elective classes are typically offered and how easy or difficult it is to register for the courses of your choice. You don't want to select a school on the basis of your interest and its expertise and then discover once you are there that you cannot get the courses you want.

If you cannot find a school that formally offers your area of interest, you may be able to find programs in which you can design your own area of specialization, tailoring a set of courses to your specifications.

Don't neglect to research specialized degrees that are related to but not the same as the M.B.A., which is a general management degree. These include the Master of Public Administration (M.P.A.), Master of Hospital Administration (M.H.A.), Master of Science in Industrial Relations (M.S.I.R.), and masters degrees in the functional areas of business themselves, such as Master of Science in Marketing or Economics. These M.S. degrees usually reside in the graduate school proper rather than the business school. Some of these degrees concentrate on a particular sector of business, such as health care, whereas others focus on a specific functional area, such as marketing, finance, or accounting.

An M.B.A. Program By Any Other Name . . .

Although the Master of Business Administration degree, the M.B.A., is the common name for a graduate management degree, many institutions offer substantially the same program with another name—Master of Management (M.M.), Master of Public and Private Management (M.P.P.M.), Master of Administrative Science (M.A.S.), and Master of Science in Business Administration (M.S.B.A.), to name a few.

Are you interested in pursuing a joint degree or augmenting your business school training with course work from another discipline? Here, too, opportunities vary from school to school. Some schools encourage you to take an interdisciplinary approach, but they may require you to wait until your second year of study.

One of the most attractive features of a formal joint-degree program is the opportunity to complete both degrees concurrently in less time than it would take to finish them consecutively. For example, the most common joint-degree program, the J.D./M.B.A., allows you to combine the two-year M.B.A. with the three-year J.D. degree in law and receive both degrees after only four years. You can also find joint-degree programs that, in addition to the M.B.A., allow you to earn degrees in such professions as health care and medicine, engineering, and architecture, as well as in traditional liberal arts fields, especially area studies programs that focus on particular regions of the world or cultures.

Outside Study

You may be able to register for courses outside the business school even if you are not in a joint-degree program. These courses may or may not fulfill part of your M.B.A. degree requirements. But by taking courses from other disciplines in the university, you may be able to design a unique program to fit your interests and complement your prior training. For example, if you have a technical background, you may be able to complement your studies in information systems within the business school with course work in computer science or electrical engineering. If your interests lie in not-for-profit management, course work drawn from public administration, education, public policy, or social work may round out your business classes.

You may even be able to take courses at another university through consortia arrangements or partnership programs. This option may allow you to take advantage of the strengths and best professors from two or more institutions, often at no additional cost.

One warning about this approach: If you take courses outside the business school that do not count toward your degree, you may add extra time to your program that will delay your graduation.

Special Program Features

You do not always need to look outside the business school for unique educational opportunities. Many special features are available within M.B.A. programs. Entrepreneurship, for example, has become very popular in recent years, and many programs now offer specialized work in this field. Such programs may offer you consulting opportunities with small businesses. And universities affiliated with technology parks may provide a chance to gain experience in technology transfer and new product development.

If you wish to pursue one subject in depth, you may want to look for a school that offers a doctoral program in business as well as the M.B.A. and explore the possibility of taking a mixture of doctoral and master's level courses.

When you venture outside the traditional disciplines of business, however, you need to inquire not only about the availability of the field, but also about the school track record in the area and the depth of its commitment. If the program has been started recently, it may have been in response to a perceived market demand without any assurance of long-term support. Specializations without roots can wither away, and the faculty who carry that area's banner may not get the support they need to continue their work.

> ### **Investigate the Special Programs**
>
> "There were lots of great lectures to go to at HBS. I would encourage folks to go to as many 'special programs,' presentations etc. as possible. This is where a lot of the learning comes in."
>
> —M.B.A., Harvard Business School

One of the areas of most substantial growth is international business. Among the opportunities open to you within M.B.A. programs are study abroad programs, language training, international internships, and double degree programs. These are in addition to a formal area of concentration or specialization in the degree program. International opportunities are described in more detail in our chapter on studying abroad.

What the Top M.B.A. Programs Say: Market Niche, Program Specialty, Distinctive Features

Cornell University, Johnson School

"We have intentionally created a very flexible core program, assuming diversity among our students' backgrounds, interests, and career objectives. Whether seeking breadth of perspective or depth in a particular discipline, students are encouraged to make the most of their two years at Cornell by tailoring their M.B.A. experience to individual goals. This gives rise to a passion for their work that students tell us is one of the most distinguishing characteristics of a Johnson School education."

University of California—Los Angeles, Anderson School

"The Anderson School has earned the reputation of having one of the top entrepreneurial programs in the country by providing more than just classroom instruction. Leading entrepreneurs share their experiences at on-campus Brown Bag Lunches and at the Breakfast Series. Students gain hands-on experience writing business plans and advising local new ventures through both the Small Business Consulting Service and academic internships. In addition, friends of the school who are willing to invest in qualified businesses have contributed substantial resources to the Entrepreneurial Studies Center. Two funds utilize these resources by providing up to $500,000 in seed capital each year to ventures founded by Anderson students."

Indiana University

"At Indiana our focus is on general management. Our students are particularly prepared for general management because of our completely integrated core program, tying together all business functions, and our emphasis on skills development. We produce graduates who not only analyze and solve problems, but can implement solutions because they have crucial leadership, teamwork, and communication skills."

Teaching Methods

Business school professors teach primarily through the case method, lectures, projects, student teams, or, in most cases, a combination of these. Everyone learns differently, so select a school with a teaching environment that will allow you to thrive.

Lectures

A lecture-based classroom is, in all likelihood, what you experienced as an undergraduate. The professor provides information, and interaction between the students and the professor, or between students, is controlled and generally limited. Students may just sit and take notes and not participate in any of the discussions, although usually participation is expected, and sometimes graded.

Case Method

In a case-method environment, on the other hand, the professor doesn't lecture but rather facilitates an open dialogue with the students by asking probing questions, expecting the students to fill most of the class time with their observations, insights, and analyses.

Each class revolves around actual business situations, and students are cast in the role of decision makers. For example, you are given the facts about a struggling business. You are placed in charge of the business and must develop a plan to improve its performance. There are a few schools, such as Harvard Business School and Virginia's Darden School, where the case method is the primary teaching tool, but you will find cases in general management courses at even the most analytical programs.

The objective of the case method is to simulate a real-world environment. Students must analyze each case and develop an action plan—i.e., what they are going to do and how they are going to do it—with limited information and time at their disposal. Occasionally, the individuals whose experience is the basis for a case may sit in on the class to share their insights.

Projects

Project classes have resulted from students' demand for classes to be closely linked to real world business situations. They are akin to the case method in the role in which they cast the student. In project courses, one student, or more often a team of students, works as a consultant with a client company on a project or problem facing the company. Whereas in a case discussion the facts of the case are assembled beforehand, a team working on a project often has to start from scratch, determining what information is needed and reviewing company documents or interviewing company employees to obtain it. Regular class meetings with the professor provide an opportunity to learn more about the subject and to discuss the particular problems and applications arising from the projects themselves. The course may end with each team presenting the project recommendations and actions to the class and to the actual clients at the company. Project courses tend to be extremely time-consuming, because of the need to consult with the clients and with the other members of the team, but are effective in bridging the usual gulf between classroom and work place.

Which Method Is for You?

Is one of these teaching methods inherently better than another? Not in and of itself. Some students prefer the more controlled, structured environment of traditional lectures. Others thrive on the unpredictable, ever-changing environment of case discussion, where many viewpoints are encouraged and no single answer provided. The hands-on application of information and theory in project classes forces students to synthesize materials independently and to deal with real-time constraints.

Most M.B.A. programs use a mix of teaching methodologies. Some, however, use one method primarily or exclusively. Even at "case schools," some students feel that the case method is better suited to some subjects than others. A marketing case, for example, on new product introductions may lead to a riveting class discussion. On the other hand, the case method can be a ponderous way to learn accounting principles.

Another issue to keep in mind is how well your learning style fits with the course expectations at programs you are considering. In a case-method classroom, as much as half of your grade will be based on class participation. If you think you may be less than eager to participate in this type of forum, you should ask yourself seriously if a case school is the appropriate environment for you.

Teaching Trends

Most schools have been trying in recent years to enhance the value of students' educational experience by exposing them to real-world situations where possible. It might be worth your while to ascertain whether or not the programs in which you are interested offer this kind of practical exposure to the world of business.

"Real World" Skills

Interactions with executives in the classroom, field studies, and student consulting assignments are becoming increasingly common in business school settings. Business simulations, computer-based programs that enable you to test your decision-making skills, are also a popular teaching tool.

In addition to the traditional business disciplines, many schools now offer courses, seminars, or workshops on contemporary issues and topics in business, such as total quality management and ethics. Many also provide opportunities within the curriculum to enhance leadership, communication, and interpersonal skills. Full-time programs often begin with a several day orientation program, during which you may receive training in the some of these areas. Both noncredit and credit classes may be offered during the academic year, and you may need to use these skills regularly in your course work.

Student Teams

One of the ways schools are mimicking the business environment in their academic programs is in the use of student teams. As corporations have increasingly turned to teams to work on projects and to solve problems, M.B.A. programs have converted an increased share of the work in the program from individual work to team work. Many programs now incorporate training in team building somewhere in the program, as part of new student orientation, in team-building workshops or as one of the topics in organizational behavior courses. Teams may be formed for the purpose of one project in one course or may remain together for months, working as a single team in multiple courses.

> ### The Benefits of Teamwork
>
> "It's really important to get into a good study group. In the study groups, you divide up the work according to your abilities. For example, there was a real poet in my group, an English major from Middlebury. He would write the introductions, and the conclusions. Our group always had the best introductions and conclusions. Two guys in the group were great at math. One of them had been a comptroller. They did all the math."
>
> —M.B.A., Stern School of Business, New York University

Although the sometimes difficult logistics of getting part-time students together to accomplish team work has made the use of teams more common in full-time programs than in part-time programs, you are likely to encounter team work somewhere during the course of your program, no matter where you study. In the sometimes competitive environment of M.B.A. programs, the cooperation required of teams does not always come naturally. Since team work is almost always time-consuming, students in schools that use teams may find that activities and even policies on work during the academic year reflect the heavy time commitment of working with others.

Theory versus Application

The tug and tension between theory and application in business school curricula are constant. Should you be learning models and paradigms and developing problem-solving frameworks, or should you be finding out the answer tonight for the issue that will be on your desk in the morning? You really do not need to choose between these two extremes, because every M.B.A. program contains both theory and application. The proportion of each varies widely, however, stretching out over a long continuum.

The benefits of application are readily apparent. You can use what you learn directly and often immediately in your job. At best, applications tie information into the context of business and cut through complexity to reveal the underlying structure and issues. At worst, applications give you a quick fix to a short-term problem that you may never again encounter and that you cannot apply to other situations.

Theory Is Practical . . . or at Least Lucrative

"Many business leaders lambast M.B.A. programs for focusing too much on academic learning and too little on practical training. [Yet research indicates] that the programmes with the best academic reputations—measured by how often the average faculty member's research is cited—tend to be those offering the highest financial returns."

—"The M.B.A. Cost-Benefit Analysis," *The Economist*, Aug. 6, 1994

On the other hand, theory can by definition be generalized. It offers a method for approaching and solving problems, even problems that cannot be imagined, much less anticipated, rather than answers to the problems themselves. Difficulty arises, however, if you do not see the connection between the theory and the problem that faces you. At best, theory gives you a tool box that will serve you well for a long time. At worst, it becomes arcane cocktail conversation.

You need to consider your personal learning style and your objectives in obtaining an M.B.A. when deciding on what balance of theory and application would serve you best in an M.B.A. program.

Faculty Matters

The quality of a school's faculty is important and is reflected in each program's reputation. Nonetheless, there are several important questions to ask. Since faculty reputation is typically based on research output, how adept are the faculty members at translating research and theory into usable information? Indeed, how much emphasis is given to teaching? Is teaching an activity in which all the faculty members engage, or is it something left to those who no longer are successful researchers? What proportion of the classes are taught by full-time faculty members, and what proportion are assigned to adjunct or part-time instructors who may not have equivalent credentials? Will you get to take classes with a school's marquee professors? With the proliferation of executive education programs, top teachers at many well-known schools are sometimes assigned to teach executive education students instead of M.B.A.'s. If one of your prime motivations in attending a certain program is to take classes from specific professors, make sure that you will have that opportunity.

Class Profile

The profile of your classmates will affect your academic, social, and professional life. Much of your learning will come from your classmates, especially in case-method classes and in programs that use a significant amount of team work or group projects. A school with a geographically, professionally, and ethnically diverse student body will expose you to many more viewpoints than will a school with a homogeneous group.

According to a former admissions official at Harvard Business School, to get an initial feel for the class profile of a particular school, you should take a look at these readily available statistics:

- Undergraduate areas of study

- Percentage of international students (countries of origin for international students)

- Percentage of women

- Percentage of minorities

- Percentage of married students

- Average years of full-time work experience at entrance

- Types of companies for which students worked prior to entrance

- Average age and age range of entering students

Two of these statistics bear a closer look. The first of these is average age. Over the past number of years, students attending M.B.A. programs have been getting older. Currently, the average age of the entering student at many programs is 26 or 27. But this average is somewhat misleading because it consists of a large number of 25- and 26-year-olds and significantly fewer 30-, 40-, and 50-year-olds, who skew the average upward. If you are an older applicant, ask yourself how you will fit in with a predominantly younger group of students. The school's social life may revolve around activities that no longer interest you, or family obligations may preclude your full participation in this important aspect of the full-time experience.

> ## Focused and Savvy
>
> "According to Bob Alig, admissions director at the University of Pennsylvania's Wharton School, today's M.B.A. candidates are two to three years older and 'much more focused, much more savvy consumers' than their counterparts a decade ago."
>
> —"Look Before You Leap," Newsweek/ Kaplan's *How to Choose a Career and Graduate School*, 1999

The average work experience statistic is subject to many of the same provisions as were just mentioned in conjunction with average age. However, the calculation of this number may be confounded by such factors as the presence of a large contingent of international students whose educational system brings them to the end of their first degree only at age 25 or 26. If you have relatively little full-time work experience, or you have ten or fifteen years in the work force, you may want to examine the composition of your prospective class with particular attention to this aspect. Refer to chapter 15 for a lengthier discussion of age and work experience issues.

Class and Section Size

Class size and structure are two factors that will have a significant impact on your business school experience. Some students prefer the intimacy of a smaller class and the opportunity to get to know everyone. Others prefer the energy of a large class and the increased resources and facilities it can support.

Many programs divide the class into sections and have students take all or most of their first-year classes with that same group. In fact, at some schools, section members actually stay in the same classroom and the professors rotate among the rooms.

There are several advantages to the section concept. By working with the same classmates day after day, you build a camaraderie borne out of a shared, often intense, first-year experience. You get to know each other in a way that is not possible in a more traditional classroom structure. More likely than not, you'll forge lasting relationships with your section mates.

The downside of the section system is that you have less exposure to classmates who are not in your section. Organized club activities, however, enable you to meet other students outside the classroom who share your interests.

Outcome Assessment

"The proof is in the pudding." The buzz words of management training and education swarm though media articles, M.B.A. program brochures, and general conversation: leadership, team building, interpersonal skills, communication skills, ethics, and quality management. It is common for M.B.A. programs to include some or all of these areas within the curriculum or to offer them as optional features. It is less common for programs to measure whether student skills or understanding have increased as a result of these efforts. Unlike the traditional academic areas, in which student knowledge is demonstrated in tests, papers, or projects, these new skill areas do not lend themselves to the traditional assessment methods. Increasingly, however, programs are turning some attention to the issue of outcome assessment, trying to measure the learning or change that has occurred. Nonetheless, the best indicator of a program's success in enhancing skills and imparting knowledge often remains its reputation among the employers who hire its graduates.

Placement

The main reason you plan to attend an M.B.A. program is probably to enhance your career prospects, both short- and long-term, just as it is for most M.B.A. students. A careful look at each school's placement records will help you decide whether it will serve you well in this last, great endeavor of your M.B.A. program.

A former admissions official from Harvard Business School has identified the following factors that you might want to consider in assessing a school's placement record:

- How many companies recruit from the school?
- Do these companies come to the campus?

- Do they request résumé referrals?

- Do they participate in other special placement functions?

- What kinds of companies recruit from the school?

- What kinds of industries recruit from the school?

- Are these companies and industries in which you might have an interest?

- What percentage of the class has job offers by graduation? Within three months of graduation?

- What is the breakdown of job offers by industry? By functional area?

- What is the geographical distribution of job offers?

- What is the average starting salary? What is the range?

- What is the average starting salary for graduates with your personal profile (technical/nontechnical background, years of prior work experience, etcetera)?

If you enroll in a traditional two-year program, find out about summer job opportunities between your first and second year. For one thing, the earnings that you receive from a summer position can alleviate some of the financial stresses of studying full time. For another, a professional internship or summer job can give you first-hand experience in a new industry or functional area that you can leverage when you graduate. Many summer jobs ultimately lead to full-time offers. In addition to all this, a substantive summer experience will make you a more attractive job candidate for prospective employers.

Finally, don't look at just the first jobs that a school's graduates take. Where are they five or ten years down the road? Did the placement program provide them with skills to manage their careers, or did it merely help them to land a first job offer? Your career is more like a marathon than a sprint. Take the long view. A strong indicator of the school's strength is the accomplishments of its alumni.

Starting Salaries

Try not to overemphasize the significance of average starting salary when you evaluate programs' placement successes. Although graduates of top-ranked schools report higher average starting salaries than the national average, there are many factors that determine the salary offered to business school graduates, including prior earnings profile, pre-

> ### Well-Paid M.B.A.'s
>
> "The median starting salary for M.B.A.'s from elite schools is approximately $80,000. 'That doesn't tell the real story, which is the extra $40,000 that we estimate students get in other benefits, like signing bonuses, tuition reimbursement and stock options,' says Steven Lubrano, Tuck's director of placement."
>
> —"Look Before You Leap," Newsweek/ Kaplan's *How to Choose a Career and Graduate School*, 1999

M.B.A. work experience, geographic location and cost of living, area of specialization, and even academic records in business school.

In addition, some industries, notably management consulting and investment banking, pay at the high end of the spectrum. Schools that send a high percentage of their students into these fields will present salary statistics skewed upward by the reports of these graduates.

What the Top M.B.A. Programs Say: Placement Issues

University of Virginia, Darden School

"Services include on-campus company briefings by recruiting companies, mock interviews with evaluations, two for-credit electives in the second year on career development and career management, participation in a West Coast job fair with Tuck (Dartmouth) and Carnegie Mellon, a computer-based library of information on recruiting companies, and special training for international students and career changers."

Thunderbird Graduate School of International Management

"Services include production and maintenance of an electronic résumé book, which is available to employers via separate software application and/or Compuserve; individual career counseling by professionals; lifetime career management instruction (a personal business plan workbook written specifically for the career planning and management needs of Thunderbird students, which gives instruction on how to use a business plan to market oneself); a resource center (company and organizational files, employer and geographic directories, videotapes, career planning publications, and the Johnson and Johnson Career Management Media Room); internship coordination and placement; and workshops focusing on learning/managerial styles, career redirection, interviewing skills, job-search techniques, and employer/faculty career panels."

Vanderbilt University, Owen School

"Owen offers a full-service placement office that actively guides students' preparation for job market encounters of all types. Videotaped practice interviews, résumé review, and network coaching are key ingredients of the program."

University of Chicago

"In addition to review of résumés and cover letters and videotaped practice interviewing, the Office of Career Services offers workshops and company presentations, lecture series, a career services library, and One Source (a computerized collection of company information).

"Student professional interest groups also bring corporate speakers to campus to discuss their jobs, their companies, and their industries. Most of these speakers are available for one-to-one discussions after their presentations."

Cornell University, Johnson School

"At Cornell we offer:

- Workshops on subjects such as career assessment, résumé writing and critiques, job search strategies, mock interviews, negotiation, personal marketing strategies and networking skills

- Individual counseling sessions with Career Services staff members that help students tailor job searches to their own interests, experience, and goals

- Networking programs, career forums, and corporate functions, both on campus and in New York City and the West Coast, that are organized in cooperation with the professional clubs, many of which also circulate résumé books and maintain lists of alumni worldwide

- A weekly newsletter, a computerized bidding process, and an e-mail bulletin board that make information readily accessible to students

- A campus-wide electronic résumé database that enables Johnson School students to response to employer inquiries to any one of Cornell's nine career services offices

- The 'CareerNetwork,' through which professionals currently working in the field offer informational interviews, résumé critiques, job search advice, on-campus recruiting, and correspondence opportunities."

University of Minnesota, Carlson School

"Among services at the University of Minnesota are individual counseling on self-assessment, career planning, and planning job search strategies; videotaped mock interviews for all M.B.A. students with professional consultants; comprehensive job search handbooks; two-day job search workshop; résumé referrals (over 18,000 per year); and M.B.A. résumé books."

Location

There are two key questions that you should consider regarding a school's location: How will it affect the overall quality of your business school experience, and how will it affect your employability? Some students prefer an urban setting. Others prefer a more rustic environment. Some want their campus to be part of the overall university campus; others would like a separate campus. Neither is inherently better, but both will have an impact on your experience.

The rural versus suburban versus urban question has ramifications beyond the size of campus and access to a major airport. The school's proximity to companies and businesses may affect your ability to interact with executives, perform field studies, and engage in on-site projects. If you have a strong interest in a certain industry, there may be advantages to studying nearby. However, you should not assume that no corporate executives will visit a school just because it is located outside a major city. Executive-in-residence programs are just one example of programs that bring M.B.A. students together with officers of companies.

See for Yourself

Whatever your initial thoughts about preferred location, it is always a good idea to visit the schools that you are seriously considering attending. Two schools in the same city may have a very different feel; one might be situated on a large campus on the outskirts of town, while another might be situated right in the middle of the financial district.

Geography may be an important criterion for you. Perhaps you are constrained by a spouse's job, or know where you want to live after graduation. You will not be limited in where you can find a job if you graduate from a school that has a national reputation, but if you attend a school with a regional name, you should be sure that your school is well regarded in the area in which you plan to settle. If you are exclusively considering nationally recognized programs, there may be relatively little advantage in the location of one versus another.

For some students, a full-time M.B.A. program is an easy way to explore an unfamiliar part of the country for two years, regardless of where they head following graduation. Proximity to recreational activities may overcome concerns about climate for some, whereas others will simply avoid areas that are too hot, too cold, or too anything for their personal temperament. Remember that if you decide to study in a part of the country with a different climate, you may need to budget for additional expenses and consider them in your decision-making. One administrator of a northern school took pains to mention the need for a "sweater allowance" to anyone interviewing from warmer climes!

What the Top M.B.A. Programs Say: Location

University of California—Los Angeles, Anderson School

"The Anderson School is located in the middle of the second-largest city in the United States and one of the most vital economic and cultural areas of the world. Los Angeles is home to numerous multi-billion dollar companies as well as thousands of start-up firms. It is also a busy port city and the country's gateway to the Pacific Rim.

"Set in the outskirts of Hollywood, the school provides students with exceptional courses and opportunities for internships and field studies in the entertainment industry."

Vanderbilt University, Owen School

"Nashville is enjoying spectacular growth fueled by health care management (Columbia/HCA), auto manufacturing and supply (Nissan, Bridgestone, Ford, and Saturn), and the entertainment industry (Gaylord and Warner Bros. Records)."

University of Virginia, Darden School

"Charlottesville/Albermarle County area has a population of approximately 110,000. Other than the summer, which is too hot and humid (but during which most students are out of town doing summer internships), the climate is wonderful—extended spring and fall, mild winters. Less than 20 minutes from the Blue Ridge Mountains, the area has large horse and cattle breeding farms. A number of writers and movie stars live in the area because of the physical beauty and proximity to a major research university, which provides cultural opportunities not typically found in a rural area.

"Charlottesville lacks the benefits as well as the problems of a major metropolitan area, and we do nothing to overcome or minimize our locational disadvantages. Academically, however, we are able to attract adjunct faculty from around the country to teach specialized elective courses, and our students have the opportunity to do both domestic and international field projects, which offer experiences beyond the limited resources of Central Virginia."

Indiana University

"Our 'college town' (Bloomington) has a permanent population of 60,000, and a student population of 35,000. In our small, Midwestern location, students are better able to focus on their education and maintain balance in their lives. Besides a relatively reasonable cost of living and ease of transportation, our location provides students with many avenues for relaxation, such as world-class cultural activities and state parks."

Cornell University, Johnson School

"In addition to the 19,000 Cornell students and the 6,000 Ithaca College students, Ithaca has approximately 30,000 year-round residents. Ithaca is located in the Finger Lakes wine district, noted for its scenic natural beauty. As one student noted about her choice of Ithaca over an urban area, 'I'd rather be worrying about my exams than about someone breaking into my car.'

"The Johnson School makes use of video conferencing to minimize the distances between itself and the world's business centers. Video conferencing has been used by students to successfully interview for jobs at Sprint, by administrators to 'meet' with consultants in New York, and by our alumni to 'attend' special workshops conducted here in Ithaca."

University of Minnesota, Carlson School

"A short ride by car or bus can put M.B.A. students in the corporate headquarters of several Fortune 500 companies. The Carlson School's location—the heart of a major metropolitan area—offers students unique opportunities. *Fortune* magazine rated the Twin Cities as one of the top 10 areas for U.S. businesses, and Minnesota ranks fifth nationally in the number of Fortune 500 companies headquartered in one place."

Distance Learning?

"After studying finance as an undergraduate, I've long wanted to pursue an M.B.A., but there are limits to how much I'll sacrifice to do it. [. . .] Traditional night courses [. . .] didn't work: travel and odd work hours interfered with classes, I knew I was apt to relocate before I completed a degree and I hated evenings apart from my family. Auburn's Graduate Outreach program, [which uses videotapes, the Internet and snail mail to replicate traditional academia], solved each ot those problems."

—Auburn University student; quoted in Newsweek/Kaplan's *Careers 2000*

The Distance Learning Option

If your list of potential programs is short because you are geographically restricted and there are few programs available in your area, you may need to investigate distance-learning opportunities or programs that require on-campus attendance only occasionally, interspersed with independent work. Such programs can be just as academically rewarding as full-time or part-time programs in which you actually attend classes, and they are far more flexible. You will, however, lose out on the opportunity to network with your classmates and the other advantages of actually being present at the school.

Corporate and Business Environment

The majority of M.B.A. programs are attempting to forge closer relations with the business community and to integrate "real life" learning experiences into the curriculum. Although students may travel the country and even the world to participate in a student consulting project, and executives can travel the same route back to the program to meet with students in formal settings or over coffee or cocktails, the most natural relations with the business community often exist in the program's backyard. Proximity to an industry or company that interests you may give you an edge in learning about the field and exploring future job prospects, including ease of interviewing for summer internships and permanent jobs.

What the Top M.B.A. Programs Say: Relationships to the Corporate Community

Cornell University, Johnson School

"Because there are not many large corporations nearby, the school leverages alumni resources to bring the corporate community here through the visiting executive program. Recent visitors have included senior executives from the Travelers, S.C. Johnson & Son, American Airlines, Sunglass Hut, and Chevron."

University of California—Los Angeles, Anderson School

"The Anderson School Board of Visitors plays a vital and active leadership role at the Anderson School. Successful entrepreneurs and business executives in their own right, board members represent a broad range of national and international industries and professions, and bring to the school a wealth of leadership, expertise, energy, and commitment. In addition, companies support the school through its Partners Program, and national and international corporate leaders visit Anderson throughout the year to interact with students and faculty."

University of Minnesota, Carlson School

"The recently redesigned program offers expanded opportunities to learn through direct experience with Twin Cities businesses. For example, small groups of M.B.A. students meet regularly with corporate executives as part of the Executive Mentor Program. They attend Top Management Perspectives, a course that features executives who share their expertise with

The Importance of Access

"We had amazing access to a huge variety of companies—to do internships, special projects, or just to get information. Definitely find companies/industries/occupations that you want to explore, and take advantage of the many opportunities to work with them on a project basis. This will make your eventual job search much more focused, and give you some work experience in interesting areas."

—M.B.A., Stanford Graduate School of Business

students in the classroom. They debate business ideas, changes, and trends with managers from the business community in the Carlson Proseminar Series."

Quality of Life Issues

There are a host of other issues that affect your quality of life during your studies and, ultimately, your satisfaction with your program. Some of them, such as workload and the competitiveness/cooperation quotient, affect primarily you, as the student in the program. Others, such as local schools, spousal support, and availability of jobs, exercise their most direct impact on your spouse and children.

Workload

Think about how hard you are prepared to work. It is generally true that the more effort you put into your program, the more you will gain from it, but some programs demand an extraordinary amount from first-year students. If the program uses teams for projects and cases, the time required can rise rapidly. Even without group or team meetings, you may need to spend 12 or more hours per week outside the classroom on each course. These demands can limit the amount of time and energy that you will have left to devote to outside activities.

Indeed, the academic requirements in some programs are such that first-year students are prohibited from holding a job. In other programs there may be a limitation on outside work. You should not assume that you will be able to work while you are in your M.B.A. program, especially during the first-year of study. Depending on your location, part-time jobs may or may not be plentiful, and even if you are able to find one, you will need to consider whether or not it contributes to your professional development. If it does not, you may be better off not working and devoting more time to study and program activities that will further your career.

Family Life

For students with families, the first year of business school requires not just a sacrifice of income but of time that you can spend with your spouse or children. Don't underestimate how all-encompassing your first year will be. At some point, these demands can become a strain on even the strongest of relationships. The time constraints of a part-time program may be even more severe, because you have to handle the rigors of your course load on top of your job and family obligations.

Compounding the problems of meshing one spouse's business school study with the other's job and family responsibilities are all the issues of relocation, if you decide to move

Keep Your Spouse Happy

Your spouse's mental state may have an effect on how successful you are in B-school. Make sure that he or she will be happy at the program you choose.

yourself and your family to attend your school of choice. A large metropolitan area is likely to offer a greater variety of employment opportunities for your spouse than a college town, where the primary businesses are a few restaurants and the campus bookstore. Although there may be employment opportunities on campus, your spouse may well be competing with the equally well-trained spouses of other graduate and professional students for a limited pool of professional and nonprofessional positions.

A related point is the availability of summer internship positions in the area in which you settle your family. If you cannot find a suitable opportunity close to home, you may be faced with the prospect of leaving your family to take a position elsewhere in the country for the summer, moving them to wherever you have found your summer job, or not being able to take full advantage of the summer to gain valuable work experience, earn money, and make contacts for your post-M.B.A. job search.

Quality of life is also an important consideration for spouses and significant others, especially if school requires a move to a new city. When the first year takes over your life, your spouse may feel left out. Find out what kind of groups and activities there are for partners. Some programs sponsor organizations aimed solely at student spouses and make a point of including the entire family in various events and activities during the year.

Is campus housing available? What is it like? Is off-campus housing convenient? Is it affordable? Where do most of the students live? If the campus offers married student housing, is it adequate for families with children? How good are the schools that your children would attend? If you are distracted by family concerns, the overall quality of your business school experience will be diminished.

One final issue to consider is that of family planning. If you plan to have a child while you are in business school, be sure that the physical and emotional demands of a new child can be managed together with the time and energy demands of your program. Although part-time students may be able to take some time away from the program to accommodate the birth of a child, most full-time students cannot.

M.B.A. plus Motherhood

"I enjoyed my M.B.A. program until my child was born. Juggling a job, child and an M.B.A. program is not something I'd advise undertaking. It's much too stressful for everyone."

—M.B.A., Stern School of Business, New York University

Cooperation versus Competitiveness

The litmus test of a program's quality of life may be the feelings of current students about the school and its environment. Beyond location and available services and amenities, these feelings will reflect issues of competition and cooperation.

The Right Atmosphere?

"Everyone wanted to do well. The atmosphere was competitive, but not cutthroat. That may be because the team structure sort of forces students to help each other."

—M.B.A., Stern School of Business, New York University

Competition is inherent to business. How can you make a product better than a competitor's? How do you provide a service more effectively? How can you get to market first? These are the questions faced by business people every day. By its nature, and by the nature of the bright, talented, and ambitious students it attracts, business school fosters a competitive environment. But business is also about cooperation and working together toward a common goal. As we have seen, business schools reflect this by encouraging students to participate in team-based learning.

Some schools have reputations for fostering an intense, competitive environment, whereas other are considered more supportive. You should determine what kind of learning environment you prefer. Then take a look at how different programs strike the balance between competition and cooperation. Find out, for example, about each school's grading system. When a program grades on a forced curve, some students feel motivated and others feel unwanted pressure. Finally, try not to base your perceptions about the academic environment at various schools on the schools' reputations alone. Sit in on first-year classes to assess the dynamics.

Facilities

A walk onto many university campuses these days will reveal a shiny new business school building. But whether or not this shiny new building is a reflection on the quality of the education you will receive in it depends on the program itself and on how you plan to use it. Ideally, the campus and business school facilities should support and enhance the academic program and should provide a comfortable environment for the time you will be spending in it.

Many older classroom buildings were built to accommodate traditional lecture courses; they may not facilitate the discussion that characterizes case method classes as well as a room designed for this particular purpose. However, the reverse is also true. Similarly, many newer buildings are wired to support computer usage in the classroom by both the instructor and by the students, allowing presentations, simulations, and other applications that cannot be easily brought into a classroom of an older vintage. But if this type of computer usage is not important to the program, it is not important to have classrooms that can handle it. Many business schools have a computer laboratory, while others require each student to acquire a computer for use in the program. If you are not dependent on the program for your computing, the state of the computer lab is of little concern. On the other hand, if you do not otherwise have access to a computer, or if you will require sophisticated computer services beyond what the typical PC or office computer offers, the availability of mainframe or supercomputer access through your program may be a highly attractive feature.

Since full-time students often "live" in the B-school building, amenities such as a lounge, snack bar or cafeteria, and group study rooms can become as much of a necessity as computer facilities and a library for research and study. Social activities, as well as individual inclination, may lead you to consider athletic facilities on campus, whether you are interested in a game of pick-up basketball, intramural sports, or individual weight training.

Part-time students often do not have sufficient time to spend on campus to worry about anything but the bare essentials of campus facilities. However, this very issue of time leads to another facilities-related question: when are they open? Can the part-time student with work and family obligations get to the library, computer lab, student services offices, or other facilities and offices when they are open? If courses are offered at more than one site, are the facilities and services equivalent at each site, or is it necessary to travel between sites to take advantage of everything the program offers?

Once you have established what you want from an M.B.A. program and have selected one that suits your needs, you'll need to think about how to get into that program. The next section of this book will tackle that question, but first, we'll take a look at studying abroad.

CHAPTER 5

Studying Abroad

The tandem rise of multinational corporations and telecommunications has made international business far more than just an elective in the world of U.S. M.B.A. programs. An M.B.A. skilled at working in a global arena is likely to be quite successful. Even a domestically posted M.B.A. will find ample opportunity to reap the benefits of an international business education in the increasingly global market of the twenty-first century.

Business schools offer a variety of electives in international business, and most U.S. business schools are developing programs to increase their presence in the global arena. Courses in international business and internationally based project courses stand beside short-term study abroad programs as common avenues for international exposure. Some institutions offer their own set of courses in another part of the world, and others work with exchange partners to provide opportunities for students to work and study in another country. Business school-organized international projects, often performed by a team of students, may involve several weeks of work with a company overseas and allow students to get a personal view of business in the other country. However, these programs don't provide enough international experience to fit the needs of some students. In these instances, U.S. students often look overseas to get an M.B.A., or for a program at a U.S. school that involves a period of study at an institution overseas.

Got to be Global

"'These days, even the plain-vanilla, master-of-the-universe MBA student needs experience overseas,' says Brandt Allen, associate dean of the University of Virginia's Darden Graduate School of Business Administration. 'You've got to be global to pick up on the best ideas, the best people, the best intelligence. Otherwise, you get smashed.'"

—"Wide Open for Business," Newsweek/ Kaplan's *How to Choose a Career and Graduate School*, 1999

Top business schools outside the United States are as competitive in reputation and prestige as the top U.S. schools. The admission requirements of these schools are just as strict as their U.S. counterparts, and their graduates are sought by the same global companies that recruit in the United States. But American students' interest in international business schools goes beyond the very best programs, extending to the less prestigious schools as well.

Options Through U.S. Programs

A source of international experience and knowledge in many schools is the group of international students who are likely to be part of your program. They bring their own perspectives and experiences to classroom discussion and individual interaction outside the classroom. Perhaps, however, you think you want more international exposure than you will get through a few courses and contact with the international students who share your U.S. classroom. Many schools offer an array of exchange programs that allow you to spend a term at a school somewhere outside the United States.

As you are investigating these options, find out the details. What are the partner institutions? Where are they located? Do you need to be fluent in a language other than English? Will you be in classes with the regular students at the partner institution or are there courses reserved just for exchange students? Will you be able to use all the credits you earn abroad to meet degree requirements back in the United States? How are students selected for the exchange programs and how many students are able to participate in exchange programs each year?

Study abroad programs typically allow you to take one semester of your M.B.A. program at a business school in another country. They range from the two-week "If this is Tuesday, it must be Belgium" whirlwind junket to a full 12 months that concludes with a battery of oral and written examinations and leads to an additional degree from the host institution. Because required core courses often consume the entire first year of the M.B.A. program, most students go abroad in the fall semester of the second year, although summer programs are also available.

Many exchange programs limit the number of students who can attend a partner institution each year. These limitations are usually set to assure that the partner school is not flooded with so many students that the educational experience is

GEMBA

"The Fuqua School of Business at Duke University has a widely admired program for midcareer executives (average age: 38) who didn't earn M.B.A.'s earlier on. The program, called Global Executive M.B.A. (GEMBA), takes a year and a half, of which only five weeks are spent at Duke and one week apiece on satellite campuses in Salzburg, Prague, Shanghai, Hong Kong, São Paolo and Buenos Aires. The rest of the time students work from their offices or homes, viewing lectures mailed to them on CD-ROMS and working on projects in teams of five people from varying disciplines and locations."

—"Wide Open for Business," Newsweek/Kaplan's *How to Choose a Career and Graduate School*, 1999

altered. Still, if you choose a U.S. M.B.A. program because it offers a study abroad program in Spain, you will want to know if there are usually 30 students competing for the two slots in the program, or only two or three.

When researching study abroad options, you should find out whether you will be in a special class with other international students or whether you will be in a regular course also taken by the students of the host institution. Programs run by U.S. schools in foreign locations may not offer the same chance to study next to someone from another country as you find in traditional exchange programs, but may have other advantages. Speakers, company tours, and cultural events may be incorporated into the program, rather than left to the initiative of the individual student to uncover or arrange. Since many of these programs are offered in English, they also provide an opportunity to experience parts of the world where you may not have the language fluency to participate in a traditional exchange program.

Since many schools open their summer programs to students from other institutions, it may not be possible to combine graduate management study at one school with an international summer program at another. Even if you find that you cannot use the academic credits earned in the summer program toward your degree at your home institution, the experience and exposure you gain may be just what you need to round out your international background.

You may also wish to consider specialized programs offered by U.S. schools, such as the Japan-focused Master of Business Administration (JEMBA) and the China-focused Master of Business Administration (CHEMBA) from the University of Hawaii. These combine core M.B.A. courses, international business courses focused on Japan or China, Japanese or Mandarin business communication classes, and an internship in a Japanese or Chinese business context. Other institutions offer the opportunity to earn two degrees, one an M.B.A. and the other an area-studies degree.

A final option is a degree program in international business. These programs seek to develop language skills and cultural understanding as well as business competence. International internships are common in this type of setting.

What the Top M.B.A. Programs Say: A Global Focus

Thunderbird Graduate School of International Management

"Thunderbird awards an MIM—Master of International Management. We prepare students to excel in management and leadership roles in a multilingual, multicultural workplace. Proficiency in speaking a second language is required, as is course work in how management practices are influenced by the political, historical, and social environment in which they are undertaken."

University of California—Los Angeles, Anderson School

"The Anderson School offers students a wide range of exciting opportunities to increase their international perspective, including working on group projects with students from among the 43 countries represented at Anderson, studying abroad, enrolling in the International Management Fellows Program, and touring a factory in Prague.

"The Anderson School encourages students to participate in academic exchange programs with universities located abroad. Currently, the school participates in 15 academic foreign exchange programs."

If you have a serious interest in international business and working outside the United States, you will want to consider whether the international options available to you through an American M.B.A. program will give you a sufficient international experience or whether you will be better served by a non-U.S. program.

Getting Your M.B.A. Outside the United States

Some U.S. students decide to travel overseas to earn a graduate management degree because the world's economy is becoming more global by the minute. Most top companies have headquarters in various parts of the world, and many of the larger firms, such as IBM and Andersen Consulting, now recruit outside the United States. Other students believe that learning business traditions and practices from different parts of the world will help them in their job searches and careers.

Career and Lifestyle Goals

Students with international career and lifestyle goals often find studying in another country appealing. If your ultimate goal is to live and work in another part of the world, then in many cases an M.B.A. from the United States is more of a hindrance than a help. A degree from a school local to a particular country generally carries more weight with foreign employers than an equivalent degree from a U.S. school. Remember, however, that most countries have restrictions on who can be hired to work in the country. A degree from a highly respected local school won't help you if you cannot be legally hired in the country of your choice. And keep in mind that if you earn a degree from a school outside the United States, however well reputed, it may carry little value back in the States, where even the best foreign programs are relatively unknown.

International Field Experience

Another advantage to attending business school abroad is the firsthand knowledge of international business culture students receive while completing their studies. Most programs require some type of field work, usually in the form of an internship or mentorship programs. The field experience teaches a lot about the industry in which a student is working as well as the subtleties of the local economy. When B-School graduates apply for the positions in the same regions in which they did their internships, their knowledge of the local business environments may give them an advantage over applicants from other areas.

Similarly, learning how businesses are run in different parts of the world gives a student a distinct advantage over those educated solely in the American way of doing business. The greater the difference between regional and U.S. business practices, the greater the advantage a student can accrue from personal knowledge of that regional system. Business practices in Asia, for example, vary significantly from those in North America and Europe. If your ultimate goal is to work for a U.S. company with close ties to Asia, knowledge of the Asian business system would be extremely helpful. One way to gain this knowledge would be to forego a U.S. business school in favor of an Asian school with ties to business in your area of interest.

Top Asian B-Schools

Schools in Asia that were highly rated in The MBA Career Guide International's 1995 recruiter survey include:

- Asian Institute of Management (Phillipines)
- Australian Graduate School of Management
- Chinese University of Hong Kong
- Hong Kong University of Science and Technology
- International University of Japan
- Keio University (Japan)
- Sasin Graduate Institute (Thailand)

—Source: *World Executive's Digest*, March 1996

Variety

International business schools may also offer programs that aren't common in U.S. schools. Most traditional U.S. business schools offer a two-year curriculum with a summer internship, although many offer accelerated, one-year and/or high-quality, part-time programs. Business schools in other parts of the world may follow tracks that are much more diverse than those of U.S. schools, increasing their appeal for some students. Although some international schools, such as London Business School, offer programs that are similar to traditional U.S. schools, most other European schools stray from the classic American model.

The typical European M.B.A. program runs from ten to fifteen months, depending on field requirements and class hours per semester. INSEAD (The European Institute of Business Administration), an institute created in 1959 by French corporations that wanted to educate people to meet corporate needs, was the first business school to run a ten-month program. INSEAD debunked the myth that the U.S. model is the only successful M.B.A. structure.

In general, European programs tend to place less emphasis on technical skills than their American counterparts and more emphasis on strategic issues and soft skills. Programs in Europe are also colored by the close ties these schools have with businesses that have influenced their development over the years. Because of business involvement, theory and research may receive less attention than they do in the

Top Recruiters' Favorites

According to a worldwide survey of more than 1,000 leading M.B.A. recruiters, these are the business schools from which they would be most likely to recruit M.B.A.'s:

- INSEAD (France)
- The Wharton School
- Harvard University
- London Business School
- IMD (Switzerland)
- University of Chicago
- Stanford University
- Rotterdam School of Management (Netherlands)
- Sloan School of Management, MIT
- IESE (Spain)

—Source: *World Executive's Digest*, March 1996

United States. A major advantage for students is that these ties often facilitate internships and permanent job placements.

An increasing number of U.S. schools are establishing campuses in other parts of the world. A recent estimate by the AACSB indicated that as many as 35 U.S. business schools sponsor international programs. The University of Chicago's B-school currently runs an executive M.B.A. program at a campus in Barcelona. Although this program is run by a U.S. school, its structure differs greatly from the classic American model. Participants in the Barcelona program take 16 courses intermittently over a span of eighteen months. Students come from many parts of Europe and the Middle East, flying in for intensive modules that last one to two weeks.

Some U.S. schools are developing partnerships with business schools from other parts of the world. The University of South Carolina and the Wirtschaftsuniversität Wien offer a 15-month program in which students start their studies in Vienna and conclude them in Columbia, South Carolina. Some of these partnerships are joint ventures with business schools in other countries, such as Northwestern University's Kellogg School program in Hong Kong, to which the Hong Kong University of Science and Technology contributes 50 percent of the faculty. Despite the international cooperation and faculty, the curriculum uses the Northwestern model. Business school partnerships may also offer the opportunity to earn more than one degree. For example, L'École Supérieure de Commerce du Havre (in Le Havre, France) has agreements with several institutions, including Wake Forest University, the University of South Florida, the University of New Mexico, and the University of Illinois/Chicago, that allow students to earn both an American M.B.A. and the French business degree.

Many schools provide students with an opportunity to study in multiple locations. ISG (Institut Supérieur de Gestion, based in Paris) offers a fourteen-month program that rotates students among campuses in Paris, New York, and Tokyo. Participants take classes in two of the three locations, and then may attend additional seminars in various location in Eastern Europe, South America, and Southeast Asia. Even though students pay additional fees for seminars (including air fare in some instances), most of the students who complete this program admit that seminars enrich their education invaluably.

IMD, in Switzerland, one of the top-rated business schools in the world, has an eleven-month program with a class size of just 80 students. This provides for plenty of individual attention for students, and 94 percent of graduates receive job offers before graduation. The IMD program focuses on students who are older and more experienced than the typical U.S. B-school students. The typical IMD student is thirty years old and has six years of work experience.

Like American M.B.A. programs, some B-schools abroad offer unique features as part of their curricula. The European Institute of Purchasing Management in France offers one-year, full-time and two- to three-year, part-time M.B.A. programs for individuals who wish to pursue a career in that particular field. ESSEC (École Supérieure des Sciences Économiques et Commerciales), on the outskirts of

> ### Queens in Canada
>
> A world leader in the use of education technology, Queens University offers an M.B.A. for Science and Technology, the first of its kind in Canada, and the National Executive M.B.A., which is delivered via interactive multi-point videoconferencing.

Paris, offers an M.B.A. program that specializes in luxury brand management and is partially organized by the world's leading luxury goods companies. For engineers who want an M.B.A., France's IEFSI runs a program designed to convert engineers to managers.

International programs come in as many different varieties as their American counterparts. Some of the variation results from the educational system and typical career path in the country where the school is located. Some differences reflect the disparate histories and expectations of management education across countries and cultures. When researching international programs, it is particularly important, and often especially difficult, to bear in mind all the factors that will shape the business school experience. For example, you should not assume that the profile of the student body will resemble that at an American institution; the students could be younger and less experienced, or they could be older and more experienced. Some programs might require an internship of their students, since the students generally have little or no formal work experience prior to their M.B.A. work. If you have a similar background, this internship gives you both work experience and an opportunity to explore another business culture. However, if you enter such a program with significant work experience, the additional time away from your career may be less valuable, and you may wish to waive this requirement, if possible.

Cost and Financial Assistance

Student may consider studying abroad to save money. Some state-supported universities in Europe and elsewhere charge no tuition and only modest fees. However, some schools carry a hefty price tag and may charge nonresidents or noncitizens more than residents and citizens.

If you're thinking about studying abroad, check out the cost of living in the city in which the school is located. Do this beforehand so that you can estimate how much you'll have to budget for your indirect costs (costs other than tuition and fees). Certain places are much more expensive than you may be accustomed to. If you are considering studying in Japan, for example, be prepared for very high housing costs. On the other hand, some European schools are located in small towns where housing and food are much more reasonably priced. This estimate becomes more difficult if you might face currency instability or high inflation. Depending on your destination, you may need to have an additional financial cushion in case the exchange or inflation rates change markedly.

The availability of financial assistance will vary from school to school. Most schools abroad don't have the same kind of grant and scholarship programs that U.S. schools do. Check out the availability of Federal Stafford Student Loans before you commit to studying abroad; most state guarantee agencies have an approval list of foreign schools. If your school of choice isn't on that list, you may not be able to take out student loans to study there.

Applying for federal funds to study abroad is somewhat different from applying for funds for U.S. study. In most cases, you submit the Federal Stafford Loan application directly to the guarantee agency of the state and the agency does the certification for you. Your loan proceeds are sent directly to you rather than the school, and you get the entire amount in one disbursement. You are then responsible for paying the school yourself. If your financial need goes beyond what's available from federal funding, contact private lenders individually to see if they lend to students who study abroad.

Don't Count on a Part-Time Job

Few countries outside the United States have a tradition of students working to put themselves through school, so don't expect a part-time job to be a solution to any financial problems you might have, especially since, as a foreigner, you'll have to obtain a special work permit of some type.

Handling your loan proceeds is just one of the financial areas where you may need to make arrangements for someone to assist you while you are abroad. Significant delays can occur when checks need to be mailed to another country or when money is transferred across borders. In addition to transit times, the receiving bank may not credit your account until the full amount of the funds have been received from the United States. Check clearing delays of three weeks are not unusual.

Take the time to check out both the costs and the availability of scholarships and loans before you commit to a business school abroad. Research and advance planning are the keys to financing your study abroad.

Admission Requirements

Foreign M.B.A. programs may have special language, experience, test, and undergraduate degree requirements.

Language Skills

Although some overseas business schools teach classes in English, most teach strictly in the local language (or a combination of the local language and English). For instance, INSEAD teaches some classes in French and other in English, and therefore requires fluency in both. INSEAD administers a French fluency test that students must pass to be admitted. The University of National and World Economy in Sofia, Bulgaria, teaches all its class in Bulgarian, and doesn't have an English language requirement. Obviously, unless you're fluent in Bulgarian, this school is not for you.

Schools that demand fluency in English require the TOEFL (Test of English as a Foreign Language) of students whose first language is not English, and most require a score of 550 or better. If you are required to take the TOEFL as a condition of business school admission, make sure that you're prepared for it. It would be disastrous to be rejected from a school because of your TOEFL score. Applicants needing to take the TOEFL should call schools of interest and ask if they have minimum TOEFL score requirements.

Even though some schools abroad teach all classes in English, and thus don't require fluency in the country's native language, U.S. students there are immersed in a new society and need to be sufficiently proficient in the local language to live comfortably. So if you plan to attend business school in a non-English-speaking country, you should learn the language, whether or not the school requires it.

Experience

B-school programs abroad are split between those that require little or no work experience and may lead directly to an M.B.A. or M.B.A.-equivalent, and those that require a certain amount of experience. Often, schools require students to have work experience in management or some other executive position. For executive M.B.A. programs, the rule of thumb for applicants is ten years' experience; for regular M.B.A. programs, it's usually significantly less.

GMAT

Virtually all U.S. business schools require the GMAT, but that isn't the case abroad. Although it's true that many of the top schools do require it, some have decided against using GMAT scores, and others use them in nontraditional ways.

Some schools, such as the University of Bradford Management Centre and Cranford School of Management in Great Britain, and the Wits Business School in South Africa, require the GMAT in lieu of another part of the application (school-administered admission test, interview, and so forth). The University of Otago in New Zealand, EAP European School of Management in France, and the Norwegian School of Management have established minimum GMAT scores, and will not accept applicants who do meet this minimum. Most schools, however, follow the Educational Testing Service's recommendation. They use the GMAT to help them make admissions decisions, but they have no established cutoff score. Make sure you find out the average GMAT score of schools that interest you, whether or not there is a minimum score requirement, and if your GMAT score can substitute for another piece of the application.

Undergraduate Degree Requirements

U.S. business schools generally require students to have bachelor's degrees and many look for a mixture of humanities, business, and technology majors to add diversity to their classes. Even though it's true that certain schools attract certain types of students (for example, MIT's Sloan School of Management attracts a high percentage of students with undergraduate degrees in technology), it is quite rare for a school to establish programs that target a single undergraduate major. In Europe, however, such specialized programs are more common, and some schools even admit students without undergraduate degrees. For example, Lancaster University's Management School in Britain admits individuals without undergraduate degrees, provided they have acquired equivalent professional experience.

When applying to a school outside the United States, remember that the schools and conventions that are familiar to U.S. admissions officers may not be known internationally. Relatively few American colleges and universities have international reputations, so your degree from a first-rate liberal arts college may make no more of an impression than the local community college. You may need to distinguish yourself on the basis of other factors or provide additional information about your undergraduate program. Establishing the quality of your prior academic performance may be a particular challenge if your alma mater did not use a traditional American grading scale. Sensitivity to issues of educational culture will assist you in presenting a strong

Want to Specialize?

- IEFSI offers an M.B.A. specifically for professional engineers who wish to move into management positions.

- Britain's Imperial College Management School specializes in training ambitious civil servants to be effective managers in the bureaucratic system.

- M.B.A. Science Po in Paris offers pre-M.B.A. courses so that engineers can be brought up to speed in business concepts before entering its M.B.A. program alongside business professionals.

application and show that you already have an understanding of some of the factors affecting international business.

Is It Really for You?

Even though attending business school abroad is an option to be considered, it isn't for everyone. Even those who know that they want to study abroad will find that not every school fits their needs. When deciding which programs are best for you, do the same kind of research you do when comparing U.S. schools—but go even further. The rewards of finding an international school that fits your needs can be tremendous, but going to school so far away from home can also be a big risk. So talk to alumni, read as much as you can about the schools, check out career placement services, and visit the schools if you can.

The decision to study internationally should also be based on a careful review of what you want from a program and your ability to adapt to the demands of a rigorous educational program in another culture. One predictor of your likely success in an international program is the success of prior stays in another country. Indeed, admission offices may question your true level of interest in international study and your ability to adapt, if you have never spent time abroad prior to applying to an international M.B.A. program. In this instance, it may still be possible to satisfy your international curiosity through shorter exchange programs or in-country residency courses.

PART THREE

Admissions

CHAPTER 6

How Do Schools Evaluate Applicants?

Each business school has its own admissions policies and practices, but most programs evaluate applications using a range of objective and subjective criteria. Regardless of which schools you are pursuing, understanding how admissions officers judge your candidacy can give you a leg up on the competition, enhancing your prospects for being admitted to the school of your choice.

Generally, admissions officers use the application process to measure your intellectual abilities, management skills, and personal characteristics. When you submit your application, admissions officers will evaluate the total package. Most admissions officers look for reasons to admit candidates, not for reasons to reject them. Your challenge, therefore, is to distinguish yourself positively from the other candidates in a variety of arenas.

Academic Record

Admissions officers are likely to start their review by looking at your prior academic record. They want to see evidence of your ability to handle the academic rigors of their program. Also, your academic record enables admissions officers to compare you to other students, albeit imperfectly.

This is why your admissions application must include official copies of your academic transcripts from every post-secondary school you attended, whether or not you received a degree. You must request that these transcripts be sent to you in sealed envelopes for you to include in your self-managed application. Even if you have an official copy of your college transcript, the B-school requires that you submit an official copy in an envelope sealed by the registrar of your college. Colleges usually charge a fee for copies

Ask Yourself . . .

- Do my grades show an upward trend?

- Did I perform well in my major?

- Did I fare well in calculus and other quantitative courses?

If the answer to any of these questions is no, you may have to take action to improve your transcript.

of your transcript, so contact the college registrar's office to find out the costs and request the transcripts.

Your grade point average (GPA) is important, but it's just part of the picture. Admissions officers will consider the reputation of your undergraduate institution and the difficulty of your courses. Admissions officers are well aware that comparing GPAs from different schools and even different majors from the same school is like comparing apples and oranges. So they'll look closely at your transcript.

Calculus, statistics, and other quantitative courses may be prerequisites for your intended program. Quantitative skills are considered essential in completing M.B.A. coursework, and your record in these areas will be carefully scrutinized for difficulty, currency, and overall quality by admissions committees. If your transcript does not show any evidence of quantitative skills, you should consider taking courses in accounting and statistics to demonstrate your aptitude and to reinforce your commitment to pursuing a business degree.

A strong performance in your advanced courses and major is interpreted as an indication that you can handle difficult work and that you can excel in your field of choice. An admissions officer may pay particularly close attention to your GPA in your last two years of undergraduate study, since most students complete work in their major as college juniors and seniors. But don't think an attempt to raise your GPA by taking introductory level courses your last term will not be recognized for what it is.

Brush up on Your Skills

"Since I had been out of school for more than 20 years, I took an algebra course at a local community college before starting my GMAT preparation. This not only started me thinking mathematically, but also helped me do well on the GMAT."

—Current EMBA student, Stern School of Business, New York University

The weight that is given to your undergraduate grades in the admission decision is affected in part by the length of time you have been out of school. If you have been out of school for some time, the passage of years makes it easier to argue that low grades can be attributed to youthful inexperience, now replaced by maturity. Unfortunately, it also raises the question of maintenance over time of skills that once brought impressive grades but that may now be rusty, if not in total disrepair. Admissions officers will look for evidence in other parts of your application to support their reading of a transcript earned many years earlier.

For recent graduates, meanwhile, the transcript is seen as a likely predictor of current skills and performance. This implies that strong grades may help offset weakness in other areas, but weak grades are much harder to dismiss or counter.

Admissions officers focus primarily on your undergraduate performance, but they will consider graduate studies and nondegree coursework that you have completed. If you have a weak undergraduate record, you may want to take additional courses to demonstrate your ability to succeed in the classroom. You may be inclined to enroll for nondegree courses in an M.B.A. program rather than in a community college or four-year undergraduate program to show your ability to handle this type of work. Be aware, though, that some top-tier programs will not accept students who have substantially completed another M.B.A. program, even from a nonaccredited program, and that admissions officers will examine these transcripts with as much care as they will use for transcripts of your undergraduate degree.

If you have a poor academic record, it will be tougher to get into a top school, but by no means impossible. Your challenge is to find other ways to demonstrate your intellectual horsepower. A high GMAT score, intelligently written essays, and recommendations that highlight your analytical abilities will help. Your work experience may show a record of promotion and success in meeting new intellectual challenges.

GMAT

The second criterion that admissions officers use to measure your intellectual ability is the Graduate Management Admission Test (GMAT). An integral part of the admissions process at virtually all schools, the GMAT measures verbal, quantitative, and analytical writing skills that are developed over your educational career. It does not test business competence or specific subject knowledge beyond general mathematics and English usage. The GMAT is designed to predict academic success in the first year of a graduate business school program.

Unlike undergraduate grades, which vary in their meaning from institution to institution and from discipline to discipline, GMAT scores use a consistent standard for all test takers. Thus the GMAT can be a useful guide in comparing the credentials of candidates from widely different backgrounds. Used by itself, the GMAT may not be a highly reliable predictor of academic performance, but it is the single best one available. Many schools routinely perform studies to gauge the effectiveness of the GMAT and other admission criteria in predicting performance in their program, and use this information to help them interpret the scores applicants present.

Description of the GMAT

The GMAT is now administered in a computerized format in North American and in many other parts of the world. This new type of test is called the Computer Adaptive Test (CAT), and is more than just a computerized version of a traditional paper-and-pencil test. The CAT allows you to see only one question at a time; you must answer that question to continue the test. Each question is chosen from a large pool of questions of varying degrees of difficulty. The first question is of medium difficulty. The selection of each subsequent question is determined by your response to all previous questions. If you keep answering questions correctly, the test will increase in difficulty; if you slip and make some mistakes, the test will adjust and start giving you easier problems. If you answer the easier questions correctly, the CAT will return to the harder ones.

One of the major differences between the CAT and a traditional paper-and-pencil test is that the CAT doesn't permit you to skip around within a section and do questions in any order. You also cannot go back and change your answer. Instead, you have to do your best to get a question right the first time you see it.

The purpose of the CAT is to give you a score based on the level at which you answer questions correctly about half the time. Hence the overall number you get right is not as important as the level at which you start getting about half the questions wrong. In spite of all these differences, computer-based test scores are considered comparable to paper scores.

There are a number of advantages to the new testing format. Among these are:

Convenience

Unlike the paper-and-pencil GMAT, which was administered only four times a year, the CAT is available throughout the year on an appointment basis. You can take it at hundreds of computer centers around the country.

Additional Time Per Question

The CAT allows you more time per question than the traditional test did.

Immediate Scoring and Faster Score Reporting

Once you have completed the computer-adaptive GMAT, you can choose to see your scores for the multiple-choice sections of the test at the test center. If you are not happy with your performance, you may cancel your scores before you see them.

Faster Score Reporting

An official score report, including scores for the Analytical Writing Assessment, will be mailed to you and your designated institutions about two weeks after testing. Scores for the paper-based GMAT take four to ten weeks after the testing date.

Individualized Environment

When you take the CAT, you are alone with a computer in the quiet and privacy of a separate testing station, not elbow to elbow with many other people in a large room. This no-distractions environment is very beneficial to some people.

You do not need to be computer-literate to take the CAT. Before beginning the test, you'll complete a tutorial to ensure that you are comfortable at the keyboard. It covers such areas as using a computer mouse, entering a response, using the word processor, accessing the help function, and moving on to the next question. The help function will be available throughout the actual test.

The GMAT CAT includes verbal, quantitative, and analytical writing questions that you answer on the computer. You will have 75 minutes to complete 37 quantitative questions, 75 minutes for 41 verbal questions and 30 minutes for each of the two analytical writing topics. The types of questions are the same as in the paper-based test, but the multiple choice questions are not grouped into sections by specific question types. Instead, Data Sufficiency and Problem Solving questions are interspersed throughout the quantitative section, and Sentence Correction, Reading Comprehension, and Critical Reasoning questions can be found throughout the verbal section.

> ## Test Your Best on the GMAT
>
> Kaplan's GMAT course teaches you the content and strategies you'll need to maximize your GMAT score and provides you with the opportunity to practice on authentic computer-adaptive tests. Call 1-800-KAP-TEST or visit www.kaplan.com (AOL keyword: Kaplan) to find out more details. You can also find Kaplan/Simon & Schuster's test prep guide, *GMAT CAT 1999-2000*, in most bookstores.

Analytical Writing Assessment

The GMAT contains an essay section, the "Analytical Writing Assessment" (AWA), that asks you to write two essays—one an analysis of an issue and the other an analysis of an argument. The AWA is designed to provide schools with information about your communications skills that is not otherwise captured by the GMAT.

Essentially, the AWA is another tool that schools can use to evaluate you. Although it won't reduce the importance of the essays on your applications, it does provide you with an opportunity to demonstrate your ability to think critically and communicate complex ideas in a very limited time period. For that reason, admissions officers may be as interested in reading your writing samples as they are in relying on your overall GMAT score.

On the other hand, admissions officers at top-tier schools already struggle to get through all their applications. That will limit the time they can spend reviewing these hand-written essays. Remember also that some applicants are still submitting old GMAT scores that do not include writing samples. Admissions officers are careful not to discriminate for or against candidates based on which GMAT they've taken.

Even though the AWA is scored separately from the multiple-choice sections, you should prepare for it with the same intensity that you put into preparing for the rest of the GMAT. Outstanding writing samples can help you stand out from the crowd. Conversely, seriously flawed essays can reduce your admissions chances.

What Your GMAT Scores Mean

You will receive a total of four scores on the GMAT: one each for the verbal, quantitative, and analytical writing sections and an overall score. It is this overall score that is used when programs report an "average GMAT score" for candidates accepted to the program, and the overall score that receives the most attention when admissions officers review your application. If you've taken the GMAT more than once, schools will generally credit you with your highest score, though some may average the scores or take the most recent one.

The total score is reported an a 200 to 800 scale, with an average score of 500. Each standard deviation from the mean (average) equals 100 points. According to this scale, a score of 700 is two standard deviations above the mean, indicating that approximately 97 percent of all scores fall below this mark.

In addition to the actual score you receive on the 200 to 800 scale, you will get a "percentile ranking" that tells you what percentage of test takers had scores below yours. You will also receive a percentile ranking for your performance on the verbal portion of the test and a second percentile ranking for the quantitative section. Although these scores typically do not receive as much attention from schools as your overall score, they can be very helpful in corroborating impressions from other parts of your application or filling in gaps in the information. For example, if you have never taken a college-level quantitative course, your score on the quantitative section of the GMAT may provide evidence of your current skills in that area.

The score on the Analytical Writing Assessment is reported separately from the score on the multiple choice sections of the GMAT. Reported on a scale of zero to six in half-point increments, a score of six is defined as "outstanding," whereas a four is considered "adequate," and a score of one is "fundamentally deficient." A zero score is given if the essay is off-topic, in a foreign language, or merely attempts to copy the topic. The average score is about 3.5. As with the scores on the verbal and quantitative sections, the AWA score provides additional information about this important skill. It will be reviewed more closely if there are questions about your critical thinking and writing skills than if you have clearly demonstrated expertise in these areas from your credentials.

Registering for the GMAT

In the United States, U.S. Territories, Puerto Rico, and Canada, you can register for the GMAT by phone using a credit card. If you don't have a credit card, you can submit a registration form by mail and receive a voucher that will then allow you to schedule your GMAT CAT appointment by phone. Phone registration is available at (800) GMAT-NOW ((800) 462-8669) or at a local Sylvan Technology Center. Phone registration is available through regional registration centers located around the world.

Although the computer adaptive test is given on many days during the month and it is typically possible to get a testing time within 30 days of your request, the most popular times are filled quickly.

Advance booking will allow you to get the time and place you want. Moreover, since you can take the GMAT CAT only once per calendar month, taking it early will allow you to repeat it, if necessary, and still have scores before the end of the admission season.

Score reports are mailed weekly to the schools that you indicate on your registration form should receive your test results. Additional information on GMAT registration, both in the United States and internationally, is available through the Graduate Management Admission Council's Web site at http://www.gmat.org.

Repeating the GMAT

Although some people repeat the GMAT because a management school requests more recent scores than currently on record, the most common reason for repeating the test is to attempt to improve test scores. Although mere familiarity with the test may push scores slightly higher the second time, scores can also drop. Unless your scores seem unusually low compared with other indicators of your ability to succeed in an M.B.A. program or there are other reasons to believe you have not performed your best, such as illness or lack of preparation, taking the GMAT more than once may not be helpful.

If you choose to repeat the test, your scores from the latest test date and the two most recent administrations in the past five years will be reported to the institutions you designate as score recipients.

Management Skills

To evaluate your management skills, admissions officers look at work experience and other relevant activities. They generally believe that the best way to measure your management potential is to look at what you've actually done. Many graduate business programs expect candidates to have several years of work experience prior to entrance. If your credentials fall outside the typical range of work experience for the program, you may need to compensate with the quality of your experience in other arenas.

You can communicate some of your management abilities through the straightforward "data" part of your application. Be sure to describe your job responsibilities. Don't just list your title and assume that an admissions officer knows what you do or the level of your responsibilities. This is especially important if your job is nontraditional for an aspiring M.B.A.

Many M.B.A. candidates come from the traditional areas of consumer goods, financial institutions, consulting, and

> ## Show Career Progress
>
> "I believe that M.B.A. programs are looking for candidates that have shown progress in their current jobs—increased responsibility, promotions, salary increases etc. The work recommendation should complement what the candidate says about himself."
>
> —M.B.A., Stanford Graduate School of Business

Leadership Challenges

"I had only a 580 on my GMAT, but I was in ROTC as an undergraduate. I spent six months on active duty as a lieutenant leading a tank squad, with $2 billion in equipment under my control. I had very interesting leadership challenges to bring up in my essays, which I think was one of the reasons I got into Wharton."

—Current Bschool student, Wharton School

accounting. This background is good training ground for management education, especially since there is demand in these industries for M.B.A. graduates. However, applicants from one of these fields will be competing with many others with similar backgrounds, and will need to distinguish themselves through their achievements and the presentation of their other qualities.

Although major companies are a natural path into a graduate management program, they are by no means the only route. If you have experience in a not-for-profit organization, government agency, small or medium-sized enterprise, or some other institution, your application will already stand out in contrast to those from candidates with large company experience. However, you still face the challenge of translating your experience for the admissions officer and showing why you are a good candidate for an M.B.A. degree.

Admissions officers will look at your overall career record. Have you been an outstanding performer? What do your recommendation writers say about your performance? Have you progressed to increasingly higher levels of responsibility? If you have limited work experience, you will not be expected to match the accomplishments of an applicant with ten years' experience, but you will be expected to demonstrate your abilities.

As you are thinking about your work experience, ask yourself the following questions:

- *How can I show that I have been successful in accomplishing my job responsibilities?* Additional responsibilities, promotions, salary increases, and leadership assignments might form part of your answer.

- *Do I work well with people?* M.B.A. programs that stress teamwork are particularly interested in your ability to work well with others, but the general tendency in business to use teams makes this attribute important in all settings.

- *What have I managed?* Not all jobs involve direct management of people. Perhaps you have managed projects or financial assets, or perhaps you have accomplished goals through other people, even though you have not had direct management authority over them.

- *What is the range of my experience?* Have you demonstrated abilities in a variety of areas? An M.B.A. is a general management degree. Both during the program and after graduation, M.B.A.'s are expected to be able to work in a variety of disciplines, using a variety of skills.

- *Have I excelled in what I do and worked beyond average expectations for the position?*

The essays also provide an opportunity to demonstrate your management aptitude. Many essay questions specifically ask you to discuss your professional experiences and how you handled different situations. With thoughtful, well-written essays, you can highlight your management strengths.

Extracurricular Activities and Community Involvement

Extracurricular activities and community involvement also present opportunities for you to highlight your skills. For younger applicants, college activities play a more significant role than for more seasoned applicants. Your activities say a lot about who you are and what's important to you. Were you a campus leader? Did your activities require discipline and commitment? Did your work with a team? What did you learn from your involvement?

Active community involvement provides a way for you to demonstrate your management skills and to impress admissions officers with your personal character. In fact, many applications ask directly about community activities. Many programs like to see candidates who demonstrate concern for individuals other than themselves, who are willing and able to assume responsibility beyond their jobs, and who can function in a variety of settings. If you are contemplating getting involved in your community, here's a chance to do something worthwhile and enhance your application in the process.

> ### Stand Out from the Crowd
>
> "If I had a traditional career (analyst for example), I would be sure that I had an 'unusual' experience about which to write. This means spending a summer as a volunteer building homes for Habitat for Humanity, being a mentor, getting involved with a community 'do-good' organization, etc."
>
> —Current EMBA student, Stern School of Business, New York University

A good way to organize your thinking is to compile a Personal Data Sheet (PDS) on which you can list all your extracurricular activities, relevant dates of participation, and any honors or positions of leadership you won, along with basic information such as your name, address, phone, undergraduate and graduate GPAs, and GMAT scores. Give this form to your recommenders to remind them of your accomplishments.

Personal Characteristics

The most subjective criterion on which schools evaluate you is your personal characteristics. Admissions officers judge you in this area primarily through essays, recommendations, and your interview.

Although different schools emphasize different qualities, most seek candidates who demonstrate leadership, maturity, integrity, responsibility, and teamwork. The more competitive schools place special emphasis on these criteria because they have many qualified applicants for each available spot in the class. In fact, the top-tier programs generally require numerous essays so that they can get a complete feel for each applicant's personal qualities.

Your presentation of your personal characteristics is important in demonstrating how well you will fit into the program of your choice. If the program emphasizes teamwork, you will want to make sure you demonstrate interpersonal skills. If you are looking at an international focus, you will want to show that you can adapt to different cultures and environments. If the program is highly competitive, you will want admissions officers to see that you can thrive in that setting.

Business School Admissions Stereotypes

Background	Perceived Strengths	Perceived Weaknesses
Engineers	Good quantitative skills; process oriented; low risk of poor academic performance	Less developed communication/ interpersonal skills; weaker writing skills
Consultants	Smart; well-grounded in fundamentals; good exposure to business situations	Limited management experience; many qualified applicants to top schools with similar experience
Financial Analysts	Good quantitative skills; solid understanding of business analysis/ research	Limited management experience; many qualified applicants to top schools with similar experience
Entrepreneurs	Hands-on understanding of how business works; high energy; proactive; not many in applicant pool	Impatient with classroom environment; limited interest in business theory
Human Resources People	Interpersonal skills and understanding of employee-related issues; strong team players	Weak quantitative skills; less competitive approach may create academic pressure at top schools
Salespeople	Great "in the trenches" experience; understanding of the customer; strong interpersonal/communication skills	Limited exposure to management; sales sometimes not viewed as training ground for management
Artists, "Poets"	Strong creative skills; unique backgrounds increase classroom diversity	Weaker quantitative skills; limited business exposure; questionable fit; academic risk
Military Personnel	Strong leadership; excellent discipline; hands-on management experience	Inflexible; may have trouble adjusting to a less hierarchical business environment
Accountants	Good numbers skills; understand "language" of business; background helpful for most classes	Quiet; may not participate much in class; not creative

Overcoming Stereotypes

Admissions officers know that all applicants are unique, each with his or her own strengths and weaknesses, and they will judge you on that basis. But after evaluating thousands of applications, stereotypes do emerge, as you can see from the table on the previous page. Understanding how admissions officers will initially perceive your experience—and what it says about you—can help you think strategically about ways to differentiate yourself from other applicants with similar backgrounds.

Increasing Classroom Diversity

Your "personal characteristics" also encompass your gender and ethnic background. Admissions officers work hard to maximize classroom diversity. Each year, they invest significant time and effort to recruit candidates from underrepresented groups. Nevertheless, women and minorities remain underrepresented at most programs. Schools will not admit students they feel are not academically qualified, but diversity goals will help some students stand out in the applicant pool.

Admissions officers encourage applications from international candidates because they add to classroom diversity and provide a fresh perspective. Because all students must be able to communicate effectively, applicants whose native language is not English may be required to take the Test of English as a Foreign Language (TOEFL), Test of Written English (TWE), and/or Test of Spoken English (TSE). Although some schools have minimum test requirements and others use the scores as a guideline, 600 on the TOEFL is generally considered a measure of adequate English skills. Some schools may require or recommend that international students who are admitted with marginal language skills take English coursework before matriculating. See the chapter on international students for more details.

Be aware that diversity extends beyond nationality, race and gender. It may encompass such factors as geography, professional experience, and college studies. The following programs, chosen by their programmatic and geographical diversity, were asked to describe their class profiles in a survey. Their responses should help you identify what the schools are looking for in M.B.A. candidates, and to consider how you can leverage various aspects of your background to your advantage.

> ### *Diversity Valued*
>
> "I'm pretty sure that Stanford valued my nontraditional background (Peace Corps volunteer, demographer, etc.). I also had international work experience and was an active member of my community."
>
> —M.B.A., Stanford Graduate School of Business

What the Top M.B.A. Programs Say: Class Profile

University of Chicago

"The typical student at the Graduate School of Business is able to combine superior intellectual skills with excellent interpersonal skills. The typical incoming class that we strive to put together is quite diverse in terms of educational and ethnic backgrounds, career paths and social experience, and country of origin. Many students say they learn as much from the diversity of the other students they meet and work with at the school as they do from their course work. Because each class represents a wide variety of undergraduate majors and backgrounds, the curriculum is wide-ranging enough to satisfy any interest. The faculty is drawn from a variety of disciplines as well, and this diversity is reflected in teaching styles.

"The school seeks candidates with strong potential for success in both an academically demanding program of study and a professional career. We accept applications from students in all fields of undergraduate study and evaluate work experience on an individual basis as well."

Broadening Applicant Bases

"At the Carnegie Mellon Graduate School of Industrial Administration, the proportion of entering students with liberal-arts degrees has gone from approximately zero two decades ago to roughly half. Of the 487 students who entered Columbia's M.B.A. program in fall 1998, only 21 percent were business majors, compared with 23 percent who studied economics and 33 percent with degrees in humanities and the social sciences."

—"Help! I Majored in Beer,"
Newsweek/Kaplan's *Careers 2000*

Indiana University

"Diversity in terms of race, gender, ethnicity, leadership ability, work experience, and evidence of management potential is important to our matrix. We look for individuals who buy into the team work concept, too. Whether they are Peace Corps volunteers or engineers, it's important for students to have a focus and vision of who they are and where they are going. A rich and diverse profile makes the educational environment beneficial.

"We seek to bring in people who fit our institution. We have a sense of who we are and we project that. We look for a mixture of those with backgrounds in liberal arts and science and engineering as well as business. That way, different approaches to problem solving can be achieved."

Cornell University, Johnson School

"The 'typical' Johnson School student cannot be easily labeled or categorized. Each year we work to put together a class that emphasizes diversity—in background, interests, experience, and career goals. As we put together a diverse class—one in which students can expect to learn as much from their peers as from the faculty—we look for strong leadership skills, the maturity and initiative to use the resources of the Johnson School and Cornell, solid academic ability, and potential for career success.

"In looking for indicators of management potential, we consider prior academic performance, GMAT scores, the range and depth of work experience, demonstrated leadership and interpersonal skills, writing skills, interviewing ability, extracurricular and community involvement, career aspirations, recommendations, and previous achievements.

"Undergraduate majors of our students break down as follows: engineering (20 percent), economics (20 percent), math and science (10 percent), humanities (10 percent), social sciences (15 percent), and business (25 percent)."

Unorthodox Backgrounds at Kellogg

- A Renaissance English major worked in catalog production at Sotheby's auction house in New York City before being accepted to Kellogg Graduate School of Management.

- A pastor at the Fourth Presbyterian Church of Chicago attended Kellogg in order to learn how to manage the church's finances and to rise to the top of her profession.

—adapted from Newsweek/Kaplan's *How to Choose a Career and Graduate School,* 1999 and *Careers 2000*

University of California—Los Angeles, Anderson School

"The Anderson School admission policy emphasizes academic ability, leadership, and work experience. The Admissions Committee evaluates applicants' prospects as effective managers and their projected ability to succeed in and profit from the M.B.A. Program. Committee members carefully consider biographical and academic background information, GMAT and TOEFL (for most international applicants) scores, achievements, distinctions, awards and honors, employment history, letters of recommendation, and college and community involvement, especially when candidates have served in a leadership capacity."

University of Virginia, Darden School

"The defining characteristics of the program—case method, general management, and integrated curriculum—define the admissions considerations. Diversity is a pedagogical necessity given the importance of class participation in the learning process; and so too, for similar reasons, are strong communication and interpersonal skills. General management requires individuals with both broad balanced capabilities and wide-ranging interests. Given the somewhat unique nature of the program, 'fit' is one of the most important considerations—finding those individuals who not only possess the requisite capabilities but the desire to learn general management in a small, highly interactive, community-oriented program."

Tulane University, Freeman School

"In the Freeman School's most recent full-time class, students' academic backgrounds were extremely diverse. Specifically, 29 percent of the class came from engineering/science, 29 percent from social sciences, 22 percent from business, and 20 percent from humanities and arts. This combination of backgrounds leads to a curriculum that emphasizes teamwork and participation. Faculty expect students to actively contribute in the classroom, while students expect faculty to capitalize on student diversity and to use it as a teaching tool. A dose of theory is balanced with extensive use of the case method, which capitalizes on students' past experiences."

The Admissions Review Process

To understand the review process, you will need a basic grasp of the review committee, their procedures, and their decisions.

Admissions Committees

Knowing what kind of people are likely to review your application will help you find the appropriate tone for it. Admissions committees vary by school, but, despite common perception, they don't consist entirely of old men with long white beards. At most schools, the committee includes professional admissions officers whose primary responsibility is to select the M.B.A. class from among the applicant pool. Some schools include faculty members on the committee, but many do not. Some schools hire recent graduates to sit on the committee, believing these individuals are in a good position to judge which candidates will benefit from and contribute to the overall business school experience. And at some schools, second year students and/or alumni play a role in reviewing applications and interviewing candidates.

As with most things, knowing the right people helps. But when it comes to the admissions process, it's hard to predict how much benefit you'll receive from an inside connection. If a school's faculty member, administrator, or respected alumnus can put in a good word for you, great. Depending on how influential that person is and how heavily they'll go to bat for you, they can have an impact. But be careful. Generally, the impact is negligible, and you risk antagonizing the admissions committee if you pursue this tactic.

Admissions officers are not always representative of the group of students they admit. Many committees contain a high percentage of women and minorities, and are likely to recognize the importance of diversity in the classroom. Although some admissions officers have had management training and business experience, many have not. They tend to be people-oriented and have strong interpersonal skills. They want to get to "know" you through your application, and they are partial to well-written essays. They're dedicated to maintaining their objectivity in an inherently subjective process, but they all have their "pet" biases (sometimes related to their own academic or professional experience).

Review Procedures

Just as the composition of the admissions committee varies by school, so does the process by which decisions are made. Some schools make decisions by committee, but many use a system in which each application, or "file," is routed from one committee member to another. Here is a standard procedure:

- Application materials are received. The file is compiled by operations staff, who ensure that all components have been received.

- Based on an initial review, the application is put in categories ranging from strong to long-shot. This process varies by school and may involve calculating a weighted average of GPA, GMAT, and work experience. Alternatively, the application may be reviewed by an individual committee member.

- The application is routed to admissions officers, who carefully read it and make written evaluations and recommendations.

- The application goes to the director, who reviews committee members' comments, personally evaluates the application, and makes a final decision.

> ### University of Chicago's Review Procedures
>
> "The admission process at the Graduate School of Business is personalized, deliberate, and time-consuming. Three people read and evaluate every application, and one of these three is the director of admissions.
>
> "If questions arise from the material submitted, admissions officers contact the applicant to clarify. The goal of the admissions process is to make each class the best possible."
>
> —Admissions Officer, University of Chicago

Evaluations of individual applications are typically "blind," that is, made without knowledge of any prior evaluation, shielding the reviewer from possible effects of bias from the other readers. If all the reviews recommend admission, the application may not go to the director or committee for a final review; applications with split decisions are passed to the committee or director for a decision.

Application Review Cycles

There are two primary models for admission cycles: "rolling" admissions and "rounds." Under the rolling admissions model, applications are reviewed as they are received and completed. They are processed in a stream and are not grouped for review with large numbers of other applications. In applications rounds, on the other hand, applications received and completed by the given deadline are reviewed together and decisions are announced by a specified date. Both these models provide a system for the admissions office to cope with the flood of paper and a structure for careful review of all applications.

Schools that use admission rounds typically have three or four decision periods. The deadline for the first cycle is often in early or mid-December, with decisions due three or four weeks later. If you submit your application in late October for a cycle with a December 1 deadline, you will not receive your decision until several weeks after that deadline. Under rolling admissions, however, your decision would usually reach you within a few weeks of your submission of your completed application.

It is important to remember that an application will not be reviewed until it is entirely complete. If a deadline for an admissions cycle arrives and your application is still missing one letter of recommendation, your application will be considered incomplete and held until the next decision cycle.

Review Decisions

Upon reviewing your application, the admissions committee may make any number of decisions, including:

Admit

Congratulations, you're in. But read the letter carefully. The committee may recommend or, in some cases, require you to do some preparatory coursework to ensure that your quantitative or language skills are up to speed.

Want to Reapply?

If you are considering reapplying, try to find out why you were rejected and whether you have a reasonable chance of being admitted the next time around. Some schools will speak to you about your application, but you may find these conversations unsatisfying because admissions decisions are subjective and cannot be quantified.

Reject

At the top schools, there are far more qualified applicants than there are spaces in the class. Even though you were rejected, you can reapply at a later date. If you are intent on reapplying, the onus is on you to demonstrate why you are a better candidate than you were previously. Depending in your situation, this may include raising your GMAT, taking additional coursework, gaining substantive new work experience, and/or writing better essays.

Deferred Admit

This decision is reserved for situations in which the admissions committee considers you a strong candidate, but believes you would benefit from an additional year or two of work experience before attending. Because most applicants now have at least two years experience before applying to school, deferred admission is not as common now as it once was.

Reject with Encouragement to Reapply

This isn't just a polite rejection. One step down from a deferred admit, it's a way for a school to say, "we like you, and we think that with more experience, you'll be a strong candidate."

Hold Over Until the Next Decision Period

Sometimes the admissions committee isn't comfortable making a decision by the scheduled reply date. Perhaps you are right on the borderline, and the committee wants to see how you stack up with the next group of applicants. In this case, all you can do is wait, but frequently, the end result is positive.

Waiting List

Schools use the waiting list—the educational equivalent of purgatory—to manage class size. The good news is that you wouldn't be on the list if you weren't considered a strong candidate. The bad news is that there is no way to know with certainty whether you'll be accepted. Be aware, though, that schools do tend to look kindly upon wait-listed candidates who reapply in a subsequent year.

Request for an Interview

Schools that do not require an interview may request that you interview with them before they make their final decision. Your application may have raised some specific issues that you can address in an interview, or perhaps the committee feels your essays did not give them a complete enough picture to render a decision. Look at this as a positive opportunity to strengthen your case. We'll talk later about how to use an interview to your best advantage.

This chapter has given you a behind-the-scenes look at the admissions process. The next chapters will discuss the secrets of successful applications.

Preparing Your Application

A key part of getting into the business school of your choice is to develop a basic application strategy so that you can present yourself in the best possible light. In this chapter and the chapters to come, we'll show you how to make the most of every aspect of your application, ranging from timing strategies to essay-writing tips.

When to Apply

Understanding how each school's application cycle operates can help you determine the optimum time to submit your application. The same guidelines as to when to send in your application may be used whether a school uses admissions rounds or a rolling cycle.

The Best Time

There are potential risks and rewards regardless of when you apply. However, the general rule is: *It's better to apply early than late.* Because so many candidates wait until the final deadline to apply, you'll be evaluated in a larger pool if you wait. Although schools are committed to judging all applicants on the same set of criteria throughout the year, they have no obligation to admit the same number of students from each cycle. So the prospects of being admitted from the later period may be worse than if you apply earlier.

Apply Early

"I was not successful my first year of applying to B-school. The next time around, I applied earlier in the application cycle. For schools that had rounds, I sent in my application for the second of three rounds."

—Current EMBA student, Stern School of Business, New York University

Applying too early can work against you, however. First of all, at the start of the admissions season, admissions committees need time to "calibrate" the yardstick by which they measure candidates. As a result, they may be less consistent in their judgments. This need to get a sense of the year's applicant pool applies to smaller programs more so than to programs that consistently, year after year, have a very large number of applicants and are very selective, admitting as few as one in every ten applicants. Second, because there are fewer applicants in the early stages, you may be scrutinized more closely than you would otherwise be. Third, the first period typically contains very strong applicants. And finally, because the application season is just starting, there's no pressure to fill class slots. Overall, however, if you are a strong candidate, it does make sense to apply early, because there are plenty of open slots. If your application stands out, you'll be accepted.

If you are planning to apply for scholarships, grants, or other merit-based financial assistance, early submission of your completed application can be very important. Some of these awards have very early deadlines; you cannot even be considered for the award unless all required application materials have been received.

The middle admissions periods are the "safest" times to apply. By then, the admissions committee has a good sense of what the applicant pool is like and has hit its stride in making consistent evaluations. Plus, there are still many spots available. Although the admissions office is typically awash in files at this time of year, the committee will still pay careful attention to your application.

Your chances of being admitted to your program of choice at the end of the admissions cycle are hard to predict. Programs that receive an abundance of applications typically have few spaces still available in the class at this stage. Backgrounds and credentials that stood out early in the year may not now appear so fresh and different. Still, if your background is highly unusual, it may be just what the admissions office is seeking to round out the class. On the other hand, if the office did not receive as large a flood of applications during the middle period as it expected, more seats may be available than anticipated, increasing your chances of being accepted. However, targeting the end of the application cycle is a risky move. Programs keep good records of application trends at their school so that they can plan appropriately and matriculate the best class possible; openings in the late cycle are created only when this planning has not produced the expected results.

All timing strategies aside, the best time of all to apply is whenever you can devote the time necessary to prepare your

The Worst Strategy

Regardless of when you make your decision to go to business school, the very worst thing you can do is wait until the last minute. Your school application is made up of many different pieces, including some that need outside attention, such as transcripts and recommendations. Each piece of the application that is beyond your control is one more disaster waiting to happen. You need to be prepared for the worst, and you need plenty of time to recover if and when things go wrong.

best application. This entails completing and submitting all your application materials in a careful and timely manner.

Make a Schedule

There are perfect times to begin and end the application process, and some people are able to move smoothly from step to step on the road to B-school admissions. Set time aside on a regular basis to complete the application materials. The key is to spread out the work. If the process is gradual and relaxed, it will be much less painful, and every piece of your application will get the attention that it deserves.

You should begin a year before you plan to enter school, preferably in the summer. Don't worry if the following schedule doesn't exactly meet your needs. You may just have to rush things a little more than some of your colleagues, or you may have several extra months to think and explore possibilities. Keep in mind, though, that a few dates are written in stone. You should find out what they are as early as possible and incorporate them into your own personal application schedule, which should include the following dates:

- Standardized test registration deadlines

- Transcript deadlines (some schools send out transcripts only on particular dates, so check with your records office to find out when you have to make requests)

- Letters of recommendation (be sure to give your recommendation writers plenty of time!)

- Application deadlines (submit your application as early as possible to ensure that you get a fair and comprehensive review)

- Financial aid forms (federal and state programs have definite deadlines, and you should also check deadlines from individual universities and independent sources of aid)

A former assistant director for admissions at Harvard Business School has drawn up the following "seasonal" schedule to help you understand how to proceed through the admission process. Within each section, you have plenty of room to move around, but the order of the sections is crucial. All the actions you need to take in each section are described in more detail in the relevant chapters elsewhere in this book.

Summer

- Request applications from schools. Ask for the current application packet to be sent to you. Although it is permitted to use schools' applications from the prior year, subtle changes are made in the application each year, and you should submit the most recent forms available.

- Start thinking about your M.B.A. goals and how you will express these in your application essays.

- Research M.B.A. programs.

- Register for the GMAT. Scores from on early fall GMAT will give you plenty of time to submit your scores with your application, rather than mailing them later. Test takers for other dates risk missing application deadlines or being evaluated late in the admissions process.

- Research your options for test preparation. There is an array of books and courses available to help you ace the GMAT.

> ### Request Your Application Early Because:
>
> - The closer it gets to the application deadline, the longer it takes for the school to get an application mailed to you, and you want to familiarize yourself with the application itself so you have time to figure out exactly what the school is asking for.
>
> - Most B-schools require a self-managed application, one in which you put together the parts of the application yourself and send it to the school as one big packet. It takes time to assemble these various parts.

Early Fall
- Make sure that your recommendation writers know enough about you to write a meaningful letter. Discuss your personal and academic goals with them. Let them know when deadlines will be to avoid any timing conflict.

Mid Fall/Late Fall
- Take the GMAT, if you have not already done so.

- Request applications from schools, if these requests have not already been made.

- Request institutional, state, and federal financial aid materials from school aid offices.

- Request information on independent grants and loans.

- Order transcripts from your undergraduate (and graduate) institutions.

Late Fall/Winter
- Process your admissions materials.

- Make sure recommenders send letters out.

- Schedule school visits and interviews.

Spring
- Await schools' decisions.

- Solidify your financial plans as you begin to receive any offers of aid.

Targeting Your Application

When it comes to applying to business school, you're the product. Your application is your marketing document. Marketing yourself doesn't mean that you should lie or even embellish; it just means that you need to make a tight and coherent presentation of the facts. Everything in your application should add up and underscore the fact that you are not only qualified to be in the class—you should be in the class!

Many application forms have a certain tone, one that's comforting and accepting. "Why would you like to come to our school?" they seem to be asking. They do want an answer to that question, but what's even more important—the subtext for the whole application process—is a bigger question: "Why should we accept you?" This is the question that your application will answer. And with some effective marketing strategies, your answer will be clear, concise, coherent, and strong.

> ## Be "Reader-Friendly"
>
> Try to make things as easy as possible for those who are reviewing your application. Part of marketing yourself is making sure the presentation of your application is flawless. Small type fonts or narrow margins can become real irritants, especially during the long days and nights of "crunch time." Whenever you submit your application, make sure it is "reader-friendly."

So what sort of image should you project? First of all, it should fit who you are; it should be natural. Don't bother to try to sell yourself as something you're not. The strategy will just make you uncomfortable, and it probably won't work. Besides, part of what readers do when they evaluate your application is to form an image of you from the various parts of your application. Your job is to help them, not hinder them.

Assembling Your Application

Before we go into detail about marketing strategies, let's recap the basic elements of the business school application. Whatever school you apply to, you will probably be required to supply:

- Completed application data form
- Your most recent résumé
- The application fee
- Your GMAT test score(s)
- TOEFL scores (if required)
- Official transcripts from all postsecondary schools that you have attended (whether or not you graduated)

- Letters of recommendations

- Personal interview

- Essays

Of the documents listed above, the only one(s) that will not be in the packet you provide are your GMAT and TOEFL scores. You need to contact the Educational Testing Service in Princeton, NJ at (609) 921-9000 to have these sent to your school(s).

Don't Be a Laughing Stock

Some of the more "entertainment-oriented" admissions committees save the videos they receive until the end of the season, cook up some popcorn, and have their own screening of B-School's Funniest Home Videos. If you decide to send in a video in support of your application, make sure it isn't unintentionally amusing.

Each school has its own policy about accepting supplemental materials that are not requested in the application packet, such as videotapes, audiotapes, and project samples. Most schools with large applicant pools either discourage them or simply don't consider them. They believe you should be able to make your case within the framework of the application. Other schools are more receptive to reviewing supplemental materials. If you have something you feel would strengthen your candidacy and you would like to submit it, call the school and ask about their policy.

The GMAT, TOEFL, college grades, and your work experience are those parts of your application that are pretty settled before you even start the important work on your application. The following chapters will examine how you should strategically approach the remaining crucial parts of your application—recommendations, your essay, and the interview.

CHAPTER 8

Recommendations

Whether a school requires one, two, or three recommendations, it will generally look to them as supporting documents that will confirm the substance of your other application materials. You should not neglect this portion of your application.

Choosing a Recommender

One of your tasks in preparing your application materials is to think strategically about the selection of individuals you ask to write on your behalf. Choose recommendation writers who can write meaningfully about your strengths and, whenever possible, match the perspective of the writer with your overall strategy for the particular application.

One of the most common mistakes applicants make is to sacrifice an insightful recommendation from someone who knows them well for a generic recommendation from a celebrity or an alumnus. Admissions officers are not impressed by famous names. So unless a famous individual knows you and can write convincingly on your behalf, this is not a strategy worth pursuing. Similarly, since admissions officers are looking for an objective confirmation of your qualifications, you should also avoid submitting letters from relatives and family friends, unless they can clearly base their assessment on professional criteria.

Good choices for recommendation writers include current and past supervisors, professors, academic and nonacademic advisors, and people you work with in community activities. In some cases, professional peers and/or subordinates can write effective recommendations, but such approaches are reserved for special circumstances. Remember that you do not need to use the same set of letter writers for each application. You will want to have at least one recommender who can speak to your work experience, but you may choose your other writers to complement the information in your application. If you have highlighted volunteer or community involvement, you can ask someone who has worked with you in this area.

If the school is particularly interested in leadership or team-work skills, you may want to choose a recommender who can address this side of you. Make sure, however, that the individuals you choose have recent knowledge of you and can relate it to your professional goals. Your high school basketball coach, for example, would not be a good choice as a writer, unless you have worked extensively with the coach in the last few years and this work is a good demonstration of your capabilities and skills.

If a school requests an academic recommendation but you aren't able to provide one, try to identify someone who can discuss your intellectual attributes, particularly if your academic record is not your forte. Similarly, if requesting a recommendation from your employer would create an awkward situation, look for someone else who can comment on your management skills. Your recommendations are not likely to make or break your application, but they will confirm your strengths and in some cases help you overcome perceived weaknesses in your application.

> ### Don't Burn Bridges
>
> "Never burn bridges when you leave jobs. My feeling from talking to friends was that if you return to school after being out of college for a while (for me it was 7 years), work references are more important than ones from college professors. I used only work references."
>
> —M.B.A., Stern School of Business, New York University

If you wish to submit an extra recommendation, it's generally not a problem. Most schools will include the letter in your file, and those that don't will not penalize you for it. You should, however, send a note explaining why you have requested an additional recommendation so it doesn't appear that you can't follow instructions.

Asking for Recommendations

There are two fundamental rules of requesting recommendations: ask early and ask nicely. As soon as you decide to go to business school, you should start sizing up potential recommendation writers and let them know that you may ask them for a recommendation. This will given them plenty of time to think about what to say. Once they've agreed, let them know about deadlines well in advance to avoid potential scheduling conflicts. The more time they have, the better job they'll do recommending you. As for asking nicely, you should let the person know you think highly of their opinion and you'd be happy and honored if they would consider writing you a recommendation.

Help Them Get to Know You

It is your responsibility to make sure that your recommendations writers know enough about you to write a meaningful letter. Discuss your personal and academic goals with them; help them get to know you well enough to write excellent recommendations. It is also helpful to tell your recommenders exactly why you are applying to a specific program, so they can understand your fit with it and emphasize this in their letters. If you are selected this writer to complement a specific aspect of your application, be sure to mention this connection, particularly if the school has an interest in this aspect.

Make Things Easy for Them

Make the task of writing a letter as easy as possible for your recommenders by organizing materials and information. Be sure that have all the necessary forms and instructions and have a stamped, addressed envelope to use for each letter. If the school uses a recommendation form, find out whether a letter on letterhead may be substituted for the form. Most schools will accept a letter, but many want the recommender to address the specific questions on the form and want to receive the form in addition to any formal letter. Some schools provide an acknowledgment card that the recommender is to include in the return envelope. Make sure that it is correctly addressed and stamped as well before you give it to the recommender. These steps will help show your appreciation for the effort being made on your behalf and will help ensure that the correct materials get sent to each school.

In addition to the required materials themselves, it is often helpful to provide your recommenders with a written summary of your background, a copy of your current résumé, and your application essays. Copies of any written feedback that they might have given you in the past can also be useful, in order to help them remember the details of your achievements. Reviewing the recommendation forms or questions yourself before sending them to the letter writer will help you determine what information may be useful. Providing your recommenders with the exact dates of employment or names of specific courses will save them from needing to research information or to rely on memories that might not be absolutely accurate.

Helpful Actions

Take the following actions to help your recommenders help you:

- Tell them about deadlines early
- Arrange a meeting to discuss your background and goals
- Clue them in on the marketing image you're using

—Former admissions official, Harvard Business School

Give Them the Highlights

"I would have ready some personal pointers/highlights that you want included in the letter of recommendation. Be sure to include examples of leadership, growth, and initiative."

—Current E.M.B.A. student, Stern School of Business, New York University

---

Under most self-managed application processes, your recommenders will return their letter to you, in a sealed envelope, for you to enclose when you submit the rest of your application materials. In this case, you will know when and whether the recommendation letters are complete. If an application deadline is looming and you are still missing a letter, you will need to follow up with your desired recommender—but be polite and discreet. On occasion, someone who has agreed to write will not be able to do so before your deadline, even though you have given that person adequate notice. You can inquire about submitting your application without one of your letters, but typically an application will not be reviewed until all materials have been received, including all required letters of recommendation. In some cases, you are better advised to seek a letter from someone else.

Confidentiality

One last issue with regard to recommendations is confidentiality. You'll need to decide whether or not to waive your right to read letters written about you. Many writers will only write confidential letter, and, unless you have serious reservations, you should waive this right. Some schools request confidentiality in recommendations, so pay close attention to each school's requirements.

What Will the Recommender Say about You?

In many cases, your recommenders will be asked to fill out a reference form for each B-school. The following are some of the most common questions recommenders are asked in these forms about the students they are recommending. Think about the responses the person you have chosen to recommend you might have to the following questions before you take the plunge and commit to him or her.

1. How long have you (i.e., the writer of the reference letter) known the applicant and in what capacity?

2. What are the applicant's primary strengths and weaknesses?

3. Discuss the applicant's competence in his/her area of responsibility.

4. Are the applicant's achievements thus far a true indication of his/her ability? Please explain your response.

5. How carefully has the applicant considered his/her plans for MBA study and subsequent career?

6. Rate the applicant on the following abilities or traits, using a scale of below average, average, good, excellent, superior. Please indicate the reference group being used.

   - Analytical ability and problem-solving skill
   - Ability to work in a team
   - Ability to work independently
   - Writing skill
   - Speaking skill
   - Motivation
   - Maturity
   - Leadership potential

CHAPTER 9

Interviewing Successfully

In the mid to late '80s, many top business schools began requiring their applicants to attend a personal interview before making a final decision on acceptance into their programs. Before that time, not only were interviews not required, but many schools would not even accommodate an interview request.

As the top schools began strongly recommending or requiring interviews, other schools followed suit. The rush to emulate programs that first established interview requirements was motivated by more than a desire to imitate the leaders. There was a heightened recognition that success in business is not always correlated with academic success. This was accompanied by an increased interest in attracting students who were not only qualified to perform well in a rigorous academic program, but who also possessed the personal qualities that would contribute to a successful post-M.B.A. job search and greater likelihood of rapid career advancement. The current emphasis on leadership, teamwork, communication, and interpersonal skills within M.B.A. programs is an outgrowth of the insights and goals that originally led to the admissions interview.

Most schools will say that the interview gives the admission committee a chance to evaluate aspects of the candidate that are not apparent or that cannot be judged on the basis of the written application alone. These attributes include poise, self-confidence, social skills, ability to think on one's feet, reaction to stress, maturity, and communication skills. A clear understanding of what the school expects to accomplish in an admissions interview and what you wish to gain from it will help you to prepare appropriately and gain maximum benefit from the interview experience.

Interview Format

The interview format you encounter will depend on whether you requested the interview or it was recommended/required by the school. If you requested the interview, you need to go into it with a firm idea of what you want to discuss. Schools that do not routinely grant interviews will expect you to provide them with information that was not included in your application. The school may wonder why you feel the information is so important that it couldn't be written up and included as an additional essay. You'd better be prepared to do more than just chat with the interviewer.

When the interview is recommended/required by the admissions office, on the other hand, the school is much better prepared to handle it. You had better be prepared also. Most interviews follow the same basic format: introduction, some welcoming comments and relaxed conversation, a little information about the school and how the interview will be conducted, detailed questions about your educational and work experience, future plans and goals, and so forth, followed by your chance to ask questions, and finally the wrap-up. They usually last 30 to 60 minutes. You need to make sure that you use the time wisely, that you make the points you want to convey and ask the questions you want to get answered, without seeming to take control of the interview. The only way to ensure success is to prepare.

How to Prepare for Your Interview

The very first thing you should do is review your application. What did you say and how did you present yourself? You need to remind yourself of these items before you go into to your interview so that you can give the interviewer some value-added information. Always assume that the interviewer has read your application thoroughly and reviewed it before the interview began. You can (and should) refer to details that you covered in your application, but you need to be able to discuss them in more depth if asked. If you refer back to your essay drafts, you should find that there is much more information to impart that you edited out in the name of length or simplicity. This is good information to have on hand for the interview portion of the application process.

You should also review everything that you know about the school with which you are about the interview. Nothing irritates an interviewer more than an unprepared interviewee who obviously hasn't read the catalog or done enough research to confirm that he or she has chosen the right school. It will also help you if you have read some other material about the school that will show that you were interested enough to do further research. Knowing which departments are strong or well known will allow you to discuss why you have chosen to apply to this school and why you will be a good choice as a student.

It is certainly helpful if you know something about the background and education of students who are already attending the school. You may find that you fit the mold of the accepted student quite well, or that you need to convince the interviewer that you can add something to the school.

In order to get an impression of what an interviewer might be looking for, take a look at the following interview form from Carnegie Mellon University. This form should help you identify the skills and demeanor required to impress the interviewer. Review the categories and make sure that you can express yourself in a manner that will convince your interviewer to rate you on the "5" end of the scale for each quality.

Interview Report

Name of Applicant				Date of Interview	
				Name of Interviewer	
APPEARANCE	Inappropriate Attire; Poor Grooming			Appropriate Attire; Presents Self Attractively	
	1	2	3	4	5
PERSONALITY	Abrasive or Bland			Charismatic, Likable; Participative Temperament	
	1	2	3	4	5
POISE	Awkward, Threatened by Interview Situation, Excessively Reticent			At Ease, Polished, Sophisticated, Easily Able to Maintain Social Conversation	
	1	2	3	4	5
SELF-CONFIDENCE	Defensive; Poorly Defined or Negative Self-Image			Outgoing, Strong Sense of Self, Forthright	
	1	2	3	4	5
SOCIAL SKILLS	Inappropriate or Ill-Mannered Responses			Handshake, Eye Contact, Appropriate Display of Manners	
	1	2	3	4	5
MATURITY	Irresponsible Attitude, Dependent, Immature			Clearly Responsible, Industrious, Conscientious, Decisive	
	1	2	3	4	5
INITIATIVE	Passive, Withdrawn, Took No Verbal Initiative, Uninformed About Program			Persistent, Formulated Specific Questions About Program, Assertive	
	1	2	3	4	5

INTERVIEW REPORT CONTINUED

DICTION	Poor Enunciation & Grammar			Enunciates Well, Structurally Correct	
	1	2	3	4	5
VERBAL FACILITY	Difficulty Expressing Self, Uses Slang, Substandard Vocabulary			Articulate; Excellent Vocabulary and Word Choice	
	1	2	3	4	5
LOGICAL PRESENTATION	Not Cohesive, Erratic Thought Patterns			Precise, Logical Continuity of Ideas	
	1	2	3	4	5
LISTENING SKILLS	Inattentive, Does Not Comprehend Questions Easily, No Clear Thought Development			Attentive, Alert, Perceptive, Skilled Comprehension of Questions, Emphatic Listener	
	1	2	3	4	5
PROFESSIONAL AMBITIONS	Confused, Unplanned, Displays Little Need for Achievement			Realistic, Clearly Defined Goals; Shows Need for Clear Ascendency	
	1	2	3	4	5
REASONS FOR APPLYING	Vaguely Defined, Naive			Qualified by Experience and Future Goals, Formulated Thoughtfully	
	1	2	3	4	5
COMMITMENT TO GRADUATE STUDIES	Unrealistic, No Sense of Strong Commitment			Determined, Realistic Appraisal of Time and Discipline Involved	
	1	2	3	4	5
ENERGY/ENTHUSIASM	Self-Restrained, Pessimistic, Lethargic			Involved, Optimistic, Vibrant, Alert, Enterprising	
	1	2	3	4	5

Work on your body language—don't fidget or present barriers between yourself and the interviewer (such as leaning back and crossing your legs). Maintain eye contact. Good, nondistracting body language will help you come across as confident, poised, and mature.

If you are concerned about your presentation, you may want to practice your interviewing skills before the actual event. You should select someone to practice with who will give you good feedback and understands what is involved in this type of interview. The best choice would be an M.B.A. grad who has gone through this process himself, or someone who is also applying to B-school and understands the importance of this exercise. You may also want to give a copy of the form to your interview partner. Ask him or her to give you both positive and negative feedback so that you can work on the weak portions of your presentation.

What about the Interviewer?

Your presentation of yourself is very important, but how you are perceived may depend somewhat on the interviewer. You may find yourself being interviewed by a permanent member of the admissions staff, a faculty member, another administrator, an alumni, a part-time admissions person, or even a student.

Many B-schools, especially those who conduct numerous interviews, have extensive training sessions for their interviewers and may even require that questions be asked in a certain order. Other schools are more flexible, allowing their interviewers to conduct the interview in whatever way is comfortable for them. It's important to keep in mind that different types of interviewers may have different approaches to the interview and different sets of primary interests. For example, a student may assess you as a potential fellow member of a group for a class project and feel free to ask pointed questions that admission staff, who are also recruiters, would not. Similarly, current students and alumni may provide you with insights about the program that you won't get from the admissions office.

> ### Ask Questions
>
> The interview is as much an opportunity for you to learn about the school as for the school to learn about you. Good questions demonstrate your knowledge of a particular program and your thoughtfulness about the entire process.

Although students and alumni may be able to spend more time with you than admissions staff charged with conducting hundreds of interviews each, be just as respectful of their time as you are of everyone else's. Business schools want these volunteers to feel good about the time and effort they spend interviewing applicants and will take any complaint about demeanor or behavior very seriously.

Interview Logistics

Going to campus to interview allows you to visit the school, see the town, and talk to current students at the same time you interview. However, an on-campus interview is not possible for everyone. To accommodate candidates who cannot come to campus, many business schools schedule interviews in cities around the United States and around the world. Often, admissions offices schedule interviews in conjunction with the M.B.A. Forums schedule, when staff will be in those cities for these events.

For applicants who cannot come to campus or meet with admissions staff at an interview site off campus, M.B.A. programs typically offer the option of interviewing with an alumnus/a who lives or works near the applicant. Some schools offer telephone interviews.

If you are finishing a Peace Corps assignment in Nepal, you may not have the option of interviewing in person. But you should make the effort to do so if at all possible. It is easy for the admissions committee to equate your failure to appear for an in-person interview with a lack of interest in the program. Moreover, since the interview is designed to evaluate attributes not easily measured by the paper application, an applicant who interviews well will have an edge over an applicant with similar academic and professional qualifications who did not interview or interviewed over the phone.

Some schools screen applications and invite only final candidates to interview. Others interview everyone. If interviews are by invitation only, you have relatively little control over their timing; you have to wait until you are invited. However, if the school interviews everyone, you need to take the initiative to schedule your interview. Remember, there may be thousands of other applicants who have to get on the interview schedule. If you delay requesting your interview time, the earliest date may be late in the spring, after most admit decisions have been made. The application materials will give you specific information on interview policy and scheduling procedures.

Depending on the availability of interview slots, you may want to interview first at schools further down your preference list, and use these experiences as practice runs. Don't jeopardize admission at your top choices by waiting too long, however!

What Questions Will You Be Asked?

Some general areas are often covered by interviewers. Here are a range of questions that they might ask:

- *College Career:*

    How did you plan your course of study in college?

    How did you decided which college to attend?

    If you had it to do again, would you make the same choice and why?

    What extracurricular activities did you participate in?

    Describe a project that you completed for one of your courses.

    What elective courses did you take and why did you choose them?

- *Motivation:*

    Tell me about an instance/incident in which you were particularly motivated.

    What are your career goals?

    What do you plan to do to achieve these goals?

- *Management Potential:*

  Have you developed a managerial style? If so, what is it?

  How would the people who report to you describe you?

  What are your weaknesses as a manager?

- *Intellectual Capacity:*

  What courses did you do best in?

  Do your grades reflect your capacity to succeed in this program?

- *Work Experience:*

  What are your current job responsibilities?

  Describe your changes in responsibilities since you started the job.

  How have you handled the changes in responsibilities?

  What have your major successes been?

> ### It's Not Just Luck
>
> "Some of what happens in the interview is luck, but you can prepare for it to a certain extent. I would suggest that you call each school that suggests an interview *early* for an appointment. Usually you are asked why now and why this particular school, what you can contribute to the school, and how you plan to use the degree, so you should know how to respond to those questions before you go in."
>
> —Current E.M.B.A. student, Stern School of Business, New York University

- *Interpersonal Relations:*

  What kind of people do you find it most difficult to work with?

  What is it about them that you would like to change?

  What do you normally do about such people?

  How would your co-workers describe you?

- *Perseverance:*

  In your first job, what were the drawbacks in pursuing it as a career?

  What were some of the problems you ran into in doing your job?

  Which one frustrates you the most?

  What do you usually do about it?

- *Communication Skills:*

  Tell me about an instance when you had to persuade someone to do something he did not want to do.

  How did you do it?

  What were the results? Were you successful?

Remember that this is just a general description of some of the types of questions that you may be asked. You can't prepare for every possibility, but as long as you feel confident about your background and application, you should do fine. You do not need to "script" or overrehearse your responses, but you should go into the interview confident that you can field any question.

Some interviewers won't ask you any of these questions. Instead, some experienced interviewers feel that they can carry on a general conversation with you, drawing you out to talk about yourself and your interests, and get enough information to make an admissions decision. Professionally trained interviewers are more likely to ask you about specific situations than they are to ask broad open-ended questions. They can learn more by asking what you've done in situations than by asking what you think you would do. Be prepared to discuss specifics—what you did and why you did it that way.

If you experience this type of interview, you may walk away wondering what just happened! Don't worry. Even if the interview seems somewhat unconventional, it doesn't mean that it was unfair or incomplete. Just be glad that you were given the opportunity to express yourself.

What the Top M.B.A. Programs Say: Interviews

Cornell University, Johnson School

"Although interviews are not required, they are an important part of the admissions process, because they provide us with a more comprehensive picture of applicants and their abilities than we could glean from academic records and test scores alone. The admissions staff will interview on campus any candidates who have submitted Part I of their applications and two copies of their résumé. For competitive applicants unable to travel to Ithaca, we can arrange alumni interviews. Staff and alumni interviews are given equal importance by the Admissions Committee.

"In addition to affording the opportunity for an interview, visiting the Johnson School offers prospective applicants the chance to talk with students and faculty and staff members. Current students tell us that seeing the campus and experiencing the Johnson School environment firsthand was crucial to making their decision. If you choose to interview on campus, we will assign a student-host to take you to classes and introduce you to current students and faculty members in your area of interest."

> ### The "Right" Answers
>
> Don't struggle to think of "right" answers to the questions you're asked in the interview. The only right answers are those that are right for you. By responding openly and honestly, you'll find the interview less stressful, and you'll come across as a more genuine, attractive candidate.

Tulane University, Freeman School

"The Freeman School requires interviews of all applicants living in the United States or Canada, and encourages interviews for international applicants as well. All interviews are conducted by a member of the admissions staff. The interview may be completed on campus, by phone, or off campus, if admissions representatives will be in the applicant's area. The candidate's application is not reviewed prior to the interview; therefore, the interview can be conducted at any time during the admission process.

"The advantages and disadvantages of each interview option greatly depend on the preferences of the candidates. I feel most candidates believe they can make a stronger impression in person and prefer the on-campus or off-campus interview. However, the Admissions Committee has no preference as to how the interview requirement is satisfied. "

Indiana University

"We encourage interviews prior to admission—either on- or off-campus—at forums and receptions. On-campus interviews are preferable, because the applicant can get a feel for who we are, learn our culture, and sit in on classes. The interview process is a two-way street. We're each looking for a good fit."

University of California/Berkeley, Haas School of Business

"Interviews are strongly recommended. Both on-campus and off-campus alumni interviews are available. On the east coast, alumni interviews are available in Washington, D.C., New York, and Boston. As regards assessment value, no particular advantage or disadvantage applies to either type of interview. However, because a campus visit is highly recommended, applicants who are able to visit the school, meet with students, and attend classes are at a distinct advantage in making an informed decision about the school that best meets their requirements and expectations."

Emory University, Roberto C. Goizueta Business School

"Interviews are strongly encouraged. The majority of interviews are conducted on campus, but admissions officers conduct interviews (by appointment) in selected U.S. cities in the spring. Phone interviews are available upon request. Trained alumni also conduct off-campus interviews. Face-to-face interviews (be they with admissions officers on campus or with officers or alumni off campus) are preferred because they provide the most interactive, and therefore, typically, the most fruitful discussions."

The Complete Picture

"The best advantage of an on-campus interview is that it allows the candidate to see the school, meet with students, sit in on classes, and explore the city. This complete picture of the school is not possible with other interview options."

—Admissions Officer, Tulane University

Columbia University

"While not required, we encourage face-to-face interviews. While the majority of interviews take place on campus, should an applicant not be able to visit the campus, we will arrange, through Project Interview, an interview with an alum located in close proximity to the applicant. Phone interviews may be conducted if there are no other alternatives."

Northwestern University, J. L. Kellogg Graduate School of Management

"All applicants are required to interview as a part of the admissions process. Applicants may interview on campus with a staff member or student or in their area with a member of the 1,200-member alumni admissions organization. All interviews are given equal consideration."

Final Thoughts about Admissions Interviews

The most important thing to remember is to be yourself. Present yourself in as positive and professional a manner as you are able, but don't try to make yourself into someone that you are not. The interviewer will pick up on that and try to pin you down or catch you in an untruth. Be as relaxed as possible.

Don't ramble through your answers. Be as concise as you can be without shortchanging yourself in providing the information. Try to listen to the questions you are asked so that you answer appropriately.

Finally, dress as you would for any job interview. Be courteous to the support staff. Be on time for the interview. Follow up with thank-you letters.

Remember that this is one of the areas of your application over which you have control, so do everything in your power to make the interview a positive experience for both you and the interviewer.

CHAPTER 10

Writing Your Essay

One of the most crucial components of your admissions application is your essays. Admissions officers use these essays to get to know more about you than can be seen through your undergraduate grades, your GMAT scores, and your work experience.

Many B-school applicants look upon the essay requirement as a part of the admissions application to be gotten through as quickly as possible. They throw something together that may or may not answer the questions asked and send it in, assuming that the rest of their credentials will be more important than the essays. They couldn't be more wrong. You can make or break an admissions application by writing outstanding or awful essays. Taking the time to compose an impressive essay can only help your chances of getting into the B-school of your choice.

Before you begin crafting your essays for any application, take a look at the big picture.

- What are your competitive strengths?

- Are there any weaknesses you'll have to overcome?

- How do your grades, scores, and experience stack up against the overall class profile?

What Makes an Essay Effective?

Writing effective essays requires serious self-examination and sound strategic planning. You will need to pay close attention to the content, style and mechanics, and distinctive qualities of your essay.

Content

Most B-school applications require that you write one to three essays. The essay questions asked probe for information the school thinks is important to know in evaluating future students. They often relate to characteristics of the program as a whole. You are, for example, more likely to find a question about your work in teams in the application of a program that emphasizes teamwork than in the application of one that does not. Reading the essay questions carefully is vital in constructing an effective essay. "Making do" by using an essay written in response to one question to answer a somewhat similar question posed by another school only indicates to the second school that you are not a serious applicant.

> ### *Parts of a Package*
>
> Most business schools require multiple essays. In order to put your candidacy in the strongest light, think of each response as part of a package rather than an individual statement on which your entire application hinges. Be bold; stick to the subject; use strong imagery; and let admissions officers get to know you.
>
> —adapted from "The Write Stuff," Newsweek/Kaplan's *Careers 2000*

Think about what will set you apart, make you memorable and attractive as a student. If you are asked what your greatest strengths are, you don't want to say they are hard work and punctuality. Since no one will say he is lazy or late for work, hard work and punctuality do not distinguish you from the rest of the applicants. Instead of being just another financial analyst in a sea of financial analyst applicants, perhaps you are the financial analyst who raises dogs and volunteers at the local animal shelter, or the one who had to assume operational responsibilities during a strike, or the one who has applied her political science background to looking at emerging Eastern European markets. Whatever you say, be sure you have examples to back it up.

Much of this self analysis should have occurred during your search for an M.B.A. program with an appropriate fit. If it didn't, you need to do it now. By cross-referencing your employment record, your personal characteristics, and desired M.B.A. program attributes, you should be able to find good examples and strong material for your essays.

Don't hesitate to go beyond your current job experience for essay topics. Although ignoring your job completely will raise a red flag, feel free to discuss other events that help define who you are. For example, if a question asks you to discuss three significant accomplishments, you might consider choosing one professional, one community, and one personal experience. Although this approach may not be exactly right for you, strategically, it does enable you to provide a range of personal insights as you answer a single question.

Style and Mechanics

Start by outlining your answers to each essay question. Consider what you want to say and take the time to outline the major points that you wish to make. Then write your first draft. Beginning with a strong lead will get the reader interested in what you are trying to say. Once you have written the first draft, put it away for a while before you begin to edit in successive rounds. Editing your essays is a very important step; you need to have gotten away from the essay and allowed it to settle before you sit down and take it apart.

Schools are pretty specific about how long they want your essays to be. Adhere to their guidelines. Short and clear is good; long and wordy is bad. One of the first mistakes that some applicants make is in thinking that "thorough" and "comprehensive" are sufficient qualities for their essays. They try to include as much information as possible, without regard for length limitations or strategic intent. Application officers dread reading these bloated essays. You're aiming for a crisp, precise style with which you can convey your message in the limited space allowed. You want to tighten your language to a point at which you have not used any extraneous words. At the same time, you want the essay to flow and be interesting to read. Extra-small margins and tiny type are not the solution, either. Keep your essays reader-friendly. Remember that your essays are just two or three of thousands the reviewer may read.

Candidates who write well have an advantage in the application process because they can state their case in a concise, compelling manner. Write in an active voice; less effective writers commonly write passively. Strong writing will not compensate for a lack of substance, but poor writing can bring down an otherwise impressive candidate.

To deliver your message effectively, you must also strive for clarity of content. You should be clear in what you are trying to convey without using slang or jargon. Endeavor to make your sentences shorter, eliminate any repetition, and make sure you have articulated your thoughts well. Give the reader more information than can be found in the other parts of your application. You don't need to restate information that you have already provided.

Finding the right tone is an important component of writing effective essays. On the one hand, you want to tout your achievements and present yourself as a poised, self-confident applicant. On the other hand, arrogance and self-importance will not go over well with admissions officers. You're trying to convey a personal message, but don't refer to yourself in the first person too much. Tell the reader what you have learned or contributed with-

---

Use the Right Terms

"I thought I was merely selling art [at my previous job in catalog production at Sotheby's]. But in B-school terms, I was 'developing important communication skills, refining my ability to prioritize and demonstrating my potential to be a self-starter.'"

—Current B-school student, Kellogg Graduate School of Management; quoted in Newsweek/Kaplan's *How to Choose a Career and Graduate School,* 1999

out sounding pompous. Before you submit your application, be sure that you're comfortable with its tone as well as its content.

If you choose to submit a humorous or creative application, you are employing a high-risk, high-reward strategy. You may not be the best judge of your creative talents, but if you're confident you can pull it off, go for it. Be aware, though, that what may work for one admissions officer may fall flat, or worse, with another. Admissions officers may consider your approach gimmicky or simply find it distracting.

> ### Be Consistent
>
> "When writing your essay, be sure to make your story consistent with what your recommenders are saying about you."
>
> —M.B.A., Stanford Graduate School of Business

Remember, your challenge is to stand out in the applicant pool in a positive way. Don't let your creativity obscure the substance of your application.

Be sure to read your essays in the context of your entire application. Does the total package make sense? Does it represent you favorably? Is everything consistent? Have you demonstrated your intellectual ability, management skills, and personal characteristics? Most importantly, do you feel good about the application? After all, you don't want to be rejected with an application that you don't believe represents the real you.

Finally, get someone you trust to read over the essays. Make sure that you have conveyed what you were trying to convey. This is the one area of your application that you have complete control over and (hopefully) ample time to do your best. Although well-written essays cannot always overcome a poor academic record or GMAT, it is your chance to impress the admissions committee with your thoughtful, well-written response to the essay topic.

Making Your Essay Distinctive

The discussion above describes the qualities of a good essay, one that won't be dismissed by even the most critical reader. But what if you want or need a great essay? Depending on the amount of time you have and the amount of effort you're willing to put in, you can write an essay that will stand out from the crowd.

Like other parts of your application, your essay is a marketing tool. The difference is that the essay gives you more freedom than any other component to present yourself in the best possible light. This is not the time to be blasé. Unless they ask for it, don't dwell on your weak points. You want to highlight your most marketable qualities. Draw attention to your achievements and explain their significance so that the reader's potential questions are answered.

One of the best ways to be distinctive is to sell your image briefly and accurately, including real-life examples to back up your points. A strong essay, for example, about how much you learned in your current position and how the experience and knowledge you've gained inspired you to apply to business school will give readers what they want—a quick image of who you are, how you got that way, and why you want to go to their school.

"Distinctive" means that your essay should answer the questions that admissions officers think about while reading essays: What's different about this applicant? Why should we pick this applicant over others? Authentic enthusiasm can be a plus, and writing about parts of your life or career that are interesting and relevant will help grab a reader's attention.

> ### *Be Introspective*
>
> "I was very introspective in my essays. I think schools want to see a high degree of self-understanding and self-reflection, as these are typically traits of great leaders, and B-schools want to graduate tomorrow's leaders."
>
> —M.B.A., Harvard Business School

Common Essay Questions

Every application is unique, but most will include essay questions that fall into one of several basic types. The good news is that once you've crafted responses to these questions, you won't have to start each application from scratch. You will, however, need to make sure that every application (especially the ones with fewer questions) provides the level of insight that you wish to present. Here are the kinds of questions you can expect to see:

1. **Describe (one, two, or three) significant accomplishments, and discuss why you view them as such.** Here, the admissions committee is looking to get a sense of what you consider important. Throughout the application review process, the committee will be gauging not only your management aptitude but also the kind of person you are. The events you choose to write about say a lot about you, as do the reasons you consider them significant.

2. **Why are you pursuing an M.B.A.? Where do you hope to be five years from now? Ten years?** Admissions officers want to see that you've thought through the reasons for going to business school, that you're committed to it, and that you have a clear understanding of what the experience is all about. Although they don't expect you to necessarily map out your entire career path, they will look for you to demonstrate forward thinking.

3. **What are your strengths and weaknesses?** Answer truthfully. Don't settle for "pat" responses. When discussing your strengths, you may want to include a brief example of an experience that highlights your strengths, if length permits.

    Writing about weaknesses can be tricky. The committee is looking for evidence of self-awareness and maturity, but be careful about raising red flags. For example, if you apply to a case method school that requires classroom participation and you write that you are uncomfortable speaking in front of a group, the committee will question whether you can thrive in that environment. Of course, you should be asking yourself the same question, anyway. Describing a weakness that's really a strength ("I'm so honest that . . ." or "I'm so committed to my employees that . . .") is a common, safe approach, but doesn't provide much insight—and it may turn off some admissions officers.

4. **Describe an ethical dilemma you've faced, and discuss how you handled it.**
   With this question, admissions officers will evaluate not just your ethical "compass," but also your thoughtfulness, maturity, and integrity. They want to see how you think through situations in which there are no easy solutions. Remember, not all dilemmas involve ethics, and not all ethical situations are dilemmas.

   Admissions officers know that applicants won't all have faced the same situations. What's most important is that you demonstrate your ability to exercise responsible judgment and learn from difficult personal circumstances.

Don't Be Defensive

When dealing with weak aspects of your application, do so in a straightforward, non-defensive manner. Discussing the weak grades, unpleasant professional experiences, or difficult personal circumstances you've faced in the right way can help you turn a potential pitfall into a strength.

---

5. **Is there anything else you would like the admissions committee to know about you?**
   If you believe that you've presented everything you need to make a strong case for admission, don't feel compelled to add anything here. With thousands of essays to read, admissions officers will not hold it against you. However, this question is also your opportunity to discuss anything you haven't yet had the chance to present. For example, if your undergraduate performance is the weak link of your application, you can use this space to explain it. Alternatively, if there's a gap in your employment record that is likely to attract attention, now is the time to discuss it.

Don't ignore something in your application that the admissions officers will question, thinking that they will not notice it. They read thousands of applications and are trained to notice the unexplained inconsistency. Write about it here—you may not get an interview to explain yourself.

6. **Describe a setback or failure and discuss what you learned from it.**
   This question acknowledges that people learn as much from their failures as they do from their successes. You may be asked to select a professional situation. Regardless of the event you choose to discuss, here is an opportunity to demonstrate your thoughtfulness and maturity, as well as your capacity for growth and change.

7. **If you could effect one change at your current job, what would it be?**
Admissions officers recognize that many (especially younger) applicants have not yet reached levels at which they could make fundamental changes at work. This question lets you flex your brain power in talking about changes you'd like to see. It reveals how knowledgeable you are about business in general and your business in particular. It also provides clues about how you think. For example, do you think about big picture issues, or do you focus on the details?

8. **Describe a situation in which you demonstrated . . . (teamwork/leadership/responsibility).**
A question like this will give you insight into the personal qualities that a school considers especially important in its students. Be sure to discuss the specifics of the situation. Answer such questions as: How did you demonstrate it? Did you have group meetings? Individual meetings? How did you motivate people? What was the end result? By discussing the details, you'll provide the admissions committee with valuable insight into your management style and aptitude.

Common Mistakes

We've asked two admissions officials from different schools and with different backgrounds to list what they consider to be the most common mistakes that business school applicants make in their essays. The results of our mini-survey are reported below. Make sure you don't make these mistakes in your B-school applications!

Admissions Official #1:

1. Not Getting to the Point Right Away

Don't force your readers to plow through a lot of irrelevant material before they reach the meat of your essay—they will lose patience with you.

2. Not Getting to the Point at All

This is even more fatal than Mistake #1. Make sure that your essays are clear and concise.

3. Using Buzzwords and Business Clichés

Using the most ubiquitous phraseology possible won't set you apart from the other candidates.

4. Not Providing an Appropriate Level of Detail

Applicants often provide either too much or too little detail in their essays.

5. Failing to Proofread

Spelling and grammatical errors are unacceptable.

Admissions Official #2:

1. Writing What You Think Someone Wants to Read

This short-sighted strategy might gain you admission into an M.B.A. program, but beware. If you provide an inaccurate reflection of who you are, but are admitted and choose to enroll in a program, you may be very uncomfortable. This can impact your ability to do well and to develop academically and personally, and can also inhibit the establishment of valuable connections for the future.

> ### Show Them Who You Are
>
> "I did not tell the business schools what I thought they wanted to hear but instead focused on who I am as a person. By being honest about my experience and goals, I think I showed the schools my ambition and drive. I feel I took a risk in opening up and it paid off."
>
> —M.B.A., Yale University

2. Failing to Explain Crises in an Appropriate Level of Detail

There is a fine line between too much and insufficient in such cases. Explanations of crises and misfortune, for example, are essential if they impacted the student's personal and academic development and perspective. A superficial mention without providing the reader with insight is useless and often detrimental, but too much "gore" and destruction also impacts the reader negatively. I once read an essay that described how the death of a roommate affected the student's ability to concentrate. The circumstances were horrific, and they were described in "bloody" detail. There are better ways to accomplish the same purpose.

3. Failing to Relate Goals and Plans to a Realistic Time Table

You don't have to know it all, and it is naive to believe that you do. Naiveté, especially at the graduate level, is not a valued commodity.

4. Failing to Check Spelling and Grammar Carefully

This should go without saying, but many people omit this vital proofreading step.

5. Failing to Respond to the Questions Asked

Admissions officials pose certain essay questions in order to obtain answers to questions they have about you as a candidate. If you don't answer the questions asked, you will not be providing them with the answers they need, and it will appear that you can't follow instructions.

Sample Essays

In order to give you a better idea of the different kinds of things that a B-school admissions officer might be looking for in as essay, we asked the two admissions officers quoted above to read and critique three actual B-school application essays. Each sample essay is followed by two critiques.

Essay A

Question: What are your career goals? How will an M.B.A. help you achieve these goals? Why are you applying to ****? (Limit: 1,000 words)

During my senior year in college, while other students were making definitive decisions about their career paths, I decided to implement a five-year plan of development for myself. The plan was designed to allow me to examine any career path during that period that I thought might interest me. I chose to focus primarily on three different fields: marketing, education, and the law. Although I am currently only in year four of my plan, I have made my decision regarding which career path to follow. After sampling each of the three areas, I have discovered that the field of marketing provides the most enjoyment for me and best complements my skills and personality.

I am now embarking on another five-year plan, during which I hope to achieve a few specific career goals. First, I would like to be a part of the team that establishes an accurate metric for measuring Internet advertising effectiveness. As computers play a more important role in people's everyday lives, corporations have begun to look for a method to analyze the effectiveness of their interactive advertising dollars. To date, no one has been able to accurately measure the impact that interactive marketing has on consumers. Although there are a few systems of measurement currently in use, they are rarely comparable and therefore provide little information in terms of the effectiveness of an online advertisement. The development of a standardized metric, similar to the Nielson Rating for television viewers, is likely to revolutionize the way corporations advertize on the Internet. I hope to help develop this new metric and to consult with corporations about the metric's results. The advice that I will be able to offer clients through the use of this system will be as important as the system itself. After all, the system will only be as effective as the results that it drives.

Beyond the five-year scope, I plan to establish my own market research firm that will focus on the burgeoning technology sector. I believe that we have only seen the beginning of the growth that the technology industry will experience in the future. Personal computers have penetrated approximately 40 percent of American households, and only approximately half of those personal computers have the capacity to connect to the Internet. We have only scratched the surface of the advancements possible through the usage of technology, and I believe that this field will continue to grow with greater acceleration as we enter the twenty-first century. My market research firm will provide support and information to companies who are affected by the increased use of technology. This market has tremendous potential and I hope to provide a necessary resource that will enhance my clients' success as well as my own.

I believe that an M.B.A. is the cornerstone to achieving my goals. First, an M.B.A. will give me the academic background necessary to successfully return to the field of marketing. Through classroom instruction and interaction with marketing professionals, I will be better suited to participate in the ever-changing global marketing environment. Additionally, I believe that an M.B.A. will provide me with the management skills necessary to effectively run a business on all levels. Whether my position is as a member of a large corporation or as an entrepreneur, I believe that the skills garnered from an M.B.A. are essential to becoming a successful manager. In addition, I believe that an M.B.A. will provide me with an enhanced thought process or a better business sense. I feel that as a student, I will be continually challenged to "think outside the box" and to analyze all available options before making an informed business decision. I believe that this process of thinking, learning, and challenging preconceived notions is an important aspect of earning an M.B.A.

I am applying to **** for a number of reasons. I believe that **** is the best environment for me to achieve my goals while gaining exposure to, and experience with, a diverse student body and faculty. It is my belief that everyone continues to learn throughout their lives, and one of the most effective methods of learning is through interaction with others. ****'s diversity offers an environment for learning both inside and outside the classroom. I hope to share my diverse knowledge with classmates and to take from them a new understanding of topics that are currently foreign to me. I believe that no other business school provides students with the opportunity to share and learn in an environment similar to that which is fostered by ****.

Academically, **** offers a comprehensive curriculum that will allow me to focus on my Marketing concentration through classes like Marketing Research, Marketing Planning and Product Management, and Strategic Marketing Planning. In addition, through core courses such as Managerial Studies and Managing Human Behavior in Organizations, I will be able to learn about business from a broader perspective. I believe that the outstanding academic reputation of **** combined with its diverse environment and thriving **** location create an opportunity that is second to none.

I have many ambitions for myself as I embark on the next stage in my life. I believe that an education from **** will provide invaluable experiences and skills that will allow me to grow into a successful business leader for the next century.

Critiques of Essay A

Admissions Official #1:

Essay A asks the candidate to address career goals, the importance of an M.B.A. toward those goals, and the specific relevance of the particular program in attaining those goals. A successful response should address these points in order, and culminate in an explanation of why the program in question is an eminently suitable choice. The essay should also provide evidence of a focused career objective and examples of ways in which the candidate might stand out from other candidates. The accompanying example succeeds in setting forth clearly organized and well-ordered points. However, the candidate is less successful in setting herself apart from other applicants. Let's look at organization first, and then examine the content of this essay.

This candidate presents her points in a very well-organized manner. The first paragraph identifies marketing as a general career interest of career. The following paragraphs define short- and long-term goals respectively, in this case describing ambitions in Internet-related marketing research with the ultimate goal of setting up a new marketing research company. The candidate then indicates that an M.B.A. is useful in the pursuit of these objectives because coursework will provide a deeper understanding of marketing. The applicant then concludes by enumerating the reasons why the program in question is the right choice. It is easy for the reader to follow these points, and the supporting information clearly addresses the major points.

Unfortunately, the points themselves vary in terms of their effectiveness. In the topic paragraph, for example, the candidate asserts that she embarked on a five-year plan of unbridled exploration. This rings hollow—and suggests that some abortive forays into careers were in fact part of an intentional strategy. That's not much of a plan. It would be more credible simply to state that after some career exploration, the candidate discovered that marketing was a good fit, and that the Internet provided an interesting opportunity to explore.

In addition, the reasons the candidate provides for choosing the school are very generic, and could apply equally to most reputable full-time M.B.A. programs. To assert that no other program offers a similar experience is not only patronizing, but probably untrue. Admissions officers expect that smart candidates will apply to multiple schools. In this particular case, the candidate missed an opportunity to incorporate the Internet-related or entrepreneurial goals in the reason for selecting the school in question. This might have helped set her apart from other applicants.

On a similar note, candidates are well advised to avoid clichés and buzzwords and to not parrot brochure copy. No admissions committee member will miss talk of "five-year plans" (fine for Stalin or *Star Trek*), being a "manager for the next century" (given that the millennium is fast approaching, we can assume most M.B.A.'s plan to manage after 2000), or the "ever-changing global environment." Using the most ubiquitous phraseology possible won't set a candidate apart from anyone.

Admissions Official #2:

There is no one answer to the issue of addressing career goals. A variety of participants with a range of personalities and skill sets are required to ensure a functioning world. M.B.A. classes are no different. And beyond the crafting of a class, an institution is choosing a set of alumni to enhance and/or maintain its reputation. Thus regardless of what the applicant writes about his or her career goals, it must be real and logical.

This essay intelligently divides a complicated issue into short- and long-range goals. However, the respondent conveys a naive and superficial understanding of his/her chosen field. The goals of being involved in an initiative that breaks new ground, of meeting a need, and of being part of a team are admirable. But it is essential, in all cases, to identify the skills, expertise, and/or abilities that would enable you to accomplish those goals. Unfortunately, in this case, I see plans without strategies.

This point is also applicable as we move to the question, "Why an M.B.A.?" What is it about an M.B.A. that will enable the author to accomplish her goals? The sections should be linked in a logical manner. Just because questions are asked sequentially, the responses do not have to be given sequentially.

There are subtexts to these questions. It is important to provide a sense of who you are, what you will bring, and why we should feel confident that you will contribute to your fellow students and class interaction. The author does understand that the class is composed of people with different strengths and that learning does come from diversity. However, I have gained no sense of who the author is as a person from this essay. Thus an opportunity has been lost.

And finally, as to the question of why the author has selected the specific institution in question, I don't see that he or she has taken the argument to the next level. A citing of courses doesn't do anything for me. Are the cited courses distinctive? In this case, they aren't. What is "diverse" about this program's "environment?" Why is being in a thriving city important? The components of this section aren't bad; they just don't provide insight into why they are important to this person. Why this program?

In summary, this essay needs more integration, logic, and focus. Make it easy to understand; don't force complicated leaps and assumptions. The author didn't capitalize on the opportunity to make a case for admission and to differentiate herself from other applicants.

Essay B

Question: In reviewing the last five years, describe one or two accomplishments of which you are most proud. (Limit: 500 words)

I have always had a sense of organization and order. As a child, every toy had its place and every book had its nook. I have consistently worked toward certain goals and implemented the appropriate plan to achieve them. Therefore, it was no surprise when I decided to develop a plan for my postcollegiate success in which I would sample a variety of different fields before deciding on which to focus. The manner in which I would execute this plan, however, was a challenge.

In order for it to be a success, my plan necessitated that I switch companies and fields several times. Being a creature of habit, this was at first a very difficult notion for me to accept. At the time, I would have preferred to have taken a job with one company and worked there for my entire career. However, that plan of action would never result in the full realization of my goal. In order for me to be successful, it was necessary for me to break out of my comfort zone and to explore a variety of fields.

As my plan progressed, I began to realize that I had created an opportunity for myself to gain a wealth of experience while also gaining new insights into my capabilities. As I faced each new experience, I was no longer daunted by its unfamiliar nature but rather enthused by its challenge. I began to relish the unknown as a chance to learn more about myself and my goals. As a result, I now understand that my plan was more than a quest for a career but also a journey of discovery and growth.

I consider the completion of my plan to be a major accomplishment. The pursuit of new positions and opportunities required a great deal of hard work and dedication. I am proud of myself for accepting my self-initiated challenge and for seeing my plan to its fruition. More importantly, I am proud that I encouraged myself to leave my comfort zone in order to achieve my goal.

In a different light, but also important to me, is my chili. I know that this sounds bizarre, but I am a dreadful cook. When I got engaged two years ago I decided that it was time to improve. I bought a cookbook and started at the beginning with the "Appetizers." I decided, however, to refocus my efforts when I unsuccessfully assembled a crudité platter. Instead, I planned to master one recipe. I chose chili because it is not overly complicated and I enjoy it. Throughout the entire winter, I toiled over my chili, perfecting the spices and the exact quantity of vegetables. Finally, when spring had arrived, I had done it: I had created the perfect chili. Although my chili has yet to win any accolades, I am proud nonetheless because I worked hard, achieved my goal, and I married a man who can cook!

Critiques of Essay B

Admissions Official #1:

Essay B asks the candidate to provide succinct accounts of one or two personal accomplishments. The candidate should begin by briefly describing the accomplishments in the topic paragraph. The body of the essay should then describe each of the accomplishments in more detail, providing insight into their significance. A concluding paragraph is probably not necessary, unless there is some common thread in the examples that the candidate wishes to underscore. The response should ideally provide the admissions committee with some insight into the candidate's values.

In this example, the candidate did not lay out the format of the essay in the topic paragraph. She instead commenced with a description of her first accomplishment. It was difficult to discern what she was describing because she didn't indicate that her "plan for postcollegiate success" was indeed one of her accomplishments until she wrapped up the description in the fourth paragraph. She spent the balance of the description saying little more than that she held jobs in a few different fields. This was not an effective tactic for differentiating herself from other applicants, since many candidates have held jobs that challenged them to grow professionally. Another problem with this accomplishment is that she provided no specific information or examples drawn from her experience.

The second "accomplishment" was also flawed. If the point of discussing her foray into cooking was to show her ability to rise above adversity, she did so by trivializing the process.

Beyond the issues of content, this essay used pronouns with unclear antecedents and preferred the passive over the active voice (i.e., "in order for it to be a success, my plan . . .," instead of "In order for my plan to succeed . . .").

The admissions committee was asked to consider a candidate whose greatest accomplishments were exploring several career paths and perfecting a chili recipe. If this essay does set the candidate apart, it does so at the expense of her candidacy relative to other candidates, who will have undoubtedly accomplished much more.

Admissions Official #2:

An essay can't address everything. The author made a choice as to topics and, in the process, she provided me with an insight into who she is. Willingness to break out of a comfort zone is a trait that I value because the business world is constantly changing and change necessitates the learning of new skills. The author recognizes that this is an uncomfortable process. I could see how she developed. I recognized that she can handle change, and even respond in positive, growth-producing ways.

Both this respondent, and the previous one, had a plan and experimented with different paths. But in this case, the author shared her internal conflicts, those created by personal preference and reality, and what she learned from the experience. The choice of this topic provided an answer to an unasked question. If I have a limited number of places in the class, and the world is constantly in flux, my best students and most successful alumni will typically be able to manage change and grow from it. The author provided evidence that she can do both. I also know that she can handle uncertainty, and that attention to detail and order are important to her. Since teams have become the predominant organizational structures in business school and business, the aforementioned abilities and values are ones that at least some team members must possess to bring a project to successful fruition.

The author's second accomplishment provided humor and addressed other dimensions. I now know that she is married and that, in her choice of a partner, she found someone who has skills that she doesn't have. That is the benefit of a team. I also know that she is organized and methodical as she assumes new tasks and responsibilities.

This was, to me, a relatively solid essay. It was informative and insightful. As a bonus, it was amusing which, while not essential, can be different. I do have one caution. This essay does not explain what experiences she had, how/why she chose them, how long she stayed, and what she learned from them. And it doesn't reassure me that the author doesn't assume that jobs and people are expendable—that once they serve their purpose you move on. The purpose of this essay was not to probe such issues. However, these questions arise as one reads the essay, and thus the answers to them should be integrated into the essay or created as an addendum if they don't appear elsewhere in the credentials.

Essay C

Question: Describe an ethical dilemma you have faced in the workplace and how you resolved it. (Limit: 500 words)

*One of the students I counseled while working for the Jewish Public School Youth Movement (JPSY) was a 16-year-old student named ****. **** had joined our club as a freshman and participated in almost all our events. When I first met him, **** seemed to be a well-adjusted teenager in good academic standing and with many friends. During his sophomore year, I noticed that **** seemed increasingly disturbed, and I was informed that his grades were suffering. Repeated attempts to question **** about his problems were rejected. I debated approaching some of his friends but decided that his desire for privacy was more important.*

*At 11 o'clock one night I received a call for help from ****. He was calling from a pay phone after wandering around town for hours. His parents had been fighting with each other consistently and had become directly hostile towards him. When he brought home a failing grade, his mother locked him out of the house. My first reaction was disbelief. Aren't a mother's instincts always correct— especially a mother who is trained as a child psychologist? Don't parents always do what they believe is best for their child? Was it right for me in my role as a friend to interfere with the way the parents were raising their son? But their son had confided in me and was asking for help. I could not bear to let him wander the streets all night. I picked up **** and took him to another advisor's apartment for the night. Meanwhile, I decided that I would speak to his mother the next day. I would approach her as an advisor of ****'s school club and offer to help him with his schoolwork. I was hoping to somehow learn the reasons for her behavior without seeming too inquisitive or intrusive.*

*When I contacted her the next day, she politely thanked me for the offer and informed me that it was no longer necessary since **** was being sent to reform school. Inquiries made at the public high school and of various JPSY officials confirmed that my involvement had to end. During the subsequent year I heard reports of ****'s deteriorating behavior. In the end, he ran away from the school, and has yet to be found. Unfortunately, I could not control the outcome of the situation, but it taught me two lessons: how naive certain childhood assumptions may be, and to be more confident in following my instincts.*

Critiques of Essay C

Admissions Official #1:

This question poses two unusual problems. The first is that it's badly worded—a dilemma isn't just any difficult problem. By definition, a dilemma is a problem that requires a person to choose between equally undesirable alternatives. A dilemma cannot, therefore, be resolved. One school that uses an "ethical dilemma" question asks how the candidate managed and resolved the attending situation, and not the dilemma itself. That was probably the intent of this question as well.

The second problem is that the question assumes that all applicants have faced ethical dilemmas in the workplace. That may not be true unless the dilemma is sought out intentionally. Author Robert Reid, who recounted his first year in a top M.B.A. program in a recent book, noted that "have you had your ethical dilemma yet?" is something of a standard workplace joke among the M.B.A.-bound. Unfortunately, candidates don't have control of the questions, just their answers.

With these problems noted, a concise (approximately 500-word) response should describe the dilemma in an introductory paragraph or two, explain each of the alternatives and their consequences, and conclude with a paragraph describing the choice the author has made and why that choice, while imperfect, was nevertheless preferable to other choices.

Here's an example. Imagine that you are an M.B.A. applicant who has never encountered an ethical dilemma in your workplace. What are your choices in answering this question? You can deliberately stretch or misrepresent events to conform to the question (i.e., lie—unethical), or indicate that you haven't had such an experience, potentially hurting your chances for admission. Both alternatives are bad—hence, a dilemma.

To his credit, the candidate in the example chose a third alternative, to do the best he could with an actual situation, even though it wasn't truly a dilemma. In this essay, the candidate is counseling a high school student who is having problems at home. The candidate adheres to his advisee's right to confidentiality until the situation turns more serious, and then attempts to intervene with the parents when the advisee's welfare might be at stake. While the situation the candidate describes is certainly unfortunate and obviously difficult, it isn't a dilemma, since there isn't a forced choice between flawed alternatives. Instead, the candidate has followed the highly ethical practice in counseling of honoring confidentiality until the advisee's welfare may be compromised by continuing to do so.

While this response isn't perfect, it is certainly preferable to lying or dismissing the question. With any luck, the admissions committee will understand the limitations of its question.

Admissions Official #2:

Unfortunately, there is little that I liked about this essay. I would caution the reader, however, that an Admissions Committee is composed of a group of people with various values and orientations, and each member reacts, more or less strongly, to different issues.

The author never really, or at least not clearly at the beginning of the essay, outlined what the ethical dilemma was. What ethics were involved in this case? The recounting of the circumstances appeared to have no overarching point. This was unfortunate, because there were real tensions inherent in this story that could have been addressed. Among them are:

- Can we ever truly understand a situation to which we are outsiders, and what role do we play when we see problems?

- What happens when the world as you experience it is inconsistent with the world as you come to see it?

- What options exist to respond to the situation, and why was this particular option chosen?

It is appropriate to set the stage or lay out the situation (one-quarter of the essay) and then proceed to analysis (three-quarters of the essay.) Since the author neglected to do this, I am unsure as to why certain items were included and why they were included in the ways that they were. There has to be logic. Why, for example, did the author say that he "picked **** up and took him to another adviser's house?" What really mattered is that the student was in need and the author found him a place to stay. It is a bad idea to provide opportunities for the reader to get side-tracked with other issues. In this case, the question arises as to why didn't the author just take the student home with him.

The essay's conclusion could have been interesting. Even when not in control, you can learn things. In the author's case, he learned that childhood assumptions could be naive and that sometimes you need to be more confident in following your instincts. Unfortunately, I don't know what his assumptions or instincts were.

This was a missed opportunity. I see someone who didn't know how to use resources that were there, i.e., a school-connected agency, and insisted on "going it alone" instead of being a member of a team. While independence is important, at times, it is essential to know when to use the resources of a system. I don't see clarity of thought; I don't see someone who knows what is important. I have no real sense of who this person is and what he or she values, and that is, in my opinion, part of the purpose for which this question was designed.

I am not saying that this student wasn't admitted to the schools to which he applied. But for me the admission would have occurred in spite of the essay, not because of it, and in a competitive environment where test scores, grades, and work experience were equal and spaces limited, this student would have suffered in comparison.

PART FOUR

Financing Your M.B.A.

CHAPTER 11

Planning Your Investment

Whether you plan to attend school full time or part time, getting an M.B.A. requires a substantial financial commitment. Graduate business schools offer financial aid programs that may include fellowships, scholarships, graduate assistantships, and low-interest loans for students who qualify. Often, this "free" money is only available to full-time students. Loans may be the only source of support for part-time students.

The harsh truth: Not everyone seeking aid will receive it. There aren't enough grant and low-interest loans to go around. Federal funding for financial aid programs, such as the Federal Perkins Loans (formerly NDSL) and the Federal Work Study Program, is always uncertain.

You may plan on working to support yourself once you start your program, as you perhaps did in college. However, be aware that even if full-time students work part time, their earnings typically defray only a portion of their tuition and living expenses. Two factors conspire against full-time students earning enough to support themselves in an M.B.A. program. Universities often charge higher tuition for these programs than for undergraduate programs. And graduate management courses typically require significantly more

Chilling Figures

"The cost of attending an elite school runs very high: $25,000 a year is typical. Factor in two, three or four years of lost income from the job you decided not to take, and the total investment can be chilling. 'I tell students they should plan on spending $40,000 each year,' says [Bob Alig, admissions director at the Wharton School]."

—"Look Before You Leap,"Newsweek/
Kaplan's *How to Choose a Career and Graduate School*, 1999

study time than college courses. Some programs strongly discourage full-time students from working, particularly in the first year of study.

Schools may offer grants and scholarships, but they expect that graduate business students will fund part of their education through loans. Because you'll probably have to pay for most of your M.B.A. yourself, don't wait until you get accepted or start registering for classes to figure out how you'll pay the bills.

Assess Your Financial Situation

Look at your current income, assets and expenses: Are you spending every cent that you make? Do you need to? Often, college grads feel the need to reward themselves for the financial sacrifices they made during college. If this is the first time that you have a regular paycheck coming in, it's understandable that you want to spend it. But since there's not as much funding available for graduate students as there is for undergrads, the more money you can start with, the less you'll have to borrow.

> ## Get Ready to Pay
>
> The primary funding source for graduate management education is the resources of the students themselves. The heavy reliance on savings, earnings, and loans distinguishes the financing of an M.B.A. from that of most other graduate degrees. A careful assessment of your financial situation is in order.

Are you spending a large portion of your net pay in housing? Can you get a roommate? Move to a less upscale neighborhood? You may not want to go back to your college lifestyle, but housing is a good place to start cutting your expenses so that you can save something toward business school.

Review all of your current expenses and try to figure out where you can cut now so that you can save something toward school. Many students don't bother to save anything before going for the M.B.A. But these are the students who graduate with the highest levels of debt, to the point of limiting their career choices. You don't want salary to be the sole criterion in your post-M.B.A. job search. You want to be able to choose a job that you're actually interested in—a job that has a future.

Helpful Money Tips

Saving money doesn't have to involve cutting back on your standard of living. Here are some concrete strategies you can use to stockpile money for business school without making sacrifices.

Pay Down Your Consumer Debt

This is one of the most important things you can do. If you don't pay off your entire balance on a credit card, you pay interest not only on that balance but also on every charge made from the date it is posted. You get no grace period. If you have no balance, then you get the approximately 25-day grace period before a payment is due. Significant consumer debt can limit your ability to obtain private educational loans to pay for tuition. Also, financial aid officers rarely consider credit card and car payments when they calculate your student living expense budget.

Look for Opportunities to Earn More Money

You may be able to accumulate some additional funds before you start school by scheduling regular overtime in the months before you enroll. Or you may be able to find some weekend or freelance work.

Stay at Your Job as Long as Possible

Nothing could be more seductive than the thought of a last fling in the month or two before starting a demanding course of study. But this is when you should be beefing up your bank account as much as possible for graduate school, not depleting it by taking an extended break. Many financial aid officers will calculate personal resources based on earnings up until the start of school, even if you quit your job before then. If you really need a break between your job and graduate school for your mental health, go ahead. Just remember that your holiday has a price tag. You'll probably have to increase your loans.

Avoid Major Purchases

Now is not the time to incur major expenses or make any major purchases. Don't make the mistake of thinking that you'll qualify for more financial aid if you wipe out your bank account. The financial aid office will probably have your federal income tax form from the year before. They'll expect that any savings your reported are still available. Alternatively, they might calculate a percentage of your income as savings. You don't want to have to explain to a financial aid officer why you made a major, nonessential purchase just before enrolling. However, it you incur a justifiable major expense that would reduce your contribution, don't hesitate to contact the financial aid office. They may be able to help. Ask if they will review your application based on the new information.

Ask Your Family for Help

So, you're in your twenties or thirties and you feel squeamish about asking your parents for money. This is not the time to assert your independence. If you feel funny about borrowing from your parents (or any other benefactor), draw up a repayment agreement with clearly stated installments. Even if your family agrees to help you financially, you'll still be considered an independent student for federal aid. You may have to report your parents' contribution on a financial aid form, but it may only affect the size of the loans you'll need. Your parents' generosity won't affect your scholarship allocation at most schools. You need to know, however, that some schools will reduce your scholarship to reflect family aid.

Liquidate Your Assets

If you've invested your savings in stocks, bonds, or other financial instruments, make sure that you can liquidate these assets in time to pay your tuition. You may want to reorder your investments in order to make them more liquid, even if that means reducing your profit margin. Plan for your cash flow requirements. Often, students must pay their spring tuition in the preceding November or December. You'll need to have your funds available well before the semester begins.

Make Smart Purchases

You may want to acquire a computer, for example, before school starts. Consider several things before you make this investment:

- Does the school require that you purchase a computer?

- Is the cost of the computer built into the student expense budget that the school has estimated for you?

- Does the school purchase computers for their students and add the cost to the tuition charges?

- Does the school have a special deal with a distributor who could sell you a computer at a discount, perhaps already loaded with the necessary software?

- Will the financial aid officer subtract the price of the computer from your expected contribution?

The bottom line is, it's smart to find out the school policy before you purchase any equipment.

Plan for Moving Costs

Remember to budget in the cost of moving and other relocation expenses, if necessary. These expenses can mount up and are usually not taken into account in the financial aid budget used to calculate your grants and loans. Investigate various moving options well in advance to get the best price. If you'll be renting, don't forget that you might need to pay your first and last month's rent plus a security deposit, depending on where you're moving.

Investigate the Lifetime Learning Tax Credits

This tax credit is available for graduate and professional students (along with other adults) who want to upgrade their job skills, acquire new ones, or pursue a new course of study. It's available to all students, even if they are taking just one course. This tax credit is worth up to $1,000—20% of the first $5,000 paid in qualified tuition and fees (tuition and fees actually paid after deducting any grants and scholarships). You can only claim one Lifetime Learning credit per year, not one per semester of payment. Check with the IRS for the income requirements to qualify for the credit. This credit will go up to $2,000 per year in 2003–20% of the first $10,000 paid in qualified tuition and fees.

You can take advantage of this tax credit by doing the following:

- Complete IRS Form 8863

- Call IRS Help Line at (800) 829-1040 for info

- Read IRS publication 970
- Check out the IRS Web site at www.irs.ustreas.gov

Calculating Your Costs

Before you can determine what resources you will need, you must calculate what your costs will be. You'll have to look at more than the tuition and fees published by the school. You'll need to calculate the cost of tuition and fees cost per semester, book expenses, and transportation expenses, plus room and board if you live on campus. If you're a part-timer, you may need to include the cost of child care on the nights that you have school, additional meals away from home, or other considerations.

Student Expense Budget

Your cost of attendance (COA) or student expense budget, includes tuition and fees, room and board, books and supplies, transportation, and personal expenses for nine months or however long you plan to be in school that year. The following budgets reflect two different types of living arrangements. Budget A shows the expenses for a full-time commuter, living with his or her parents. Budget B shows the expenses of a full-time student living in a dorm or off-campus apartment. Both budgets are based on a nine-month period. In the commuter budget, the room and board and personal expenses are substantially lower, since it's assumed that parents will cover many of these expenses.

Sample Student Expense Budgets

Budget Item	Budget A: Commuter	Budget B: Dormitory
Tuition and Fees	$15,690	$15,690
Room and Board	$1,500	$6,975
Books and Supplies	$700	$700
Transportation	$500	$500
Personal Expenses	$1,500	$2,150
TOTAL	$19,890	$26,015

Schools calculate your cost of attendance by combining standard school cost and living expense budgets. Use the sample student expense budgets above to get an idea of what your personal costs might be. These budgets lists both fixed and flexible personal expenses, apart from the cost of tuition and fees. You will encounter both types of costs at any B-school you choose to attend. Typically, while tuition will vary, your living expenses will not vary that much whether you attend a private or public school, full time or part time.

Now that you have an idea of how much money you will need to pursue M.B.A. studies, it's time to research ways to come up with that money. The next three chapters in this section will lead you through the processes of applying for financial aid, obtaining scholarships and other "free" money, and taking out loans.

CHAPTER 12

Applying for Financial Aid

Financial aid application procedures can vary more from school to school than the procedures for admissions. This chapter will give you an overview of the general application requirements, including the documentation, that's usually required.

To be eligible for need-based aid, you must:

- Be a U.S. citizen or permanent resident

- Not be in default on any prior student loan

- Be registered for Selective Service, if required

- Submit the required forms by the stated financial aid deadline, which differs from school to school

Forms

Get the admissions material and read it thoroughly. Usually, general financial aid information appears in the admissions application, including the financial aid deadline(s). These deadlines drive the rest of the process for you. The admissions application deadline may be earlier or later than the financial aid application deadline. In the case of multiple financial aid deadlines, the first one is usually for students interested in scholarship and fellowship assistance. A later deadline may be set for those students who are only interested in campus-based aid and federal loans.

Key Materials

The Free Application for Federal Student Aid (FAFSA) form is always required to request any federal financial aid. This form is used for need analysis, the calculation that determines your financial need. The detailed financial information you provide on the FAFSA form is run through a federal formula to arrive at an expected family contribution (EFC) figure. The calculations are explained in more detail in the next chapter.

If you are in school the year before you plan to attend B-school and you apply for financial aid, chances are that you'll receive a Renewal Application in the mail. This form is basically a FAFSA preprinted with the information that you provided the year before. All you need to do is update the information and sign the form. (If you're in college, change your class year to "graduate.") List the schools to which you're applying for the M.B.A. program. The information will be electronically transmitted to them.

Both of these forms (the FAFSA and the Renewal Application) allow you to send your financial information to a maximum of six institutions. If you're applying to more than six schools, you need to list your top six choices. If you subsequently want to add a school to this list, you'll have to drop one from your list. Make your life easier—try to limit your financial aid application to just your six top choices.

Other required forms may include (but are not limited to):

- A separate school financial aid application

- Private need analysis form, such as the PROFILE from the College Scholarship Service or the NeedAccess disk

- Your prior year's IRS 1040 form

- Financial aid transcripts from every postsecondary school that you attended (this requirement has been replaced at many schools by the National Student Loan Database System (NSLDS); check with your school to see if it participates)

Since many deadlines are as early as January 15, you probably won't be able to complete your federal tax form before the deadline. Most schools recommend that you estimate the numbers and then correct them once you get your taxes filed. But other schools may want you to wait until you have all the actual numbers. A school's policy about estimating tax figures versus waiting for the real figures may be stated in the financial aid application materials. Otherwise, check with the school's financial aid office.

Even though you should be careful on your financial aid application forms, don't work yourself into a panic about them. It's usually better to estimate a number than to miss a deadline while you're trying to verify it. You can always submit the actual figure to the financial aid officer when you get it. He or she will make the appropriate correction for you and recalculate your need analysis contribution.

How to File FATs and Other Forms

In the Fall of 1996, the FAT requirement changed. Schools are now able to access FAT information on the National Student Loan Database System (NSLDS). Because of this access, most schools have eliminated the requirement for prospective students to supply FATs. However, some schools are not yet comfortable using the NSLDS information and are still requesting students to supply FATs. Contact each school you are interested in to find out what its current policy is. Don't necessarily believe what you read in the admissions material, since more and more schools are dropping the FAT requirement every day; as of January 1, 1998, all schools were required to have electronic access to NSLDS in their offices.

If FATs are still required, the school financial aid application material will contain a single copy of the FAT form. You'll need to make a copy for every school within the United States that you have attended since high school, even if you didn't apply for or receive any financial aid. Remember that refresher course in calculus you took one summer at your local community college? You have to get a FAT from that school, too.

Complete the top section of the FAT and then send the form to the financial aid offices at all your previous schools. They'll send the form directly to the graduate business schools to which you're applying. If you're applying to a lot of schools, you'll get a lot of practice filling out these forms. Give your previous schools a reasonable amount of time to send your forms out. After about a month, check that the financial aid offices at the schools to which you are applying have received all the pertinent information.

Forms: Round Two

Once you've submitted all the required forms, you'll have to wait about a month before anything else happens regarding your financial aid. You might hear from admissions offices during this time.

Meanwhile, the federal processor, a number-crunching center for the government currently based in Iowa, is working on the information you provided on your FAFSA.

Where Do They Go?

Form	Where to Send It
FAFSA	Federal processor (address on the envelope enclosed with the form)
School's financial aid application	School's financial aid office
CSS Profile Form	College Scholarship Service, Princeton, New Jersey
NeedAccess disk	Access Group, Delaware
Signed federal tax form	School's financial aid office
Financial aid transcript requests (if required)	Financial aid offices of undergraduate or graduate schools attended (even if you didn't get a degree)

They rub your numbers through a formula called Federal Methodology that is revamped every six years (although the numbers are changed yearly). Their calculations result in a Student Aid Report (SAR). You'll get a copy of it in the mail. Your SAR contains both the financial information that you provided on your FAFSA plus the results of the federal need analysis calculation. The schools that you listed on the FAFSA will receive the data electronically, but may need you to sign an additional form to activate the financial aid process (especially if the school does not have its own financial aid application). The actual need-analysis calculation parallels the process of estimating your EFC that we discuss late in this chapter.

Remember to keep track of your financial aid applications in the same way that you're keeping track of your admissions application material. If you need money to attend school, this process is just as important as the process of getting admitted.

Calculating Your Need

The calculation of how much a student (and family) can contribute toward graduate business education is made using the following guidelines:

Federal Methodology

Federal Methodology (FM), the formula used in need analysis to determine eligibility for most federal financial aid programs, was written into law by the U.S. Congress. Congress reviews this formula every several years and recommends changes to it. The federal formula was established to set objective standards that would be uniformly applied to all applicants.

Broadly, FM tries to take the income that is received by the members of the student's household, subtract the taxes paid and the cost of maintaining the members of the family other than the student, add in a portion of the assets, and then take a percentage of the result to produce an expected family contribution. Although this formula may not take into account all the vagaries of an individual student's situation, it produces generally comparable data on all students applying for financial aid. The financial aid officer at the school then has the option of adjusting data elements (through professional judgment) to make the contribution realistic for each student.

Basic Guidelines

The first concept to understand is financial need. Think of it as a simple matter of subtraction:

Cost of Attendance – Family Contribution = Financial Need

As we discussed previously, the cost of attendance is determined by the school and consists of the tuition and fees, room and board, books and supplies, transportation, and personal expenses. The federal processor (a selected firm under government contract) runs your FAFSA figures through the FM formula and produces the EFC.

For federal aid eligibility (Federal Stafford Loan, Federal Perkins Loan, and Federal Work-Study), the income and assets of your parents will not be assessed. The school does have the right to assess a parental contribution when calculating your eligibility for its own scholarship and loan funds. Very few B-schools currently require that you provide parental information, but this practice could change in the future as the demand for financial aid becomes greater.

The components reviewed in assessing EFC include the following:

> ### EFC and Your Kin
>
> As a graduate student, you're automatically considered to be independent of your parents, even if you live with them. However, if you're married, your spouse is considered to be part of your family, and his/her income and assets will be assessed in the calculation of your EFC. On the other hand, if you have children, your EFC will be reduced.

- Total family income from the previous calendar year (base year income)
- Net value of any assets (value minus debt)
- Taxes paid (federal, state, and local)
- Asset protection for retirement
- Number of family members
- Number of family members in college at least half time
- Costs associated with both spouses working
- Income protection allowance (IPA) for basic living expenses

Before going on to the actual calculation, you need to understand the components listed above and why they are considered.

Base Year Income

The FM formula requires the use of the prior calendar year income to determine your contribution. This means that if you enroll in the fall of 2000, you'll be asked to provide your 1999 income. For the majority of the population, the best predictor of current year income is prior year income.

Income Protection Allowance (IPA)

This allowance provides for basic living expenses not included in the standard student expense budget. This allowance will vary according to the number of family members and the number in college at least half time. For a single student with no dependents, the IPA is $3,000; a married student with no dependents other than a spouse is allowed $6,000; for students with dependent children, the amount varies depending on the number of family members.

Asset Protection Allowance

The FM formula includes an allowance for protection of assets, depending on your age. This means that a portion of your assets will not be considered in the calculation because they're protected for your retirement. The older you are, the more of your assets are protected.

Employment Allowance

The concept of an employment allowance grows from the realization that it costs to have both members of a married couple work outside the home. The formula allows 35 percent of the lower income, up to $2,700, to be deducted as an allowance against total income.

Estimating Your EFC

We can't explain all the ins and outs of the FM in this book. The instructions for using the FM that financial aid officers receive would take up a few chapters of this book. Instead, we've done some research on the World Wide Web and found several sources that allow you to do an estimate of your family contribution online. The two best that we have found are:

- http://www.finaid.org—select CALCULATORS and then select Financial Aid Estimation under Needs Analysis

- http://www.kaplan.com—select the EFC Calculator for Graduate Students

These two sites each have EFC calculators that will do the job for you. You don't need to manually do all the calculations and have access to all the charts, because it's all automatic. What you do need is your most recent tax form and some idea of the value of your assets. All you have to do is enter the financial information that they ask for and your EFC will be calculated. You can even print out the results for reference. These results represent what the federal government considers to be the money you have available for your education. We can't guarantee that the figure you arrive at using the worksheet will exactly match the figure used in the financial aid office at your B-school, but it should give you a reasonable estimate. Use this estimated figure in your financial planning.

Your Financial Aid Package

Once the financial aid office has all the forms and data that they need, they'll wait for the admissions decision before they review your application. During this waiting period, it's a good idea to check with the schools to make sure that everything is complete and ready for processing once the admissions decision has been made.

When the financial aid office finds out that you've been admitted, they'll review your application and offer you an award package. This financial aid package can include scholarships and grants, Federal Work-Study, Federal Perkins Loans, Federal Stafford or Federal Direct Loans, and suggested private loans.

Now you need to review the financial aid packages and decide where you'll attend school. Your choice might not be the school that offered you the largest scholarship. You need to weigh the merits of the financial aid package against the desirability of the school itself and your match with it.

Before You Decide . . .

Get the answers to these questions about your financial aid package:

- What is your contribution expected to be?

- How much will you be expected to borrow?

- What kinds of loans are offered, and do they have attractive rates?

- Will you have to work while you're attending school?

CHAPTER 13

Scholarships and Other Sources of Funding

Financial aid for professional school or graduate school is less abundant than it is for college. And financial aid for B-school students is even tighter than for other types of grad students, since prospective M.B.A.'s are seen as being involved in lucrative fields. But bargains in financial aid for M.B.A. students do exist—scholarships, fellowships, and grants, along with campus-based federal aid programs.

Don't be unduly discouraged by the prospect of high debt and lack of grant and scholarship money. Many individuals find the M.B.A. degree a worthwhile investment. Most M.B.A. grads would agree that this degree made professional growth possible and was well worth the time and expense.

Aid for Full-Time Students

Although funds are limited, full-time students who meet the application deadlines will usually be considered for all available "free" monies, which may include grants, scholarships, and fellowships. Award packages usually include a combination of grants, part-time work, and loans. Offers of financial aid are determined by a number of factors:

- Merit relative to other applicants

- Financial need

- Eligibility for outside resources, such as state scholarships and state loans

Some schools offer only need-based scholarships, while others offer only merit-based awards. Since every institution's policies in awarding financial aid are different, talk to the schools that you are considering about their award policies. Scholarships can range from small amounts to full tuition, depending on the type of funding the school has available.

Unfortunately, "free money" for graduate business students is very limited, since starting salaries for graduates of business programs are relatively high—donors often prefer to assist students entering less lucrative professions. But don't let this deter you from investigating the possibilities. The following titles will help you to identify the opportunities available:

- Yale Daily News *Guide to Fellowships and Grants* (Simon & Schuster)

- *Worldwide Graduate Scholarship Directory* (Career Press)

- *Money for Graduate Students in the Social Sciences* (Reference Service Press)

Additional funding is available for certain groups. Two useful guides on this type of funding are *Directory of Financial Aids for Women* and *Financial Aid for the Disabled and Their Families*, both published by Reference Service Press.

Minority students are also eligible for special funding opportunities through business schools and outside funding sources. You'll find more information on such opportunities in the section entitled "Financial Aid for Minority Applicants" at the end of this chapter.

Sources of "Free Money"

Scholarships, fellowships, and grants are the best kind of funding to receive. They're "free money"— dollars that you don't have to work for or pay back. Of course, this is the most sought-after kind of funding, and the most difficult to receive. You'll need to do some advance planning to land this type of aid.

State Governments

State scholarship funds for graduate students exist, but on a limited basis, and usually there are strings attached. For example, states that do give scholarships to graduate and professional students may require that the funds be used at a school within the state offering the award. Check with your state government or with the schools in which you're interested for specific information about state-offered scholarships.

Graduate Business Schools

Many schools have scholarships, fellowships, and grants. Private graduate business schools have more free money than state schools, but, on the other hand, they usually cost more. The free money is needed to make private schools accessible to prospective students. It also attracts top students to B-school programs that are working hard to rebuild, revamp, and upgrade themselves. More and more B-schools are offering scholarships based solely on merit to prospective students to encourage them to attend their school. This is being done at schools hoping to upgrade their student population but also at top many schools who are still competing for students. Always look for merit scholarships even at schools you wouldn't think would be offering this type of award.

Employers

Although part-time students are generally not eligible for institutional gift aid, they have an important source of support not available to full-time student: their employers. Many companies provide educational benefits that subsidize tuition expenses for employees who pursue additional study.

These benefits may be limited to a certain amount per year or per course or may be offered only in areas of study approved by the company. When restrictions on area of study exist, the primary criterion for approval is usually the direct applicability of the program to the requirements of the employee's job. If you are a sales representative for a pharmaceutical company, for example, the company may not reimburse you for a course in music history, although marketing and chemistry might be approved. There may be additional eligibility requirements, such as length of employment with the firm prior to receiving benefits or contractual requirements to remain with the company for a specified period of time after receipt of educational benefits. In this latter case, employees who leave before the specified time may be required to repay the tuition benefits.

Many companies are now limiting the amount of reimbursement that they offer. Some companies set a dollar amount cutoff. In many cases the limitation reflects the former federal tax law in which the first $5,250 in company tuition reimbursement was exempt from taxes. This law has expired, although colleges and universities are still trying to have it reinstated.

> ### Don't Forget the Fees
>
> Some companies will reimburse you for the cost of tuition, but not mandatory student fees. If your program charges only minimal fees, the lack of reimbursement may not be important. However, fees at some institutions run hundreds of dollars per term and may become a major expense over the course of study.

Another possible snag is that companies often reimburse employees only after their courses are completed. You may have completed your first time and started your second term (and had to pay for it) before you receive any reimbursement.

Individuals, Businesses, and Philanthropic Organizations

These sources recognize the value of investing in the future of business professionals, and they provide fellowships and scholarships for outstanding students who otherwise would be unable to pursue graduate studies. You might receive this type of award through the school of your choice. Organizations often give money to schools to set up "named" scholarships. These scholarships usually go to students selected by the admissions/financial aid officers or faculty members. Often, you'll be considered for these scholarships on the strength of your admissions application or your interview. Sometimes a separate application is required. If so, the extra steps will be outlined in the admissions or financial aid application materials.

Students who receive named scholarships might also be offered internships or be honored at receptions where they meet the officers of the sponsoring organization. Some organizations and companies award scholarships directly to students. There are various free scholarship search databases on the web which you can use to identify scholarship sources that you can pursue. This kind of research could turn up one or two small grants to help offset the cost of your M.B.A.

The most comprehensive scholarship search is fastWEB, the Internet's first, largest and fastest free scholarship search service. You can even submit a preliminary application to some of the scholarships listed here directly via the Web through fastWEB's E-Scholarships Program.

Some other free scholarship databases that you may want to investigate are:

- Peterson's COLLEGEQUEST, which presents 800,000 awards from about 2,000 sources in 69 academic subject areas.

- Sallie Mae's Online Scholarship Service. This service offers free access to the College Aid Sources for Higher Education (CASHE) database, which lists private sector awards from 3,600 sponsors.

- The College Board's FUND FINDER scholarship database, also known as ExPAN Scholarship Search, lists scholarships and other types of financial aid programs from 3,300 national, state, public and private sources.

- CollegeNET MACH25 is a free web version of the Wintergreen/Orchard House Scholarship Finder database. The database lists awards from 1,570 sponsors.

- SRN Express is a free web version of the Scholarship Resource Network (SRN) database. The SRN database focuses on private-sector, non-need-based aid, and includes information about awards from more than 1,500 organizations.

All these scholarship databases can be accessed on the web through www.finaid.org under Scholarships.

Veteran's Benefits

If you've served in the U.S. military, you may be eligible for educational benefits. Check with the Office of Veteran's Affairs at your school, if your school had one. If budget cuts have closed the Veteran's Affairs office at your school, you can obtain information through the following sources:

- Department of Veteran's Affairs

- On the Internet, you can access the Federal Benefits for Veterans and Dependents Web site at http://www.va.gov/publ/benman95/index.htm

Veterans' Educational Benefits

	SURVIVORS'/DEPENDENTS' EDUCATIONAL ASSISTANCE PROGRAM (DEAP) CHAPTER 35	POST-VIETNAM ERA VETERANS' EDUCATIONAL PROGRAM (VEAP) CHAPTER 32	NEW G.I. BILL: MONTGOMERY G.I. BILL–ACTIVE DUTY CHAPTER 30
Eligible	Child or spouse of veteran who died or is permanently disabled as a result of active service; spouse eligibility extends for 10 years; children are eligible between ages of 18 and 26	Entered service between 1/1/77 and 6/30/85 Enrolled in VEAP before 4/1/87 Completed two years of active duty Served continuously for 181 days Received honorable discharge	Entered service after 6/30/85 Completed 2 years of active duty Received $100 per month reduction in military pay for 12 months
Maximum Term	Forty-five months (including undergraduate school)	Up to 36 months (including undergraduate school)	Up to 36 months (including undergraduate school)
Rate	Monthly amount fixed by the government	Voluntary; may contribute $25–$100 per month Government matches 2:1	Varies based on the length of service; depends upon enrollment status

Graduate Assistantships

Many B-schools offer some graduate assistantships to qualified M.B.A. students. These assistantships may or may not be based on financial need. Often, hiring decisions are based on your qualifications—your experience or completed course work.

Usually an assistantship provides a basic stipend for the academic year and remission of some portion of tuition for the fall and spring terms. The tuition remission may cover a certain number of credit hours, fill the gap between the resident and nonresident tuition rates, or rebate a percentage of the full tuition. Grad assistants hold teaching, research, or administrative positions. Usually graduate assistants must be registered as full-time students (registered for 12 credits). If you receive a graduate assistantship, you may not be eligible to receive any other school-funded financial assistance.

Federal Work-Study Program

The Federal Work-Study (FWS) Program provides financial aid by funding jobs for students. The U.S. federal government gives funds to the school, and the school matches a percentage of these funds. The joint fund pays student salaries for selected jobs. Under this program, you receive a salary or stipend, which usually can't be applied directly to tuition and fee charges. The program is administered by schools, but unfortunately, not all schools have FWS funds for graduate and professional students.

Eligibility

The college or university determines eligibility for FWS funds based on financial need (calculated through the FAFSA/SAR), and the availability of funds. Students must be enrolled at least half time and maintain satisfactory progress toward a degree. Funds from this program often go to undergraduate students first.

Earning Limits

Your earnings are limited to the FWS award figure listed in your financial aid package. The figure includes both the federal funds and the school's matching funds. FWS students are eligible for a variety of jobs, both on and off campus. Off-campus jobs usually involve non-profit institutions. Some schools have work-study agreements with private sector employers, though. Schools might also fund graduate assistantships with FWS money.

Application Procedures

There are generally no separate application procedures for FWS. You'll be automatically considered for FWS when you apply for financial aid. If you've been offered a work-study allocation, you can select from the various approved positions available on and off campus.

In addition to federal work-study funds, schools also admister the Federal Perkins Student Loan Program. Turn to the next chapter, "Borrowing the Money," for more information on this program.

Financial Aid for Minority Applicants

There are a number of fellowships and scholarships available for specific ethnic groups. If you are an African American or Hispanic American applicant, for example, it might be worth your while to take the time to investigate fellowships offerings at your local chapter of the National Black M.B.A. Association and the National Society of Hispanic M.B.A.'s. You might also want to check into fellowships from the organizations listed below. The Consortium for Graduate Study Management provides fellowships at selected M.B.A. programs, while the Robert A. Toigo Foundation offers fellowships, internships, and mentorship for M.B.A.'s interested in the financial services industry.

> Consortium for Graduate Study in Management
> 200 S. Hanley Road, Suite 1102
> St. Louis, MO 63105
> phone: (314) 935-8714
> fax: (314) 935-5014
> e-mail: cgsm@wuolin.wustl.edu

Robert A. Toigo Foundation
1230 Preservation Park Way
Oakland, CA 94612
phone: (510) 763-5771
fax: (510) 763-5778
e-mail: rtfmailbox@aol.com
Web site: http://www.rtf.org

Reference Service Press publishes a number of guides on scholarships and other funding that are written with specific minority groups in mind, including:

- *Financial Aid for African Americans*

- *Financial Aid for Asian Americans*

- *Financial Aid for Hispanic Americans*

- *Financial Aid for Native Americans*

Final Thoughts

"Free money"—grants, scholarships, and fellowships—are great, but they're hard to get. To give you the complete financial aid picture, we'll cover loan sources in the next chapter.

CHAPTER 14

Borrowing the Money

Student loans are an important source of support for graduate business students. This chapter provides you with the information you'll need to decide which loan programs fit your particular situation.

It can take up to eight to 12 weeks from the date you apply to receive any loan proceeds, so planning is essential. Also, since the rules and regulations for borrowing through each of these programs differ, you should read each section carefully.

The good news is that educational loans typically have more favorable terms than consumer loans, particularly unsecured loans, and they're usually easier to obtain. However, you can't assume that you'll be able to get a student loan whatever your financial circumstances. Remember, federal student loan programs have eligibility requirements. Many private loan programs have some type of credit criteria that you must meet before you can borrow, and virtually all programs establish some borrowing limits.

The trick is to make sure that you don't borrow so much that you reduce the return on your investment once you graduate. With planning, you can avoid that problem.

Kaplan/American Express Student Loan Program

A valuable resource for prospective borrowers is the Kaplan/American Express Student Loan Program. This program provides students and their parents with information and step-by-step assistance in how to meet the high cost of business school. Through an affiliation with one of the nation's largest student loan lenders, the Kaplan/American Express Student Loan Program connects you with a resource for the financing you need to reach your educational goals.

You can get information about the Kaplan/American Express Student Loan Program at seminars, in written materials, and through online services. Additional benefits include:

- *Free Assistance Available Toll-Free.* Educational Finance Specialists (EFSs) are available 12 hours a day to answer any questions you may have. You can reach an EFS toll-free at (888) KAP-LOAN, Monday through Sunday, from 10:00 A.M. to 10:00 P.M. Eastern time.

- *Money-Saving Features.* Both Federal PLUS and Stafford Loans come with valuable borrower benefits that can save you money at repayment time.

- *Easy Application.* You can access financial aid information, and even apply for a student loan online at the Kaplan/American Express Student Loan Program Web site (www.kaploan.com).

- *Credit Reevaluation Program.* The Second Review helps previously denied borrowers to reverse their credit-denied status. Borrowers are guided through the process of gathering documentation that might clear up incorrect and/or outdated credit report listings.

Credit and Credit Reporting

A poor credit history could be a large stumbling block to financing your M.B.A. degree. While the U.S. federal loan programs for graduate students don't really check your credit history, many of the private loan programs do. If your credit record is weak, your previous actions may come back to haunt you and make attending B-school a financial impossibility.

Federal Loans

In order to qualify for federal student loans (Federal Stafford or Federal Direct loans), you cannot be in default of any previous federal loans. If you are, you can't take out another federal student loan until you make six consecutive payments on the loan you're in default on, or completely pay it off. If you're only delinquent rather than in default on your loan payments, you must pay off any past-due balance before you can borrow again.

Private Loans and Credit Reports

Private loan programs are much stricter about their lending guidelines than the federal government. When a private loan program checks your credit history, it requests a credit report from one of the three major credit bureaus in the United States.

Your credit history shows a record of all your prior debts and your history of repayments. This list will include your credit cards, mortgage, and any other consumer loans you might have. Your repayment history on any previous student loans will be listed, too. Private loan programs look for a record of on-time, consistent repayment of any financial obligations. If your track record as a borrower is not up to its standards, a lender will deny your loan application.

Key Credit Terms

Most private loan programs require that you have no adverse credit and that you be at least credit-ready, if not credit-worthy. Credit-ready simply means that your credit record is clean, that there are no indications of credit problems. You can be credit-ready even if you have no credit history at all, because you have nothing adverse in your credit record. Some private loan programs may require that you get a cosigner if you have no previous credit history. Credit-wor-

> ### *Check Your Credit Report*
>
> We recommend that you obtain a copy of your credit report well before you apply for any loans. We've all heard horror stories about someone's bad credit history getting mixed up with someone else's good one. It's a good idea to get a copy of your credit report periodically and verify that the information is correct.

thy means that you have both a clean credit history and that you currently have the means to make payments on the loan. A mortgage is an example of a loan that requires you to be credit-worthy.

Federal Loan Programs

The two U.S. federal loan programs available to graduate business school students are generally considered the core loan programs, since they carry certain attractive features defined by law. These features include a low interest rate, low fees, and defined deferment provisions. The two programs are:

- Federal Stafford Student Loan Program (part of the Federal Family Education Loan Program)
- William D. Ford Federal Direct Student Loan Program

The terms of these loan programs are similar. The eligibility criteria, interest rates, fees, grace period, deferment and cancelation provisions, and other terms are all basically the same. There are, however, minor differences in the application process and certain repayment options.

The key differences lies in who provides the loan funds. The Federal Stafford Student Loan is part of the Federal Family Education Loan Program (FFELP), through which loans are made by a private lender (such as a bank, a savings and loan association, a credit union, or an insurance company) and are insured by a state or private guarantee agency sponsored by the U.S. federal government. Under the William D. Ford Federal Direct Student Loan Program, the U.S. federal government is the lender.

Many schools participate in the Stafford program, but some participate in the Ford Direct program. The school you attend will determine which of these two loans you can apply for.

In order to be eligible for these programs, you must:

- Be a citizen, a permanent resident, or eligible noncitizen of the United States

- Be enrolled at least half time (usually six credits)

- Be in good academic standing, and be making satisfactory progress toward the degree (as defined by the school)

- Not be in default of any previous loans without being in an approved repayment program

- Have progressed a class year since receiving your last Federal Stafford Loan (for example, fourth-year undergrad to first-year grad student)

- Show financial need based on the information provided on your FAFSA in order to qualify for the interest subsidy

Federal Stafford Student Loans

The Federal Stafford Student Loan Program provides two types of loans: subsidized and unsubsidized. The subsidized loans are a better deal, but you have to meet the government's financial need criteria. For either type of loan, you may defer payments of principal and interest until you graduate or drop below half-time enrollment. Depending on when you first borrowed, there's a grace period of six or nine months before you'll have to start repayment.

The Federal Stafford Loan Program evolved from the Guaranteed Student Loan Program (GSL) that you may have borrowed under in college. The concept of a federal loan program originated in 1965 as the Federally Insured Student Loan Program (FISL). The Federal Stafford Loan Program has the same purpose as these previous programs—to make loan funds available for students to attend post-secondary school—but the amounts available, interest rates, and deferment provisions have been modified.

Federal Subsidized Stafford Loans are available to all students who meet the financial need criteria. A federally mandated needs analysis, based on information provided on the FAFSA, determines a student's Federal Subsidized Stafford Loan eligibility. Students who don't qualify for the subsidized loan or need to borrow beyond the limit can take out an Unsubsidized Federal Stafford Loan.

Borrowing Limits

Graduate students may borrow up to their demonstrated need with a maximum $8,500 per year in the Federal Subsidized Stafford Loan Program, with a total borrowing limit (including undergraduate Federal Stafford Loans) of $65,500. The Federal Unsubsidized Stafford Loan Program allows an eligible student to borrow up to $18,500 per year, minus any Federal Subsidized Stafford Loan approved. The total cumulative maximum is $138,500 (including the Federal Subsidized Stafford Loans).

Interest Rate

As the program's name indicates, the federal government subsidizes the interest on the Federal Subsidized Stafford Loan. You're not required to pay interest on these loans until after you leave school. If you have a Federal Unsubsidized Stafford Loan, you're responsible for the interest while you're in school, but most lenders will allow you to capitalize the interest, and not pay it until you leave school. Capitalization means that the interest accrues while you're still in school and is added to the principal at a predetermined time (often at the point of repayment). Applications and information about current interest rates and repayment schedules are available at participating lending institutions.

Fluctuating Interest Rates

The current interest rate on these loans is the 91-day Treasury Bill rate plus 3.1 percent with a cap of 8.25 percent. This rate is supposed to change during the summer of 1998, but there is a movement to keep the same rate. You should check with your school and/or lender to find out whether or not the rate has changed.

Fees

There's a loan origination fee that is equal to 3 percent of the loan. If you borrow $5,000, for example, the loan origination fee will be $150. The fee, required by law, is sent to the U.S. federal government to offset a portion of the federal interest subsidy. In addition, the guarantee agency may charge you an insurance fee of up to 1 percent of the loan. Both of these fees would be deducted from the loan proceeds when the check is issued. All lenders are required to deduct the federal government's 3 percent loan origination fee, but they're allowed to reduce or eliminate their own 1 percent guarantee fee. Some lenders reduce this fee as an incentive for borrowers. Shop around for the best deal.

Sources of Federal Stafford Student Loans

Federal Stafford Student Loans are made through participating banks, savings and loan associations, credit unions, pension funds, and insurance companies.

Application Procedures

To apply for a Federal Stafford Student Loan, you should complete the FAFSA and mail it to the federal processor, and fill out a Common Loan Application and submit it to the school you plan to attend. The B-school will certify your application and either mail it to the bank or electronically send them the certification information. The bank will electronically forward that information on to the guarantee agency who will approve or deny the loan and send that info back to the bank. The bank will either cut a check made payable to you and the school, or will transmit the funds to the school via Electronic Funds Transfer (EFT). Once the funds are available at the B-school, the funds are credited against any unpaid balance you have and the difference is refunded to you. This whole process can take up to three months, so plan for the time lag.

Repayment

The amount of your monthly payment will depend on the total amount you borrowed, the number of months in the repayment schedule, and whether or not you elected to pay interest on the unsubsidized portion of the loan while in school. The maximum repayment period is usually ten years, with repayment generally in equal monthly installments. You'll have a shorter repayment term if you borrow a small amount, since there's a minimum monthly installment of $50.

> ### The Good Will of Lenders
>
> Check with your lender to see if it has developed any innovative ways for you to repay your debt. Lenders are trying to make it possible for students to keep in good standing with their repayments, and are willing to work with them to help manage their debt.

If you don't meet the repayment terms of the loan, you go into default and the entire balance of the loan becomes due. If your loan goes into default, your lender may refuse to allow you to borrow again until the entire debt is satisfied.

Deferments/Forbearance/Cancelations

Under certain circumstances you may be able to defer, or postpone, the payments of your Federal Stafford Loan. Deferments are not automatic; you must apply for them. You can also request forbearance in situations that aren't covered by normal deferments. Forbearance means the lender agrees to grant you a temporary suspension of payments, reduced payments, or an extension of the time for your payments. As a final option, you can get a portion of your loans canceled under special circumstances. Read your promissory note for details of all of these provisions. They should also have been covered in your entrance and exit interviews.

William D. Ford Federal Direct Loan Program

The Ford Federal Direct Loan Program was authorized by the U.S. Congress in 1993. In this program, the federal government is the lender. Individual schools, rather than banks or other financial institutions, originate the loans. This program includes two types of loans: the Federal Direct Stafford Loan and the Federal Direct Unsubsidized Stafford Loan.

The eligibility criteria, borrowing limits, interest rate, fees, grace period, and deferment and cancellation provisions for this program are the same as for the Federal Stafford Loan Program, covered above. The Federal Direct Loan Program has different application procedures and repayment options for students.

Application Procedures

The FAFSA and the other required documents that were discussed earlier must be completed. Usually, the Federal Direct Loan will be offered as part of your financial aid package. Once you accept the loan as part of the package, the financial aid officer creates a Loan Origination Record and electronically transmits it to the federal servicer for approval. The approval is transmitted back to the school, and the school produces a promissory note for you to sign. Once the promissory note is signed, the school can disburse the first semester portion of the loan (minus fees) to your student account. Any funds remaining after any unpaid balance you have with the university will be refunded to you. The entire process, from the point of loan certification to disbursement of the check, can take as little as a week to complete.

Repayment

Most of the conditions of repayment are the same as for the Federal Stafford Loan Program. Although the same standard repayment plan (fixed payment for up to ten years) is offered in both programs, students who participate in the Federal Direct Loan Program have three additional repayment options: the extended repayment plan, the income contingent repayment plan, and the graduated repayment plan.

Option 1: Extended Repayment

Similar to the standard repayment plan, it allows the student to repay a fixed amount over a period longer than ten years.

Option 2: Income Contingent Repayment

Students pay a percentage of their salary no matter how much they've borrowed. If they have large debts, this option require many more years of repayment than the standard ten years. As their salaries increase, so do their loan repayments. The drawback to this option is that the longer they stay in repayment, the more interest they pay on the loan. Indeed, if their payment does not cover the current interest due, unpaid interest is capitalized, increasing the amount of principal they owe.

Option 3: Graduated Repayment

This allows students to opt for lower payments at the beginning of the repayment cycle when their salaries are lower. The payments automatically increase as the years progress. The repayment term remains ten years, but the payments are more manageable in the beginning.

No matter which repayment option you select, the plan will be explained in the promissory note you sign. Repayments will be made to a federal loan servicer contracted by the U.S. Department of Education.

Federal Perkins Student Loan

In addition to the Federal Stafford Student Loan Program and the William D. Ford Federal Direct Student Loan Program, there is another federal student loan program that merits your consideration. Like the Federal Work-Study Program described in the last chapter, the Federal Perkins Student Loan Program is administered by colleges and universities. It is made possible through a combination of resources: an annual allocation from the U.S. Department of Education, a contribution from the participating institution, and repayments by previous borrowers. You may have taken advantage of this program under its previous name, the National Direct Student Loan (NDSL) Program. This program, one of the first federal financial aid programs, was instituted more than 30 years ago.

Eligibility

As with FWS, the college or university determines eligibility for Federal Perkins Loans based on your financial need (calculated through the FAFSA/SAR) and the availability of funds. Besides demonstrating financial need, you have to be enrolled at least half time, and maintain satisfactory progress toward a degree. Keep in mind that Federal Perkins Loans are reserved for the neediest students.

Borrowing Limits

Federal policy allows the maximum annual loan of $5,000 per graduate student. Actually, though, many schools lack the funds to allocate this much to any one student. A graduate student may borrow up to a cumulative total of $30,000, including all outstanding undergraduate and graduate Federal Perkins Loans.

Interest Rate

The terms are very good. The annual interest rate is currently 5 percent. Interest does not accrue while the borrower remains enrolled at least half time.

Fees

Another perk of the Federal Perkins Loan: no fees.

Application Procedures

Usually, you're automatically considered for this loan when you apply for financial aid. If you've been offered and have accepted a Federal Perkins Loan, you'll sign a promissory note for each semester of the loan. The promissory note lists the amount of the loan and states your rights and responsibilities as a borrower. When the signed note is received, either you will be credited for one semester's portion of the loan, or a check will be cut for you directly.

Deferments

You can defer payments of your Federal Perkins loan while you are enrolled until you graduate or drop below half time. This deferment is not automatic; you must request the deferment forms from either your school or the billing agency to which you're repaying the loan.

Grace Period

A Federal Perkins Loan has a six-month grace period after a student graduates or drops below half-time attendance. During this period, no repayment is required and no interest accrues. If you borrowed under the NDSL Program, you may have a different grace period. You need to check with the school that granted you the loan to find out what the specific grace period for your loan is.

Repayment

Borrowers under the Federal Perkins Loan program repay the school, although there may be an intermediary. Many schools contract with outside agencies for billing and collection. Repayment may extend up to ten years, beginning six months (your grace period) after you cease to be enrolled at least half time. The amount of the monthly payment and the maximum number of months allowed for repayment is based on the total amount borrowed. The federal government has set the minimum monthly payment at $40. Under some special circumstances, borrowers may make arrangements to repay a lower amount or to extend the repayment period. There is no prepayment penalty.

Cancelations

The entirety of your Federal Perkins Loans and/or NDSLs will be canceled if you become permanently disabled or die. Check your promissory note. Your loan may have additional cancellation provisions. Also, if you have "old" Federal Perkins Loans or NDSLs, there may be some different conditions depending on when the original loan was made. Check with your previous school for any special circumstances.

Federal Loan Consolidation

Federal Loan Consolidation allows students with substantial debt to combine several federal loans into one larger loan with a longer repayment schedule. The new loan has an interest rate based on the weighted average of the rates of the consolidated loans. Students who borrowed under the Federal Stafford Loan (or the earlier Guaranteed Student Loan), the Federal Perkins Loan (or the earlier National Direct Student Loan), the Federal Supplemental Loan for Students, the Auxiliary Loan to Assist Students (ALAS), and the Health Professions Student Loan Program can consolidate all these loans into one new loan.

To qualify for federal loan consolidation, you must be in your grace period or in repayment of your loans, and not be delinquent by more than ninety days. Apply to one of the lenders of your current loans. They'll negotiate to purchase your other loans from the lenders who hold them so your loans will be consolidated. If none of your lenders offers federal loan consolidation, you can go to another lender who does. Arrange to have that lender purchase your loans.

You have the option of consolidating all or only part of your loans. Often, students consolidate their higher interest loans, but keep their Federal Perkins Loans separate since the interest rate is so low. No fees are charged to participate in this program.

You may be eligible for a deferment of principal, but you must continue to pay the interest on your consolidated loan. Deferment of principal is available if you are:

- Enrolled at least half time in a postsecondary school or graduate program

- Enrolled in an approved graduate fellowship or rehabilitation training program for persons with disabilities

- Temporarily totally disabled, or unemployed because you're taking care of a temporarily totally disabled dependent

- Unable to find full-time employment

Consolidation Federal Loan Repayment

Total Consolidation Federal Student Loan Debt	Maximum Repayment Period
Less than $7,500	10 years
$7,500 to 9,999	12 years
$10,000 to 19,999	15 years
$20,000 to 39,999	20 years
$40,000 to 59,999	25 years
$60,000 or more	30 years

Information about time limitations for repayment is shown in the Consolidation Loan Repayment chart above. Consolidation has several advantages. The monthly payment is reduced while the length of time allowed for repayment is extended. Also, keeping track of payments is easier since there's only one payment for several loans. Prepay all or part of your federal consolidated loan at any time without penalty, reducing the amount of interest you'll end up paying.

Private Loan Programs

Many M.B.A. students find that scholarship funds and the federal loan programs are not adequate to meet their expenses in a full-time M.B.A. program. Over the last few years, several private loan programs have emerged to fill the gap.

As the economic environment changes, new loan private programs are added and some older programs are discontinued. Check with the individual programs for their current provisions.

The TERI Supplemental Loan Program

This is a private educational loan program designed to help students make up the difference between their cost of education and their grants or loans. Approval is based on the creditworthiness of the applicant.

Business Access

This is a private loan program sponsored by The Access Group. Business Access offers private and federal loan funds up to the cost of attendance to students attending graduate business schools accredited by the American Assembly of Collegiate Schools of Business.

The GradEXCEL Program

This is an education loan program through Nellie Mae, a private loan agency, designed to meet the needs of students enrolled in graduate and professional degree programs. GradEXCEL offers graduate students an educational loan based on projected future earnings rather than on current credit-worthiness.

Tuition Loan Program (TLP)

This private educational loan plan was designed specifically as part of a service called M.B.A. LOANS for graduate business students who need additional funds to support their educational expenses. Students may borrow on their own or use a cosigner. The program was designed by the Graduate Admissions Management Council (GMAC), the people who bring you the GMAT, in association with Norwest Bank and HEMAR Insurance Corporation of America.

Debt Management

You've read the material on financial aid and loans. How much did you calculate you'd need to borrow? This is the time to figure out if you'll actually be able to manage your projected debt. Don't wait until you're in over your head. If your projected indebtedness seems unmanageable, identify ways to reduce either your borrowing or your payments.

Step One: Calculate Your Monthly Payments

Use the following Monthly Loan Payments table to calculate your monthly repayments after graduating. In estimating your indebtedness, remember that you're likely to need similar funding for each year you're in school. Will you be enrolling full time? Double all the loan amounts in your financial aid award letter; you'll probably borrow the same amount for two years. If you're enrolling part time, you may need to multiply your loan amount by three, four, or even five to cover the number of years it'll take you to finish the program.

Use the Monthly Loan Payments table to help you calculate most monthly payments on a level-payment plan over five to thirty years. For example, suppose you had a $5,000 loan at 8 percent and a ten-year payment term. As the table shows, the monthly payment for a $1,000 loan would be $12.13. Multiply this by five to get $60.65.

Bear in mind, however, that you may need to calculate several payments. Each lender, under each loan program, should be calculated separately. For example, if you have several Federal Stafford Student Loans issued by a single lender, add them up to arrive at a single balance. But, if you have two additional loans issued under a private supplemental loan program, consider them separately. Calculate the payments for the two different programs separately, then add them together to determine your total payment responsibility.

Step Two: Estimate Your Starting Salary

You probably have several schools in mind by now; get average starting salary information for each of them. Look for their average starting salaries in the "Directory of Business Schools" section at the end of this book.

Step Three: Calculate Whether or Not Your Paycheck Will Cover Your Expenses

Taking into account all mandatory and discretionary expenses, calculate exactly how much money you will have left over each month. You should take into account such expenses as child care, health insurance, credit card payments, travel, car payments, gifts, etcetera. Try not to underestimate your expenses, since this will give you problems later when you realize you haven't budgeted for all of them.

Work as Much as Possible

The more you can earn both before and while in the program, the less you'll need to borrow. A summer job or internship can help a lot. Consider this: If you earn just $1,000 per year in a two-year, full-time program and borrow $2,000 less, you can reduce your monthly loan repayment by $25 per month for ten years, saving you a total of $3,000.

Step Four: Consider Your Financial Options

If things look tight in your post-M.B.A. financial picture, you could plan to reduce items in the "Discretionary Expenses" category. Another option is to lower your monthly loan payments. The only way to have lower loan payments is to adjust your living expenses before you start school and while you are in school so you can borrow less. Otherwise, you will need to try to live on less when you get out of school because your loan payments will now be

Monthly Loan Payments*

FOR A $1,000 LOAN

Rate	60 Months	120 Months	180 Months	240 Months	300 Months
5%	$18.87	$10.61	$7.91	$6.60	$5.85
6%	19.33	11.10	8.44	7.16	6.44
7%	19.80	11.61	8.99	7.75	7.07
8%	20.28	12.13	9.56	8.36	7.72
9%	20.76	12.67	10.14	9.00	8.39
10%	21.25	13.22	10.75	9.65	9.09
11%	21.74	13.77	11.37	10.32	9.80
12%	22.24	14.35	12.00	11.01	10.53
13%	22.75	14.93	12.65	11.72	11.28
14%	23.27	15.53	13.32	12.44	12.04
16%	24.32	16.75	14.69	13.91	13.59
18%	25.39	18.02	16.10	15.43	15.17
20%	26.49	19.33	17.56	16.99	16.78

* Minimum monthly payments may apply regardless of the loan amount.

fixed. Potential employers won't increase your starting salary to cover your expenses and loan repayments!

When you're projecting your loan repayments, remember this: While the payments will stay relatively stable, your salary will (presumably) increase over the repayment term of the loan. The loan payments will be less onerous as your salary goes up. On the other hand, the longer you're out of school, the more major expenses you're likely to have: a house, a car, children, vacations, and so on.

If your loan repayments are very high, you may have to evaluate post-graduation job offers strictly in terms of salary. Any investment involves some risk and some level of sacrifice, but you don't want to be paying for it with a reduced living standard for ten years.

Your M.B.A. degree is an investment that should produce considerable professional and financial returns. Make sure that you will be getting the returns you want and need from your M.B.A. investment before you commit yourself to a program.

PART FIVE

Special Considerations

CHAPTER 15

Students Directly Out of College

Conventional wisdom has it that you need work experience, and often substantial work experience, before starting an M.B.A. program. This belief is both true and false. Some B-schools won't even consider you without a minimum of two years of full-time work experience. Other schools would like you to come into their program with at least some relevant work experience, although they will still seriously consider you without it. Finally, some schools accept the majority of their class directly out of college. You need to do the research required to figure out which schools fall into which categories. In most cases, you will find that the most competitive schools fall into the "work experience required" category. Why do schools have different views on this topic?

Schools That Require Work Experience

Business schools that require work experience think they have good reasons to do so. These reasons are outlined below.

Understanding of Subject Material

Schools typically want candidates with experience because they bring a broader understanding of subject material to the classroom (helping to counteract the "Why am I learning this?!" syndrome), and because they can contribute to classroom discussion and enrich the learning of their fellow students. Many schools feel that it is preferable to have "many instructors in the classroom, not just one professor in front." There is a perception that students who have worked full time for one or more years have gained perspective and maturity in dealing both with work and personal situations.

Placement Issues

Employers often want experience; therefore, students with nothing beyond summer work experience will have a more difficult time getting a job. Employers feel that work experience makes you a more valuable employee. A student with little experience may be given relatively few opportunities to interview through the placement office if the companies are looking for and expecting someone with experience.

There are exceptions to the work experience requirement. Candidates from family firms, who have worked in those firms perhaps since before they were of legal age to work and who will return directly to the family company after B-school, probably won't benefit from additional work experience. Even in this, the school's attitudes will differ, so don't count on not needing any full-time work experience if you are associated with a family firm.

The 90 Percent Range

One well-known B-school has its placement director interview every candidate who is too young or too old to fall within the 90 percent age range for the program. If the placement director feels that the candidate would be placeable at the end of two years, he or she is admitted.

There are of course some individuals who are accepted into B-schools right out of college (for example, one Northwestern University woman, aged 21 with no full-time experience, wowed Northwestern in an interview, and got accepted). However, this is the exception rather than the rule. B-school directors point to an unusual level of maturity and understanding, very significant summer experience, or an unusual degree of goal-orientation in students who are accepted under these circumstances.

Salaries

M.B.A. candidates are generally very interested in the starting salaries published by business schools. In consequence, B-schools like to report high starting salaries. Students who were already relatively well paid when they entered B-school are more likely to be command high starting salaries after graduation. The salaries offered to younger, less experienced graduates, meanwhile, are likely to be on the lower end of the salary range, dragging average starting salary statistics down and making these students less attractive to B-schools.

Networking

One of most important aspects of any B-school program is the people you meet, the networks you form, and the friendships you make. B-schools are aware that an inexperienced student who is admitted to a program in which students average three or four years of experience will have more than the age difference issue to deal with. He or she might not understand what is going on in classroom, be able to make friends with classmates, or contribute to the classroom discussions and keep up with the group work. If you are such an applicant, don't take such issues lightly. You don't want to be the one person who can't contribute and is considered the drain on the group. Your credibility is at stake.

Younger students sometimes recognize the drawbacks of not having full-time work experience midyear and withdraw (or take a leave of absence) from the M.B.A. program. Most intend to work for a year or two and then return to complete the program. But this approach has its perils. Despite the best intentions of these students, it may not be possible for them to return later. Even if they do, the interruption of their studies can have financial implications. The best course is to think about these issues ahead of time before making a commitment.

Schools That Don't Require Work Experience

Not all schools require that you work for two or more years before starting your M.B.A. program; some schools, in fact, welcome inexperienced students, for a variety of reasons.

Internships

Programs that don't require work experience often make internships available. They help facilitate placements that will give their students meaningful experience before they graduate. The classroom experience at these schools is also geared toward students without significant experience. Students are less likely to be given an assignment that requires them to apply a theory from the course to their prior work experience.

For those students who haven't had significant experience, summer internships may be a make-or-break factor; it is the one chance for these students to prove their ability to compete. B-schools that accept inexperienced students will make every effort to place these students in summer jobs or internships that will help compensate for the lack of prior work experience when their students come onto the job market. Some programs have formal cooperative education possibilities that place students in a company for six months or even longer. These longer placements, whether they are called cooperative education or internships, provide students with experience similar to a full-time position.

Placement in Different Companies

Look at the B-school's placement record; presumably, these schools have identified opportunities for their candidates that are appropriate. There are lots of companies out there that look for graduates from less well known B-schools that still turn out high-quality graduates. These companies may want to bring in new employees who will grow with the company or are more willing to embrace the company culture. For these reasons, these schools establish relationships with companies that expect B-school grads to have less work experience.

No Experience Required

Most want ads specify that they are looking for applicants who are experienced. Yet many companies actually prefer to hire inexperienced employees, because this enables them to keep costs down and to train workers in the company ethos more easily.

More Flexible Salary Requirements

The average starting salary for students graduating from these schools may not be as high as at a school with students with significant experience. These salaries are probably more reflective of what inexperienced students would earn coming out of any program. But this can be a plus. Many companies can't afford to pay the huge salaries and bonuses commanded by graduates of the top-tier B-schools. These companies turn to B-schools that produce graduates who are willing to start a little lower on the wage scale, with the potential of increasing their salaries as they prove their worth.

Deferred Admission

There is one more option available for students with little work experience. Some B-schools will get applications from students who look like they would be good additions to their program, but are lacking the work experience requirement. Deferred admission may be the B-school's answer. In deferred admission, students are accepted for a later term/year than the one for which they applied. In the meantime, they are told to go get some more work experience in a professional job that will pertain to their B-school studies. You may need to pay a tuition deposit to retain a deferred position in the class. The deposit is expected when you are admitted rather than just before you enter.

What the Top M.B.A. Programs Say: Age and Work Experience

University of Virginia, Darden School

"The demographics of our entering classes is very broad and balanced. We publish this profile every year and would encourage prospective applicants to look at the profile as part of their application process.

"At Darden the average age of entering students is 27+ years. Historically, Darden doesn't admit U.S. citizens without full-time work experience. Given the case-method pedagogy, experience is vital for class activities, as is diversity of experiences.

"Important for all schools, regardless of pedagogical method, is the issue of placement and starting salaries. Most major recruiters won't hire or pay top dollar for M.B.A.'s without full-time work experience. In 1995, we began to offer a limited number of openings in the entering class for exceptional students coming directly from undergraduate school (the Direct

Admit Program). After the first-year, required curriculum, these students will have 15-month (versus regular summer 3-month) internships with the same companies that hire our graduates and summer interns. After completing the year-and-a-summer internship, the students return and complete the second year of the M.B.A. program. In 3 years, these students get full-time work experience and an M.B.A., which will allow them to compete for traditional work experience-based M.B.A. jobs."

University of Minnesota, Carlson School

"M.B.A. students typically have 2–4 years of work experience. This experience is highly valued because of the extensive class participation and group projects in our program."

Cornell University, Johnson School

"Our students have over three years of post-college work experience, on average. While seven percent of our students do not have any full-time experience, they would need to make up for that with very high scores, a stellar academic record at a very selective college, an unusual level of maturity, and a compelling reason for starting the M.B.A. sooner rather than later. We expect our students to use their previous work experience to contribute to classroom discussions and team projects. A record of achievement in the work world also helps an M.B.A. student in her search for a summer internship and a post-M.B.A. job."

Indiana University

"Our M.B.A. students on average have four years of work experience prior to matriculation. Peer-to-peer learning in our program works best when there are a variety of perspectives and insights the students can share, and from which they can learn. Students with prior work experience can make more sense of the principles discussed, have greater self awareness, and possess a better understanding of what they want to do and who they are—which is critical for success. Those with less work experience often don't have as sharp a focus as their peers who have a more seasoned career background. The M.B.A. experience is richer and more meaningful for those with work context."

What Should You Do?

If you have decided to pursue an M.B.A. directly out of college, you need to be sure that your goals are well defined and that you have done the appropriate self-examination. Is there a good reason for going to B-school right now? Can you convince the admissions committee that you are ready for the M.B.A. program? Do you want to get one of those big starting salaries or are you willing to start with less and grow? All these questions need to be answered before you finally decide where to apply.

CHAPTER 16

Students with Disabilities

by Chris Rosa

The decision to go to business school involves a major commitment of time, money, energy, and the development of a professional sense of self. It is an enormous commitment for any individual, but especially for individuals with disabilities. In choosing an M.B.A. program, people with disabilities not only commit the same personal resources that all students devote to the business school endeavor, they must also realign all of the access resources upon which they rely for independence and success in other parts of their lives in order to support their efforts in business school. This reallocation of independent living resources to support study in business school often significantly diminishes quality of life for people with disabilities in other life domains.

If one is truly ready for business school and chooses the right program, these sacrifices are surely worth it. However, in order to avoid regrettable decisions, candidates with disabilities must understand what it takes to be ready academically, logistically, physically, and emotionally for the rigors of business school. If you are such a candidate, you must be willing look at yourself self-critically and ask, "Am I ready for this?"

The Right Stuff

Like all candidates for business school, students with disabilities must ensure that their candidate profiles meet the criteria for admission to the programs to which they apply and that their profiles are sufficiently attractive to earn serious consideration from admission committees. In constructing candidate profiles, people with disabilities should consider disability issues that will affect their presentation of self as candidates.

Undergraduate Performance

Undergraduate performance is always a significant factor in whether or not candidates are admitted to their programs of choice. If your undergraduate performance was affected by a disability issue (i.e., an undergraduate institution's failure to adequately meet your needs for reasonable accommodation, or a learning disability that went undiagnosed throughout most of a college career), you might be able to use other aspects of your candidate profile—your personal statement, letters of reference, admissions committee interviews, and so on)—to explain away a relatively low GPA. While such explanations may improve your chances for admission, they often do so at the cost of disclosing your identity as a candidate with a disability.

To Tell or Not to Tell?

While your personal statement, letters of reference, GMAT scores, and interviews with admissions committees offer candidates with disabilities the opportunity to demonstrate their richness and strengths as applicants, these dimensions of the candidate profile are fraught with opportunities for others to learn about your status as a candidate with a disability. For those of you who are concerned about disability disclosure, these aspects of your candidate profile must be carefully managed.

> ### Cover All Bases
>
> If you decide not to disclose your status as a candidate with a disability, make sure you cover all the bases. Speak to those providing you with letters of reference who are aware of your disability and let them know how you feel about disability disclosure, so that they do not unwittingly disclose information that you're uncomfortable with in their reference letters.

The decision of whether or not to disclose a disability in a personal statement is a very difficult, very personal one. This decision pits people's pride in their disability identity against their concerns that lingering cultural biases against people with disabilities will cause candidates who have disclosed their disabilities to be perceived as somehow less viable by admissions committees. If you are at all concerned about the possible repercussions of disability disclosure, follow this general rule: Unless it is central to your personal statement's thesis or to your ability to explain away a sub-par undergraduate performance, leave it out!

If you would rather not reveal your disability, do not feel obliged to volunteer any information about it during interviews with admissions personnel or program representatives. Asking questions like "Do you have a disability?" is illegal in most admissions contexts. However, if you are asked such an inappropriate question during an interview, asserting your Americans with Disabilities Act right to confidentiality will probably not help your admissions chances. If you are asked about your disability, you may consider simply and honestly informing the interviewer that you have a disability that, with the necessary reasonable accommodations, in no way limits your ability to be successful in graduate school.

Taking the GMAT Under Accommodative Conditions

Reasonable accommodations are available to test takers with documented disabilities in both the paper-based or computer-based exam formats of the GMAT. Among the accommodations available are exams in accessible formats, readers and amanuenses, access to assistive technologies, and extended exam time.

An official request for exam accommodations must include a completed Documentation Certificate of Nonstandard Testing Accommodations (completed by a licensed or certified professional, the Director of Human Resources at your place of employment, or the Office of Disability Services at your academic institution) and a completed Examinee's Eligibility Questionnaire.

Beware of the "Maris Effect"

In 1961, Roger Maris of the New York Yankees hit home runs at a furious pace that enabled him to eclipse Babe Ruth's single season record for round-trippers, a record that the experts swore would never be broken. In breaking Ruth's record of 60 home runs, Maris was the subject of much controversy and criticism among contemporaries who thought his accomplishment was less valid because he hit his 61 Homers during a 162-game schedule, while Ruth reached 60 home runs during a 154-game schedule. As a result of this controversy, Baseball Commissioner Ford Frick placed an asterisk next to his home run total of 61, which forever stigmatized and diminished Maris' record-setting total.

When candidates with disabilities take the GMAT under accommodative conditions, they run the risk of experiencing the "Maris Effect." Even though reasonable exam accommodations do not provide testers with disabilities a distinct advantage over standard exam takers, the GMAT includes a statement in exam reports indicating that accommodative exams were taken under nonstandard conditions. There are also no interpretive data for such GMAT scores. This distinction may cause even the highest GMAT scores to be considered less valid and may raise a red flag, alerting programs to these candidates' status as applicants with disabilities.

If you are considering taking the GMAT under nonstandard conditions and are concerned about the issue of disability disclosure, you should take into account the "Maris Effect" and weigh the benefits of accommodative testing against the potential costs of disclosing your disability.

Alternatives

There are two possible alternatives to disclosing your disability through the nonstandard examination process. One option would be to test under standard conditions with minor modifications to the exam setting; if ETS determines

Accommodations Info

For additional information on accommodations for the GMAT, contact:

Special Testing Accommodations
1425 Lower Ferry Rd.
Mail Stop 05-Q
Ewing, NJ 08618
Phone: (609) 771-7780
Fax: (609) 771-7165
Web site: http://www.gmat.org/
OR www.ets.org/disabilities.html

that you can test in the standard setting with minor reasonable adjustments (i.e. a wheelchair-accessible setting, or exam materials in an alternative format) by taking your exam under these conditions, your scores will reported in the standard way, with no red flags provided to your disability status. Another option would be to contact the graduate school or fellowship sponsors to which you are applying and ask if they are willing to waive the GMAT requirements and evaluate your application based upon other criteria.

Narrowing the Field

Once you have taken the necessary steps to ensure that you are prepared for business school and have sufficiently honed your candidate profile, you are ready to make a list of factors to consider when narrowing your choice of programs. In addition to the factors covered in this book that pertain to all prospective business school candidates, the following are some issues of particular relevance to candidates with disabilities:

Home or Away?

Limiting their choices of business programs to those available locally offers students with disabilities the opportunity to draw upon the support of a familiar network of resources in their efforts to meet the very rigorous demands of M.B.A. programs. However, by limiting their choices in this manner, they often exclude themselves from programs in other regions that would represent a better fit for them academically and professionally.

Sunbelt or Snowbelt?

There are distinctive regional benefits for people with disabilities to attending business schools in different locales. For example, many graduate students have found that when they have moved to the northeast and midwest, they often enjoy a comparatively higher rate of disability benefits than those available in many southern and western states. They also often find that M.B.A. programs located in northeastern and midwestern cities tend to offer them proximity to more accessible mass transit than those in many southern and western cities.

However, business schools in the northeast and midwest are also frequently situated in cold and snowy climates and on hilly terrain that tends to undermine access for individuals with physical disabilities. Schools in the south and west are more likely to have newer, more accessible facilities, are situated in places that are warm, flat, and dry, and are more likely to be near off-campus, accessible housing units than those in the northeast and midwest.

Full Time or Part Time?

Most M.B.A. programs offer students the option of attending full or part time. Given the rigorous demands of most full-time programs, students with disabilities may find that attending part time offers them greater opportunity to perform to their potential. For example, students with learning disabilities, or those who are blind or have visual impairments, may find it easier to keep up with the large amount of reading that M.B.A. programs demand by attending part time. The major drawbacks to part-time study are that in the long run, part-time study costs more (both in terms of tuition costs and lost earnings from time out of the workforce); vocational rehabilitation agencies will often not subsidize the tuition of business school students with disabilities who attend part time; and part-time students may lose some of the networking opportunities fostered by attending business school with their cohort.

One-Year or Two-Year Programs?

One-year programs are more cost-effective (in terms of tuition and time out of the workforce) than two-year programs. However, they are extremely rigorous, requiring a large volume of intellectually demanding work over a very short time period. These conditions offer students with disabilities very little margin for error. Any difficulty in working out the logistics of reasonable accommodations or any health-related difficulties could cause a student with a disability to fall way behind.

Big or Small Classes?

Class size and structure are factors that will have a significant impact on the business school experience for students with disabilities. Smaller classes tend to offer the opportunity for more individualized instruction—a setting in which it is often much easier to provide for effective, highly individualized, reasonable academic adjustments for students with disabilities. They are also less impersonal and are administered less bureaucratically than large classes. However, smaller classes are much less conducive to student anonymity, so it's often more difficult to preserve your confidentiality as a student with a disability in this setting.

Larger classes, on the other hand, usually offer greater diversity and the opportunity for students with disabilities to blend into the fabric of the class. They also often offer students with disabilities greater opportunities to meet students like themselves.

Cooperation or Competitiveness?

Each business school has a distinctive culture, with some programs privileging an ethic of competitiveness and others promoting a culture of cooperation. While a competitive setting may help prepare students with disabilities for the culture of the business world, such an environment may not be very a supportive of the provision of effective reasonable accommodations. In such a setting, a student's request for reasonable accommodations might be perceived as an attempt to gain an unfair advantage in a very competitive environment. Such environments are also not as conducive to the development of natural supports that promote access for students with disabilities.

Business schools that feature a strong emphasis on the cooperation essential to business success, on the other hand, tend to be more supportive of the accommodation needs of students with disabilities. Indeed, the team-based approach to learning, which emphasizes the integration of people with varying abilities and strengths to achieve the most productive outcome, is more conducive to the development of natural supports.

Assessing Accessibility

Once you've narrowed the field and have a short list of business schools you're interested in, you'll have to make some tough choices. But before you make those choices, there's more work to be done. Here are the main factors to consider in judging how accessible the M.B.A. programs on your short list are to people with disabilities.

Physical Access

The architectural and technological accessibility of a campus should play a significant role in your evaluation of business programs. The following questions will help you to evaluate the physical accessibility of a school.

1. What is the campus terrain like? Is it hilly or flat?

2. What is the campus infrastructure like? Are walkways and roadways well paved, or riddled with cracks and potholes?

3. Are the buildings you will need to use accessible to students with mobility-related disabilities? If not, what is the institution's policy regarding moving classes and other business student activities to accessible sites to accommodate students with disabilities?

4. The institution's library will play a central role in your business education. How accessible are its facilities and services to students with disabilities?

5. Are the assistive technologies that you need available, and are the academic computing facilities accessible to students with disabilities?

6. Many M.B.A. programs offer internships in business and other institutional settings. Are these institutions' facilities accessible to people with disabilities?

Programmatic Access

For all students with disabilities, but particularly for students with learning, sensory, and psychiatric disabilities, the programmatic accessibility of business schools will significantly impact school selection. When assessing the programmatic access of business schools and M.B.A. programs, keep the following questions in mind:

1. Most M.B.A. programs demand large volumes of assigned and unassigned reading. What are the institution's policies regarding the provision of reading and other course materials in accessible formats?

2. What are the institution's policies on the provision of reader, notetaker, and sign language interpreter services?

3. What are the M.B.A. program's policies on incomplete grades and leaves of absence?

4. What are the institution's policies on accommodative testing?

5. Where does the institution keep confidential student disability documentation? It should not store such records in your graduate program student files. This file is a quasiprofessional file to which faculty may have access; it is not appropriate for disability documentation to be kept here.

Office of Services for Students with Disabilities

Effective services and accommodations for business students with disabilities is usually an indicator that an institution has a high-quality Office of Services for Students with Disabilities (OSSD). Effective OSSDs will work closely with you and business school faculty and administration to ensure that your accommodation needs are met. The commitment of significant resources to accommodate students with disabilities through an OSSD is often indicative of an institution's larger commitment to equal access and opportunity for individuals with disabilities in all aspects of business school life.

It is perfectly feasible to succeed in business school as a student with disabilities. If you take all of the factors discussed in this chapter into account when you choose your M.B.A. program, you should be set to make the most of this rewarding opportunity.

Where's the Office?

A good indicator of the quality of OSSDs is whether or not the institution has established an actual office that coordinates the provision of reasonable accommodations and support services to students with disabilities, as opposed to assigning this responsibility to a person or office that has multiple responsibilities.

CHAPTER 17

International Students

by James Stevens

While M.B.A. programs continue to emphasize their global and international focus, simply being an international student no longer provides the guaranteed advantage that it once did when applying to top business schools. International applicants should apprise themselves of the changing conditions in M.B.A. admissions and adjust their application strategies accordingly.

When reviewing applications from international candidates, admissions committees consider the same factors that they consider for domestic applicants—intellectual abilities, management skills, and personal characteristics. They may also need to assess your level of English proficiency if English is not your native language, as well as how you will contribute to the class.

So how do you, as an international applicant, improve your chances of being admitted, preferably to your program of choice? You may have some extra work to do. From taking the Test of English as a Foreign Language (TOEFL) to securing "official" transcripts (and possibly translations) to explaining an unfamiliar educational or employment system to arranging for a student visa, requirements for international applicants often exceed those for domestic ones.

Application Requirements

There are a number of application requirements that international M.B.A. applicants must fulfill. Some are identical to those faced by all applicants, while others are specific to prospective students of international origin.

Test of English as a Foreign Language (TOEFL)

Since English is the medium of instruction for M.B.A. programs in the United States, you will need to demonstrate your ability to function at a high level in this environment. If English is not your native language, most programs will require you to take the TOEFL to measure your proficiency. The TOEFL measures your ability to communicate in English. The total score ranges from 200 to 677. The three sections of the TOEFL are listening comprehension, structure and written comprehension, and reading comprehension; each section has scores ranging from 20 to 68. Most M.B.A. programs look for scores within the 550–600 range, and top programs typically require at least 600, preferably higher. If you take the TOEFL more than once, most programs will take your most recent TOEFL score as evidence of your current proficiency. Others will consider the highest score if you took the tests within a few months of each other.

TOEFL Info

To find out more about TOEFL, call ETS (Educational Testing Service) at (609) 921-9000 and ask for TSE Services. To find out about taking a course or getting a book to help you prepare for the TOEFL, call (800) KAP-TEST. Kaplan/Simon & Schuster's *TOEFL for the Computer* guide is another useful resource.

The Educational Testing Service (ETS), which administers the GMAT, also administers the TOEFL. The test lasts two and a half hours (three and a half hours total time) and is offered monthly at locations around the world. Individual testing sites fill up quickly, so you need to register well in advance. Just as with the GMAT and GRE, the TOEFL has recently been converted to a computer-based test format. The TOEFL is typically valid for two years, and ETS will not send score reports more than two years old. Some schools calculate the two years from the month you apply, while others calculate it from the month you plan to enroll.

Some schools are willing to accept an alternative to the TOEFL for assessing your language proficiency. You may also qualify for a waiver of the TOEFL if your primary, secondary, and tertiary education was conducted entirely or mostly in English, even if your native language is not English. If you believe you may qualify, make your request as early as possible so that you still have time to take the TOEFL if your request is denied. Because it is not specifically designed to measure language proficiency, most programs will not consider the GMAT as an alternative to the TOEFL.

For information about the TOEFL, contact ETS at:

> Test of English as a Foreign Language
> P.O. Box 6151
> Princeton, NJ 08541-6151 USA
> Telephone: (609) 771-7100
> Fax: (609) 771-7500
> Web site: http://www.toefl.org

GMAT

As noted elsewhere, most programs will require you to take the GMAT. Most schools publish general information about their GMAT averages and ranges. When considering international applicants, admissions officers take into account that the test format (several multiple-choice sections and two essays) may be unfamiliar to you and that English may not be your native language. While programs will not use an explicitly different standard for an international applicant, most do realize that average scores may be lower, and adjust their expectations according to the country from which you are applying. For some applicants, this means greater flexibility in the evaluation process. However, you should not assume that the admissions committee will overlook your lower score, and you should address it directly in your essays.

Securing Transcripts

Potentially, one of the most difficult aspects of preparing your application will be securing an "official" transcript from a non-U.S. institution. Many schools outside the United States are unfamiliar with the application process for graduate school and simply do not have a system in place for issuing transcripts. The most common problems are excessive, seemingly endless delays and uncooperative institutions. Foreign institutions may also require a personal appearance by you (or your agent) before they will issue your transcripts.

If you are unable to obtain an official transcript directly from your institution, you can suggest several other options to the admissions office to meet this requirement:

- If you have an original transcript, you can have the ministry of education in your home country or your consulate in the United States verify its authenticity and provide a copy to submit directly to the M.B.A. program.

- If you have already submitted an official transcript to another institution, you can ask that institution to provide a copy in a sealed envelope. This usually works best if you have already completed another degree in the United States and can make the request as an alum. We don't recommend that you ask that one M.B.A. program to provide a transcript to another M.B.A. program.

Some programs will require an official transcript before beginning the evaluation process, while others will evaluate your application using a copy of your transcript and require an official copy only if you are admitted. Plan for sufficient time to secure your transcript(s) and translation(s), and it's always a good idea to get an extra copy.

Degree Eligibility

When applying for a master's program, you will need to have earned the equivalent of a U.S. bachelor's degree, generally representing 16 years of primary, secondary, and tertiary study. While there may be some flexibility for otherwise outstanding candidates, the accrediting agency that certifies the educational institution's eligibility has specific guidelines and standards that the admissions committee must follow.

You cannot assume that a bachelor's degree from your home country will be considered the equivalent of a U.S. bachelor's degree. For example, most programs do not consider the Bachelor of Commerce degree to be the equivalent because it is only a "three-year" degree. If you are not certain, ask the individual schools what they are willing to accept.

World Education Services

World Education Services can evaluate your credentials and determine their equivalency for a fee. Most programs will follow their recommendations. For more information, contact:

World Education Services
P.O. Box 745
Old Chelsea Station
New York, NY 10113-0745
USA
Telephone: (212) 966-6311
Fax: (212) 966-6395
E-mail: info@wes.org
Web site: http://www.wes.org

Essays

This is your opportunity to demonstrate to the admissions committee your unique qualities and characteristics. It's also a way for you to demonstrate your command of English. Most M.B.A. programs specifically instruct you to write your own essay without any outside help. This can present a significant challenge if English is not your native language. However, admissions officers have read thousands of applications and can usually tell if someone has helped you write your essays, so resist the temptation to have someone "fix" your essays.

In sharing your background and experiences in your essays, the admissions committee wants to get to know you not only as an individual but also as a representative of your country. Rather than comparing you to the general pool of applicants, most programs will compare you to other applicants from your country. If you have had unique opportunities or experiences, you can share them with the admission committee in your essays.

Historically, Asia has supplied the largest number of international applicants to M.B.A. programs, with Europe coming in a close second. Recently, more Latin Americans have been applying to, and enrolling in, M.B.A. programs. However, Africa, the Middle East, and the rest of the world are still not widely represented in graduate business education programs. Your home country can play a key role in how the admissions committee will view your application. If only a few individuals from your country are applying to a particular program, your chances of admission may be higher. Most programs want to offer a broad perspective in the classroom, and the more countries represented in the incoming class, the greater the diversity. Conversely, if there are many applicants from your country, it may be more difficult to distinguish yourself from the crowd. Emphasizing how you can broadly represent both cultural and business practices in your essay and the other components of your application will enhance your appeal and strengthen your chances of receiving an offer of admission.

Interviews

In the 1980s, very few M.B.A. programs interviewed candidates for their programs. Today, you will be hard put to find a top program that does not include an interview as part of their admissions evaluation. The interview provides admissions officers with a good opportunity to assess the language ability of international applicants.

To increase your chances for a successful interview, you need to be as comfortable as possible conversing in English. Practicing with a native speaker will give you an opportunity to develop both your comprehension and your speaking skills. Some applicants try to prepare for every possible question and will compose answers in advance. While you should think about the kinds of questions you may be asked, each interviewer will pose questions differently, and an experienced interviewer can tell if you have memorized your answers. Too many times a candidate sounds rehearsed or worse, or will misunderstand and begin answering an entirely different question. If necessary, it's acceptable to ask the interviewer to repeat the question, but you should not need to ask this for every question.

Finally, while it can very expensive to travel to the United States, the school will appreciate the commitment you demonstrate by taking the time, effort, and expense to visit them. Also, an alumni or telephone interview may not effectively convey all that you want the admissions committee to know about you. A face-to-face meeting with one of the people who will be making the decision can tip the scale in your favor. It is also to your benefit to visit the program, preferably when classes are in session, so you can visit a class and talk to current students from you own country.

Work Experience

As more M.B.A. programs expect postundergraduate work experience of their students, it becomes increasingly important for you to demonstrate not only your unique experience, but also to explain the overall pattern for education and work in your country. In Asia, most individuals attend undergraduate school, finish their degree, and then begin working. This follows the traditional pattern in the United States. However, in Europe and Latin America, it is more typical to attend school and work full time simultaneously. When presenting yourself to the admission committee, you cannot assume that its members will be familiar this pattern. Unless you clarify this for them, they may not give adequate consideration to your experience.

If your country requires you as a citizen to perform national or military service, presenting this experience so that it "counts" can be a challenge. Individuals usually do not have their choice of assignments, but some people are able to excel and can use this experience to highlight their leadership and maturity. If your assignment was unusual or particularly challenging, the admission committee will consider this, but only if you tell them about it. Again, without information from you, this experience may not be given the weight it deserves when your credentials are assessed.

Recommendations

A particular challenge faced by international applicants is securing a letter of recommendation from a non-English speaker. Although your language skills may be fine, if your recommender cannot communicate in English, the recommendation may lose its effectiveness. As a solution, you should consider suggesting that your recommender compose the recommendation in his or her own language, and then have the recommendation translated. This can be a difficult request that requires your utmost diplomacy to avoid offending the individual in question.

Evaluating Your Academic Credentials

With the increase in international applicants, more admissions officers are becoming familiar with the educational systems of various countries. However, you should not assume that the admissions committee will be familiar with your country's system. While the guidelines to determine the eligibility of your educational credentials are relatively straightforward, it is often difficult to assess the strength and selectivity of your school as well as your performance in the program. Most U.S. institutions use a 4.0 (A to F) grading scale, but many programs use a scale that is not readily convertible to this scale. There may be a tendency to simply force this 4.0 scale onto the one used by your school, and the strength of your academic record could be underestimated as a result.

> ## *Will They Understand Your Credentials?*
>
> While admissions officers are reluctant to admit to prospective applicants that they are not familiar with a country's educational system, most will tell you approximately how many applications they have received from your country. Hence you can find out whether or not admissions officers are familiar with your country's educational system by asking how many candidates from your country have applied in recent years. If that number is low, you may want to include additional explanatory materials in your application package.

Admissions officers may not be familiar with the nuances of your country's educational system, including the strength of individual schools and the variations in grading patterns across countries and schools. If available, you should provide your rank within the class, particularly if you ranked highly within your university, department, or program. You need to ensure that the admissions committee understands the grading system and how you performed. Including written information from the institution about the grading system and typical marks can provide basic guidelines for the admissions committee and ensure that you receive the credit that you deserve.

Pointers for Preparing Your Application

1. When submitting your application, include photocopies of your TOEFL and GMAT reports, even though ETS will send them directly to your school and the application may not require them. Since some names may be unfamiliar to admissions staff, receiving an exact copy of the report from you may help the admissions department to match your test reports with your application.

2. Include a photocopy of your transcript and diploma with an English translation. While you need to supply an official transcript, you can't be sure that your school will send all the information that the admissions committee wants to see. If some information is missing, you may be able to expedite the review of your application by including these copies.

3. When preparing your application, your research should include speaking with people who have completed an M.B.A. abroad. They can offer advice and insights based on direct experience. If possible, talk to alumni from the programs to which you will be applying.

4. Be certain that your language skills are sufficient for you to be admitted as well as to be successful once you enroll. An M.B.A. in the United States can be an expensive undertaking, and you want to get the maximum benefit from your studies.

Student Visas

To study in the United States as an international student, you will need a valid passport and student visa from the U.S. Immigration and Naturalization Service (INS), and you may need an exit visa from your country's government. Typically, you will have an F-1 visa and your spouse and children will have an F-2 visa. If a company, government agency, or foundation will sponsor your education, J-1 and J-2 visas are needed.

To secure your F-1 and F-2 visas, you will need a document called an I-20 that your school will provide after you have been admitted. To issue the I-20, the school requires documentation of your ability to pay for your studies, both your direct educational costs and your travel and living expenses. If you have sufficient funds in your own bank account, a simple letter from your bank verifying this will usually be enough. If an organization will sponsor all or part of your M.B.A. studies, a letter from the sponsoring organization will work. Finally, if another individual plans to assist with your expenses, you will need a letter of support from that individual and a copy of the individual's bank statement(s).

Access America

The Access America™ program was created by Kaplan Educational Centers to help students and professionals from outside the United States to enter the U.S. university system. For more information on this program, visit www.kaplan.com (AOL Keyword: Kaplan).

You then present the I-20 and the documentation of your ability to pay to the U.S. embassy or consulate. Upon acceptance of this documentation, your student visa will be issued. In some countries, particularly where foreign exchange is problematic, it may difficult to secure your visa even if you have all your documentation.

Conclusion

As with domestic applicants, applying early is important in order to minimize the effects of unanticipated delays. You should always plan for things to take longer than you expect, whether it is securing your transcript, registering for the GMAT or TOEFL, or just waiting for your application to arrive through international mail.

The difficulties in preparing an application for study in another country can seem insurmountable. But don't lose sight of the fact that the potential rewards of gaining admission to an M.B.A. program in the United States are incalculable. Good luck!

PART SIX

Directory of Business Schools

Directory of Business Schools

*An asterisk following the school name in this directory indicates the school did not respond to our request to confirm or correct the data listed. Please contact the school directly to verify the information provided here.

School Name and Contact Information

Here you'll find the information you need to contact each school by mail, phone, fax, or e-mail. The Web site is also given.

Student Body

This section provides statistics on how many and what kind of students attend the school. The categories African American, Asian American, and Latino refer to the ethnic background of U.S. residents. The international category refers to students who are citizens of other countries and not permanent residents of the United States.

Academics

This section contains data related to the academic offerings of the school. You'll find statistics on full-time and part-time faculty, a listing of graduate degrees offered by the school, and information on an evening program, if any.

Finances

The tuition and fees the school charges are provided for the 1998–99 academic year. Figures for the 1999–2000 academic year have also been provided by schools that had finalized these by press time. Note that amounts listed for 1999–2000 are subject to change. Information on financial aid and average student debt upon graduation is also provided.

Admissions Requirements

Most—but not all—business schools require a bachelor's degree and the GMAT. These requirements plus application deadline dates are included in this section. Students living outside the United States should note that some schools have special application deadlines for international students. Many schools also have earlier deadlines for special programs.

Selectivity

The information in this section will help you determine your chances of being accepted by the school. For most schools the information is for the fall 1998 entering class. However, when this was not available, we have printed information from a prior year.

Placement

Ultimately, you'll want a job. The placement rate is the percentage of students accepting a job offer out of the total number of students who sought job placement through the school's placement office. For most schools, the figures provided are for the class graduating in spring 1998. However, when these were not available, we have used figures from a prior year. Job placement rates are those reported by the school and have not been independently verified by Kaplan or *Newsweek*.

Alabama

AUBURN UNIVERSITY

College of Business
Lowder Business Building
Suite 503
Auburn University, AL 36849
Phone: (334) 844-4060
Fax: (334) 844-2964
E-mail: mbainfo@business.auburn.edu
http://www.auburn.edu
Student Body: Full-time enrollment: 152.
Men: 61%. Women: 39%. African
American: 3%. Asian American: 2%. Latino:
1%. International: 12%. Average age: 26.
Students living on campus: 15%. Part-time
enrollment: 244. Men: 62%. Women:
38%.
Academics: Full-time faculty: 90. Part-time
faculty: 5. Degrees awarded: M.B.A.,
M.A.C., M.S., Ph.D., M.M.I.S. Evening
program is not offered. For fall 1996 entering class: 56% completed program within 2
years. 21% continued towards degree.
Finances: Tuition (1998–99): In-State:
$3,760, Out-of-State: $11,280. Estimated
tuition (1999–2000): In-State: $3,950.
Out-of-State: $11,850. 40% of students
receive non-need-based aid. 10% of students receive need-based aid. Average student debt incurred by graduation: $5,500.
Admission Requirements: GMAT is required.
Application deadline for fall: August 1.
Selectivity: Applications received (full-time):
128. Admitted: 68. Enrolled: 54.
Applications received (part-time): 65.
Admitted: 46. Enrolled: 32. Average
GMAT: 580. Average undergraduate GPA:
3.1. GMAT section weighed most heavily:
weighed equally.
Placement: School has placement office.
Placement rate at time of graduation: 65%.
Placement rate 6 months after graduation:
98%. Average starting salary: $43,500.

AUBURN UNIVERSITY— MONTGOMERY*

School of Business
7300 University Drive
Montgomery, AL 36117
Phone: (334) 244-3565
Student Body: Full-time enrollment: 112.
Men: 58%. Women: 42%. International:
9%. Part-time enrollment: 112. Men: 66%.
Women: 34%.
Academics: Full-time faculty: 40. Part-time
faculty: 1. Degrees awarded: M.B.A.
Finances: Tuition (1998–99): In-State:
$2,540. Out-of-State: $7,620.
Admission Requirements: GMAT is
required. Application deadline for fall:
June 1.
Selectivity: Applications received (full-time):
100. Admitted: 95. Enrolled: 78. Average
GMAT: 532. Average undergraduate GPA:
3.0.
Placement: School has placement office.

UNIVERSITY OF ALABAMA

Manderson Graduate School of Business
P.O. Box 870223
Tuscaloosa, AL 35487
Phone: (205) 348-6517,
(888) 863-3622
Fax: (205) 348-4504
E-mail: mba@cba.ua.edu
http://www.cba.ua.edu/~mba
Student Body: Full-time enrollment: 107.
Men: 70%. Women: 30%. African
American: 4%. Asian American: 1%. Latino:
1%. International: 8%. Average age: 25.
Students living on campus: 1%.
Academics: Full-time faculty: 87. Degrees
awarded: M.B.A., M.S., M.A., Ph.D. Joint
degree programs: M.B.A./J.D. Evening pro-
gram is not offered. For fall 1996 entering
class: 86% completed program within 2
years. 4% continued towards degree.
Finances: Tuition (1998–99): In-State:
$4,284. Out-of-State: $8,816. Estimated
tuition (1999–2000): In-State: $4,284.
Out-of-State: $8,816. 50% of students
receive merit-based aid.

Admission Requirements: GMAT is
required. Application deadline for fall:
May 15.
Selectivity: Applications received (full-time):
168. Admitted: 80. Enrolled: 57. Average
GMAT: 592. Average undergraduate GPA:
3.4. GMAT section weighed most heavily:
weighed equally.
Placement: School has placement office.
Placement rate at time of graduation: 97%.
Placement rate 6 months after graduation:
98%. Average starting salary: $47,791.

UNIVERSITY OF ALABAMA— BIRMINGHAM

Graduate School of Management
1150 10th Avenue, South
Birmingham, AL 35294-4460
Phone: (205) 934-8817
Fax: (205) 934-9200
E-mail: gradschool@uab.edu
http://138.26.83.65/school/
school.htm
Student Body: Average age: 27. Part-time
enrollment: 334.
Academics: Full-time faculty: 28. Part-time
faculty: 2. Degrees awarded: M.B.A.,
M. Acc. Joint degree programs:
M.B.A./M.S.H.A., M.B.A./M.P.H.
Evening program is offered.
Finances: Tuition (1998–99): In-State:
$99/credit. Out-of-State: $198/credit. 1%
receive some type of aid.
Admission Requirements: GMAT is
required. Application deadline for fall:
August 1.
Selectivity: Applications received (part-time):
185. Admitted: 138. Enrolled: 82.
Average GMAT: 510. Average undergradu-
ate GPA: 3.0.
Placement: School has placement office.
Average starting salary: $36,625.

UNIVERSITY OF SOUTH ALABAMA

College of Business and Management Studies
University Boulevard
Mobile, AL 36688
Phone: (334) 460-5990
Student Body: Full-time enrollment: 22.
Men: 55%. Women: 45%. Part-time enrollment: 136. Men: 52%. Women: 48%.
Academics: Full-time faculty: 46. Part-time faculty: 3. Degrees awarded: M.B.A., M. Acc.
Admission Requirements: GMAT is required. Application deadline for fall: September 1.
Selectivity: Applications received (full-time): 69. Admitted: 64. Enrolled: 42. Average GMAT: 475.
Placement: School has placement office.

Alaska

UNIVERSITY OF ALASKA— FAIRBANKS

School of Management
P.O. Box 957480
Fairbanks, AK 99775-6080
Phone: (907) 474-7500
Fax: (907) 474-5379
E-mail: fyappply@uaf.edu,
famba@som.uaf.edu
http://www.uafsom.alaska.edu
Student Body: Full-time enrollment: 14.
Men: 64%. Women: 36%. African American: 14%. Latino: 7%. International: 7%. Average age: 29.4. Students living on campus: 10%. Part-time enrollment: 22. Men: 18%. Women: 82%.
Academics: Full-time faculty: 27. Part-time faculty: 1. Degrees awarded: M.B.A., M.S. Evening program is offered. For fall 1996 entering class: 83% completed program within 2 years. 17% continued towards degree.
Finances: Estimated tuition (1999–2000): In-State: $3,724. Out-of-State: $6,496.

Admission Requirements: GMAT is required. Application deadline for fall: rolling.
Selectivity: Enrolled (full-time): 6. Enrolled(part-time): 7. Average GMAT: 560. Average undergraduate GPA: 3.3.
Placement: School has placement office.

Arizona

ARIZONA STATE UNIVERSITY

College of Business
P.O. Box 874906
Tempe, AZ 85287-4906
Phone: (602) 965-3332
Fax: (602) 965-8569
E-mail: asu.mba@asu.edu
http://www.cob.asu.edu/mba/mba.html
Student Body: Full-time enrollment: 330.
Men: 70%. Women 30%. African American: 4%. Asian American: 5%. Latino: 4%. Native American: 1%. International: 23%. Average age: 28. Part-time enrollment: 523. Men: 71%. Women: 39%.
Academics: Full-time faculty: 64. Degrees awarded: M.B.A., M.S., M.H.S.A., Ph.D. Joint degree programs: M.B.A./M.H.S.A., M.B.A./J.D., M.B.A./M.I.M., M.B.A./M.S.I.M., M.B.A./M.Arch., M.B.A./M.S. Acc., M.B.A./M.S. E.C.N., M.B.A./M.S.Tax. Evening program is offered.
Finances: Tuition (1998–99): In-State: $4,408. Out-of-State: $11,360. Estimated tuition (1999–2000): In-State: $4,408. Out-of-State: $11,360.
Admission Requirements: GMAT is required. Application deadline for fall: May 1.
Selectivity: Applications received (full-time): 775. Admitted: 332. Enrolled: 167. Applications received (part-time): 463. Admitted: 318. Enrolled: 272. Average GMAT: 628. Average undergraduate GPA: 3.3.
Placement: School has placement office. Placement rate at time of graduation: 94%.

Placement rate 6 months after graduation: 100%. Average starting salary: $70,019.

NORTHERN ARIZONA UNIVERSITY

College of Business Administration
Box 15066
Flagstaff, AZ 86011-5066
Phone: (520) 523-7342
Fax: (520) 523-7331
E-mail: cba-mba@mail.cba.nau.edu
http://www.cba.nau.edu
Student Body: Full-time enrollment: 48.
Men: 63%. Women: 37%. African American: 4%. Asian American: 21%. Latino: 15%. International: 44%. Average age: 27. Students living on campus: 10%. Part-time enrollment: 35. Men: 60%. Women: 40%.
Academics: Full-time faculty: 53. Part-time faculty: 1. Degrees awarded: M.B.A. Evening program is offered. For the entering class of 1996: 100% completed program within 2 years.
Finances: Tuition (1998–99): $3,608. Estimated tuition (1999–2000): In-State: $4,533. Out-of-State: $11,484. 5% of students receive need-based aid. 50% of students receive non-need-based aid. Average student debt incurred by graduation: $6,600.
Admission Requirements: GMAT is required. Application deadline for fall: March 1.
Selectivity: Applications received (full-time): 80. Admitted: 57. Enrolled: 48. Applications received (part-time): 34. Admitted: 22. Enrolled: 35. Average GMAT: 525. Average undergraduate GPA: 3.2. GMAT section weighed most heavily: weighed equally.
Placement: School has placement office. Placement rate at time of graduation: 80%. Placement rate 6 months after graduation: 92%. Average starting salary: $50,500.

THUNDERBIRD, THE AMERICAN GRADUATE SCHOOL OF INTERNATIONAL MANAGEMENT

15249 North 59th Avenue
Glendale, AZ 85306-6000
Phone: (602) 978-7210
Fax: (602) 439-5432
E-mail: tbird@t-bird.edu
http://www.t-bird.edu
Student Body: Full-time enrollment: 1,512.
Men: 63%. Women: 37%. African
American: 1%. Asian American: 3%. Latino:
4%. International: 47%. Average age:
27.4. Students living on campus: 25%.
Academics: Full-time faculty: 102. Part-time
faculty: 20. Degrees awarded: M.I.M.,
M.S. International Health Management,
M.S. International Management Technology,
E.M.S. International Management. Joint
degree programs: M.I.M./M.B.A. Evening
program is not offered.
Finances: Tuition (1998–99): $21,200.
67% of students receive some type of aid.
Average student debt incurred by gradua-
tion: $38,000.
Admission Requirements: GMAT is
required. Application deadline for fall:
January 31.
Selectivity: Applications received (full-time):
1,317. Admitted: 896. Enrolled: 454.
Average GMAT: 601. Average undergradu-
ate GPA: 3.4.
Placement: School has placement office.
Placement rate at time of graduation: 92%.
Placement rate 6 months after graduation:
100%. Average starting salary: $62,648.

UNIVERSITY OF ARIZONA

Eller Graduate School of Management
P.O. Box 210108
Tucson, AZ 85721
Phone: (520) 621-4008
Fax: (520) 621-2606
E-mail: Ellernet@bpa.arizona.edu
http://www.bpa.arizona.edu
Student Body: Full-time enrollment: 257.
Men: 71%. Women: 29%. African
American: 3%. Asian American: 5%. Latino:

7%. International: 13%. Average age: 27.
Part-time enrollment: 64. Men: 64%.
Women: 36%.
Academics: Full-time faculty: 64. Degrees
awarded: M.B.A., M.B.A./M.S.,
M.B.A./J.D., M.B.A./M.I.M.,
M.S./M.I.S., M. Acc. Joint degree pro-
grams: M.B.A./M.I.S., M.B.A./J.D.,
M.B.A./M.I.M. Evening program is
offered.
Finances: Tuition (1998–99): In-State:
$4,162. Out-of-State: $11,114. Estimated
tuition (1999–2000): In-State: $5,263.
Out-of-State: $12,405. 95% of students
receive some type of aid.
Admission Requirements: GMAT is required
Application deadline for fall: March 1.
Selectivity: Applications received (full-time):
852. Admitted: 177. Enrolled: 121.
Applications received (part-time): 50.
Admitted: 35. Enrolled: 31. Average GMAT:
634. Average undergraduate GPA: 3.4.
GMAT section weighed most heavily: Math.
Placement: School has placement office.
Placement rate at time of graduation: 78%.
Placement rate 6 months after graduation:
99%. Average starting salary: $56,835.

Arkansas

ARKANSAS STATE UNIVERSITY*

College of Business
P.O. Box 970
State University, AR 72467
Phone: (870) 972-3024
E-mail: toroach@cherokee.astate.edu
http://www.asu.edu
Student Body: Full-time enrollment: 32.
Men: 75%. Women: 25%. International:
119%. Average age: 23. Students living on
campus: 0%. Part-time enrollment: 57. Men:
54%. Women: 46%.
Academics: Full-time faculty: 52. Part-time
faculty: 2. Degrees awarded: M.B.A.,
M.S.E. Evening program is offered.

Finances: Tuition (1998–99): In-State:
$1,170. Out-of-State: $3,060.
Admission Requirements: GMAT is
required. Application deadline for fall:
Before first week of term.
Selectivity: Applications received (full-time):
146. Admitted: 73. Enrolled: 73. Average
GMAT: 491. Average undergraduate GPA:
3.3.
Placement: School has placement office.

UNIVERSITY OF ARKANSAS— FAYETTEVILLE

Sam M. Walton College of
Business Administration
BADM 475
Fayetteville, AR 72701
Phone: (501) 575-2851
Fax: (501) 575-8721
E-mail: gso@comp.uark.edu
http://www.uark.edu/depts/
mba/public
Student Body: Full-time enrollment: 99.
Men: 65%. Women: 35%. International:
32%. Average age: 26. Students living on
campus: 2.8%. Part-time enrollment: 49.
Men: 69%. Women: 31%.
Academics: Full-time faculty: 59. Part-time
faculty: 5. Degrees awarded: M.B.A.,
M.S., M.T.L.M., M. Acc., M.E.L.O.N. Joint
degree programs: J.D./M.B.A. Evening pro-
gram is offered.
Finances: Tuition (1998–99): In-State:
$3,912. Out-of-State: $9,192. Estimated
tuition (1999–2000): In-State: $4,499.
Out-of-State: $9,779.
Admission Requirements: GMAT is
required. Application deadline for fall:
February 15 (prog. begins in July).
Selectivity: Applications received (full-time):
128. Admitted: 77. Enrolled: 60.
Applications received (part-time): 16.
Admitted: 11. Enrolled: 10. Average GMAT:
549. Average undergraduate GPA: 3.4.
GMAT section weighed most heavily: equally.
Placement: School has placement office.
Placement rate at time of graduation: 90%.
Placement rate 6 months after graduation:
98%. Average starting salary: $50,000.

UNIVERSITY OF ARKANSAS—LITTLE ROCK

College of Business Administration
Little Rock, AR 72204
Phone: (501) 569-3206
Fax: (501) 569-8898
http://www.ualr.edu
Student Body: Full-time enrollment: 25. Men: 60%. Women: 40%. International: 72%. Average age: 28. Part-time enrollment: 225. Men: 56%. Women: 44%.
Academics: Full-time faculty: 40. Degrees awarded: M.B.A. Joint degree programs: J.D./M.B.A. Evening program is offered.
Finances: Tuition (1998–99): In-State: $149/credit. Out-of-State: $292/credit.
Admission Requirements: GMAT is required. Application deadline for fall: none.
Selectivity: Applications received (part-time): 87. Admitted: 57. Enrolled: 42. Average GMAT: 525. Average undergraduate GPA: 3.2. GMAT section weighed most heavily: weighed equally.
Placement: School has placement office.

UNIVERSITY OF CENTRAL ARKANSAS

College of Business Administration
Burdick #222
Conway, AR 72032
Phone: (501) 450-3124
Fax: (501) 450-5339
E-mail: dougc@mail.uca.edu
Student Body: Full-time enrollment: 31. Part-time enrollment: 32.
Academics: Full-time faculty: 19. Degrees awarded: M.B.A. Evening program is offered.
Finances: Estimated tuition (1999–2000): $161/credit hour (in-state); $150/credit hour (out-of-state). 25% of students receive some type of aid.
Admission Requirements: GMAT is required. Application deadline for fall: July 15.
Selectivity: Average undergraduate GPA: 3.2.
Placement: School has placement office. Average starting salary: $40,000.

California

CALIFORNIA POLYTECHNIC STATE UNIVERSITY—SAN LUIS OBISPO

College of Business
Graduate Management Programs
San Luis Obispo, CA 93407
Phone: (805) 756-2637
Fax: (805) 756-0110
E-mail: spahlow@calpoly.edu
http://www.cob.calpoly.edu
Student Body: Full-time enrollment: 95. Men: 71%. Women: 29%. International: 4%. Average age: 27. Students living on campus: 1%. Part-time enrollment: 4. Men: 50%. Women: 50%.
Academics: Part-time faculty: 54. Degrees awarded: M.B.A., M.B.A./M.S. Joint degree programs: M.B.A./M.B. in Eng., M.B.A./B.S. Arch. Evening program is not offered. For fall 1996 entering class: 95% completed program within 2 years. 5% continued towards degree.
Finances: Tuition (1998–99): In-State: $2,250. Out-of-State: $7,872.
Admission Requirements: GMAT is required. Application deadline for fall: July 1.
Selectivity: Applications received (full-time): 135. Admitted: 70. Enrolled: 55. Average GMAT: 550. Average undergraduate GPA: 3.1. GMAT section weighed most heavily: weighed equally.
Placement: School has placement office. Placement rate 6 months after graduation: 100%. Average starting salary: $54,982.

CALIFORNIA STATE UNIVERSITY—BAKERSFIELD

School of Business & Public Administration
9001 Stockdale Highway
Bakersfield, CA 93311
Phone: (805) 664-3036
Fax: (805) 664-3389
http://www.csubak.bpa
Student Body: Total enrollment: 92. Men: 57%. Women: 43%. African American:

2%. Asian American: 9%. Latino: 2%. International: 18%. Average age: 29. Students living on campus: 10%.
Academics: Full-time faculty: 16. Degrees awarded: M.B.A. Evening program is offered.
Finances: Tuition (1998–99): $1,953. Estimated tuition (1999–2000): In-State: $1,953 (assumes 30 units per year). Out-of-State: $6,873 (assumes 30 units per year).
Admission Requirements: GMAT is required. Application deadline for fall: July 1.
Selectivity: Average GMAT: 520. Average undergraduate GPA: 3.2. GMAT section weighed most heavily: equal.
Placement: School has placement office. Average starting salary: $32,000.

CALIFORNIA STATE UNIVERSITY—CHICO

College of Business
Graduate & International Programs
Chico, CA 95929-0680
Phone: (530) 898-6880
Fax: (530) 898-6889
E-mail: gs_student@macgate.csuchico.edu
http://www.csuchico.edu
Student Body: Full-time enrollment: 40. Men: 73%. Women: 28%. Asian American: 5%. Latino: 8%. International: 23%. Average age: 33. Part-time enrollment: 22. Men: 50%. Women: 50%.
Academics: Full-time faculty: 15. Degrees awarded: M.B.A., M.S. Acc. Evening program is offered.
Finances: Tuition (1998–99): In-State: $1,059 per semester. Out-of-State: $4,100 (approximately). Estimated tuition (1999–2000): In-State: $1,054. Out-of-State: $4,100.
Admission Requirements: GMAT is required. Application deadline for fall: April 1.
Selectivity: Average GMAT: 530. Average undergraduate GPA: 3.1.
Placement: School has placement office. Average starting salary: $45,000.

CALIFORNIA STATE UNIVERSITY—FRESNO

The Craig School of Business
5245 N. Backer Avenue
Fresno, CA 93740-8001
Phone: (559) 278-2107
Fax: (559) 278-4911
E-mail: pennyt@csufresno.edu,
mkeppler@csufresno.edu
http://www.craig.csufresno.edu/mba1
Student Body: Full-time enrollment: 48.
Men: 60%. Women: 40%. Asian
American: 27%. Latino: 6%. International:
85%. Average age: 25. Students living on
campus: 5%. Part-time enrollment: 169.
Men: 64%. Women: 36%.
Academics: Part-time faculty: 23. Degrees
awarded: M.B.A. Evening program is
offered.
Finances: Tuition (1998–99): In-State:
$1,806. Out-of-State: $5,904. Estimated
tuition (1999–2000): In-State: $1,806.
Out-of-State: $5,904.
Admission Requirements: GMAT is required.
Application deadline for fall: June 1.
Selectivity: Applications received (total):
132. Admitted: 72. Enrolled (full-time): 60.
Enrolled (part-time): 169. Average GMAT:
550. Average undergraduate GPA: 3.4.
GMAT section weighed most heavily:
weighed equally.
Placement: School has placement office.

CALIFORNIA STATE UNIVERSITY—FULLERTON

School of Business Administration &
Economics
800 N. State College Boulevard
P.O. Box 34080
Fullerton, CA 92834-9480
Phone: (714) 278-2300
E-mail: admissions@fullerton.edu
http://sbaeweb.fullerton.edu
Student Body: Average age: 28. Part-time
enrollment: 546. Men: 56%. Women: 44%.
Academics: Full-time faculty: 44. Part-time
faculty: 3. Degrees awarded: M.B.A.,
M.S., M.A. Evening program is offered.

Finances: Tuition (1998–99): In-State:
$1,947 for 12 units. Out-of-State: $7,851.
Admission Requirements: GMAT is required.
Application deadline for fall: open.
Selectivity: Applications received (part-time):
498. Admitted: 315. Enrolled: 163.
Average GMAT: 511. Average undergraduate GPA: 3.2. GMAT section weighed most
heavily: weighed equally.
Placement: School has placement office.

CALIFORNIA STATE UNIVERSITY—HAYWARD

School of Business and Economics
Hayward, CA 94542
Phone: (510) 885-3828
Fax: (510) 885-3816
http://www.csuhayward.edu
Student Body: Full-time enrollment: 644.
International: 31%. Average age: 30.
Academics: Full-time faculty: 75. Degrees
awarded: M.B.A., M.A. Economics,
M.S.B.A., M.S. Taxation, M.S.
Telecommunication Systems. Evening program is offered.
Finances: Tuition (1998–99): 4 units:
$387; 8 units: $609. Estimated tuition
(1999–2000): In-State: 4 units: $387; 8
units: $609. Out-of-State: 4 units: $1,043;
8 units: $1,921.
Admission Requirements: GMAT is required.
Application deadline for fall: June 1.
Selectivity: Average GMAT: 517. Average
undergraduate GPA: 3.1.
Placement: School has placement office.

CALIFORNIA STATE UNIVERSITY—LONG BEACH

College of Business Administration
M.B.A. Program
1250 Bellflower Boulevard
Long Beach, CA 90840
Phone: (562) 985-1797
Fax: (562) 985-5590
http://www.csulb.edu
Student Body: Full-time enrollment: 100.
Men: 39%. Women: 61%. International:

87%. Average age: 29. Students living on
campus: 3%. Part-time enrollment: 306.
Men: 41%. Women: 59%.
Academics: Full-time faculty: 22. Part-time
faculty: 5. Degrees awarded: M.B.A.
Evening program is offered. For fall 1996
entering class: 70% completed program
within 2 years. 30% continued towards
degree.
Finances: Tuition (1998–99): In-State:
$1,982. Out-of-State: $246 per credit
hour. Estimated tuition (1999–2000): In-State: $1,982. Out-of-State: $246 per
credit hour.
Admission Requirements: GMAT is required.
Application deadline for fall: May 30.
Selectivity: Applications received (full-time):
200. Admitted: 71. Enrolled: 37.
Applications received (part-time): 230.
Admitted: 84. Enrolled: 68. Average
GMAT: 560. Average undergraduate GPA:
3.2. GMAT section weighed most heavily:
all sections weighed equally.
Placement: School has placement office.

CALIFORNIA STATE UNIVERSITY—LOS ANGELES*

School of Business & Economics
5151 State University Drive
Los Angeles, CA 90032-8120
Phone: (323) 343-5156
Fax: (323) 343-2813
E-mail: deansbe@calstatela.edu
Student Body: Average age: 31. Part-time
enrollment: 330.
Academics: Full-time faculty: 85. Part-time
faculty: 20. Degrees awarded: M.B.A.,
M.S. Acc., M.A. Economics. Evening program is offered.
Finances: Tuition (1998–99): In-State:
$2,339. Out-of-State: $261 per unit.
Estimated tuition (1999–2000): In-State:
$2,339. Out-of-State: $261 per unit.
Admission Requirements: GMAT is required.
Application deadline for fall: July 1.
Selectivity: Applications received (full-time):
200. Admitted: 90. Enrolled: 62. Average
GMAT: 550. Average undergraduate GPA:

3.0. GMAT section weighed most heavily: Verbal, Analytical.

Placement: School has placement office. Placement rate at time of graduation: 85%. Placement rate 6 months after graduation: 90%.

CALIFORNIA STATE UNIVERSITY—NORTHRIDGE

College of Business Administration & Economics
18111 Nordhoff Street
Northridge, CA 91330
Phone: (818) 677-2467
Fax: (818) 677-3188
E-mail: hfbus033@csun.edu
http://www.csun.edu/cobaegrad
Student Body: Part-time enrollment: 317. Men: 60%. Women: 40%.
Academics: Part-time faculty: 108. Degrees awarded: M.B.A., M.S. Taxation. Evening program is offered.
Finances: Tuition (1998–99): $985. Estimated tuition (1999–2000): In-State: $985. Out-of-State: $985 plus $246 per unit.
Admission Requirements: GMAT is required. Application deadline for fall: April 1.
Selectivity: Applications received (part-time): 181. Admitted: 80. Enrolled: 53. Average GMAT: 540. Average undergraduate GPA: 3.2. GMAT section weighed most heavily: weighed equally.
Placement: School has placement office.

CALIFORNIA STATE UNIVERSITY—SACRAMENTO

College of Business Administration
Office of Graduate Programs
Sacramento, CA 95819-6088
Phone: (916) 278-6722
Fax: (916) 278-5767
E-mail: sbagrad@csus.edu
http://www.csus.edu/sbagrad

Student Body: Part-time enrollment: 505. Men: 55%. Women: 45%. Minority: 26%. International: 13%.
Academics: Part-time faculty: 24. Degrees awarded: M.B.A., M.S., M.S.B.A. Joint degree programs: J.D./M.B.A., M.S.B.A. Taxation, M.S. Accounting, M.S.B.A./M.I.S. Evening program is offered.
Finances: Tuition (1998–99): In-State: $2,012. Out-of-State: $3,220. Estimated tuition (1999–2000): In-State: $2,012. Out-of-State: $3,220.
Admission Requirements: GMAT is required. Application deadline for fall: May 1.
Selectivity: Applications received (part-time): 296. Admitted: 178. Enrolled: 108. Average GMAT: 540. Average undergraduate GPA: 3.2. GMAT section weighed most heavily: weighed equally.
Placement: School has placement office.

CLAREMONT GRADUATE UNIVERSITY

Peter F. Drucker Graduate School of Management
1021 North Dartmouth Avenue
Claremont, CA 91711
Phone: (909) 607-7810
Fax: (909) 607-9104
E-mail: drucker@cgu.edu
http://www.cgu.edu/Drucker
Student Body: Full-time enrollment: 125. Men: 66%. Women: 34%. African American: 2%. Asian American: 13%. Latino: 2%. International: 46%. Average age: 27. Students living on campus: 18%. Part-time enrollment: 78. Men: 68%. Women: 32%.
Academics: Full-time faculty: 14. Part-time faculty: 11. Degrees awarded: M.B.A., M.S. in Financial Engineering. Joint degree programs: M.B.A./M.A. in Humanities, M.B.A./Ph.D., M.B.A./M.S.I.S., H.R.D., Financial Engineering. Evening program is offered. For fall 1996 entering class: 100% completed program within 2 years.
Finances: Tuition (1998–99): $20,250. Estimated tuition (1999–2000): $20,860. 12% of students receive need-based aid.

40% of students receive non-need-based aid. Average student debt incurred by graduation: $17,500.
Admission Requirements: GMAT is required. Application deadline for fall: February 15.
Selectivity: Applications received (full-time): 415. Admitted: 170. Enrolled: 43. Applications received (part-time): 49. Admitted: 36. Enrolled: 29. Average GMAT: 565. Average undergraduate GPA: 3.2. GMAT section weighed most heavily: Math.
Placement: School has placement office. Placement rate at time of graduation: 80%. Placement rate 6 months after graduation: 100%. Average starting salary: $70,000.

LOYOLA MARYMOUNT UNIVERSITY

College of Business Administration
M.B.A. Program
7900 Loyola Blvd
Los Angeles, CA 90045-8387
Phone: (310) 338-2848
Fax: (310) 338-2899
E-mail: mbapc@lmmail.lmu.edu
http://www.lmu.edu/colleges/cba.mba
Student Body: Full-time enrollment: 104. Men: 55%. Women: 45%. African American: 15%. Asian American: 63%. Latino: 39%. International: 35%. Average age: 24. Part-time enrollment: 314. Men: 55%. Women: 45%.
Academics: Full-time faculty: 38. Part-time faculty: 10. Degrees awarded: M.B.A. Joint degree programs: J.D./M.B.A. Evening program is offered.
Finances: Tuition (1998–99): $17,000. Estimated tuition (1999–2000): $17,800.
Admission Requirements: GMAT is required. Application deadline for fall: Rolling.
Selectivity: Applications received (full-time): 110. Admitted: 63. Enrolled: 36. Applications received (part-time): 333. Admitted: 190. Enrolled: 107. Average GMAT: 570. Average undergraduate GPA: 3.2. GMAT section weighed most heavily: weighed equally.
Placement: School has placement office.

SAN DIEGO STATE UNIVERSITY

Graduate School of Business
5300 Campanile Drive
San Diego, CA 92182
Phone: (619) 594-8073
Fax: (619) 594-1863
E-mail: sdsumba@mail.sdsu.edu
http://www.rohan.sdsu.edu/dept/cbaweb/
Student Body: Full-time enrollment: 407.
Men: 61%. Women: 39%. International:
18%. Average age: 27. Part-time enroll-
ment: 395. Men: 61%. Women: 39%.
Academics: Full-time faculty: 82. Part-time
faculty: 20. Degrees awarded: M.B.A.,
M.S.B.A., M.S.A. Evening program is
offered. For fall 1996 entering class: 86%
completed program within 2 years. 14%
continued towards degree.
Finances: Tuition (1998-99): $1,916.
Admission Requirements: GMAT is required.
Application deadline for fall: April 15.
Selectivity: Applications received: 874.
Admitted: 417. Enrolled: 277. Average
GMAT: 590. Average undergraduate GPA:
3.0. GMAT section weighed most heavily:
weighed equally.
Placement: School has placement office.
Average starting salary: $45,000.

SAN FRANCISCO STATE UNIVERSITY

Graduate School of Business
1600 Holloway Avenue
San Francisco, CA 94132
Phone: (415) 338-1935
Fax: (415) 338-6237
E-mail: mba@sfsu.edu
http://www.sfsu.edu/~mba
Student Body: Total enrollment: 823.
International: 29%. Average age: 28.
Academics: Full-time faculty: 128. Part-time
faculty: 81. Degrees awarded: M.B.A.,
M.S.B.A., M.S. Tax. Evening program is
offered.
Finances: Tuition (1998-99): In-State:
$991/semester. Out-of-State:
$3,943/semester. Estimated tuition

(1999-2000): In-State: $991/semester.
Out-of-State: $3,943/semester.
Admission Requirements: GMAT is required.
Application deadline for fall: May 15.
Selectivity: Applications received: 543.
Admitted: 292. Enrolled: 156.
Average GMAT: 535. Average undergradu-
ate GPA: 3.3.
Placement: School has placement office.
Average starting salary: $50,000.

SAN JOSE STATE UNIVERSITY*

College of Business
One Washington Square
BT 250
San Jose, CA 95192-0162
Phone: (408) 924-3423
Fax: (408) 924-3426
E-mail: 408 924-3426
http://http://www.cob.sjsu.edu/graduate
Student Body: Full-time enrollment: 60.
Men: 58%. Women: 42%. International:
27%. Part-time enrollment: 604. Men: 60%.
Women: 40%.
Academics: Full-time faculty: 20. Part-time
faculty: 5. Degrees awarded: M.B.A., M.S.
Evening program is offered.
Finances: Tuition (1998-99): $4,291.
Admission Requirements: GMAT is
required. Application deadline for fall:
June 1.
Selectivity: Applications received (full-time):
813. Admitted: 442. Enrolled: 283.
Average GMAT: 570. Average undergradu-
ate GPA: 3.3.
Placement: School has placement office.
Average starting salary: $60,000.

SANTA CLARA UNIVERSITY

Leavey School of Business & Administration
200 Kenna Hall
Santa Clara, CA 95053
Phone: (408) 554-4500
Fax: (408) 554-2332
E-mail: mbaadmissions@scu.edu
http://www.scu.edu
Student Body: Full-time enrollment: 173.
Men: 66%. Women: 34%. International:

41%. Average age: 29. Part-time enroll-
ment: 846. Men: 66%. Women: 34%.
Academics: Full-time faculty: 63. Part-time
faculty: 30. Degrees awarded: M.B.A.,
M.B.A. Agribusiness, E.M.B.A. Joint degree
programs: J.D./M.B.A. Evening program is
offered.
Finances: Tuition (1998-99): $458/credit.
Admission Requirements: GMAT is required.
Application deadline for fall: June 1.
Selectivity: Applications received (part-time):
521. Admitted: 210. Enrolled: 147.
Average GMAT: 648. Average undergradu-
ate GPA: 3.2. GMAT section weighed most
heavily: weighed equally.
Placement: School has placement office.

STANFORD UNIVERSITY

Graduate School of Business
518 Memorial Way
Stanford, CA 94305-5015
Phone: (650) 723-2766
Fax: (650) 725-7831
E-mail: mbainquiries@gsb.stanford.edu
http://gsb-www.stanford.edu
Student Body: Full-time enrollment: 726.
Men: 70%. Women: 30%. Minorities:
25%. International: 25%. Average age: 26.
Academics: Full-time faculty: 87. Part-time
faculty: 18. Degrees awarded: M.B.A.,
M.S., Ph.D. Joint degree programs:
J.D./M.B.A., M.S.E./M.B.A., others by
arrangement. Evening program is not
offered. For fall 1996 entering class: 98%
completed program within 2 years. 2% con-
tinued towards degree.
Finances: Tuition (1998-99): $24,990.
Estimated tuition (1999-2000): $24,990.
70% of students receive some type of aid.
Average student debt incurred by graduation: $46,400.
Admission Requirements: GMAT is
required. Application deadline for fall:
November 4, January 13, March 24.
Selectivity: Applications received (full-time):
7,061. Admitted: 70%. Enrolled: 364.
Average GMAT: 722. GMAT section
weighed most heavily: weighed equally.

Placement: School has placement office. Placement rate at time of graduation: 99%. Average starting salary: $85,685.

UNIVERSITY OF CALIFORNIA— BERKELEY

Haas School of Business
M.B.A. Admissions
Berkeley, CA 94720-1902
Phone: (510) 642-1405
Fax: (510) 643-6659
E-mail: mbaadms@haas.berkeley.edu
http://www.haas.berkeley.edu
Student Body: Full-time enrollment: 484. Men: 65%. Women: 35%. African American: 2%. Asian American: 10%. Latino: 6%. International: 30%. Average age: 28.2. Students living on campus: 2%. Part-time enrollment: 325. Men: 76%. Women: 24%.
Academics: Full-time faculty: 66. Part-time faculty: 43. Degrees awarded: M.B.A. Joint degree programs: J.D./M.B.A., M.B.A./M.P.H., M.B.A./M.I.A.S., M.B.A./M.A. in Asian Studies. Evening program is offered. For fall 1996 entering class: 98% completed program within 2 years. 2% continued towards degree.
Finances: Tuition (1998–99): In-State: $10,408. Out-of-State: $19,792. 43% of students receive some type of aid. Average student debt incurred by graduation: $33,938.
Admission Requirements: GMAT is required. Application deadline for fall: March 30.
Selectivity: Applications received (full-time): 4,162. Admitted: 459. Enrolled: 240. Applications received (part-time): 445. Admitted: 140. Enrolled: 115. Average GMAT: 674. Average undergraduate GPA: 3.4. GMAT section weighed most heavily: varies, depending on other factors.
Placement: School has placement office. Placement rate at time of graduation: 95%. Placement rate 6 months after graduation: 99%. Average starting salary: $77,800.

UNIVERSITY OF CALIFORNIA— DAVIS

Graduate School of Management
One Shields Avenue
Davis, CA 95616
Phone: (530) 752-7399
Fax: (530) 752-2924
E-mail: gsm@ucdavis.edu
http://www.gsm.ucdavis.edu
Student Body: Full-time enrollment: 125. Men: 65%. Women: 35%. Average age: 28. Students living on campus: 3%.
Academics: Full-time faculty: 27. Part-time faculty: 19. Degrees awarded: M.B.A. Joint degree programs: J.D./M.B.A., M.B.A./M.E., M.B.A./M.D., M.B.A./M. Ag. Econ. Evening program is offered.
Finances: Tuition (1998–99): In-State: $10,483. Out-of-State: $19,862. 55% of students receive some type of aid.
Admission Requirements: GMAT is required. Application deadline for fall: February 7, April 7.
Selectivity: Applications received (full-time): 387. Admitted: 118. Enrolled: 62. Average GMAT: 663. Average undergraduate GPA: 3.2.
Placement: School has placement office. Placement rate at time of graduation: 90%. Placement rate 6 months after graduation: 98%. Average starting salary: $61,000.

UNIVERSITY OF CALIFORNIA— IRVINE

Graduate School of Management
M.B.A. Admissions
202 GSM
Irvine, CA 92697-3125
Phone: (949) UCI-4MBA
Fax: (949) 824-2944
E-mail: gsm-mba@uci.edu
http://www.gsm.uci.edu
Student Body: Full-time enrollment: 251. Men: 73%. Women: 27%. Asian American: 23%. Latino: 2%. International: 25%. Average age: 28. Part-time enrollment: 320. Men: 69%. Women: 31%.

Academics: Full-time faculty: 35. Part-time faculty: 36. Degrees awarded: M.B.A., Ph.D. Joint degree programs: M.D./M.B.A. Evening program is offered.
Finances: Tuition (1998–99): In-State: $11,193. Out-of-State: $20,577. Estimated tuition (1999–2000): In-State: $11,193. Out-of-State: $20,577. 70% of students receive non-need-based aid. 55% of students receive need-based aid. Average student debt incurred by graduation: $32,000.
Admission Requirements: GMAT is required. Application deadline for fall: Dec. 14, Jan. 25, Mar. 1, May 1.
Selectivity: Applications received (full-time): 823. Admitted: 222. Enrolled: 127. Applications received (part-time): 299. Admitted: 210. Enrolled: 126. Average GMAT: 652. Average undergraduate GPA: 3.3. GMAT section weighed most heavily: weighed equally.
Placement: School has placement office. Placement rate at time of graduation: 76%. Placement rate 6 months after graduation: 99%. Average starting salary: $63,200.

UNIVERSITY OF CALIFORNIA— LOS ANGELES

John E. Anderson Graduate School of Management
110 Westwood Plaza, Suite B201
Box 951481
Los Angeles, CA 90095-1481
Phone: (310) 825-6944
Fax: (310) 825-8582
E-mail: mba.admissions@anderson.ucla.edu
http://www.anderson.ucla.edu/
Student Body: Full-time enrollment: 655. Men: 71%. Women: 29%. Total Minority: 20%. International: 25%. Average age: 27.8. Students living on campus: 5%. Part-time enrollment: 547. Men: 75%. Women: 25%.
Academics: Full-time faculty: 82. Part-time faculty: 54. Degrees awarded: M.B.A., E.M.B.A., F.E.M.B.A., Ph.D., M.S. Management. Joint degree programs: M.D./M.B.A., J.D./M.B.A. Evening program is offered.

Finances: Tuition (1998–99): In-State: In-state $11,580. Out-of-State: Out-of-State $20,964. Average student debt incurred by graduation: $45,000.
Admission Requirements: GMAT is required. Application deadline for fall: April 3.
Selectivity: Applications received (full-time): 4,366. Admitted: 611. Enrolled: 330. Applications received (part-time): 502. Admitted: 158. Enrolled: 137. Average GMAT: 690. Average undergraduate GPA: 3.5.
Placement: School has placement office. Placement rate at time of graduation: 97%. Placement rate 6 months after graduation: 99.5%. Average starting salary: $77,000.

UNIVERSITY OF SAN DIEGO*

School of Business
5998 Alcala Park
San Diego, CA 92110
Phone: (619) 260-4524
Fax: (619) 260-2393
E-mail: grads@acusd.edu
http://http://www.acusd.edu
Student Body: Full-time enrollment: 162. Men: 66%. Women: 34%. International: 21%. Average age: 25. Students living on campus: 0%. Part-time enrollment: 225. Men: 56%. Women: 44%.
Academics: Full-time faculty: 61. Part-time faculty: 30. Degrees awarded: M.B.A., M.I.B. Joint degree programs: J.D./M.B.A., J.D./M.I.B., M.B.A./M.S.N. Evening program is offered.
Finances: Tuition (1998–99): $13,320. Estimated tuition (1999–2000): $13,986. Average student debt incurred by graduation: $11,000.
Admission Requirements: GMAT is required. Application deadline for fall: May 1.
Selectivity: Applications received (full-time): 490. Admitted: 256. Enrolled: 131. Average GMAT: 542. Average undergraduate GPA: 3.2.
Placement: School has placement office. Average starting salary: $50,000.

UNIVERSITY OF SAN FRANCISCO

McLaren Graduate School of Management
Ignatian Heights
2130 Fulton Street
San Francisco, CA 94117-1080
Phone: (415) 422-6563
Fax: (415) 422-2502
E-mail: mbausf@usfca.edu
http://www.usfa.edu/usf/mclaren
Student Body: Full-time enrollment: 248. Men: 70%. Women: 30%. African American: 4%. Asian American: 35%. Latino: 7%. International: 58%. Average age: 27. Students living on campus: 15%. Part-time enrollment: 230. Men: 61%. Women: 39%.
Academics: Full-time faculty: 45. Part-time faculty: 32. Degrees awarded: M.B.A., E.M.B.A., E.M.R.A. Joint degree programs: J.D./M.B.A., M.A.P.S./M.B.A., Masters in Asia Pacific Studies. Evening program is offered. For fall 1996 entering class: 89% completed program within 2 years. 12% continued towards degree.
Finances: Tuition (1998–99): $15,827. Estimated tuition (1999–2000): $16,739.
Admission Requirements: GMAT is required. Application deadline for fall: June 1.
Selectivity: Applications received (full-time): 309. Admitted: 210. Enrolled: 86. Applications received (part-time): 267. Admitted: 187. Enrolled: 81. Average GMAT: 560. Average undergraduate GPA: 3.3. GMAT section weighed most heavily: weighed equally.
Placement: School has placement office. Average starting salary: $51,000.

UNIVERSITY OF SOUTHERN CALIFORNIA

Marshall School of Business
BRI 101B
Los Angeles, CA 90089-1421
Phone: (213) 740-7846
Fax: (213) 740-8520
E-mail: uscmba@marshall.usc.edu
http://www.marshall.usc.edu
Student Body: Full-time enrollment: 547. Men: 71%. Women: 29%. African American: 5%. Asian American: 22%. Latino: 5%. International: 19%. Average age: 28. Part-time enrollment: 682. Men: 73%. Women: 27%.
Academics: Full-time faculty: 174. Part-time faculty: 43. Degrees awarded: M.B.A., M. Acc., M.S.B.A., M.B.T., M.S.I.O.M. Joint degree programs: M.B.A./M.A. East Asian Studies, J.D. M.B.A., M.B.A./M.A. Planning, M.B.A./M.A. Real Estate Dev., M.B.A./M.S. Gerontology, M.B.A./M.S. Industrial & Systems Eng. Evening program is offered. For fall 1996 entering class: 94% completed program within 2 years. 6% continued towards degree.
Finances: Tuition (1998–99): $24,852. Estimated tuition (1999–2000): $25,500. 75% of students receive need-based aid. 10% receive non-need-based aid. Average student debt incurred by graduation: $40,000.
Admission Requirements: GMAT is required. Application deadline for fall: April 1.
Selectivity: Applications received (full-time): 2,150. Admitted: 544. Enrolled: 280. Applications received (part-time): 310. Admitted: 195. Enrolled: 190. Average GMAT: 650. Average undergraduate GPA: 3.3. GMAT section weighed most heavily: weighed equally.
Placement: School has placement office. Placement rate at time of graduation: 86%. Placement rate 6 months after graduation: 100%. Average starting salary: $71,000.

Colorado

COLORADO STATE UNIVERSITY

College of Business
Rockwell Hall
Fort Collins, CO 80523
Phone: (970) 491-3704
Fax: (970) 491-0596
http://www.biz.colostate.edu
Student Body: Full-time enrollment: 152.
Men: 57%. Women: 43%. African
American: 2%. Asian American: 9%. Latino:
1%. International: 19%. Average age: 30.
Part-time enrollment: 537. Men: 68%.
Women: 32%.
Academics: Part-time faculty: 52. Degrees
awarded: M.B.A., M.S.B.A. Concentrations
in Actg/Tax/C.I.S. Evening program is
offered.
Finances: Tuition (1998–99): In-State:
$1,670 per semester. Out-of-State: $5,462
per semester. Estimated tuition
(1999–2000): In-State: $1,750 per semes-
ter. Out-of-State: $5,950 per semester.
Admission Requirements: GMAT is required.
Application deadline for fall: April 1.
Selectivity: Applications received (full-time):
288. Admitted: 116. Enrolled: 58.
Applications received (part-time): 243.
Admitted: 193. Enrolled: 169. Average
GMAT: 580. Average undergraduate GPA:
3.2. GMAT section weighed most heavily:
weighed equally.
Placement: School has placement office.
Placement rate at time of graduation: 79%.
Placement rate 6 months after graduation:
95%. Average starting salary: $45,731.

UNIVERSITY OF COLORADO— BOULDER

Graduate School of Business Administration
Campus Box 419
Boulder, CO 80309-0419
Phone: (303) 492-1831
Fax: (303) 492-1727
E-mail: busgrad@colorado.edu

http://bus.colorado.edu
Student Body: Full-time enrollment: 170.
Men: 70%. Women: 30%. African
American: 3%. Asian American: 5%. Latino:
2%. International: 12%. Average age: 29.
Part-time enrollment: 148. Men: 68%.
Women: 32%.
Academics: Full-time faculty: 69. Part-time
faculty: 3. Degrees awarded: M.B.A.,
M.S., Ph.D. Joint degree programs:
J.D./M.B.A., M.B.A./M.S.
Telecommunications. Evening program is not
offered. For fall 1996 entering class: 82%
completed program within 2 years. 15%
continued towards degree.
Finances: Tuition (1998–99): In-State:
$4,052. Out-of-State: $15,450. 32%
receive non-need-based aid. 78% of stu-
dents receive need-based aid. Average student debt incurred by graduation:
$24,337.
Admission Requirements: GMAT is
required. Application deadline for fall: Dec.
15, Feb. 15, May 1.
Selectivity: Applications received (full-time):
360. Admitted: 183. Enrolled: 85.
Applications received (part-time): 85.
Admitted: 60. Enrolled: 54. Average GMAT:
624. Average undergraduate GPA: 3.2.
Placement: School has placement office.
Placement rate within 3 months of graduation: 88%.
Average starting salary: $59,514.

UNIVERSITY OF COLORADO— COLORADO SPRINGS

College of Business and Administration
P.O. Box 7150
1420 Austin Bluffs Parkway
Colorado Springs, CO 80933-7150
Phone: (719) 262-3408
Fax: (719) 262-3494
E-mail: busadvsr@uccs.edu
http://www.uccs.edu
Student Body: Average age: 29. Part-time
enrollment: 306. Men: 59%. Women:
41%. International: 8%
Academics: Full-time faculty: 26. Part-time
faculty: 11. Degrees awarded: M.B.A. (on

campus or through Distance Learning).
Evening program is offered.
Finances: Tuition (1998–99): $145/credit
hour (for residents).
Admission Requirements: GMAT is required.
Application deadline for fall: June 1.
Selectivity: Applications received (part-time):
78. Admitted: 69. Average GMAT: 545.
Average undergraduate GPA: 3.1. GMAT
section weighed most heavily: weighed
equally.
Placement: School has placement office.

UNIVERSITY OF COLORADO— DENVER

Graduate School of Business Administration
Campus Box 165
P.O. Box 173364
Denver, CO 80217-3364
Phone: (303) 556-5900
Fax: (303) 556-5904
E-mail: Connie_Cornwell@maroon.
cudenver.edu
http://www.cudenver.edu/
public/business
Student Body: Full-time enrollment: 440.
Men: 56%. Women: 44%. African
American: 5%. Asian American: 18%.
Latino: 12%. International: 36%. Average
age: 33. Part-time enrollment: 976. Men:
59%. Women: 41%.
Academics: Full-time faculty: 70. Part-time
faculty: 20. Degrees awarded: M.B.A.,
M.S. Joint degree programs: M.B.A./M.S.
Evening program is offered.
Finances: Tuition (1998–99): In-State:
$3,750. Out-of-State: $12,900.
Admission Requirements: GMAT is required.
Application deadline for fall: July 1.
Selectivity: Applications received (full-time):
189. Admitted: 137. Enrolled: 84.
Applications received (part-time): 440.
Admitted: 321. Enrolled: 196. Average
GMAT: 525. Average undergraduate GPA:
3.2.
Placement: School has placement office.
Average starting salary: $49,471.

UNIVERSITY OF DENVER

Daniels College of Business
2020 S. Race #122
Denver, CO 80208
Phone: (303) 871-3416, (800) 622-4723
Fax: (303) 871-4466
E-mail: dcb@du.edu
http://www.dcb.du.edu
Student Body: Full-time enrollment: 528.
Men: 65%. Women: 35%. African
American: 2%. Asian American: 3%. Latino:
2%. International: 23%. Average age: 29.
Part-time enrollment: 188. Men: 55%.
Women: 45%.
Academics: Full-time faculty: 80. Part-time
faculty: 15. Degrees awarded: M.B.A.,
M.I.M., M.S.F., M. Acc., M.S.M., M.S.R.T.,
M.R.C.M., M.S.I.T. Joint degree programs:
M.B.A./J.D., M.I.M./J.D., M. Tax. Evening
program is offered. For fall 1996 entering
class. 95% completed program within 2
years. 6% continued towards degree.
Finances: Tuition (1998–99): $19,250.
Estimated tuition (1999–2000): $20,115.
Admission Requirements: GMAT is required.
Application deadline for fall: May 1.
Selectivity: Applications received (full-time):
529. Admitted: 416. Enrolled: 184
Applications received (part-time): 150.
Admitted: 138. Enrolled: 83. Average
GMAT: 530. Average undergraduate GPA:
3.1. GMAT section weighed most heavily:
weighed equally.
Placement: School has placement office.
Placement rate at time of graduation: 85%.
Placement rate 6 months after graduation:
99%. Average starting salary: $46,093.

Connecticut

FAIRFIELD UNIVERSITY

School of Business
Fairfield, CT 06430-5195
Phone: (203) 254-4180
Fax: (203) 254-4029
E-mail: mba@fair1.fairfield.edu
http://www.fairfield.edu

Student Body: Full-time enrollment: 17.
Men: 65%. Women: 35%. African
American: 9%. Asian American: 36%.
Latino: 36%. International: 81%. Average
age: 24. Students living on campus: 2%.
Part-time enrollment: 280. Men: 60%.
Women: 40%.
Academics: Full-time faculty: 40. Part-time
faculty: 1. Degrees awarded: M.B.A., M.S.
in Financial Management. For fall 1996
entering class: 100% continued towards
degree. Evening program is offered.
Finances: Tuition (1998–99): $7,500.
Admission Requirements: GMAT is required.
Application deadline for fall: August 15.
Selectivity: Applications received (full-time):
15. Admitted: 6. Enrolled: 6. Applications
received (part-time): 99. Admitted: 83.
Enrolled: 77. Average GMAT: 530.
Average undergraduate GPA: 3.2.
Placement: School has placement office.
Placement rate 6 months after graduation:
100%.

UNIVERSITY OF BRIDGEPORT

College of Business
126 Park Avenue
Bridgeport, CT 06601
Phone: (203) 576-4552
Fax: (203) 576-4941
E-mail: admit@cse.bridgeport.edu
http://www.bridgeport.edu
Student Body: Full-time enrollment: 246. Men:
61%. Women: 39%. Average age: 24.
Students living on campus: 25%. Part-time
enrollment: 35. Men: 57%. Women: 43%.
Academics: Full-time faculty: 12. Part-time
faculty: 10. Degrees awarded: M.B.A.
Evening program is offered.
Finances: Tuition (1998–99): $360/credit.
Estimated tuition (1999–2000):
$360/credit.
Admission Requirements: GMAT is
required. Application deadline for fall:
open.
Selectivity: Applications received (full-time):
820. Admitted: 300. Enrolled: 60.
Applications received (part-time): 12.
Admitted: 8. Enrolled: 6. Average GMAT:
480. Average undergraduate GPA: 3.1.

GMAT section weighed most heavily:
weighed equally.
Placement: School has placement office.
Placement rate at time of graduation: 40%.
Placement rate 6 months after graduation:
85%.

UNIVERSITY OF CONNECTICUT

School of Business Administration
368 Fairfield Road, U-41.MBA
Storrs, CT 06269-2041
Phone: (860) 486-2872
Fax: (860) 486-5222
E-mail: mbagen@sba.uconn.edu
http://www.sba.uconn.edu
Student Body: Full-time enrollment: 108.
Men: 58%. Women: 42%. African
American: 3%. Asian American: 2%. Latino:
2%. International: 31%. Average age: 28.
Students living on campus: 31%. Part-time
enrollment: 898. Men: 61%. Women: 39%.
Academics: Full-time faculty: 88. Part-time
faculty: 23. Degrees awarded: M.B.A.,
M.S. Acc. Joint degree programs:
M.B.A./M.D., M.B.A./M.S.W.,
M.B.A./M.A. Int'l, M.B.A., M.P.H.,
M.B.A./M.P.A., M.B.A./J.D.,
M.B.A./M.S. Nursing. Evening program is
offered. For fall 1996 entering class: 88%
completed program within 2 years. 10%
continued towards degree.
Finances: Tuition (1998–99): In-State:
$6,066. Out-of-State: $14,246. Estimated
tuition (1999–2000): In-State: $6,157.
Out-of-State: $14,460.
Admission Requirements: GMAT is
required. Application deadline for fall: June
1 (domestic), January 1 (international).
Selectivity: Applications received (full-time):
252. Admitted: 123. Enrolled: 46.
Applications received (part-time): 151.
Admitted: 121. Enrolled: 110. Average
GMAT: 601. Average undergraduate GPA:
3.3. GMAT section weighed most heavily:
approximately equally.
Placement: School has placement office.
Placement rate at time of graduation: 84%.
Placement rate 6 months after graduation:
98%. Average starting salary: $52,000.

YALE UNIVERSITY

Yale School of Management
2 Whitney Avenue
3rd Floor
New Haven, CT 06511
Phone: (203) 432-5932
Fax: (203) 432-7004
E-mail: som.admissions@yale.edu
http://www.yale.edu/som/
Student Body: Full-time enrollment: 430.
Men: 67%. Women: 33%. African
American: 3%. Asian American: 17%.
Latino: 3%. International: 28%. Average
age: 27.5.
Academics: Full-time faculty: 41. Part-time
faculty: 43. Degrees awarded: M.B.A.,
Ph.D. Evening program is not offered. For
fall 1996 entering class: 95% completed
program within 2 years. 3% continued
towards degree.
Finances: Tuition (1998–99): $25,250 +
$4,190 in fees. Average student debt
incurred by graduation: $44,218.
Admission Requirements: GMAT is
required. Application deadline for fall:
March 15.
Selectivity: Applications received (full-time):
1,777. Admitted: 458. Enrolled: 216.
Average GMAT: 682. Average undergraduate GPA: 3.4. GMAT section weighed most
heavily: Math is weighted more heavily due
to the quantitative nature of the program.
Placement: School has placement office.
Placement rate at time of graduation: 90%.
Placement rate 3 months after graduation:
98.5%. Average starting salary: $76,332.

Delaware

UNIVERSITY OF DELAWARE

College of Business and Economics
103 MBNA America Hall
Newark, DE 19716
Phone: (302) 831-2221
Fax: (302) 831-3329
E-mail: mbaprogram@udel.edu
http://www.mba.udel.edu

Student Body: Full-time enrollment: 139.
Men: 67%. Women: 33%. African
American: 1%. Asian American: 1%. Latino:
1%. International: 50%. Average age: 26.
Part-time enrollment: 295. Men: 68%.
Women: 32%.
Academics: Full-time faculty: 100. Part-time
faculty: 2. Degrees awarded: M.B.A. Joint
degree programs: M.B.A./M.A.
Economics, M.B.A./M.I.B. Evening pro-
gram is offered.
Finances: Tuition (1998–99): In-State:
$5,360. Out-of-State: $12,250. Estimated
tuition (1999–2000): In-State: $5,500.
Out-of-State: $12,750. 10% of students
receive non-need-based aid.
Admission Requirements: GMAT is required.
Application deadline for fall: May 1.
Selectivity: Applications received (full-time):
279. Admitted: 182. Enrolled: 61.
Applications received (part-time): 138.
Admitted: 109. Enrolled: 85. Average
GMAT: 600. Average undergraduate GPA:
3.1. GMAT section weighed most heavily:
weighed equally.
Placement: School has placement office.
Placement rate at time of graduation: 80%.
Placement rate 6 months after graduation:
98%. Average starting salary: $51,595.

District of Columbia

AMERICAN UNIVERSITY

Kogod College of Business Administration
4400 Massachusetts Avenue NW
Washington, DC 20016
Phone: (202) 885-1913
Fax: (202) 885-1078
E-mail: JSUGAR@american.edu
http://www.american.edu
Student Body: Full-time enrollment: 225.
Men: 58%. Women: 42%. International:
45%. Average age: 25. Students living on
campus: 20%. Part-time enrollment: 175.
Men: 55%. Women: 45%.

Academics: Full-time faculty: 58. Part-time
faculty: 12. Degrees awarded: M.B.A.,
M.S., M.S.A., M.S.F., M.S.H.R., M.S. Tax.,
M.S. Acc., M.S. Finance, M.S. Human
Resource Management. Joint degree programs: J.D./M.B.A., M.B.A./M.A. Evening
program is offered. For fall 1996 entering
class: 94% completed program within 2
years. 6% continued towards degree.
Finances: Tuition (1998–99): $19,080.
3.5% of students receive non-need-based
aid. Over 80% of students receive need-
based aid. Average student debt incurred
by graduation: $33,000.
Admission Requirements: GMAT is required.
Application deadline for fall: June 1.
Selectivity: Applications received: 554.
Admitted: 469. Enrolled (full-time): 85.
Enrolled (part-time): 72. Average GMAT:
552. Average undergraduate GPA: 3.2.
GMAT section weighed most heavily:
weighed equally.
Placement: School has placement office.
Placement rate at time of graduation: 54%.
Placement rate 6 months after graduation:
91%. Average starting salary: $55,000.

GEORGE WASHINGTON UNIVERSITY

School of Business & Public Management
710 21st Street NW
Washington, DC 20052
Phone: (202) 994-6584
Fax: (202) 994-6382
E-mail: sbpmapp.gwu.edu
http://www.sbpm@gwu.edu
Student Body: Full-time enrollment: 980.
Men: 61%. Women: 39%. Minorities:
17%. International: 46%. Average age: 27.
Part-time enrollment: 1,058. Men: 57%.
Women: 43%.
Academics: Full-time faculty: 128. Part-time
faculty: 53. Degrees awarded: M. Acc.,
M.B.A., E.M.B.A., M.S. Ist., M.T.A., M.S.
Project Management, M.S. Acquisition
Management, Ph.D., M.P.A., M. Public
Policy. Joint degree programs: M.B.A./J.D.,
M.P.A./J.D., M.B.A./M.A., International
Affairs. Evening program is offered. For fall

1996 entering class: 71% completed program within 2 years. 29% continued towards degree.
Finances: Tuition (1998–99): $19,292 (based on 27 credit hours). Estimated tuition (1999–2000): $20,264 (based on 27 credit hours). 70% of students receive some type of aid.
Admission Requirements: GMAT is required. Application deadline for fall: May 1.
Selectivity: Applications received (full-time). 1,873. Admitted: 950. Enrolled: 486. Applications received (part-time): 803. Admitted: 585. Enrolled: 284. Average GMAT: 601. Average undergraduate GPA: 3.2. GMAT section weighed most heavily: weighed equally.
Placement: School has placement office. Placement rate at time of graduation: 90%. Placement rate 6 months after graduation: 93%. Average starting salary: $59,000.

GEORGETOWN UNIVERSITY

The McDonough School of Business
105 Old North Building
Box 571148
Washington, DC 20057-1148
Phone: (202) 687-4200
Fax: (202) 687-7809
E-mail: MBA@gunet.georgetown.edu
http://www.georgetown.edu/gsb/gsb-home.html
Student Body: Full-time enrollment: 519. Men: 66%. Women: 34%. African American: 3%. Asian American: 7%. Latino: 4%. International: 28%. Average age: 28.
Academics: Full-time faculty: 79. Part-time faculty: 47. Degrees awarded: M.B.A. Joint degree programs: J.D./M.B.A., M.B.A./M.P.P., M.B.A./M.S.F.S., M.B.A./B.S.F.S., M.D./M.B.A., M.B.A./M.S.F.S. Evening program is not offered. For fall 1996 entering class: 97% completed program within 2 years. 3% continued towards degree.
Finances: Tuition (1998–99): $25,678. 60% of students receive need-based aid. 25% of students receive non-need-based aid.
Admission Requirements: GMAT is required. Application deadline for fall: April 15.

Selectivity: Applications received (full-time): 1,829. Admitted: 666. Enrolled: 262. Average GMAT: 637. Average undergraduate GPA: 3.2. GMAT section weighed most heavily: weighed equally.
Placement: School has placement office. Placement rate at time of graduation: 75%. Placement rate 6 months after graduation: 92%. Average starting salary: $70,338.

HOWARD UNIVERSITY

School of Business
Office of Graduate Studies
2600 Sixth Street, NW
Washington, DC 20059
Phone: (202) 806-1725
Fax: (202) 806-1625
http://www.bschool.howard.edu
Student Body: Full-time enrollment: 128. Men: 51%. Women: 49%. International: 30%. Average age: 27.
Academics: Full-time faculty: 17. Part-time faculty: 1. Degrees awarded: M.B.A. Joint degree programs: J.D./M.B.A. Evening program is offered.
Finances: Tuition (1998–99): $10,604. 19% of students receive some type of aid.
Admission Requirements: GMAT is required. Application deadline for fall: April 1.
Selectivity: Applications received (full-time): 225. Enrolled: 63. Average GMAT: 517. Average undergraduate GPA: 3.0.
Placement: School has placement office. Placement rate at time of graduation: 93%. Average starting salary: $61,500.

Florida

FLORIDA ATLANTIC UNIVERSITY

College of Business
Graduate Studies
Admissions, ADM 297
777 Glades Road
Boca Raton, FL 33431-0091
Phone: (561) 297-2618

Fax: (561) 297-2117
E-mail: gradadm@fau.edu
http://www.fau.edu
Student Body: Full-time enrollment: 162. Men: 57%. Women: 43%. African American: 20%. Asian American: 13%. Latino: 29%. Average age: 29. Part-time enrollment: 333. Men: 52%. Women: 48%.
Academics: Full-time faculty: 116. Part-time faculty: 8. Degrees awarded: M.B.A., M. Acc., M. Tax., M.S. Econ.
Finances: Tuition (1998–99): In-State: $140 per credit hour. Out-of-State: $484 per credit hour.
Admission Requirements: GMAT is required. Application deadline for fall: June 1.
Selectivity: Applications received: 215. Admitted: 165. Enrolled: 117. Average GMAT: 538. Average undergraduate GPA: 3.3. GMAT section weighed most heavily: Verbal.
Placement: School has placement office. Average starting salary: $50,580.

FLORIDA INTERNATIONAL UNIVERSITY

College of Business Administration
University Park
Charles E. Perry Building
Miami, FL 33199
Phone: (305) 348-2363
On-line Application:
http://www.fiu.edu/orgs/admiss
http://www.fiu.edu
Student Body: Total enrollment: 4,422. Men: 51%. Women: 49%. International: 2%. Average age: 35.
Academics: Full-time faculty: 116. Part-time faculty: 24. Degrees awarded: M.B.A., M.S.F., M. Acc., M.S., E.M.B.A., M. Tax. Evening program is offered.
Finances: Tuition (1998–99): In-State: $130/credit. Out-of-State: $435/credit.
Admission Requirements: GMAT is required. Application deadline for fall: April 1.

FLORIDA STATE UNIVERSITY

College of Business, Graduate Office
Room 318 RBA
Tallahassee, FL 32306-1110
Phone: (850) 644-6458
Fax: (850) 644-0915
E-mail: smartin@cob.fsu.edu
http://www.cob.fsu.edu/mba
Student Body: Full-time enrollment: 28.
Men: 75%. Women: 25%. African
American: 4%. Latino: 4%. Average age:
26. Part-time enrollment: 92. Men: 64%.
Women: 36%.
Academics: Faculty: 55 (also teachers at
undergraduate level). Degrees awarded:
M.B.A., M. Acc., Ph.D., M.S.M. in M.I.S.
Joint degree programs: J.D./M.B.A.
Evening program is offered. For fall 1996
entering class: 100% completed program
within 2 years.
Finances: Tuition (1998–99): In-State:
$139/graduate hour. Out-of-State:
$483/graduate hour. Estimated tuition
(1999–2000): In-State: $153/graduate
hour. Out-of-State: $531/graduate hour.
Admission Requirements: GMAT is
required. Application deadline: October 1
(PT), March 1 (FT); no admissions for fall.
Selectivity: Applications received (full-time):
51. Admitted: 31. Enrolled: 28.
Applications received (part-time): 116.
Admitted: 85. Enrolled: 70. Average
GMAT: 549. Average undergraduate GPA:
3.1. GMAT section weighed most heavily:
weighed equally.
Placement: School has placement office.
Placement rate at time of graduation: 38%.
Placement rate 6 months after graduation:
100%. Average starting salary: $43,602.

ROLLINS COLLEGE

Crummer Graduate School of Business
1000 Holt Avenue 2722
Winter Park, FL 32789-4499
Phone: (407) 646-2405
Fax: (407) 646-2402
E-mail: sgauthier@rollins.edu
http://www.crummer.rollins.edu

Student Body: Full-time enrollment: 174.
Men: 68%. Women: 32%. African
American: 3%. Asian American: 15%.
Latino: 4%. International: 24%. Average
age: 27.3. Part-time enrollment: 206. Men:
65%. Women: 35%.
Academics: Full-time faculty: 23. Part-time
faculty: 4. Degrees awarded: M.B.A.
Evening program is offered. For fall 1996
entering class: 96% completed program
within 2 years.
Finances: Tuition (1998–99): $20,400.
50% of students receive non-need-based aid.
50% of students receive need-based aid.
Admission Requirements: GMAT is required.
Application deadline for fall: April 1.
Selectivity: Applications received (full-time):
326. Admitted: 201. Enrolled: 117.
Applications received (part-time): 68.
Admitted: 50. Enrolled: 36. Average
GMAT: 590. Average undergraduate GPA:
3.2. GMAT section weighed most heavily:
weighed equally.
Placement: School has placement office.
Placement rate at time of graduation: 80%.
Placement rate 6 months after graduation:
100%. Average starting salary: $60,000.

UNIVERSITY OF CENTRAL FLORIDA

College of Business Administration
Suite 240
Orlando, FL 32816-0991
Phone: (407) 823-2766
Fax: (407) 823-6442
E-mail: graduate@mail.ucf.edu
http://www.ucf.edu
Student Body: Average age: 29. Part-time
enrollment: 714. Men: 51%. Women:
49%. International: 12%
Academics: Full-time faculty: 63. Part-time
faculty: 11. Degrees awarded: M.B.A.,
M.A.E.E., M.S.A., M.S.T. Evening program
is offered.
Finances: Tuition (1998–99): In-State:
$137/hour. Out-of-State: $481/hour.
Estimated tuition (1999–2000): In-State:
$137/hour. Out-of-State: $481/hour.

Admission Requirements: GMAT is required.
Application deadline for fall: Nov. 1.
Selectivity: Applications received (part-time):
267. Admitted: 176. Enrolled: 142.
Average GMAT: 545. Average undergraduate GPA: 3.3. GMAT section weighed most
heavily: weighed equally.
Placement: School has placement office.

UNIVERSITY OF FLORIDA

Warrington College of Bus. Florida MBA
Programs
134 Bryan Hall
P.O. Box 117152
Gainesville, FL 32611-7152
Phone: (352) 392-7992
Fax: (352) 392-8791
E-mail: floridamba@cba.ufl.edu
http://www.floridamba.ufl.edu
Student Body: Full-time enrollment: 299.
Men: 74%. Women: 26%. African
American: 3%. Asian American: 7%. Latino:
7%. International: 15%. Average age: 27.
Students living on campus: 1%.
Academics: Full-time faculty: 106. Degrees
awarded: M.B.A., Ph.D., M.A., M.S. Joint
degree programs: M.B.A./J.D.,
M.B.A./Pharm., M.B.A./M.S.
Biotechnology, M.B.A./M.S. Exercise &
Sport Science, M.B.A./M.I.M.,
M.B.A./I.M.B.A., M.B.A./M.H.A.,
M.B.A./B.S.I.S.E. Evening program is not
offered. For fall 1996 entering class: 73%
completed program within 2 years. 22%
continued towards degree.
Finances: Tuition (1998–99): In-State:
$3,982. Out-of-State: $12,914. Estimated
tuition (1999–2000): In-State: $4,411.
Out-of-State: $14,415.
Admission Requirements: GMAT is required.
Application deadline for fall: June 1.
Selectivity: Applications received (full-time):
479. Admitted: 201. Enrolled: 116.
Average GMAT: 610. Average undergraduate GPA: 3.3. GMAT section weighed most
heavily: Quantitative.
Placement: School has placement office.
Placement rate at time of graduation: 80%.
Placement rate 6 months after graduation:
95%. Average starting salary: $54,179.

UNIVERSITY OF MIAMI

School of Business Administration
P.O. Box 248505
Coral Gables, FL 33124-6520
Phone: (305) 284-4607
Fax: (305) 284-1878
E-mail: gba@bus.miami.edu
http://www.bus.miami.edu
Student Body: Full-time enrollment: 359.
Men: 65%. Women: 35%. African
American: 6%. Asian American: 4%. Latino:
26%. International: 37%. Average age: 26.
Students living on campus: 6%. Part-time
enrollment: 120. Men: 58%. Women: 43%.
Academics: Full-time faculty: 93. Part-time
faculty: 40. Degrees awarded: M.B.A.,
M.A., M.P.A., M.P.Acc., M.S., Ph.D. Joint
degree programs: J.D./M.B.A. Evening pro-
gram is offered.
Finances: Tuition (1998–99): $815/credit.
Estimated tuition (1999–2000):
$852/credit. Average student debt
incurred by graduation: $27,500.
Admission Requirements: GMAT is
required. Application deadline for fall:
July 1.
Selectivity: Applications received (full-time):
531. Admitted: 256. Enrolled: 84.
Applications received (part-time): 72.
Admitted: 34. Enrolled: 17. Average
GMAT: 610. Average undergraduate GPA:
3.1. GMAT section weighed most heavily:
weighed equally.
Placement: School has placement office.
Placement rate at time of graduation: 68%.
Placement rate 6 months after graduation:
97%. Average starting salary: $47,760.

UNIVERSITY OF NORTH FLORIDA*

College of Business Administration
4567 St. John's Bluff Rd. South
Jacksonville, FL 32216
Phone: (904) 620-2624
Student Body: Full-time enrollment: 106.
Men: 58%. Women: 42%. International:
5%. Part-time enrollment: 420. Men: 53%.
Women: 47%.

Academics: Full-time faculty: 53. Part-time
faculty: 0. Degrees awarded: M.B.A.,
M. Acc., M.H.R.M. Evening program is
offered.
Finances: Tuition (1998–99): In-State:
$2,000. Out-of-State: $6,000.
Admission Requirements: GMAT is required.
Application deadline for fall: July 1.
Selectivity: Applications received (full-time):
183. Admitted: 146. Enrolled: 135.
Average GMAT: 510. Average undergradu-
ate GPA: 3.1.
Placement: School has placement office.
Average starting salary: $35,000.

UNIVERSITY OF SOUTH FLORIDA*

College of Business Administration
4202 East Fowler Avenue, FAO 100N
Graduate Admissions
Tampa, FL 33620-7900
Phone: (813) 974-8800
Fax: (813) 974-7343
E-mail: eagee@grad.usf.edu
Student Body: Full-time enrollment: 168.
Men: 58%. Women: 42%. International:
17%. Average age: 28. Students living on
campus: 10%. Part-time enrollment: 383.
Men: 61%. Women: 39%.
Academics: Full-time faculty: 104. Part-time
faculty: 5. Degrees awarded: M.B.A.,
M.A.Econ., M.A.C., M.A.N., I.S.T.
Evening program is offered.
Finances: Tuition (1998–99): In-State:
$135. Out-of-State: $440. Estimated tuition
(1999–2000): In-State: $135. Out-of-State:
$440.
Admission Requirements: GMAT is required.
Application deadline for fall: May 15.
Selectivity: Applications received (full-time):
343. Admitted: 241. Enrolled: 123.
Average GMAT: 542. Average undergradu-
ate GPA: 3.2. GMAT section weighed most
heavily: Quantitative.
Placement: School has placement office.
Average starting salary: $49,000.

Georgia

CLARK ATLANTA UNIVERSITY

School of Business Administration
323 James P. Brawley Drive
at Fair Street, S.W.
Atlanta, GA 30314
Phone: (404) 880-8479
Fax: (404) 880-6159
E-mail: cechols@sbus.cau.edu
http://www.cau.edu/business/
index.htm
Student Body: Full-time enrollment: 150.
Men: 40%. Women: 60%. African
American: 89%. Latino: 1%. International:
11%. Average age: 28. Students living on
campus: 10%. Part-time enrollment: 16.
Men: 44%. Women: 56%.
Academics: Full-time faculty: 30. Part-time
faculty: 4. Degrees awarded: M.B.A.
Evening program is offered. For fall 1996
entering class: 95% completed program
within 2 years
Finances: Tuition (1998–99): $12,090.
90% of students receive need-based aid.
32% of students receive non-need-based
aid. Average student debt incurred by grad-
uation: $36,000.
Admission Requirements: GMAT is required.
Application deadline for fall: April 1.
Selectivity: Applications received (full-time):
250. Admitted: 117. Enrolled: 78.
Applications received (part-time): 20.
Admitted: 18. Enrolled: 16. Average
GMAT: 415. Average undergraduate GPA:
2.8. GMAT section weighed most heavily:
weighed equally.
Placement: School has placement office.
Placement rate at time of graduation: 80%.
Placement rate 6 months after graduation:
85%. Average starting salary: $65,000.

EMORY UNIVERSITY

Goizueta Business School
1300 Clifton Rd, NE
Atlanta, GA 30322
Phone: (404) 727-6311
Fax: (404) 727-4612
E-mail: Admissions@bus.emory.edu
http://www.emory.edu/BUS/
Student Body: Full-time enrollment: 324.
Men: 69%. Women: 31%. Minority: 10%.
International: 27%. Average age: 27.
Students living on campus: 18%. Part-time
enrollment: 191. Men: 66%. Women: 34%.
Academics: Full-time faculty: 59. Part-time
faculty: 12. Degrees awarded: M.B.A. Joint
degree programs: J.D./M.B.A.,
M.B.A./M.P.H., M.B.A./M.D.I.V. Evening
program is offered.For fall 1996 entering
class: 98% continued towards a degree.
Finances: Tuition (1998–99): $24,200.
80% of students receive need-based aid.
40% of students received non-need-based
aid. Average student debt incurred by graduation: $31,666.
Admission Requirements: GMAT is required.
Application deadline for fall: March 31.
Selectivity: Applications received (full-time):
1,106. Admitted: 378. Enrolled: 150.
Applications received (part-time): 154.
Admitted: 86. Enrolled: 60. Average GMAT:
640. Average undergraduate GPA: 3.3.
Placement: School has placement office.
Placement rate at time of graduation: 86%.
Placement rate 6 months after graduation:
99%. Average starting salary: $70,641.

GEORGIA INSTITUTE OF TECHNOLOGY

DuPree College of Management
755 Ferst Drive
212 DuPree College of Management
Atlanta, GA 30332-0520
Phone: (404) 894-8722,
(800) 869-1014
Fax: (404) 894-4199
E-mail: msm@mgt.gatech.edu
http://http://www.iac.gatech.edu/

Student Body: Full-time enrollment: 210.
Men: 72%. Women: 28%. International:
28%. Average age: 27.
Academics: Full-time faculty: 50. Degrees
awarded: I.E.M., M.S.M., Ph.D. Evening
program is not offered. For fall 1996 enter-
ing class: 94% completed program within 2
years. 2% continued towards degree.
Admission Requirements: GMAT is required.
Application deadline for fall: May 1.
Selectivity: Applications received (full-time):
500. Admitted: 220. Enrolled: 103.
Average GMAT: 632. Average undergradu-
ate GPA: 3.2.
Placement: School has placement office.
Placement rate at time of graduation: 93%.
Placement rate 6 months after graduation:
99%. Average starting salary: $56,100.

GEORGIA SOUTHERN UNIVERSITY

College of Business Administration
P.O. Box 8050
Statesboro, GA 30460-8050
Phone: (912) 681-5767
Fax: (912) 486-7480
E-mail: eleverni@gsaix2.cc.gasou.edu
http://www.gasou.edu/mba.main.htm
Student Body: Full-time enrollment: 62.
Men: 55%. Women: 45%. African
American: 16%. Asian American: 26%.
Latino: 3%. International: 47%. Average
age: 30. Part-time enrollment: 198. Men:
55%. Women: 45%.
Academics: Full-time faculty: 56. Degrees
awarded: M.B.A., M. Acc. Joint degree
programs: M.B.A./M. Acc. Evening pro-
gram is offered.
Finances: Tuition (1998–99): In-State: $83
per semester hour. Out-of-State: $322 per
semester hour plus fees. Estimated tuition
(1999–2000): In-State: $83 per semester
hour. Out-of-State: $250 per semester.
Admission Requirements: GMAT is
required.
Selectivity: Enrolled (full-time): 23. Enrolled
(part-time): 72. Average GMAT: 498.
Average undergraduate GPA: 3.1.
Placement: School has placement office.

GEORGIA STATE UNIVERSITY

J. Mack Robinson College of Business
Office of Master's Admissions
Atlanta, GA 30303
Phone: (404) 651-1913
Fax: (404) 651-0219
http://www.cba.gsu.edu
Student Body: Full-time enrollment: 599.
Men: 63%. Women: 37%. African
American: 7%. Asian American: 8%. Latino:
2%. International: 6%. Average age: 27.
Part-time enrollment: 1,163. Men: 63%.
Women: 37%.
Academics: Full-time faculty: 180. Part-time
faculty: 122. Degrees awarded: M.B.A.
(and eight specialized master's programs).
Joint degree programs: M.B.A./M.H.A.,
M.B.A./J.D. Evening program is offered.
Finances: Tuition (1998–99): In-State:
$1,908. Out-of-State: $7,632.
Admission Requirements: GMAT is required.
Application deadline for fall: May 1.
Selectivity: Applications received: 995.
Admitted: 580. Enrolled (full-time): 144.
Enrolled (part-time): 279. Average GMAT:
570. Average undergraduate GPA: 3.1.
GMAT section weighed most heavily:
weighed equally.
Placement: School has placement office.
Placement rate at time of graduation: 90%.
Placement rate 6 months after graduation:
100%. Average starting salary: $51,138.

STATE UNIVERSITY OF WEST GEORGIA

Richards College of Business
The Graduate School-Cobb Hall
1600 Maple Street
Carrollton, GA 30118-4160
Phone: (770) 836-6419
Fax: (770) 830-2301
E-mail: gradsch@westga.edu
http://www.westga.edu/~gradsch/
Student Body: Full-time enrollment: 46.
Men: 61%. Women: 39%. Students living
on campus: 1%. Part-time enrollment: 47.
Men: 62%. Women: 38%.

Academics: Full-time faculty: 35. Part-time faculty: 3. Degrees awarded: M.B.A., M.P. Acc. Evening program is offered.

Finances: Tuition (1998–99): In-State: $8,665. Out-of-State: $13,225.

Admission Requirements: GMAT is required. Application deadline for fall: June 29.

Selectivity: Applications received (full-time): 55. Admitted: 49. Average GMAT: 557. Average undergraduate GPA: 3.0. GMAT section weighed most heavily: weighed equally.

Placement: School has placement office. Placement rate at time of graduation: 85%. Placement rate 6 months after graduation: 98%. Average starting salary: $38,500.

UNIVERSITY OF GEORGIA

Terry College of Business
346 Brooks Hall
Athens, GA 30602-6264
Phone: (706) 542-5671
Fax: (706) 542-5351
E-mail: ugamba@cba.uga.edu
http://www.cba.uga.edu/mba

Student Body: Full-time enrollment: 156. Men: 81%. Women: 19%. African American: 4%. Asian American: 1%. Latino: 1%. International: 21%. Average age: 26.5. Students living on campus: 5%.

Academics: Full-time faculty: 85. Degrees awarded: M.B.A., M.A., M. Acc., M.M.R., Ph.D. Joint degree programs: J.D./M.B.A., Nijenrode/U. of Georgia M.B.A. Evening program is not offered. For fall 1996 entering class: 91% completed program within 2 years. 4% continued towards degree.

Finances: Tuition (1998–99): In-State: $3,290. Out-of-State: $11,300. 65% of students receiving non-need-based aid.

Admission Requirements: GMAT is required. Application deadline for fall: March 1 (recommended).

Selectivity: Applications received (full-time): 642. Admitted: 174. Enrolled: 97. Average GMAT: 640. Average undergraduate GPA: 3.2. GMAT section weighed most heavily: slightly more weight on Quantitative.

Placement: School has placement office. Placement rate at time of graduation: 81%. Placement rate 6 months after graduation: 93%. Average starting salary: $57,000.

Hawaii

UNIVERSITY OF HAWAII— MANOA

College of Business Administration
2404 Maile Way
BUSAD, A303
Honolulu, HI 96822
Phone: (808) 956-8266
Fax: (808) 956-9890
E-mail: osas@busadm.cba.hawaii.edu
http://www.cba.hawaii.edu

Student Body: Full-time enrollment: 163. Men: 57%. Women: 43%. African American: 1%. Asian American: 64%. Latino: 2%. International: 25%. Average age: 32. Students living on campus: 25%. Part-time enrollment: 166. Men: 51%. Women: 49%.

Academics: Full-time faculty: /. Part-time faculty: 36. Degrees awarded: M.B.A., M. Acc., E.M.B.A., J.E.M.B.A., C.H.E.M.B.A., Ph.D./C.I.S., M.P.S. Joint degree programs: M.B.A./J.D., M.B.A./Ph.D. Economics. Evening program is offered. For fall 1996 entering class: 85% completed program within 2 years. 9% continued towards degree.

Finances: Tuition (1998–99): In-State: $3,912. Out-of-State: $9,840. Estimated tuition (1999–2000): In-State: $4,032. Out-of-State: $9,960.

Admission Requirements: GMAT is required. Application deadline for fall: May 1.

Selectivity: Applications received (full-time): 145. Admitted: 84. Enrolled: 57. Applications received (part-time): 163. Admitted: 75. Enrolled: 44. Average GMAT: 575. Average undergraduate GPA: 3.3. GMAT section weighed most heavily: weighed equally.

Placement: School has placement office.

Idaho

BOISE STATE UNIVERSITY

College of Business & Economics
1910 University Drive
Boise, ID 83725
Phone: (208) 426-1126
Fax: (208) 426-4989
E-mail: abuanchu@cobfaa.idbsu.edu
http://www.boisestate.edu/

Student Body: Full-time enrollment: 36. Men: 63%. Women: 37%. Asian American: 17%. Latino: 8%. International: 36%. Average age: 27.6. Students living on campus: 11%. Part-time enrollment: 175. Men: 61%. Women: 39%.

Academics: Full-time faculty: 54. Part-time faculty: 1. Degrees awarded: M.B.A., M.S. Acc., M.S. Tax., M.S.M.I.S., Health Administration. Evening program is offered. For fall 1996 entering class: 7% completed program within 2 years. 88% continued towards degree.

Finances: Tuition (1998–99): In-State: $3,020. Out-of-State: $8,900. Estimated tuition (1999–2000): In-State: $3,171. Out-of-State: $9,345. 12% of students received non-need-based aid.

Admission Requirements: GMAT is required. Application deadline: March 1, October 1.

Selectivity: Applications received (full-time): 21. Admitted: 16. Enrolled: 14. Applications received (part-time): 79. Admitted: 71. Enrolled: 59. Average GMAT: 553. Average undergraduate GPA: 3.1. GMAT section weighed most heavily: weighed equally.

Placement: School has placement office. Placement rate at time of graduation: 90%. Placement rate 6 months after graduation: 98%. Average starting salary: $75,000.

IDAHO STATE UNIVERSITY

College of Business
Box 8020
Pocatello, ID 83209
Phone: (208) 236-2475
Fax: (208) 236-4367
E-mail: mbaadmin@isu.edu
Student Body: Full-time enrollment: 57.
Asian American: 4%. Latino: 2%. Native
American: 4%. International: 11%. Part-time
enrollment: 45.
Academics: Full-time faculty: 36. Degrees
awarded: M.B.A. Evening program is
offered.
Finances: Tuition (1998–99): In-State:
$2,940. Out-of-State: $8,920.
Admission Requirements: GMAT is required.
Application deadline for fall: July 1.
Selectivity: Applications received: 42.
Admitted: 30. Enrolled: 20. Average
GMAT: 551.9. Average undergraduate
GPA: 3.3.
Placement: School has placement office.

Illinois

BRADLEY UNIVERSITY*

Foster College of Business Administration
Baker Hall
Peoria, IL 61625
Phone: (309) 677-1000
Student Body: Full-time enrollment: 30.
International: 7%. Part-time enrollment: 159.
Academics: Full-time faculty: 18. Degrees
awarded: M.B.A.
Admission Requirements: GMAT is required.
Application deadline for fall: March 1.
Selectivity: Applications received (full-time):
193. Admitted: 99. Enrolled: 52. Average
GMAT: 548. Average undergraduate GPA:
3.3.
Placement: School has placement office.

DePaul University

Kellstadt Graduate School of Business
1 E. Jackson
Suite 7900
Chicago, IL 60604-2287
Phone: (312) 362-8810
Fax: (312) 362-6677
E-mail: MBAInfo@wppost.Depaul.edu
http://www.depaul.edu/
Student Body: Full-time enrollment: 72.
African American: 1%. Asian American:
1%. Latino: 1%. International: 42%.
Average age: 27. Part-time enrollment:
2,537. Men: 64%. Women: 36%.
Academics: Full-time faculty: 113. Degrees
awarded: M.B.A., M.S.T., M.S.A., M.
Acc., M.I.S., M.S.F. Joint degree programs:
M.S./M.I.S. Evening program is offered.
For fall 1996 entering class: 97% complet-
ed program within 2 years. 1% continued
towards degree.
Finances: Tuition (1998–99): $21,771.
Estimated tuition (1999–2000): $22,960.
40% of students receive some type of aid.
Admission Requirements: GMAT is required.
Application deadline for fall: May 1.
Selectivity: Applications received (full-time):
155. Admitted: 76. Enrolled: 36. Average
GMAT: 591. Average undergraduate GPA:
3.1.
Placement: School has placement office.
Placement rate at time of graduation: 50%.
Placement rate 6 months after graduation:
88%. Average starting salary: $57,882.

ILLINOIS STATE UNIVERSITY

College of Business
327 Williams Hall
Campus Box 5500
Normal, IL 61790-5500
Phone: (309) 438-8388
Fax: (309) 438-5510
E-mail: isumba@ilstu.edu
http://gilbreth.cob.ilstu.edu/MBA
Student Body: Full-time enrollment: 62.
Men: 60%. Women: 40%. African
American: 16%. Asian American: 6%.
Latino: 2%. International: 69%. Average

age: 30. Part-time enrollment: 164. Men:
54%. Women: 46%.
Academics: Full-time faculty: 59. Part-time
faculty: 2. Degrees awarded: M.B.A.,
M.S.A. Evening program is offered.
Finances: Tuition (1998–99): In-State:
$2,490. Out-of-State: $6,171. Estimated
tuition (1999–2000): In-State: $2,638.
Out-of-State: $6,428.
Admission Requirements: GMAT is required.
Application deadline for fall: March 15.
Selectivity: Applications received (full-time):
111. Admitted: 81. Enrolled: 56. Average
GMAT: 556. Average undergraduate GPA:
3.3.
Placement: School has placement office.
Placement rate at time of graduation: 66%.
Placement rate 6 months after graduation:
94%. Average starting salary: $40,000.

LOYOLA UNIVERSITY CHICAGO

Graduate School of Business
820 North Michigan Avenue
Chicago, IL 60611
Phone: (312) 915-6120
Fax: (312) 915-7207
E-mail: mba-loyola@luc.edu
http://www.luc.edu.depts/mba/
Student Body: Full-time enrollment: 160.
Men: 62%. Women: 38%. International:
73%. Average age: 26. Students living on
campus: 6%. Part-time enrollment: 749.
Men: 65%. Women: 35%.
Academics: Degrees awarded: M.B.A.,
M.S.A., M.S.I.S.M. Joint degree programs:
M.B.A./J.D., M.B.A./M.S.N. Evening pro-
gram is offered. For fall 1996 entering class:
89% completed program within 2 years.
Finances: Tuition (1998–99): $17,982.
Admission Requirements: GMAT is
required. Application deadline for fall:
August 1.
Selectivity: Applications received (full-time):
215. Admitted: 112. Enrolled: 72.
Applications received (part-time): 247.
Admitted: 184. Enrolled: 129. Average
GMAT: 520. Average undergraduate GPA:
3.2. GMAT section weighed most heavily:
both weighed equally.

Placement: School has placement office. Placement rate at time of graduation: 82%. Placement rate 6 months after graduation: 97%. Average starting salary: $53,600.

NORTHERN ILLINOIS UNIVERSITY

College of Business
Graduate Studies in Business
Wirt Hall 140
De Kalb, IL 60115-2897
Phone: (815) 753-1245
(800) 323-8714 (in-state)
Fax: (815) 753-3300
E-mail: cobgrads@niu.edu
http://www.cob.niu.edu/grad/grad.html
Student Body: Full-time enrollment: 91. Men: 65%. Women: 35%. Part-time enrollment: 566. Men: 65%. Women: 35%.
Academics: Full-time faculty: 76. Part-time faculty: 11. Degrees awarded: M.B.A., M.A.S., M.S.F., M.S.M.I.S. Evening program is offered.
Finances: Tuition (1998–99): Off-campus $266/credit. Out-of-State: $154-385/credit.
Admission Requirements: GMAT is required. Application deadline for fall: June 1.
Selectivity: Applications received (part-time): 330. Admitted: 301. Enrolled: 215. Average GMAT: 551. Average undergraduate GPA: 3.1. GMAT section weighed most heavily: all are factored into decision-making process.
Placement: School has placement office. Average starting salary: $64,399.

NORTHWESTERN UNIVERSITY

Kellogg Graduate School of Management
2001 Sheridan Road
Evanston, IL 60208-2001
Phone: (847) 491-3308
Fax: (847) 491-4960
E-mail: kellogg-admission@nwu.edu
http://www.kellogg.nwu.edu
Student Body: Full-time enrollment: 1,254. Men: 68%. Women: 32%. African

American: 4%. Asian American: 9%. Latino: 2%. International: 24%. Average age: 27. Part-time enrollment: 1,300. Men: 65%. Women: 35%.
Academics: Full-time faculty: 170. Part-time faculty: 96. Degrees awarded: Master of Management. Joint degree programs: J.D./M.M., M.D./M.M., M.M.M. Evening program is offered. For fall 1996 entering class: 100% completed degree within 2 years.
Finances: Tuition (1998–99): $25,872. 60% of students receive some type of aid.
Admission Requirements: GMAT is required. Application deadline for fall: November 13, January 15, March 16.
Selectivity: Applications received (full-time): 6,128. Enrolled: 627. Applications received (part-time): 679. Enrolled: 236. Average GMAT: 695. Average undergraduate GPA: 3.4. GMAT section weighed most heavily: weighed equally.
Placement: School has placement office. Placement rate at time of graduation: 98%. Placement rate 6 months after graduation: 100%. Average starting salary: $90,000.

SOUTHERN ILLINOIS UNIVERSITY—CARBONDALE

College of Business & Administration
133 Rehn Hall
Mail Code 4625
Carbondale, IL 62901-4625
Phone: (618) 453-3030
Fax: (618) 453-7961
E-mail: mbagp@siu.edu/~mba
http://www.siu.edu
Student Body: Full-time enrollment: 137. Men: 57%. Women: 43%. African American: 6%. Asian American: 2%. Latino: 1%. International: 53%. Part-time enrollment: 7. Men: 57%. Women: 43%.
Academics: Full-time faculty: 37. Degrees awarded: M.B.A., M. Acc., D.B.A. Joint degree programs: J.D./M.B.A., M.A. Telecommunications/ M.B.A., M.B.A. Agribusiness Economics, M.B.A./B.A. Computer Science. Evening program is not offered.

Finances: Tuition (1998–99): In-State: $1,703 per semester. Out-of-State: $4,074 per semester. Estimated tuition (1999–2000): In-State: $1,835 per semester. Out-of-State: $3,137 per semester (based on 12 semester hours).
Admission Requirements: GMAT is required. Application deadline for fall: June 15 (domestic), April 15 (international).
Selectivity: Enrolled (full-time): 40. Enrolled (part-time): 2. Average GMAT: 520. Average undergraduate GPA: 3.2. GMAT section weighed most heavily: slightly more placed on Quantitative.
Placement: School has placement office.

SOUTHERN ILLINOIS UNIVERSITY—EDWARDSVILLE

School of Business
Box 1086
Edwardsville, IL 62026-1086
Phone: (618) 650-3840
Fax: (618) 650-3979
E-mail: fmarti@siue.edu
http://www.siue.edu
Student Body: Full-time enrollment: 40. Men: 55%. Women: 45%. African American: 3%. International: 25%. Average age: 33. Students living on campus: 25%. Part-time enrollment: 169. Men: 55%. Women: 45%.
Academics: Full-time faculty: 53. Part-time faculty: 15. Degrees awarded: M.B.A., M.S. Acc., M.M.R. Joint degree programs: M.A./M.S., M.S. in C.I.S. Evening program is offered.
Finances: Tuition (1998–99): In-State: $1,365. Out-of-State: $3,635. Estimated tuition (1999–2000): In-State: $1,607. Out-of-State: $3,895.
Admission Requirements: GMAT is required. Application deadline for fall: July 25.
Selectivity: Applications received (full-time): 11. Admitted: 5. Enrolled: 4. Applications received (part-time): 102. Admitted: 43. Enrolled: 24. Average GMAT: 510. Average undergraduate GPA: 3.5. GMAT section weighed most heavily: weighed equally.
Placement: School has placement office.

UNIVERSITY OF CHICAGO

Graduate School of Business
1101 E. 58th Street
Chicago, IL 60637
Phone: (773) 702-7369
Fax: (773) 702-9085
E-mail: admissions@gsb.uchicago.edu
http://gsbwww.uchicago.edu
Student Body: Full-time enrollment: 1,151.
Men: 79%. Women: 21%. Average age:
28. Part-time enrollment: 1,847. Men:
73%. Women: 27%.
Academics: Full-time faculty: 123. Part-time
faculty: 53. Degrees awarded: M.B.A., Intl.
M.B.A., Ph.D. Joint degree programs:
M.B.A./A.M., M.B.A./S.M.,
M.B.A./M.D., M.B.A./J.D.,
M.B.A./M.P.P. Evening program is offered.
For fall 1996 entering class: 96% complet-
ed program within 2 years. 2% continued
towards degree.
Finances: Tuition (1998–99): $26,578.
Average student debt incurred by gradua-
tion: $70,000.
Admission Requirements: GMAT is required.
Application deadline for fall: March 1.
Selectivity: Applications received (full-time):
3,517. Admitted: 835. Enrolled: 518.
Average GMAT: 690. Average undergradu-
ate GPA: 3.4. GMAT section weighed most
heavily: weighed equally.
Placement: School has placement office.
Placement rate at time of graduation: 95%.
Placement rate 6 months after graduation:
99%. Average starting salary: $79,854.

UNIVERSITY OF ILLINOIS— CHICAGO

College of Business Administration
UIC, MBA Programs (MIC 077)
817 W. Van Buren Street, Suite 220
Chicago, IL 60607-3525
Phone: (312) 996-4573
Fax: (312) 413-0338
E-mail: mba@uic.edu
http://www.uic.edu/cba/mba
Student Body: Full-time enrollment: 98.
Men: 45%. Women: 55%.

Minorities: 10%. International: 57%.
Average age: 27. Students living on cam-
pus: 10%. Part-time enrollment: 283. Men:
35%. Women: 65%.
Academics: Full-time faculty: 67. Part-time
faculty: 33. Degrees awarded: M.B.A.,
Ph.D., M.S.A., M.S. Acc., M.S.M.I.S.,
M.S. Econ. Joint degree programs:
M.B.A./M.S.A., M.B.A./M.S. Nursing,
M.B.A./M.A. Econ., M.B.A./M.P.H.
Evening program is offered. For fall 1996
entering class: 95% completed program
within 2 years.
Finances: Tuition (1998–99): In-State:
$10,116. Out-of-State: $16,752.
Estimated tuition (1999–2000): In-State:
$10,222. Out-of-State: $17,089.
Admission Requirements: GMAT is required.
Application deadline for fall: June 1.
Selectivity: Applications received (full-time):
260. Admitted: 150. Enrolled: 58.
Applications received (part-time): 130.
Admitted: 80. Enrolled: 54. Average
GMAT: 560. Average undergraduate GPA:
4.3. GMAT section weighed most heavily:
weighed equally.
Placement: School has placement office.
Placement rate at time of graduation: 47%.
Placement rate 6 months after graduation:
98%. Average starting salary: $57,102.

UNIVERSITY OF ILLINOIS— URBANA-CHAMPAIGN

College of Commerce & Business
Administration
MBA Program
410 David Kinley Hall
1407 West Gregory Drive
Champaign, IL 61801
Phone: (217) 244-7602
(800) MBA-UIUC
Fax: (217) 333-1156
E-mail: mba@uiuc.edu
http://www.mba.uiuc.edu/
Student Body: Full-time enrollment: 519.
Men: 70% Women: 30% African
American: 8%. Asian American: 8%. Latino:
3%. International: 43%. Average age: 27.

Academics: Full-time faculty: 149. Part-time
faculty: 7. Degrees awarded: M.B.A. Joint
degree programs: Architecture, Engineering,
Computer Science, Education, Journalism,
Law, Medicine. Evening program is not
offered. For fall 1996 entering class: 89%
completed program within 2 years.
Finances: Tuition (1998–99): In-State:
$11,278. Out-of-State: $18,288.
Estimated tuition (1999–2000): In-State:
$11,842. Out-of-State: $19,202. 80% of
students receive need-based aid. 35% of
students receive merit-based aid. Average
student debt incurred by graduation:
$21,000.
Admission Requirements: GMAT is
required. Application deadline for fall: April
1 (domestic), February 1 (international).
Selectivity: Applications received (full-time):
1,081. Admitted: 515. Enrolled: 195.
Average GMAT: 612. Average undergraduate GPA: 3.3. GMAT section weighed most
heavily: Quantitative.
Placement: School has placement office.
Placement rate at time of graduation: 80%.
Placement rate 6 months after graduation:
97%. Average starting salary: $61,524.

WESTERN ILLINOIS UNIVERSITY

College of Business & Technology
School of Graduate Studies
1 University Circle
Macomb, IL 61455
Phone: (309) 298-1806
Fax: (309) 298-2245
E-mail: Grad_Office@ccmail.wiu.edu
http://www.wiu.edu
Student Body: Full-time enrollment: 67.
Men: 64%. Women: 36%. Asian
American: 10%. Latino: 1%. International:
27%. Average age: 24.3. Students living
on campus: 50%. Part-time enrollment: 37.
Men: 78%. Women: 22%.
Academics: Full-time faculty: 34. Degrees
awarded: M.B.A. Evening program is
offered.
Finances: Tuition (1998–99): In-State:
$1,624. Out-of-State: $3,928.
Admission Requirements: GMAT is required.
Application deadline for fall: July 31.

Selectivity: Applications received (full-time): 165. Admitted: 98. Enrolled: 60. Applications received (part-time): 40. Admitted: 38. Enrolled: 25. Average GMAT: 538. Average undergraduate GPA: 3.5. GMAT section weighed most heavily: weighed equally.

Placement: School has placement office.

Indiana

BALL STATE UNIVERSITY

College of Business
Graduate Business Programs
WB 146
Muncie, IN 47306
Phone: (765) 285-1931
Fax: (765) 285-8818
E-mail: bsumba.bsuvc@bsu.edu
http://www.bsu.edu/business
Student Body: Full-time enrollment: 23. Part-time enrollment: 66.
Academics: Full-time faculty: 81. Part-time faculty: 8. Degrees awarded: M.B.A. Evening program is offered.
Finances: Tuition (1998–99): $5,200.
Admission Requirements: GMAT is required. Application deadline for fall: July 31.
Selectivity: Enrolled (full-time): 14. Enrolled (part-time): 28. Average GMAT: 536. Average undergraduate GPA: 3.1. GMAT section weighed most heavily: weighed equally.
Placement: School has placement office.

INDIANA STATE UNIVERSITY

School of Business
M.B.A. Office
Terre Haute, IN 47809
Phone: (812) 237-2002
Fax: (812) 237-8720
E-mail: mba@indstate.edu
http://web.indstate.edu/schbus/mba.html
Student Body: Full-time enrollment: 15. Men: 67%. Women: 33%. International:

53%. Average age: 28. Part-time enrollment: 125. Men: 60%. Women: 40%.
Academics: Full-time faculty: 30. Part-time faculty: 2. Degrees awarded: M.B.A. Evening program is not offered.
Finances: Tuition (1998–99): In-State: $144/credit. Out-of-State: $325/credit. Estimated tuition (1999–2000): In-State: $157/credit. Out-of-State: $340/credit. 17% of students receive some type of aid.
Admission Requirements: GMAT is required. Application deadline for fall: April.
Selectivity: Applications received (full-time): 35. Admitted: 15. Enrolled: 10. Applications received (part-time): 72. Admitted: 50. Enrolled: 45. Average GMAT: 490. Average undergraduate GPA: 2.9. GMAT section weighed most heavily: weighed equally.
Placement: School has placement office.

INDIANA UNIVERSITY— BLOOMINGTON

Kelley School of Business
1309 E 10th Street, Room 254
Bloomington, IN 47405-1701
Phone: (812) 855-8006
Fax: (812) 855-9039
E-mail: mbaoffice@indiana.edu
http://www.bus.indiana.edu/mba
Student Body: Full-time enrollment: 548. Men: 72%. Women: 28%. African American: 6%. Asian American: 10%. Latino: 5%. International: 20%. Average age: 28. Students living on campus: 10%.
Academics: Full-time faculty: 110. Part-time faculty: 39 Degrees awarded: M.B.A. Joint degree programs: M.B.A./J.D., M.B.A./M.A. Evening program is not offered. For fall 1996 entering class: 98% completed program within 2 years. 1% continued towards degree.
Finances: Tuition (1998–99): In-State: $8,775. Out-of-State: $17,013. 35% of students receive non-need-based aid. 78% of students receive need-based aid. Average student debt incurred by graduation: $35,906.

Admission Requirements: GMAT is required. Application deadline for fall: (domestic) December 1, January 15, March 1; (international) December 1, February 1, March 1.
Selectivity: Applications received (full-time): 1,638. Admitted: 659. Enrolled: 294. Average GMAT: 630. Average undergraduate GPA: 3.3. GMAT section weighed most heavily: weighed equally.
Placement: School has placement office. Placement rate at time of graduation: 85%. Placement rate 6 months after graduation: 98%. Average starting salary: $71,300.

INDIANA UNIVERSITY— NORTHWEST*

Division of Business and Economics
3400 Broadway
Gary, IN 46408
Phone: (219) 980-6821
Student Body: Full-time enrollment: 9. Men: 56%. Women: 44%. International: %. Part-time enrollment: 262. Men: 71%. Women: 29%.
Academics: Full-time faculty: 21. Part-time faculty: 2. Degrees awarded: M.B.A., M. Acc. Evening program is offered.
Finances: Tuition (1998–99): $132.50 per credit hour.
Admission Requirements: GMAT is required. Application deadline for fall: July 15, November 15, April 1.
Selectivity: Applications received (full-time): 46. Admitted: 37. Enrolled: 34. Average GMAT: 500. Average undergraduate GPA: 3.0.
Placement: School has placement office.

INDIANA UNIVERSITY— PURDUE UNIVERSITY AT FORT WAYNE*

School of Business & Management Sciences
Neff Hall Suite 330
Fort Wayne, IN 46805-1499
Phone: (219) 481-6498
Student Body: Full-time enrollment: 13.
Men: 62%. Women: 38%. International:
15%. Part-time enrollment: 168. Men: 74%.
Women: 26%.
Academics: Full-time faculty: 27. Degrees
awarded: M.B.A.
Admission Requirements: GMAT is required.
Application deadline for fall: July 1.
Selectivity: Applications received (full-time):
92. Admitted: 72. Average GMAT: 550.
Average undergraduate GPA: 3.0.
Placement: School has placement office.

INDIANA UNIVERSITY— PURDUE UNIVERSITY AT INDIANAPOLIS

Kelley School of Business
801 W. Michigan Street, BS 3028
Indianapolis, IN 46202-5151
Phone: (317) 274-4895
Fax: (317) 274-2483
E-mail: mbaindy@iupui.edu
http://www.iupui.edu/~business/mba
Student Body: Part-time enrollment: 312.
Men: 73%. Women: 27%.
Academics: Full-time faculty: 30. Degrees
awarded: M.B.A., M.P.A. Joint degree pro-
grams: M.B.A./J.D. Evening program is
offered.
Finances: Tuition (1998–99): In-State:
$239/credit hour. Out-of-State:
$477/credit hour.
Admission Requirements: GMAT is required.
Application deadline for fall: May 1.
Selectivity: Applications received (part-time):
123. Admitted: 72. Enrolled: 60. Average
GMAT: 618. Average undergraduate GPA:
3.2.
Placement: School has placement office.

INDIANA UNIVERSITY— SOUTH BEND*

Division of Business and Economics
1700 Mishawaka Avenue
P.O. Box 7111
South Bend, IN 46634
Phone: (219) 237-4138
Fax: (219) 237-4866
Student Body: Full-time enrollment: 46.
Men: 61%. Women: 39%. International:
152%. Average age: 29. Part-time enroll-
ment: 242. Men: 29%. Women: 71%.
Academics: Full-time faculty: 31. Part-time
faculty: 5. Degrees awarded: M.B.A.
Evening program is offered.
Finances: Estimated tuition (1999–2000):
In-State: $145.75 per credit hour. Out-of-
State: $346.40 per credit hour.
Admission Requirements: GMAT is
required. Application deadline for fall:
July 1, November 1, April 1.
Selectivity: Applications received (full-time):
65. Admitted: 60. Enrolled: 53. Average
GMAT: 513. Average undergraduate GPA:
2.9.
Placement: School has placement office.

PURDUE UNIVERSITY

Krannert Graduate
School of Management
1310 Krannert Center
West Lafayette, IN 47907-1310
Phone: (765) 494-4365
Fax: (765) 494-9481
E-mail: Krannert_ms@mgmt.purdue.edu
http://www.mgmt.purdue.edu
Student Body: Full-time enrollment: 320.
Men: 73%. Women: 27%. African
American: 6%. Asian American: 8%. Latino:
2%. International: 37%. Average age: 27.
Academics: Full-time faculty: 46. Degrees
awarded: M.B.A., M.S.M., M.S.I.A.,
M.S.H.R.M. Evening program is not
offered. For fall 1996 entering class: 99%
completed program within 2 years. 1% con-
tinued towards degree.
Finances: Tuition (1998–99): In-State:
$7,176. Out-of-State: $15,424. Estimated

tuition (1999–2000): In-State: $8,535.
Out-of-State: $17,195. Average student
debt incurred by graduation: $19,677.
Admission Requirements: GMAT is
required. Application deadline for fall: May
1 (domestic), February 1 (international).
Selectivity: Applications received (full-time):
1,450. Admitted: 415. Enrolled: 171.
Average GMAT: 623. Average undergraduate GPA: 3.3.
Placement: School has placement office.
Placement rate at time of graduation:
97.5%. Placement rate 6 months after graduation: 100%. Average starting salary:
$74,881.

UNIVERSITY OF NOTRE DAME

College of Business Administration
276 College of Business Adminstration
P.O. Box 399
Notre Dame, IN 46556-0399
Phone: (219) 631-8488,
(800) 631-8488
Fax: (219) 631-8800
E-mail: mba.1@nd.edu
http://www.nd.edu/~mba
Student Body: Full-time enrollment: 283.
Men: 72%. Women: 28%. African
American: 3%. Asian American: 2%. Latino:
6%. International: 25%. Average age: 26.
Students living on campus: 25%.
Academics: Full-time faculty: 60. Part-time
faculty: 8. Degrees awarded: M.B.A. Joint
degree programs: M.B.A./J.D.,
M.B.A/Engineering (Notre Dame UG only),
M.B.A./Science (Notre Dame UG only).
Evening program is not offered. For fall
1996 entering class: 95% completed program within 2 years. 1% continued towards
degree.
Finances: Tuition (1998–99): $21,500 +
fees. Estimated tuition (1999–2000):
$22,575 + fees. 79% of students receive
some type of aid. Average student debt
incurred by graduation: $25,066.
Admission Requirements: GMAT is
required. Application deadline for fall: Mar.
6 (1 yr.), Apr. 16 (2 yr.).
Selectivity: Applications received (full-time):
417. Admitted: 243. Enrolled: 121.

Average GMAT: 613. Average undergraduate GPA: 3.2. GMAT section weighed most heavily: slightly greater emphasis is placed on Quantitative.

Placement: School has placement office. Placement rate at time of graduation: 74%. Placement rate 6 months after graduation: 94%. Average starting salary: $60,079.

IOWA

DRAKE UNIVERSITY

College of Business &
Public Administration
2507 University Avenue
Des Moines, IA 50311
Phone: (515) 271-2188
Fax: (515) 271-4518
E-mail: nancy.gabriel@drake.edu
http://www.drake.edu/cbpa
Student Body: Full-time enrollment: 36. Men: 47%. Women: 53%. Part-time enrollment: 276. Men: 69%. Women: 31%.
Academics: Full-time faculty: 30. Degrees awarded: M.B.A. Joint degree programs: M.B.A./J.D., M.B.A./Pharm. D. Evening program is offered. For fall 1996 entering class: 75% completed program within 2 years. 25% continued towards degree.
Admission Requirements: GMAT is required. Application deadline for fall: six weeks before term.
Selectivity: Applications received (full-time): 27. Admitted: 25. Enrolled: 12. Applications received (part-time): 25. Admitted: 22. Enrolled: 19. Average GMAT: 520. Average undergraduate GPA: 3.3.
Placement: School has placement office.

IOWA STATE UNIVERSITY

College of Business
Graduate Programs Office
218 Carver Hall
Ames, IA 50011-2063
Phone: (515) 294-8118
Fax: (515) 294-2446
E-mail: busgrad@iastate.edu
http://www.bus.iastate.edu/grad
Student Body: Full-time enrollment: 96. Men: 58%. Women: 42%. African American: 1%. Asian American: 1%. International: 47%. Average age: 26. Part-time enrollment: 120. Men: 71%. Women: 29%.
Academics: Full-time faculty: 58. Degrees awarded: M.B.A., M.S. Evening program is offered. For fall 1996 entering class: 71% completed program within 2 years. 9% continued towards degree.
Finances: Tuition (1998–99): In-State: $3,374. Out-of-State: $9,532. Estimated tuition (1999–2000): In-State: $3,509. Out-of-State: $9,913.
Admission Requirements: GMAT is required. Application deadline for fall: May 1.
Selectivity: Applications received (full-time): 171. Admitted: 92. Enrolled: 42. Applications received (part-time): 63. Admitted: 53. Enrolled: 47. Average GMAT: 577. Average undergraduate GPA: 3.4. GMAT section weighed most heavily: weighed equally.
Placement: School has placement office. Placement rate at time of graduation: 76%. Placement rate 6 months after graduation: 97%. Average starting salary: $42,618.

UNIVERSITY OF IOWA

College of Business Administration School of Management
108 Pappajohn Business Administration Building
Suite C140
Iowa City, IA 52242-1000
Phone: (319) 335-1039
Fax: (319) 335-3604
E-mail: iowamba@uiowa.edu
http://www.biz.uiowa.edu/mba

Student Body: Full-time enrollment: 152. Men: 79%. Women: 21%. African American: 7%. Latino: 1%. International: 35%. Average age: 28. Students living on campus: 8%. Part-time enrollment: 631. Men: 65%. Women: 35%.
Academics: Full-time faculty: 88. Part-time faculty: 6. Degrees awarded: M.B.A. Joint degree programs: J.D./M.B.A., M.B.A./M.S.N., M.B.A./M.A. M.I.S., M.B.A./M.A. H.H.A., M.B.A./M.A. Library & Informational Science. Evening program is offered. For fall 1996 entering class: 89% completed program within 2 years. 2% continued towards degree.
Finances: Tuition (1998–99): In-State: $4,130. Out-of-State: $11,246. Estimated tuition (1999–2000): In-State: $4,337. Out-of-State: $11,808. Average student debt incurred by graduation: $19,983.
Admission Requirements: GMAT is required. Application deadline for fall: July 15 (domestic), April 15 (international).
Selectivity: Applications received (full-time): 662. Admitted: 188. Enrolled: 76. Applications received (part-time): 184. Admitted: 98. Enrolled: 95. Average GMAT: 613. Average undergraduate GPA: 3.2. GMAT section weighed most heavily: weighed equally.
Placement: School has placement office. Placement rate at time of graduation: 94%. Placement rate 6 months after graduation: 100%. Average starting salary: $61,847.

Kansas

KANSAS STATE UNIVERSITY

College of Business Administration
110 Calvin Hall
Manhattan, KS 66506
Phone: (785) 532-7190
Fax: (913) 532-7216
E-mail: flynn@ksu.edu
http://www.ksu.edu
Student Body: Full-time enrollment: 111. Men: 56%. Women: 44%. African American: 3%. Asian American: 10%.

Latino: 2%. International: 23%. Part-time enrollment: 21. Men: 48%. Women: 52%.
Academics: Full-time faculty: 32. Part-time faculty: 8. Degrees awarded: M.B.A., M. Acc. Evening program is offered. For fall 1996 entering class: 81% completed program within 2 years. 19% continued towards degree.
Finances: Tuition (1998–99): In-State: $162/per credit hour. Out-of-State: $385/credit hour.
Admission Requirements: GMAT is required. Application deadline for fall: June 1.
Selectivity: Enrolled (full-time): 248. Enrolled (part-time): 4. Average GMAT: 546. Average undergraduate GPA: 3.5. GMAT section weighed most heavily: weighed equally.
Placement: School has placement office. Placement rate at time of graduation: 85%. Average starting salary: $47,800.

UNIVERSITY OF KANSAS

School of Business
206 Summerfield Hall
Lawrence, KS 66045
Phone: (785) 864-4254
Fax: (785) 864-5328
E-mail: dcollins@bschool.wpo.ukans.edu
http://www.bschool.ukans.edu/
Student Body: Full-time enrollment: 146. Men: 71%. Women: 29%. African American: 3%. Asian American: 2%. Latino: 1%. International: 17%. Average age: 27. Students living on campus: 20%. Part-time enrollment: 301. Men: 71%. Women: 29%.
Academics: Full-time faculty: 58. Part-time faculty: 6. Degrees awarded: M.B.A., M.S., M.A.I.S. Joint degree programs: M.B.A./J.D., M.B.A./Ph.D. Nursing. Evening program is offered. For fall 1996 entering class: 62% completed program within 2 years. 28% continued towards degree.
Finances: Tuition (1998–99): In-State: $101/credit. Out-of-State: $330/credit. Estimated tuition (1999–2000): In-State: $105/credit. Out-of-State: $335/credit. 50% of students receive some type of aid.

Admission Requirements: GMAT is required. Application deadline for fall: May 1.
Selectivity: Applications received (full-time): 154. Admitted: 85. Enrolled: 45. Applications received (part-time): 94. Admitted: 63. Enrolled: 59. Average GMAT: 612. Average undergraduate GPA: 3.2. GMAT section weighed most heavily: weighed equally.
Placement: School has placement office. Placement rate at time of graduation: 64%. Placement rate 6 months after graduation: 90%. Average starting salary: $54,500.

WICHITA STATE UNIVERSITY

W. Frank Barton School of Business
Graduate Studies in Business
Box 48
Wichita, KS 67260-0048
Phone: (316) 978-3230
Fax: (316) 978-3767
E-mail: harpool@twsuvm.uc.twsu.edu
http://www.twsu.edu/~bsbwww/
Student Body: Full-time enrollment: 138. Men: 66%. Women: 34%. Average age: 25. Students living on campus: 25%. Part-time enrollment: 443. Men: 71%. Women: 29%.
Academics: Full-time faculty: 52. Part-time faculty: 10. Degrees awarded: M.B.A., M.A., M.S., E.M.B.A. Joint degree programs: M.S.N./M.B.A. Evening program is offered.
Admission Requirements: GMAT is required. Application deadline for fall: July 1.
Selectivity: Average GMAT: 508. Average undergraduate GPA: 3.2. GMAT section weighed most heavily: weighed equally.
Placement: School has placement office. Average starting salary: $37,000.

Kentucky

MURRAY STATE UNIVERSITY

College of Business & Public Affairs
University Station
P.O. Box 9
Murray, KY 42071
Phone: (502) 762-6970
Fax: (502) 762-3482
E-mail: ladonna.mccuan@murraystate.edu
http://www.murraystate.edu
Student Body: Full-time enrollment: 72. Men: 56%. Women: 44%. International: 46%. Part-time enrollment: 99. Men: 53%. Women: 47%.
Academics: Full-time faculty: 60. Part-time faculty: 13. Degrees awarded: M.B.A., M.S., M.P.A. Evening program is offered.
Finances: Tuition (1998–99): In-State: $2,500. Out-of-State: $6,740.
Admission Requirements: GMAT is required. Application deadline for fall: July 15, December 15.
Selectivity: Applications received (full-time): 57. Admitted: 46. Enrolled: 19. Applications received (part-time): 75. Admitted: 57. Enrolled: 25. Average GMAT: 500. Average undergraduate GPA: 3.1.
Placement: School has placement office.

UNIVERSITY OF KENTUCKY

Carol Martin Gatton College of Business and Economics
237 Gatton College of Business & Economics
Lexington, KY 40506-0034
Phone: (606) 257-3592
Fax: (606) 257-3293
E-mail: drball01@pop.uky.edu
http://www.gatton.gws.uky.edu
Student Body: Full-time enrollment: 149. Men: 68%. Women: 32%. African American: 11%. International: 19%. Average age: 25. Part-time enrollment: 111. Men: 78%. Women: 22%.
Academics: Full-time faculty: 77. Part-time faculty: 4. Degrees awarded: M.B.A., M.S.,

Ph.D. Joint degree programs: J.D./M.B.A., M.B.A./M.D., M.B.A./Pharm.D., M.B.A./B.S. Eng. Evening program is offered. For fall 1996 entering class: 81% completed program within 2 years. 9% continued towards degree.
Finances: Tuition (1998–99): In-State: $3,276. Out-of-State: $9,156. 11% of students receive non-need-based aid.
Admission Requirements: GMAT is required. Application deadline for fall: July 15.
Selectivity: Applications received (full-time): 163. Admitted: 86. Enrolled: 66. Applications received (part-time): 52. Admitted: 33. Enrolled: 31. Average GMAT: 599. Average undergraduate GPA: 3.2. GMAT section weighed most heavily: weighed equally.
Placement: School has placement office. Placement rate at time of graduation: 65%. Average starting salary: $46,110.

UNIVERSITY OF LOUISVILLE

College of Business and Public Administration
Department AO
Louisville, KY 40292
Phone: (502) 852-7439
Fax: (502) 852-6256
http://www.louisville.edu
Student Body: Full-time enrollment: 223. Men: 61%. Women: 39%. Average age: 32. Part-time enrollment: 429. Men: 58%. Women: 42%.
Academics: Degrees awarded: M.B.A. Joint degree programs: J.D./M.B.A., M.B.A./Eng. Evening program is offered.
Finances: Tuition (1998–99): In-State: $3,180. Out-of-State: $9,060.
Admission Requirements: GMAT is required. Application deadline for fall: June 1.
Selectivity: Applications received (full-time): 80. Admitted: 43. Enrolled: 35. Applications received (part-time): 155, Admitted: 84. Enrolled: 67. Average GMAT: 550. Average undergraduate GPA: 3.3. GMAT section weighed most heavily: weighed equally.
Placement: School has placement office.

Louisiana

LOUISIANA STATE UNIVERSITY AND A&M COLLEGE

E.J. Ourso College of Business Administration
Baton Rouge, LA 70803
Phone: (504) 388 5059
Fax: (504) 388-5256
E-mail: busmba@lsu.edu
http://www.bus.lsu.edu
Student Body: Full-time enrollment: 230. Men: 67%. Women: 33%. International: 4%. Part-time enrollment: 110. Men: 68%. Women: 32%. Average age: 25.5. Students living on campus: 15%.
Academics: Full-time faculty: 80. Part-time faculty: 23. Degrees awarded: M.B.A. Evening program is offered. For fall 1996 entering class: 79% completed program within 2 years. 10% continued towards degree.
Finances: Estimated tuition (1999–2000): In-state: $2,726. Out-of-State: $6,010.
Admission Requirements: GMAT is required. Application deadline for fall: May 15.
Selectivity: Applications received (full-time): 278. Admitted: 86. Enrolled: 62. Applications received (part-time): 47. Admitted: 41 Enrolled: 37. Average GMAT: 599. Average undergraduate GPA: 3.3.
Placement: School has placement office. Placement rate at time of graduation: 86%. Average starting salary: $48,200.

LOUISIANA STATE UNIVERSITY IN SHREVEPORT

College of Business Administration
One University Place
Shreveport, LA 71115
Phone: (318) 797-5276
Fax: (318) 797-5127
E-mail: lkrajews@pilot.lsus.edu
http://lsus.edu
Student Body: Full-time enrollment: 25. International: 12%. Average age: 28. Part-

time enrollment: 110. Men: 55%. Women: 45%.
Academics: Full-time faculty: 25. Degrees awarded: M.B.A. Evening program is offered.
Finances: Tuition (1998–99): In-State: $350 per 3-credit course. Out-of-State: $840 per 3-credit course.
Admission Requirements: GMAT is required. Application deadline for fall: June.
Selectivity: Average GMAT: 480. Average undergraduate GPA: 2.8. GMAT section weighed most heavily: weighed equally.
Placement: School has placement office. Placement rate at time of graduation: 95%. Placement rate 6 months after graduation: 97%. Average starting salary: $45,000.

LOUISIANA TECH UNIVERSITY

College of Administration and Business
The Graduate School
P.O. Box 7923
Ruston, LA 71272
Phone: (318) 257-2921
Fax: (318) 257-4487
E-mail: gschool@latech.edu
http://www.latech.edu
Student Body: Full-time enrollment: 65. Men: 58%. Women: 42%. African American: 8%. Asian American: 2%. Latino: 2%. International: 43%. Average age: 25. Part-time enrollment: 19. Men: 53%. Women: 47%.
Academics: Full-time faculty: 28. Degrees awarded: M.B.A., M.P.A., D.B.A. Evening program is offered. For fall 1996 entering class: 85% completed program within 2 years.
Finances: Tuition (1998–99): In-State: $2,468 + $160. Out-of-State: $4,868 + $160. Estimated tuition (1999–2000): In-State: $2,468 + $160. Out-of-State: $4,868 + $160.
Admission Requirements: GMAT is required. Application deadline for fall: August 1 (domestic), June 1 (international).
Selectivity: Applications received (full-time): 94. Admitted: 87. Enrolled: 45. Applications received (part-time): 23. Admitted: 23. Enrolled: 23. Average

GMAT: 514. Average undergraduate GPA: 3.1. GMAT section weighed most heavily: weighed equally.

Placement: School has placement office.

LOYOLA UNIVERSITY NEW ORLEANS

Joseph A. Butt S.J. College of Business Administration
6363 St. Charles Avenue, Box 15
New Orleans, LA 70118
Phone: (504) 865-3544
Fax: (504) 865-3496
E-mail: mba@loyno.edu
http://www.cba.loyno.edu
Student Body: Full-time enrollment: 25. Men: 68%. Women: 32%. African American: 8%. Asian American: 2%. Latino: 7%. International: 4%. Average age: 28. Part-time enrollment: 119. Men: 66%. Women: 34%.
Academics: Full-time faculty: 21. Part-time faculty: 5. Degrees awarded: M.B.A., M.Q.M. (Master of Quality Management). Joint degree programs: J.D./M.B.A. Evening program is offered. For fall 1996 entering class: 87% completed program within 2 years. 13% continued towards degree.
Finances: Tuition (1998–99): $11,216. Estimated tuition (1999–2000): $11,768. 20% of students receive need-based aid. Average student debt incurred by graduation: $30,500.
Admission Requirements: GMAT is required. Application deadline for fall: November 30.
Selectivity: Applications received (full-time): 30. Admitted: 20. Enrolled: 12. Applications received (part-time): 13. Admitted: 11. Enrolled: 8. Average GMAT: 570. Average undergraduate GPA: 3.0. GMAT section weighed most heavily: Math.
Placement: School has placement office. Placement rate at time of graduation: 92%. Placement rate 6 months after graduation: 96%. Average starting salary: $51,000.

McNEESE STATE UNIVERSITY

College of Business
M.B.A. Program Office
Lake Charles, LA 70609
Phone: (318) 475-5576
Fax: (318) 475-5986
E-mail: mbaprog@mail.mcneese.edu
http://www.mcneese.edu
Student Body: Full-time enrollment: 21. Men: 62%. Women: 38%. Asian American: 14%. Latino: 10%. International: 48%. Average age: 26. Part-time enrollment: 66. Men: 45%. Women: 55%.
Academics: Full-time faculty: 24. Degrees awarded: M.B.A. Evening program is offered.
Finances: Tuition (1998–99): In-State: $2,000. Out-of-State: $5,200. Estimated tuition (1999–2000): In-State: $2,000. Out-of-State: $5,200.
Admission Requirements: GMAT is required. Application deadline for fall: June 30.
Selectivity: Enrolled (full-time): 8. Enrolled (part-time): 18. Average GMAT: 476. Average undergraduate GPA: 3.3. GMAT section weighed most heavily: weighed equally.
Placement: School has placement office. Placement rate at time of graduation: 95%. Placement rate 6 months after graduation: 100%.

NICHOLLS STATE UNIVERSITY

College of Business Administration
Admissions
P.O. Box 2004
Thibodaux, LA 70310
Phone: (504) 448-4507
Fax: (504) 448-4922
Student Body: Full-time enrollment: 35. Men: 54%. Women: 46%. Part-time enrollment: 84. Men: 61%. Women: 39%.
Academics: Full-time faculty: 31. Degrees awarded: M.B.A. Evening program is offered.
Finances: Tuition (1998–99): In-State: $2,003.50. Out-of-State: $4,608.50.
Admission Requirements: GMAT is required.

Selectivity: Average GMAT: 475. Average undergraduate GPA: 3.0. GMAT section weighed most heavily: weighed equally.
Placement: School has placement office.

NORTHEAST LOUISIANA UNIVERSITY

College of Business Administration
700 University Avenue
Monroe, LA 71209-0100
Phone: (318) 342-5252
E-mail: econeal@alpha.nlu.edu
http://www.nlu.edu
Student Body: Full-time enrollment: 58. Men: 53%. Women: 47%. International: 59%. Part-time enrollment: 20. Men: 75%. Women: 25%.
Academics: Full-time faculty: 35. Degrees awarded: M.B.A. Evening program is offered.
Finances: Tuition (1998–99): In-State: $2,028. Out-of-State: $6,852.
Admission Requirements: GMAT is required. Application deadline for fall: varies.
Selectivity: Applications received: 86. Admitted: 56. Enrolled: 45. Average GMAT: 510. Average undergraduate GPA: 3.1. GMAT section weighed most heavily: weighed equally.
Placement: School has placement office. Average starting salary: $27,500.

SOUTHEASTERN LOUISIANA UNIVERSITY

College of Business
SLU 735
Hammond, LA 70402
Phone: (504) 549-2146
Fax: (504) 549-5038
E-mail: bohara@selu.edu
Student Body: Full-time enrollment: 126. Men: 56%. Women: 44%. African American: 7%. Asian American: 23%. Latino: 4%. International: 33%. Average age: 27.2. Students living on campus: 3%. Part-time enrollment: 71. Men: 61%. Women: 39%.

Academics: Full-time faculty: 19. Part-time faculty: 1. Degrees awarded: M.B.A. Evening program is offered.
Finances: Tuition (1998–99): In-State: $2,400. Out-of-State: $5,000.
Admission Requirements: GMAT is required. Application deadline for fall: July 15.
Selectivity: Average GMAT: 475. Average undergraduate GPA: 3.4.
Placement: School has placement office.

TULANE UNIVERSITY

A.B. Freeman School of Business
7 McAlister Drive, Suite 400
New Orleans, LA 70118-5669
Phone: (504) 865-5410
(800) 223-5402
Fax: (504) 865-6770
E-mail: Freeman.Admissions@
Tulane.edu
http://freeman.tulane.edu
Student Body: Full-time enrollment: 195. Men: 75%. Women: 25%. African American: 3%. Asian American: 1%. Latino: 2%. International: 34%. Average age: 26. Students living on campus: 2%. Part-time enrollment: 185. Men: 69%. Women: 31%.
Academics: Full-time faculty: 53. Part-time faculty: 39. Degrees awarded: M.B.A., M. Acc. Joint degree programs: M.B.A./J.D., M.B.A./M.P.H., M.B.A./M.A. (Latin American Studies), M.B.A./B.A. or B.S. Evening program is offered. For fall 1996 entering class: 98% completed program within 2 years. 2% continued towards degree.
Finances: Tuition (1998–99): $23,304. Estimated tuition (1999–2000): $24,170. 42% of students receive fellowships. 60% receive assistantships. Average student debt incurred by graduation: $30,000.
Admission Requirements: GMAT is required. Application deadline for fall: May 1 (domestic), April 1 (international).
Selectivity: Applications received (full-time): 500. Admitted: 210. Enrolled: 104. Applications received (part-time): 58. Admitted: 41. Enrolled: 37. Average GMAT: 632. Average undergraduate GPA:

3.4. GMAT section weighed most heavily: depends on candidate.
Placement: School has placement office. Placement rate 6 months after graduation: 91%. Average starting salary: $59,550.

UNIVERSITY OF NEW ORLEANS

College of Business Administration
Lakefront
New Orleans, LA 70148
Phone: (504) 280-5494
Student Body: Full-time enrollment: 102. Men: 81%. Women: 19%. International: 18%. Average age: 32. Part-time enrollment: 453. Men: 69%. Women: 31%.
Academics: Full-time faculty: 81. Part-time faculty: 11. Degrees awarded: M.B.A. Evening program is offered.
Finances: Tuition (1998–99): In-State: $2,362. Out-of-State: $6,532. Estimated tuition (1999–2000): In-State: $2,362. Out-of-State: $7,500.
Admission Requirements: GMAT is required.
Selectivity: Applications received (full-time): 341. Admitted: 133. Enrolled: 120. Average GMAT: 512. Average undergraduate GPA: 3.0.
Placement: School has placement office. Placement rate 6 months after graduation: 95%. Average starting salary: $31,000.

Maine

UNIVERSITY OF MAINE

Maine Business School
5723 Donald P. Corbett
Business Building
Orono, ME 04469-5723
Phone: (207) 581-1973
Fax: (207) 581-1930
E-mail: MBA@maine.edu
http://www.main.edu/~gibson/umocba.html

Student Body: Full-time enrollment: 52. Men: 60%. Women: 40%. Asian American: 12%. Native American 4% International: 31%. Average age: 27. Students living on campus: 11%. Part-time enrollment: 45. Men: 76%. Women: 24%.
Academics: Full-time faculty: 17. Degrees awarded: M.B.A. Evening program is offered. For fall 1996 entering class: 83% completed program within 2 years. 11% continued towards degree.
Finances: Tuition (1998–99): In-State: $194/credit. Out-of-State: $548/credit. Plus $375/fees (for both)
Admission Requirements: GMAT is required. Application deadline for fall: July 15.
Selectivity: Applications received (full-time): 55. Admitted: 45. Enrolled: 29. Applications received (part-time): 14. Admitted: 13. Enrolled: 12. Average GMAT: 520. Average undergraduate GPA: 3.1. GMAT section weighed most heavily: weighed equally.
Placement: School has placement office.

Maryland

LOYOLA COLLEGE IN MARYLAND

Joseph A. Sellinger School of Business and Management
4501 North Charles Street
Baltimore, MD 21210
Phone: (410) 617-2407
Fax: (410) 617-2002
http://www.loyola.edu
Student Body: Full-time enrollment: 239. Men: 72%. Women: 28%. African American: 8%. Asian American: 2%. Latino: 1%. International: 6%. Average age: 35. Part-time enrollment: 786. Men: 64%. Women: 36%.
Academics: Full-time faculty: 49. Part-time faculty: 21. Degrees awarded: M.B.A., M.S.F., X.M.B.A. Evening program is offered. For fall 1996 entering class: 42%

completed program within 2 years. 49% continued towards degree.

Finances: Tuition (1998–99): M.B.A. and M.S.F.: $365/credit. X.M.B.A.: $18,450. M.B.A. Fellows program $11,633. 8% of students receive some type of aid. Average student debt incurred by graduation: $12,750.

Admission Requirements: GMAT is required. Application deadline for fall: July 20.

Selectivity: Applications received (full-time): 116. Admitted: 100. Enrolled: 89. Applications received (part-time): 331. Admitted: 286. Enrolled: 160. Average GMAT: 517. GMAT section weighed most heavily: weighed equally.

Placement: School has placement office. Average starting salary: $56,000.

UNIVERSITY OF BALTIMORE*

Robert G. Merrick School of Business
1420 N Charles St.
Baltimore, MD 21201
Phone: (410) 837-4809
Student Body: Full-time enrollment: 164. Men: 63%. Women: 37%. International: 7%. Part-time enrollment: 749. Men: 65%. Women: 35%.

Academics: Full-time faculty: 65. Part-time faculty: 16. Degrees awarded: M.B.A. Evening program is offered.

Finances: Tuition (1998–99): In-State: $2,022. Out-of-State: $2,697.

Admission Requirements: GMAT is required. Application deadline for fall: July 15.

Selectivity: Applications received (full-time): 419. Admitted: 373. Enrolled: 265. Average GMAT: 502. Average undergraduate GPA: 3.0.

Placement: School has placement office.

UNIVERSITY OF MARYLAND— COLLEGE PARK

The Robert H. Smith School of Business
M.B.A./M.S. Admissions
2308 Van Munching Hall
College Park, MD 20742

Phone: (301) 405-2278
Fax: (301) 314-9862
E-mail: mba_info@rhsmith.umd.edu
http://www.rhsmith.umd.edu
Student Body: Full-time enrollment: 482. Men: 60%. Women: 40%. African American: 5%. Asian American: 5%. Latino: 3%. International: 31%. Average age: 27. Students living on campus: 5%. Part-time enrollment: 385. Men: 70%. Women: 30%.

Academics: Full-time faculty: 85. Part-time faculty: 20. Degrees awarded: M.B.A., M.S. Joint degree programs: M.B.A./M.S.W., M.B.A./M.S., M.B.A./J.D., M.B.A./M.P.M. Evening program is offered.

Finances: Tuition (1998–99): In-State: $9,818. Out-of-State: $14,048. Estimated tuition (1999–2000): In-State: $10,745. Out-of-State: $15,371. 30% of students receive non-need-based aid. Average student debt incurred by graduation: $19,200.

Admission Requirements: GMAT is required. Application deadline for fall: April 15, February 15.

Selectivity: Applications received (full-time): 1,515. Admitted: 372. Enrolled: 198. Applications received (part-time): 426. Admitted: 182. Enrolled: 114. Average GMAT: 653. Average undergraduate GPA: 3.4. GMAT section weighed most heavily: weighed equally.

Placement: School has placement office. Placement rate at time of graduation: 90%. Placement rate 6 months after graduation: 100%. Average starting salary: $62,828.

Massachusetts

BABSON COLLEGE

F.W. Olin Graduate School
M.B.A. Admissions
Babson Park, MA 02457-0310
Phone: (781) 239-4317
Fax: (781) 239-4194
E-mail: mbaadmission@babson.edu
http://www.babson.edu/mba

Student Body: Full-time enrollment: 450. Men: 68%. Women: 32%. African American: 3%. Asian American: 6%. Latino: 2%. International: 23%. Average age: 28. Students living on campus: 30%. Part-time enrollment: 1,236. Men: 66%. Women: 34%.

Academics: Full-time faculty: 155. Part-time faculty: 21. Degrees awarded: M.B.A. Evening program is offered. For fall 1996 entering class: 98% completed program within 2 years. 2% continued towards degree.

Finances: Tuition (1998–99): $22,600. 22% of students receive non-need-based aid. 37% of students receive need-based aid. Average student debt incurred by graduation: $32,640.

Admission Requirements: GMAT is required. Application deadlines: January 15, March 1, April 15 (two year).

Selectivity: Applications received (full-time): 871. Admitted: 362. Enrolled: 163. Applications received (part-time): 383. Admitted: 322. Enrolled: 238. Average GMAT: 634. Average undergraduate GPA: 3.1. GMAT section weighed most heavily: weighed equally.

Placement: School has placement office. Placement rate at time of graduation: 80%. Placement rate 3 months after graduation: 92%. Average starting salary: $68,400.

BENTLEY COLLEGE

Bentley College Graduate School of Business
175 Forest Street
Waltham, MA 02154-4705
Phone: (781) 891-2108
Fax: (781) 891-2464
E-mail: gradadm@bentley.edu
http://www.Bentley.edu
Student Body: Full-time enrollment: 278. Men: 51%. Women: 49%. African American: 2%. Asian American: 3%. Latino: 3%. Average Age: 31. International: 57%. Students living on campus: 24%. Part-time enrollment: 1,311. Men: 56%. Women: 44%.

Academics: Full-time faculty: 38. Part-time faculty: 324. Degrees awarded: M.B.A., M.S.C.I.S., M.S.F., M.S.T., M.S.P.F.P. Information Age M.B.A. Self-paced M.B.A. Evening program is offered.
Finances: Tuition (1998–99): $2,050. Tuition (I.A.M.B.A.): $22,000. 17% of students receive some type of aid.
Admission Requirements: GMAT is required. Application deadline for fall: June 1.
Selectivity: Applications received (full-time): 470. Admitted: 315. Enrolled: 125. Applications received (part-time): 371. Admitted: 299. Enrolled: 199. Average GMAT: 547. Average undergraduate GPA: 3.1. GMAT section weighed most heavily: weighed equally.
Placement: School has placement office. Placement rate 6 months after graduation: 90%. Average starting salary: $55,000

BOSTON COLLEGE

The Graduate School of the Wallace F. Carroll School of Management
140 Commonwealth Avenue
Fulton Hall 320
Chestnut Hill, MA 02467
Phone: (617) 552-3920
Fax: (617) 552-8078
http://www.bc.edu/mba
Student Body: Full-time enrollment: 192. Men: 68%. Women: 32%. Minority: 12%. International: 31%. Average age: 27. Part-time enrollment: 586. Men: 65%. Women: 35%.
Academics: Full-time faculty: 77. Part-time faculty: 8. Degrees awarded: M.B.A., M.S.F., Ph.D. Joint degree programs: M.B.A./J.D., M.B.A./M.S.W., M.B.A./M.S.N., M.B.A./M.S. Finance, M.B.A./M.S. Biology, M.B.A./Geology/Geophysics, M.B.A./M.A. Math, Slavic Languages, M.B.A./Russian Linguistics, M.B.A./Ph.D. Sociology, M.B.A./Diplome de formation (international through Robert Shuman University). Evening program is offered. For fall 1996 entering class: 45% completed program within 2 years. 5% continued towards degree.

Finances: Tuition (1998–99): $22,134. Estimated tuition (1999–2000): $22,134. 45% of students receive non-need-based aid.
Admission Requirements: GMAT is required. Application deadline for fall: March 1.
Selectivity: Applications received (full-time): 646. Admitted: 278. Enrolled: 96. Applications received (part-time): 388. Admitted: 263. Enrolled: 188. Average GMAT: 622. Average undergraduate GPA: 3.1. GMAT section weighed most heavily: Quantitative.
Placement: School has placement office. Placement rate at time of graduation: 42%. Placement rate 6 months after graduation: 92%. Average starting salary: $60,000.

BOSTON UNIVERSITY

Boston University School of Management
595 Commonwealth Avenue
Boston, MA 02215
Phone: (617) 353-2670
Fax: (617) 353-7368
E-mail: mba@bu.edu
http://management.bu.edu
Student Body: Full-time enrollment: 539. Men: 64%. Women: 36%. International: 46%. Average age: 28. Part-time enrollment: 612. Men: 60%. Women: 40%.
Academics: Full-time faculty: 105. Part-time faculty: 15. Degrees awarded: M.B.A., E.M.B.A., M.S., D.B.A. Joint degree programs: M.B.A./J.D., M.B.A./M.S. in Mgmt. Info. Sys., M.B.A./M.A. in Econ., M.B.A./M.P.H. in Health Services, M.B.A./M.A. Int'l. Rel., M.B.A./M.S. Manuf. Eng., M.B.A./M.S. T.V. Mgmt., M.B.A./M.S. in Medical Services, M.B.A./M.S. Public Health. Evening program is offered.
Finances: Tuition (1998–99): $22,830. 45% of students receive need-based aid. 36% of students receive non-need-based aid. Average student debt incurred by graduation: 38,500.
Admission Requirements: GMAT is required. Application deadline for fall: April 15.
Selectivity: Applications received (full-time): 1,166. Admitted: 515. Enrolled: 223. Applications received (part-time): 312.

Admitted: 220. Enrolled: 129. Average GMAT: 608. Average undergraduate GPA: 3.1. GMAT section weighed most heavily: weighed equally. (TOEFL is also important for international students.)
Placement: School has placement office. Placement rate at time of graduation: 80%. Placement rate 6 months after graduation: 94%. Average starting salary: $62,363.

CLARK UNIVERSITY

Graduate School of Management
950 Main Street
Worcester, MA 01610
Phone: (508) 793-7406
Fax: (508) 793-8822
E-mail: clarkmba@clarku.edu
http://www.mba.clarku.edu
Student Body: Full time enrollment: 115. Men: 64%. Women: 36%. International: 68%. Average age: 24. Students living on campus: 20%. Part-time enrollment: 168. Men: 55%. Women: 45%.
Academics: Full-time faculty: 18. Part-time faculty: 12. Degrees awarded: M.B.A., M.S.F. Joint degree programs: B.S./M.B.A. Evening program is offered.
Finances: Tuition (1998–99): $1,925 per course.
Admission Requirements: GMAT is required. Application deadline for fall: June 1.
Selectivity: Average GMAT: 560. Average undergraduate GPA: 3.2.
Placement: School has placement office. Placement rate at time of graduation: 76%. Placement rate 6 months after graduation: 97%. Average starting salary: $48,900.

HARVARD UNIVERSITY

Graduate School of Business Administration
Soldiers Field
Boston, MA 02163
Phone: (617) 495-6127
Fax: (617) 496-9272
E-mail: admissions@hbs.edu
http://www.hbs.edu

Student Body: Full-time enrollment: 1,801. Men: 70%. Women: 30%. Minorities: 18%. International: 26%. Average age: 27. **Academics:** Full-time faculty: 191. Degrees awarded: M.B.A., D.B.A. Joint degree programs: J.D./M.B.A. Evening program is not offered.
Finances: Tuition (1998–99): $26,260.
Admission Requirements: GMAT is required. Application deadline for fall: March 3, Nov. 10, Jan. 6.
Selectivity: Average GMAT: 689. Average undergraduate GPA: 3.5.
Placement: School has placement office. Placement rate 6 months after graduation: 99%. Average starting salary: $86,000.

MASSACHUSETTS INSTITUTE OF TECHNOLOGY

MIT Sloan School of Management
50 Memorial Drive, E52-126
Cambridge, MA 02142
Phone: (617) 253-3730
Fax: (617) 253-6405
E-mail: mbaadmissions@sloan.mit.edu
http://web.mit.edu/sloan/www/
Student Body: Full-time enrollment: 708. Men: 73%. Women: 27%. International: 37%. African American: 8%. Latino: 3%. Asian American: 8%. Average age: 28.
Academics: Full-time faculty: 89. Degrees awarded: M.B.A., M.S., Ph.D. Joint degree programs: Leaders for Manufacturing (L.F.M.), and System Design Manufacturing (S.D.M.). Evening program is not offered. For fall 1996 entering class: 100% completed program within 2 years.
Finances: Tuition (1998–99): $27,100. Estimated tuition (1999–2000): $27,100. 60% receive non-need-based aid.
Admission Requirements: GMAT is required. Application deadline for fall: February 14.
Selectivity: Applications received (full-time): 3,452. Admitted: 462. Enrolled: 358. Average GMAT: 690. Average undergraduate GPA: 3.5. GMAT section weighed most heavily: weighed equally.

Placement: School has placement office. Average starting salary: $80,000.

NORTHEASTERN UNIVERSITY

College of Business
474 Dodge Hall
Boston, MA 02115
Phone: (617) 373-5992
Fax: (617) 373-8564
E-mail: grba@cba.neu.edu
http://www.cba.neu.edu
Student Body: Full-time enrollment: 338. Men: 60%. Women: 40%. African American: 2%. Asian American: 2%. Latino: 1%. International: 31%. Average age: 26. Students living on campus: 15%. Part-time enrollment: 697. Men: 63%. Women: 37%.
Academics: Full-time faculty: 90. Part-time faculty: 40. Degrees awarded: M.S., M.B.A. Joint degree programs: M.S./M.B.A., J.D./M.B.A. Evening program is offered.
Finances: Tuition (1998–99): $500/credit. Full cost: $20,000. Estimated tuition (1999–2000): $500/credit. Full cost: $20,000. 60% of students receive non-need-based aid. 100% of students receive need-based aid.
Admission Requirements: GMAT is required. Application deadline for fall: rolling (45 days prior to start).
Selectivity: Applications received (full-time): 528. Admitted: 380. Enrolled: 201. Applications received (part-time): 335. Admitted: 262. Enrolled: 202. Average GMAT: 550. Average undergraduate GPA: 3.2. GMAT section weighed most heavily: varies with student.
Placement: School has placement office. Placement rate at time of graduation: 75%. Placement rate 6 months after graduation: 90%. Average starting salary: $57,000.

SUFFOLK UNIVERSITY

Sawyer School of Management
8 Ashburton Place
Boston, MA 02108-2770
Phone: (617) 573-8302
Fax: (617) 523-0116

E-mail: grad.admission@admin.suffolk.edu
http://www.suffolk.edu
Student Body: Full-time enrollment: 97. Men: 51%. Women: 49%. African American: 2%. Asian American: 3%. Latino: 1%. International: 60%. Average age: 25. Part-time enrollment: 541. Men: 56%. Women: 44%.
Academics: Full-time faculty: 62. Part-time faculty: 50. Degrees awarded: M.B.A., M.P.A., M.S.T., M.S.A., M.S.F., M.S.E.S., X.M.B.A., Accel. D.B.A. for Attorneys, M.H.A. Joint degree programs: M.B.A./J.D., M.P.A./J.D., M.S.F./J.D., M.P.A./C.J., M.P.A./M.A. Evening program is offered. For fall 1996 entering class: 69% completed program within 2 years. 7% continued towards degree.
Finances: Tuition (1998–99): $17,590. 21% of students receive some type of aid. Average student debt incurred by graduation: $14,300.
Admission Requirements: GMAT is required. Application deadline for fall: June 15, November 15.
Selectivity: Applications received (full-time): 172. Admitted: 134. Enrolled: 46. Applications received (part-time): 154. Admitted: 139. Enrolled: 115. Average GMAT: 500. Average undergraduate GPA: 3.1. GMAT section weighed most heavily: weighed equally.
Placement: School has placement office. Placement rate at time of graduation: 75%. Placement rate 6 months after graduation: 95%. Average starting salary: $40,500 (full–time), $50,700 (part–time).

UNIVERSITY OF MASSACHUSETTS—AMHERST

Isenberg School of Management
209 Isenberg School of Management
Amherst, MA 01003
Phone: (413) 545-5608
Fax: (413) 545-3858
E-mail: gradprog@som.umass.edu
http://www.som.umass.edu
Student Body: Full-time enrollment: 72. Men: 56%. Women: 44%. African

American: 3%. Asian American: 10%. International: 36%. Average age: 27. Students living on campus: 11%. Part-time enrollment: 237. Men: 56%. Women: 44%.

Academics: Full-time faculty: 56. Degrees awarded: M.B.A., P.M.B.A., M.S.A. Evening program is offered. For fall 1996 entering class: 88% completed program within 2 years. 6% continued towards degree.

Finances: Tuition (1998–99): In-State: $5,496. Out-of-State: $12,222. 94% of students receive some type of aid. Average student debt incurred by graduation: $18,965.

Admission Requirements: GMAT is required. Application deadline for fall: March 1.

Selectivity: Applications received (full-time): 230. Admitted: 59. Enrolled: 32. Applications received (part-time): 67. Admitted: 63. Enrolled: 56. Average GMAT: 602. Average undergraduate GPA: 3.3. GMAT section weighed most heavily: weighed equally.

Placement: School has placement office. Placement rate at time of graduation: 100%. Average starting salary: $60,879.

UNIVERSITY OF MASSACHUSETTS—LOWELL

College of Management
1 University Avenue
Pasteur Hall
Lowell, MA 01854-9985
Phone: (978) 934-2380
Fax: (978) 934-4058
E-mail: graduate_admissions@uml.edu
http://www.uml.edu/grad

Student Body: Full-time enrollment: 14. Men: 71%. Women: 29%. International: 86%. Average age: 28. Part-time enrollment: 287. Men: 70%. Women: 30%.

Academics: Full-time faculty: 31. Part-time faculty: 4. Degrees awarded: M.B.A., M.M.S. Evening program is offered.

Finances: Tuition (1998–99): In-State: $215/credit. Out-of-State: $431/credit.

Admission Requirements: GMAT is required. Application deadline for fall: July 15.

Selectivity: Average GMAT: 549. Average undergraduate GPA: 3.1. GMAT section weighed most heavily: weighed equally.

Placement: School has placement office. Average starting salary: $45,000.

MICHIGAN

CENTRAL MICHIGAN UNIVERSITY*

College of Business Administration
Graduate Business Studies
112 Grawn Hall
Mount Pleasant, MI 48859
Phone: (517) 774-3150
Fax: (517) 774-2372
E-mail: Pamela.Stambersky@cmich.edu

Student Body: Full-time enrollment: 208. Men: 55%. Women: 45%. International: 7%. Average age: 23. Part-time enrollment: 230. Men: 64%. Women: 36%.

Academics: Full-time faculty: 62. Part-time faculty: 0. Degrees awarded: M.B.A. Evening program is offered.

Finances: Tuition (1998–99): In-State: $4,562. Out-of-State: $8,564. Estimated tuition (1999–2000): In-State: $135.40 per credit hour. Out-of-State: $368.80 per credit hour.

Admission Requirements: GMAT is required. Application deadline for fall: July 1.

Selectivity: Applications received (full-time): 236. Admitted: 191. Enrolled: 95. Average GMAT: 513. Average undergraduate GPA: 3.2.

Placement: School has placement office.

EASTERN MICHIGAN UNIVERSITY

College of Business
Admissions Office
401 Pierce Hall
Ypsilanti, MI 48197
Phone: (734) 487-3060
Fax: (734) 487-1484
http://www.emich.edu

Student Body: Full-time enrollment: 199. Men: 52%. Women: 48%. Minority: 14%. International: 62%. Average age: 29. Part-time enrollment: 568. Men: 52%. Women: 48%.

Academics: Full-time faculty: 60. Part-time faculty: 1. Degrees awarded: M.B.A., M.S. Acc., M.S.I.S., M.S. Human Resources/Organizational Development. Evening program is offered.

Finances: Tuition (1998–99): In-State: $8,045. Out-of-State: $11,060.

Admission Requirements: GMAT is required. Application deadline for fall: May 15.

Selectivity: Applications received (full-time): 151. Admitted: 138. Enrolled: 69. Applications received (part-time): 429. Admitted: 391. Enrolled: 198. Average GMAT: 510. Average undergraduate GPA: 3.1. GMAT section weighed most heavily: weighed equally.

Placement: School has placement office.

MICHIGAN STATE UNIVERSITY

The Eli Broad Graduate School of Management
215 Eppley Center
East Lansing, MI 48824-1121
Phone: (517) 355-7604
Fax: (517) 353-1649
E-mail: mba@pilot.msu.edu
http://www.bus.msu.edu/mba

Student Body: Full-time enrollment: 303. Men: 72%. Women: 28%. African American: 4%. Asian American: 5%. Latino: 3%. International: 34%. Average age: 27. Students living on campus: 30%. Part-time enrollment: 154. Men: 78%. Women: 22%.

Academics: Full-time faculty: 104. Part-time faculty: 2. Degrees awarded: M.B.A., Ph.D., M.S., M.A. Joint degree programs: J.D./M.B.A. Evening program is not offered. For fall 1996 entering class: 97% completed program within 2 years. 1% continued towards degree.
Finances: Tuition (1998–99): In-State: $8,372. Out-of-State: $12,182. Estimated tuition (1999–2000): In-State: $8,625. Out-of-State: $12,550. 50% of students receive need-based aid. 45% of students receive non-need-based aid. Average student debt incurred by graduation: $27,028.
Admission Requirements: GMAT is required. Application deadline for fall: April 1.
Selectivity: Applications received (full-time): 713. Admitted: 194. Enrolled: 96. Applications received (part-time): 149. Admitted: 95. Enrolled: 85. Average GMAT: 628. Average undergraduate GPA: 3.3. GMAT section weighed most heavily: weighed equally.
Placement: School has placement office. Placement rate at time of graduation: 88%. Placement rate 6 months after graduation: 98%. Average starting salary: $63,862.

OAKLAND UNIVERSITY

School of Business Administration
520 O'Dowd Hall
Rochester, MI 48309-4401
Phone: (248) 370-3287
Fax: (248) 370-4275
E-mail: gbp@oak.oakland.edu
http://www.sba.oakland.edu/
Student Body: Full-time enrollment: 35. Men: 57%. Women: 43%. Asian American: 9%. Native American: 3%. International: 20%. Average age: 28. Part-time enrollment: 510. Men: 65%. Women: 35%.
Academics: Full-time faculty: 47. Part-time faculty: 40. Degrees awarded: M.B.A., M. Acc., P.M.C. Joint degree programs: B.A./M.B.A., B.A./M. Acc., B.A.-B.S./M.B.A., B.S./M. Acc. Evening program is offered. For fall 1996 entering class: 25% completed program within 2 years. 50% continued towards degree.

Finances: Tuition (1998–99): In-State: $214 per credit hour. Out-of-State: $474 per credit hour.
Admission Requirements: GMAT is required. Application deadline for fall: August 1.
Selectivity: Applications received (full-time): 44. Admitted: 28. Enrolled: 13. Applications received (part-time): 123. Admitted: 108. Enrolled: 69. Average GMAT: 530. Average undergraduate GPA: 3.1. GMAT section weighed most heavily: weighed equally.
Placement: School has placement office.

UNIVERSITY OF DETROIT MERCY

College of Business Administration
Bahaman Mirshab
P.O. Box 19900
Detroit, MI 48219-0900
Phone: (313) 993-1202
Fax: (313) 993-1052
E-mail: mirshabb@udmercy.edu
http://udmercy.edu
Student Body: Full-time enrollment: 113. Men: 65%. Women: 35%. African American: 12%. Asian American: 7%. Latino: 1%. Native American: 1%. Average Age: 30. International: 64%. Average age: 30. Part-time enrollment: 457. Men: 59%. Women: 41%.
Academics: Full-time faculty: 30. Part-time faculty: 25. Degrees awarded: M.B.A., M.S.C.I.S. Joint degree programs: J.D./M.B.A. Evening program is offered.
Finances: Tuition (1998–99): $490/credit. Estimated tuition (1999–2000): $490/credit.
Admission Requirements: GMAT is required. Application deadline for fall: July 15.
Selectivity: Applications received (part-time): 54. Admitted: 47. Enrolled: 39. Average GMAT: 520. Average undergraduate GPA: 3.0. GMAT section weighed most heavily: weighed equally.
Placement: School has placement office. Placement rate 6 months after graduation: 95%. Average starting salary: $55,000.

UNIVERSITY OF MICHIGAN

University of Michigan Business School
701 Tappan
Ann Arbor, MI 48109-1234
Phone: (734) 763-5796
Fax: (734) 763-7804
E-mail: usmbusmba@umich.edu
http://www.bus.umich.edu
Student Body: Full-time enrollment: 857. Men: 71%. Women: 29%. African American: 8%. Asian American: 8%. Latino: 6%. International: 25%. Average age: 28. Part-time enrollment: 1,070. Men: 77%. Women: 23%.
Academics: Full-time faculty: 130. Part-time faculty: 60. Degrees awarded: M.B.A., M. Acc., Ph.D. Evening program is offered. For fall 1996 entering class: 100% completed program within 2 years.
Finances: Estimated tuition (1999–2000): In-State: $20,000. Out-of-State: $25,000. 25% of students receive non-need-based aid. 49% of students receive need-based aid. Average student debt incurred by graduation: $37,511.
Admission Requirements: GMAT is required. Application deadline for fall: Nov. 15, Jan. 15, Mar. 15, Apr. 15.
Selectivity: Applications received (full-time): 4,186. Enrolled: 433. Applications received (part-time): 317. Enrolled: 170. Average GMAT: 672. Average undergraduate GPA: 3.3.
Placement: School has placement office. Placement rate at time of graduation: 99%. Placement rate 6 months after graduation: 99%. Average starting salary: $75,000.

UNIVERSITY OF MICHIGAN— DEARBORN

School of Management
4901 Evergreen Road
Dearborn, MI 48128-1491
Phone: (313) 593-5460
Fax: (313) 593-5636
E-mail: mba-umd-umd.umich.edu
http://www.umd.umich.edu

Student Body: Full-time enrollment: 29. Men: 69%. Women: 31%. African American: 7%. Asian American: 17%. Latino: 3%. International: 7%. Average age: 30. Part-time enrollment: 335. Men: 78%. Women: 12%.

Academics: Full-time faculty: 2. Part-time faculty: 3. Degrees awarded: M.B.A., M.S.A., M.S.F., M.B.A./M.S.E. Ind. & Systems Eng. Evening program offered.

Finances: Tuition (1998-1999): In-state: $252/credit + fees. Out-of-state: $728/credit + fees.

Admission Requirements: GMAT is required. Application deadline for fall: August 1.

Selectivity: Applications received (part-time): 143. Admitted: 99. Enrolled: 75. Average GMAT: 523. Average undergraduate GPA: 3.1. GMAT section weighed most heavily: weighed equally.

Placement: School has placement office.

UNIVERSITY OF MICHIGAN— FLINT*

School of Management
MBA Admissions
Room 346 CROB
Flint, MI 48502-2186
Phone: (810) 762-3160
Fax: (810) 762-0736
E-mail: gasper_k@crob.flint.umich.edu
Student Body: Average age: 30. Students living on campus: 0%. Part-time enrollment: 280. Men: 65%. Women: 35%.
Academics: Full-time faculty: 18. Part-time faculty: 10. Degrees awarded: M.B.A. Joint degree programs: B.B.A./M.B.A. Evening program is offered.
Finances: Tuition (1998–99): $5,326.
Admission Requirements: GMAT is required. Application deadline for fall: July 1 (fall), Nov. 1 (winter).
Selectivity: Applications received (full-time): 65. Admitted: 58. Enrolled: 40. Average GMAT: 502. Average undergraduate GPA: 3.0. GMAT section weighed most heavily: Quantitative.
Placement: School has placement office.

WAYNE STATE UNIVERSITY

School of Business Administration
5201 Cass Avenue
Detroit, MI 48202
Phone: (313) 577-4510
Fax: (313) 577-5299
E-mail: lzaddach@cms.cc.wayne.edu
http://www.busadm.wayne.edu
Student Body: Full-time enrollment: 181. Men: 59%. Women: 41%. Part-time enrollment: 1,558. Men: 62%. Women: 38%.
Academics: Full-time faculty: 60. Part-time faculty: 32. Degrees awarded: M.B.A., M.S.T. Evening program is offered.
Finances: Estimated tuition (1999–2000): In-State: $163/credit. Out-of-State: $355/credit.
Admission Requirements: GMAT is required. Application deadline for fall: August 1.
Selectivity: Applications received (full-time): 43. Admitted: 20. Enrolled: 13. Applications received (part-time): 500. Admitted: 403. Enrolled: 281. Average GMAT: 531. Average undergraduate GPA: 3.2.
Placement: School has placement office. Average starting salary: $52,434.

WESTERN MICHIGAN UNIVERSITY*

Haworth College of Business
1201 Oliver Street
Kalamazoo, MI 49008
Phone: (616) 387-5075
Student Body: Full-time enrollment: 135. Men: 67%. Women: 33%. International: 16%. Part-time enrollment: 483.
Academics: Full-time faculty: 68. Part-time faculty: 2. Degrees awarded: M.B.A., M.S.A. Evening program is not offered.
Finances: Tuition (1998–99): In-State: $141.75 per credit hour. Out-of-State: $344.30 per credit hour. Estimated tuition (1999–2000): In-State: $141.75 per credit hour. Out-of-State: $344.30 per credit hour.
Admission Requirements: GMAT is required. Application deadline for fall: June 1.

Selectivity: Applications received (full-time): 850. Admitted: 250. Enrolled: 200. Average GMAT: 520. Average undergraduate GPA: 3.4. GMAT section weighed most heavily: total score considered.
Placement: School has placement office.

Minnesota

ST. CLOUD STATE UNIVERSITY

College of Business
720 4th Avenue South
St. Cloud, MN 56301-4498
Phone: (320) 255 2244
Fax: (320) 255-2243
E-mail: sesu4u@stcloudstate.edu
http://www.statecloudstate.edu
Student Body: Full-time enrollment: 39. Men: 64%. Women: 36%. International: 56%. Part-time enrollment: 59. Men: 64%. Women: 36%.
Academics: Full-time faculty: 56. Degrees awarded: M.B.A., M.S. Acc. Evening program is offered. For fall 1996 entering class: 29% completed program within 2 years. 25% continued towards degree.
Finances: Tuition (1998–99): In-State: $145/credit. Out-of-State: $219/credit. Estimated tuition (1999–2000): In-State: $152/credit. Out-of-State: $230/credit.
Admission Requirements: GMAT is required. Application deadline for fall: rolling.
Selectivity: Applications received: 81. Admitted: 58. Enrolled: 46. Average GMAT: 526. Average undergraduate GPA: 3.3. GMAT section weighed most heavily: weighed equally.
Placement: School has placement office.

UNIVERSITY OF MINNESOTA

Carlson School of Management
2-210 Carlson School of Management
321 19th Ave. South
Minneapolis, MN 55455
Phone: (612) 625-5555
Fax: (612) 626-7785

E-mail: mbaoffice@csom.umn.edu
http://www.csom.umn.edu
Student Body: Full-time enrollment: 275.
Men: 73%. Women: 27%. African
American: 3%. Asian American: 7%. Latino:
2%. International: 18%. Average age: 28.
Part-time enrollment: 985. Men: 68%.
Women: 32%.
Academics: Full-time faculty: 70. Part-time
faculty: 36. Degrees awarded: M.B.A.,
Ph.D., M.B.T., M.H.A., M.A.I.R. Joint
degree programs: M.H.A./M.B.A. For fall
1996 entering class: 82% completed program within 2 years. 13% continued
towards degree.
Finances: Tuition (1998–99): In-State:
$12,150. Out-of-State: $16,882.
Admission Requirements: GMAT is
required. Application deadline for fall: Jan.
1, Mar. 1, Apr. 1, Feb. 15 (international).
Selectivity: Applications received (full-time):
656. Admitted: 299. Enrolled: 128.
Applications received (part-time): 268.
Admitted: 187. Enrolled: 162. Average
GMAT: 628. Average undergraduate GPA:
3.3. GMAT section weighed most heavily:
weighed equally.
Placement: School has placement office.
Placement rate at time of graduation: 97%.
Placement rate 6 months after graduation:
99%. Average starting salary: $67,690.

Mississippi

MILLSAPS COLLEGE

Else School of Management
1701 North State Street
Jackson, MS 39210
Phone: (601) 974-1253
Fax: (601) 974-1260
E-mail: mbamacc@millsaps.edu
http://elseschool.millsaps.edu
Student Body: Full-time enrollment: 35.
Men: 63%. Women: 37%. African
American: 11%. Asian American: 17%.
Native American: 3%. International: 17%.
Average age: 23.9. Students living on

campus: 6%. Part-time enrollment: 116.
Men: 63%. Women: 37%.
Academics: Full-time faculty: 16. Part-time
faculty: 4. Degrees awarded: M.B.A., M.
Acc. Evening program is offered. For fall
1996 entering class: 88% completed pro-
gram within 2 years. 12% continued
towards degree.
Finances: Tuition (1998–99): $550/credit.
Average student debt incurred by gradua-
tion: $21,494.
Admission Requirements: GMAT is required.
Application deadline for fall: July 1.
Selectivity: Applications received (full-time):
55. Admitted: 39. Enrolled: 22.
Applications received (part-time): 27.
Admitted: 23. Enrolled: 22. Average
GMAT: 543. Average undergraduate GPA:
3.3. GMAT section weighed most heavily:
weighed equally.
Placement: School has placement office.
Average starting salary: $44,250.

MISSISSIPPI STATE UNIVERSITY

College of Business & Industry
Office of the Graduate School
P.O. Box G
MSU, MS 39762
Phone: (601) 325-7400
Fax: (601) 325-1967
E-mail: grad@grad.msstate.edu
http://www.gsb.cbi.msstate.edu
Student Body: Full-time enrollment: 202.
Men: 50%. Women: 50%. African
American: 5%. Asian American: 15%.
International: 17%. Average age: 24.
Students living on campus: 10%. Part-time.
enrollment: 45. Men: 58%. Women: 42%.
Academics: Full-time faculty: 55. Degrees
awarded: M.B.A., M.P.A., M.S.B.A., M.
Tax., D.B.A., Information Systems, Finance,
Economics. Evening program is offered. For
fall 1996 entering class: 91% completed
program within 2 years. 9% continued
towards degree.
Finances: Tuition (1998–99): In-State:
$1,509/semester. Out-of-State:
$3,060/semester. 50% of students receive
some type of aid.

Admission Requirements: GMAT is required.
Application deadline for fall: July 1.
Selectivity: Applications received (full-time):
80. Enrolled: 60. Applications received
(part-time): 6. Average GMAT: 521.
Average undergraduate GPA: 3.3. GMAT
section weighed most heavily: weighed
equally.
Placement: School has placement office.
Average starting salary: $30,000.

UNIVERSITY OF MISSISSIPPI

School of Business Administration
253 Holman Hall
University, MS 38677
Phone: (601) 232-5483
Fax: (601) 232-5821
E-mail: holleman@bus.olemiss.edu
http://www.bus.olemiss.edu
Student Body: Full-time enrollment: 52.
Men: 67%. Women: 33%. African
American: 4%. International: 33%. Average
age: 24. Students living on campus: 25%.
Academics: Full-time faculty: 56. Degrees
awarded: M.B.A., M.S., Ph.D. Evening
program is not offered. For fall 1996 enter-
ing class: 90% completed program within 2
years.
Finances: Tuition (1998–99): In-State:
$2,731. Out-of-State: $5,551. Estimated
tuition (1999–2000): In-State: $2,850.
Out-of-State: $5,700. 85% of students
receive some type of aid.
Admission Requirements: GMAT is required.
Application deadline for fall: April 1.
Selectivity: Applications received (full-time):
116. Admitted: 47. Enrolled: 27. Average
GMAT: 550. Average undergraduate GPA:
3.4. GMAT section weighed most heavily:
weighed equally.
Placement: School has placement office.
Placement rate at time of graduation: 80%.
Placement rate 6 months after graduation:
95%. Average starting salary: $42,000.

UNIVERSITY OF SOUTHERN MISSISSIPPI

College of Business Administration
Graduate Business Programs
Box 5096
Hattiesburg, MS 39406-5096
Phone: (601) 266-4653
Fax: (601) 266-4639
E-mail: kinge@cba.usm.edu
http://www.usm.edu
Student Body: Full-time enrollment: 72. Men: 54%. Women: 46%. African American: 10%. Asian American: 3%. Latino: 3%. International: 11%. Average age: 26. Students living on campus: 5%. Part-time enrollment: 70. Men: 57%. Women: 43%.
Academics: Full-time faculty: 32. Degrees awarded: M.B.A., M.P.A., P.M.B.A. Joint degree programs: M.B.A./M.P.H. Evening program is not offered. For fall 1996 entering class: 95% completed program within 2 years. 5% continued towards degree.
Finances: Tuition (1998–99): In-State: $3,858. Out-of-State: $7,210. 45% of students receive some type of aid.
Admission Requirements: GMAT is required. Application deadline for fall: July 15.
Selectivity: Applications received (full-time): 114. Admitted: 102. Enrolled: 67. Applications received (part-time): 18. Admitted: 14. Enrolled: 10. Average GMAT: 531. Average undergraduate GPA: 3.3. GMAT section weighed most heavily: Verbal.
Placement: School has placement office. Average starting salary: $36,000.

Missouri

St. Louis University

School of Business and Administration
3674 Lindell Blvd
St. Louis, MO 63103
Phone: (314) 977-3800
Fax: (314) 977-3897
E-mail: johnsonab@slu.edu
http://www.slu.edu

Student Body: Full-time enrollment: 180. Men: 61%. Women: 39%. African American: 7%. Asian American: 8%. Latino: 7%. International: 50%. Average age: 27. Part-time enrollment: 300. Men: 65%. Women: 35%.
Academics: Full-time faculty: 61. Part-time faculty: 20. Degrees awarded: M.B.A., M.P.A., M.F.N., Executive Master in International Business, Master of International Business. Joint degree programs: J.D./M.B.A., M.H.A./M.B.A., M.S.N./M.B.A. Evening program is offered. For fall 1996 entering class: 78% completed program within 2 years. 7% continued towards degree.
Finances: Tuition (1998–99): $602/credit. Full-time day program: $22,000. 10% of students receive some type of aid.
Admission Requirements: GMAT is required. Application deadline for fall: July 15.
Selectivity: Applications received (part-time): 315. Admitted: 195. Enrolled: 89. Average GMAT: 551. Average undergraduate GPA: 3.2. GMAT section weighed most heavily: weighed equally.
Placement: School has placement office. Placement rate at time of graduation: 90%. Average starting salary: $46,595.

UNIVERSITY OF MISSOURI— COLUMBIA

College of Business & Public Administration
303 Middlebush Hall
Columbia, MO 65211
Phone: (573) 882-2750
Fax: (573) 882-0365
E-mail: grad@bpa.missouri.edu
http://tiger.bpa.missouri.edu/mba
Student Body: Full-time enrollment: 121. Men: 66%. Women: 34%. African American: 3%. Asian American: 1%. Latino: 1%. International: 25%. Average age: 25. Students living on campus: 1%. Part-time enrollment: 19. Men: 63%. Women: 37%.
Academics: Full-time faculty: 49. Part-time faculty: 8. Degrees awarded: M.B.A. Joint degree programs: M.B.A./J.D., M.B.A./Master of Health Admin.,

M.B.A./M.S. Indus. Engineering. Evening program is not offered. For fall 1996 entering class: 62% completed program within 2 years. 13% continued towards degree.
Finances: Tuition (1998–99): In-State: $163/credit + fees. Out-of-State: $489/credit + fees. 60% of students receive some type of aid.
Admission Requirements: GMAT is required. Application deadline for fall: August 1.
Selectivity: Applications received (full-time): 183. Admitted: 128. Enrolled: 85. Average GMAT: 602. Average undergraduate GPA: 3.3.
Placement: School has placement office. Placement rate at time of graduation: 58%. Placement rate 6 months after graduation: 94%. Average starting salary: $51,750.

UNIVERSITY OF MISSOURI— KANSAS CITY

H.W. Bloch School of Business & Public Administration
120 Administrative Center
5100 Rockhill Road
Kansas City, MO 64110-2499
Phone: (816) 235-1111
Fax: (816) 235-2312
http://www.bsbpa.umkc.edu/
Student Body: Full-time enrollment: 222. Men: 54%. Women: 46%. African American: 20%. Asian American: 9%. Latino: 5%. International: 10%. Average age: 30. Students living on campus: 3%. Part-time enrollment: 475. Men: 49%. Women: 51%.
Academics: Full-time faculty: 24. Part-time faculty: 12. Degrees awarded: M.B.A., M.S. Accounting, M.P.A. Joint degree programs: M.B.A./J.D. Evening program is offered.
Finances: Tuition (1998–99): In-State: $3,336.
Admission Requirements: GMAT is required. Application deadline for fall: May 1.
Selectivity: Applications received: 429. Admitted: 300. Enrolled: 213. Average GMAT: 556. Average undergraduate GPA:

3.2. GMAT section weighed most heavily: formula used including GMAT and GPA. **Placement:** School has placement office. Average starting salary: $39,600.

UNIVERSITY OF MISSOURI— ST. LOUIS

School of Business Administration
Graduate Admissions
8001 Natural Bridge Road
St. Louis, MO 63121
Phone: (314) 516-5458
Fax: (314) 516-5310
E-mail: gradadm@UMSL.edu
http://www.umsl.edu
Student Body: Full-time enrollment: 116. International: 26%. Average age: 30. Students living on campus: 30%. Part-time enrollment: 271.
Academics: Part-time faculty: 30. Degrees awarded: M.B.A., M.S. in M.I.S., M. Acc. Evening program is offered.
Finances: Tuition (1998–99): In-State: $200/credit. Out-of-State: $520/credit. 3% of students receive some type of aid.
Admission Requirements: GMAT is required. Application deadline for fall: August 1 (June 1 if not local).
Selectivity: Applications received (full-time): 141. Admitted: 69. Enrolled: 35. Average GMAT: 542. Applications received (part-time): 68. Admitted: 57. Enrolled: 39. Average GMAT: 542. Average undergraduate GPA: 3.06–4.0.
Placement: School has placement office. Average starting salary: $37,000.

WASHINGTON UNIVERSITY

John M. Olin School of Business
Campus Box 1133
One Brookings Drive
St. Louis, MO 63130
Phone: (314) 935-7301
Fax: (314) 935-6309
E-mail: mba@mail.olin.wustl.edu
http://www.olin.wustl.edu

Student Body: Full-time enrollment: 305. Men: 73%. Women: 27%. Total minority: 12%. International: 29%. Average age: 27. Part-time enrollment: 422. Men: 75%. Women: 25%.
Academics: Full-time faculty: 74. Part-time faculty: 27. Degrees awarded: M.B.A., E.M.B.A., Ph.D. Joint degree programs: J.D./M.B.A., M.B.A./M. Arch., M.B.A./M.S.W., M.B.A./M.A. in East Asian Studies. Evening program is offered. For fall 1996 entering class: 99% completed program within 2 years. 1% continued towards degree.
Finances: Tuition (1998–99): $23,980. 57% of students receive some type of aid. Average student debt incurred by graduation: $22,450.
Admission Requirements: GMAT is required. Application deadline for fall: varies.
Selectivity: Applications received (full-time): 1,091. Admitted: 361. Enrolled: 150. Applications received (part-time): 99. Admitted: 91. Enrolled: 79. Average GMAT: 624. Average undergraduate GPA: 3.1. GMAT section weighed most heavily: weighed equally.
Placement: School has placement office. Placement rate at time of graduation: 82%. Average starting salary: $66,000.

Montana

UNIVERSITY OF MONTANA

School of Business Administration
Missoula, MT 59812
Phone: (406) 243-4983
Fax: (406) 243-2086
E-mail: spritzer@selway.umt.edu
http://www.business.umt.edu
Student Body: Full-time enrollment: 74. Men: 54%. Women: 46%. International: 7%. Average age: 29. Part-time enrollment: 70. Men: 46%. Women: 54%.
Academics: Full-time faculty: 28. Part-time faculty: 10. Degrees awarded: M.B.A., M. Acct. Evening program is offered.

Finances: Tuition (1998–99): In-State: $3,137. Out-of-State: $8,508. Estimated tuition (1999–2000): In-State: $3,388. Out-of-State: $9,189.
Admission Requirements: GMAT is required. Application deadline for fall: March 1.
Selectivity: Applications received (full-time): 79. Admitted: 67. Enrolled: 48. Average GMAT: 570. Average undergraduate GPA: 3.3. GMAT section weighed most heavily: weighed equally.
Placement: School has placement office.

Nebraska

CREIGHTON UNIVERSITY

College of Business Administration
2500 California Plaza
Omaha, NE 68178-0130
Phone: (402) 280-2829
Fax: (402) 280-2172
E-mail: cobgrad@creighton.edu
http://cobgrad.creighton.edu/grad/
Student Body: Full-time enrollment: 28. Men: 54%. Women: 46%. International: 46%. Part-time enrollment: 80. Men: 60%. Women: 40%.
Academics: Part-time faculty: 24. Degrees awarded: M.B.A., M.S. Joint degree programs: M.B.A./M.S. in I.T.M., M.B.A./J.D., M.B.A./M.A. International Relations. Evening program is offered.
Finances: Tuition (1998–99): $402/credit hour. Average student debt incurred by graduation: $24,123.
Admission Requirements: GMAT is required. Application deadline for fall: rolling.
Selectivity: Average GMAT: 537. Average undergraduate GPA: 3.0. GMAT section most heavily weighed: weighed equally.
Placement: School has placement office. Placement rate at time of graduation: 70%. Average starting salary: $43,700.

UNIVERSITY OF NEBRASKA— LINCOLN

College of Business Administration
Administration 301
Lincoln, NE 68588-0434
Phone: (402) 472-2878
(800) 742-8800
Fax: (402) 472-5180
E-mail: grad_admissions@unl.edu
http://www.unl.edu/gradstud
Student Body: Full-time enrollment: 54.
Men: 63%. Women: 37%. Asian
American: 11%. Latino: 6%. International:
24%. Average age: 24 Students living on
campus: 4%. Part-time enrollment: 84. Men:
63%. Women: 37%.
Academics: Full-time faculty: 71. Degrees
awarded: M.B.A., M.P.A., M.A., Ph.D.
Joint degree programs: M.B.A./J.D.,
M.P.A./J.D., M.B.A./Arch. Evening pro-
gram is offered.
Finances: Tuition (1998–99): In-State:
$2,500. Out-of-State: $5,500.
Admission Requirements: GMAT is required.
Application deadline for fall: June 15.
Selectivity: Applications received (full-time):
83. Admitted: 40. Enrolled: 20.
Applications received (part-time): 29.
Admitted: 19. Enrolled: 16. Average
GMAT: 560. Average undergraduate GPA:
3.5. GMAT section weighed most heavily:
weighed equally.
Placement: School has placement office.
Placement rate 6 months after graduation:
98%.

UNIVERSITY OF NEBRASKA— OMAHA

College of Business Administration
60th and Dodge Streets
Room 414
Omaha, NE 68182-0048
Phone: (402) 554-4836
Fax: (402) 554-3747
E-mail: mba@unomaha.edu
http://www.unomaha.edu
Student Body: Part-time enrollment: 273.
Men: 58%. Women: 42%.

Academics: Full-time faculty: 43. Degrees
awarded: M.B.A., M.S. Economics, M.A.
Economics, M. Acc., E.M.B.A. International
Business. Evening program is offered.
Finances: Tuition (1998–99): In-State:
$95/credit. Out-of-State: $225/credit.
Estimated tuition (1999–2000): In-State:
$100/credit. Out-of-State: $235/credit.
Admission Requirements: GMAT is required.
Application deadline for fall: July 1.
Selectivity: Applications received (part-time):
71. Admitted: 63. Enrolled: 46. Average
GMAT: 533. Average undergraduate GPA:
3.3. GMAT section weighed most heavily:
weighed equally.
Placement: School has placement office.

Nevada

UNIVERSITY OF NEVADA— LAS VEGAS

College of Business
4505 S. Maryland Parkway
Las Vegas, NV 89154-6001
Phone: (702) 895-3970
Student Body: Full-time enrollment: 60.
Men: 58%. Women: 42%. Average age:
32. Part-time enrollment: 109. Men: 64%.
Women: 36%.
Academics: Full-time faculty: 97. Part-time
faculty: 25. Degrees awarded: M.B.A.,
M.S. Acc., M.A. in Economics. Evening
program is offered.
Finances: Tuition (1998–99): In-State: $93
per credit. Out-of-State: $5,770.
Admission Requirements: GMAT is
required. Application deadline for fall: June
1, November 15.
Selectivity: Average GMAT: 540. Average
undergraduate GPA: 3.2. GMAT section
weighed most heavily: weighed equally.
Placement: School has placement office.
Placement rate at time of graduation:
100%. Average starting salary: $43,500.

UNIVERSITY OF NEVADA— RENO

College of Business Administration
Reno, NV 89557
Phone: (775) 784-4912
E-mail: mgraham@unr.edu
http://www.unr.edu/unr/coba/
index.html
Student Body: Full-time enrollment: 5%. Part-
time enrollment: 95%. Men: 65%. Women:
35%. International: 14%. Average age: 29.
Academics: Full-time faculty: 23. Degrees
awarded: M.B.A. Evening program is
offered
Finances: Tuition (1998–99): In-State:
$93/credit. Out-of-State: $190/credit (for 1-
6 credits) or $2,885 (for / or more credits).
Admission Requirements: GMAT is
required. Application deadline for fall:
November 1.
Selectivity: Applications received (full-time):
46. Admitted: 25. Enrolled: 13.
Placement: School has placement office.

New Hampshire

DARTMOUTH COLLEGE

Amos Tuck School of Business
Administration
100 Tuck Hall
Hanover, NH 03755-9040
Phone: (603) 646-3162
Fax: (603) 646-1441
E-mail: tuck_admissions@dartmouth.edu
http://www.tuck.dartmouth.edu
Student Body: Full-time enrollment: 375.
Men: 71%. Women: 29%. African
American: 4%. Asian American: 10%.
Latino: 4%. International: 24%. Average
age: 27.7.
Academics: Full-time faculty: 40. Part-time
faculty: 8. Degrees awarded: M.B.A. Joint
degree programs: M.B.A./International
Affairs, M.B.A./M.D., M.B.A./
Engineering. Evening program is not
offered.

Finances: Tuition (1998–99): $26,100. Estimated tuition (1999–2000): $27,400. 66% of students receive some type of aid. Average student debt incurred by graduation: $49,845.

Admission Requirements: GMAT is required. Application deadline for fall: April 21.

Selectivity: Applications received (full-time): 2,916. Admitted: 350. Enrolled: 191. Average GMAT: 671. Average undergraduate GPA: 3.4. GMAT section weighed most heavily: each application is evaluated individually.

Placement: School has placement office. Placement rate at time of graduation: 98.7%. Placement rate 6 months after graduation: 100%. Average starting salary: $82,074.

New Jersey

RUTGERS UNIVERSITY

Graduate School of Management
92 New Street
Newark, NJ 07102
Phone: (973) 353-1234
Fax: (973) 353-1592
E-mail: admit@gsmack.rutgers.edu
Student Body: Full-time enrollment: 387. Men: 63%. Women: 37%. International: 9%. Average age: 28. Part-time enrollment: 1,159. Men: 66%. Women: 34%.

Academics: Full-time faculty: 135. Part-time faculty: 67. Degrees awarded: M.B.A., E.M.B.A., M. Acc., Ph.D. Joint degree programs: J.D./M.B.A., M.P.H./M.B.A. Evening program is offered.

Finances: Tuition (1998–99): In-State: $9,212. Out-of-State: $13,342.

Admission Requirements: GMAT is required. Application deadline for fall: May 15.

Selectivity: Applications received (full-time): 794. Admitted: 487. Enrolled: 314. Average GMAT: 564. Average undergraduate GPA: 3.1.

Placement: School has placement office. Placement rate at time of graduation: 68%. Average starting salary: $67,102.

SETON HALL UNIVERSITY

W. Paul Stillman School of Business
400 South Orange Avenue
South Orange, NJ 07079
Phone: (973) 761-9222
Fax: (973) 275-2465
E-mail: busgrad@shu.edu
http://www.shu.edu
Student Body: Full-time enrollment: 94. Men: 65%. Women: 35%. African American: 5%. Asian American: 16%. Latino: 2%. International: 15%. Average age: 27. Part-time enrollment: 581. Men: 63%. Women: 37%.

Academics: Full-time faculty: 30. Part-time faculty: 16. Degrees awarded: M.B.A., M.S. Joint degree programs: M.B.A./M.S. International Business, J.D./M.B.A. Evening program is offered.

Finances: Tuition (1998–99): $538/credit + fees.

Admission Requirements: GMAT is required. Application deadline for fall: rolling.

Selectivity: Applications received (full-time): 117. Admitted: 68. Enrolled: 38. Applications received (part-time): 237. Admitted: 151. Enrolled: 111. Average GMAT: 565. Average undergraduate GPA: 3.1. GMAT section weighed most heavily: weighed equally.

Placement: School has placement office.

New Mexico

NEW MEXICO STATE UNIVERSITY

College of Business Administration and Economics
MSC 3GSP
PO Box 30001
Las Cruces, NM 88003
Phone: (505) 646-8003
Fax: (505) 646-7977
E-mail: mbaprog@nmsu.edu
http://cbae.nmsu.edu/~mbaprog/

Student Body: Full-time enrollment: 70. Men: 57%. Women: 43%. African American: 3%. Latino: 23%. Native American: 1%. International: 23%. Average age: 27. Part-time enrollment: 55. Men: 62%. Women: 38%.

Academics: Full-time faculty: 65. Part-time faculty: 1. Degrees awarded: M.B.A., M.S., M.A., Ph.D. Joint degree programs: Engineering Management, Hotel, Restaurant & Tourism Management. Evening program is offered. For fall 1996 entering class: 28% completed program within 2 years. 32% continued towards degree.

Finances: Tuition (1998–99): In-State: $1,257. Out-of-State: $3,985. Estimated tuition (1999–2000): In-State: $1,257. Out-of-State: $3,985. 17% of students receive non-need-based aid. 21 students are on graduate assistantships.

Admission Requirements: GMAT is required. Application deadline for fall: July 1.

Selectivity: Applications received (full-time): 94. Admitted: 73. Enrolled: 24. Enrolled (part-time): 13. Average GMAT: 494. Average undergraduate GPA: 3.2.

Placement: School has placement office.

UNIVERSITY OF NEW MEXICO

Robert O. Anderson Graduate School of Management
Albuquerque, NM 87131
Phone: (505) 277-2446
Fax: (505) 277-9356
E-mail: chastain@anderson.unm.edu
http://asm.unm.edu
Student Body: Full-time enrollment: 240. Men: 60%. Women: 40%. African American: 4%. Asian American: 5%. Latino: 18%. Native American: 5%. International: 12%. Average age: 33. Part-time enrollment: 197. Men: 60%. Women: 40%.

Academics: Full-time faculty: 51. Part-time faculty: 15. Degrees awarded: M.B.A., M.S. Acc. Joint degree programs: J.D./M.B.A., M.B.A./Latin American Studies. Evening program is offered.

Finances: Tuition (1998–99): In-State: $1,221/semester. Out-of-State: $4,345/semester.

Admission Requirements: GMAT is required. Application deadline for fall: July 1. **Selectivity:** Applications received: 163. Admitted: 123. Enrolled: 77. Average GMAT: 567. Average undergraduate GPA: 3.5. GMAT section weighed most heavily: weighed equally.
Placement: School has placement office. Placement rate at time of graduation: 86%. Placement rate 6 months after graduation: 100%. Average starting salary: $51,050.

New York

CANISIUS COLLEGE

Richard J. Wehle School of Business
2001 Main Street
Buffalo, NY 14208
Phone: (716) 888-2140
E-mail: dsully@canisius.edu
http://www.canisius.edu
Student Body: Full-time enrollment: 45. Men: 60%. Women: 40%. Part-time enrollment: 405. Men: 60%. Women: 40%.
Academics: Full time faculty: 45. Degrees awarded: M.B.A., M.B.A.P.A. Evening program is offered.
Finances: Tuition (1998–99): $499 per credit hour.
Admission Requirements: GMAT is required. Application deadline for fall: July 1.
Selectivity: Average GMAT: 500. Average undergraduate GPA: 3.0.
Placement: School has placement office.

CITY UNIVERSITY OF NEW YORK—BARUCH COLLEGE

Zicklin School of Business
17 Lexington Avenue
Box H-0880
New York, NY 10010
Phone: (212) 802-2330
Fax: (212) 802-2335
E-mail: graduate_admissions@baruch.cuny.edu
http://www.bus.baruch.cuny.edu

Student Body: Full-time enrollment: 80. Men: 60%. Women: 40%. International: 38%. Average age: 27. Part-time enrollment: 1,714. Men: 60%. Women: 40%.
Academics: Full-time faculty: 185. Part-time faculty: 100. Degrees awarded: M.B.A., Ph.D., M.S. Joint degree programs: J.D./M.B.A. Evening program is offered.
Finances: Tuition (1998–99): In-State: $185/credit; $2,175 per semester. Out-of-State: $320/credit; $3,800 per semester. Estimated tuition (1999–2000): In-State: $185/credit; $4,350 per semester. Out-of-State: $ 320/credit; $7,600 per semester. 5% of students receive non-need-based aid. 20% of students receive need-based aid.
Admission Requirements: GMAT is required. Application deadline for fall: April 1 (full-time M.B.A.), May 1 (International), June 1 (flex/part-time programs).
Selectivity: Applications received (full-time): 907 Admitted: 72. Enrolled: 50. Applications received (part-time): 1,767. Admitted: 965. Enrolled: 496. Average GMAT: 580. Average undergraduate GPA: 3.2. GMAT section weighed most heavily. Math (Verbal for non-native English speakers).
Placement: School has placement office. Average starting salary: $55,000.

CLARKSON UNIVERSITY

School of Business
P.O. Box 5770
Potsdam, NY 13699-5770
Phone: (315) 268-6613
Fax: (315) 268-3810
E-mail: gradprog@clarkson.edu
http://phoenix.som.clarkson.edu
Student Body: Full-time enrollment: 94. Men: 64%. Women: 36%. Latino: 1%. International: 31%. Average age: 26. Students living on campus: 10%. Part-time enrollment: 46. Men: 65%. Women: 35%.
Academics: Full-time faculty: 30. Part-time faculty: 3. Degrees awarded: M.B.A., M.S. Joint degree programs: M.E./M.B.A. Evening program is offered. For fall 1996 entering class: 100% completed program within 2 years. (1 year program)
Finances: Tuition (1998–99): $20,352.

Admission Requirements: GMAT is required. Application deadline for fall: rolling.
Selectivity: Applications received (full-time): 163. Admitted: 102. Enrolled: 94. Applications received (part-time): 4. Admitted: 4. Enrolled: 4. Average GMAT: 513. Average undergraduate GPA: 3.1. GMAT section weighed most heavily: all weighed equally.
Placement: School has placement office. Placement rate at time of graduation: 58%. Placement rate 6 months after graduation: 97%. Average starting salary: $47,800.

COLUMBIA UNIVERSITY

Columbia Business School
Office of Admissions
105 Uris Hall, 3022 Broadway
New York, NY 10027
Phone: (212) 854-1961
Fax: (212) 662-6754
E-mail: gohermes@claven.gsb.columbia.edu
http://www.columbia.edu/cu/business/
Student Body: Full-time enrollment: 1,373. Men: 63%. Women: 37%. African American: 8%. Asian American: 9%. Latino: 5%. International: 28%. Average age: 27.
Academics: Full-time faculty: 111. Part-time faculty: 81. Degrees awarded: M.B.A., E.M.B.A., Ph.D. Joint degree programs: M.B.A./M.S. Urban Planning, M.B.A./D.D.S, M.B.A./M.S. Industrial Engineering, M.B.A./B.A., M.B.A./B.S., M.B.A./M.I.A., M.B.A./M.S. Journalism, M.B.A./J.D., M.B.A./M.D., M.B.A./M.S. Nursing, M.B.A./M.P.H., M.B.A./M.S. Social Work, M.B.A.
Finances: Tuition (1998–99): $27,700.
Admission Requirements: GMAT is required. Application deadline for fall: April 20 (domestic), March 1 (international).
Selectivity: Applications received (full-time): 5,719. Admitted: 658. Enrolled: 487. Average GMAT: 680. Average undergraduate GPA: 3.5. GMAT section weighed most heavily: weighed equally.
Placement: School has placement office. Placement rate at time of graduation: 98%.

Average starting salary: $132,000 (including bonuses).

CORNELL UNIVERSITY

Johnson Graduate School of Management
Sage Hall
Ithaca, NY 14853
Phone: (607) 255-4526,
(800) 847-2082
Fax: (607) 255-0065
E-mail: mba@cornell.edu
http://www.johnson.cornell.edu
Student Body: Full-time enrollment: 576.
Men: 77%. Women: 23%. African
American: 3%. Asian American: 13%. Latino:
2%. International: 19%. Average age: 30.
Academics: Full-time faculty: 50. Part-time
faculty: 10. Degrees awarded: M.B.A.,
Ph.D. Joint degree programs: J.D./M.B.A.,
M.Eng./M.B.A., M.I.L.R./M.B.A.,
M.A.Asian Studies/M.B.A. Evening program
is not offered. For fall 1996 entering class:
99% completed program within 2 years. Less
than 1% continued towards degree.
Finances: Tuition (1998–99): $24,400.
58% of students receive non-need-based
aid. 66% of students receive need-based
aid. Average student debt incurred by
graduation: $47,634.
Admission Requirements: GMAT is
required. Application deadline for fall:
batch decision process; November 15,
January 15, March 15.
Selectivity: Applications received (full-time):
2,045. Admitted: 547. Enrolled: 282.
Average GMAT: 648. Average undergraduate GPA: 3.3. GMAT section weighed most
heavily: both are considered along with
many other factors.
Placement: School has placement office.
Placement rate at time of graduation: 95%.
Placement rate 3 months after graduation:
98%. Average starting salary: $76,000.

FORDHAM UNIVERSITY

Graduate School of Business Administration
113 West 60th Street
New York, NY 10023
Phone: (212) 636-6200
Fax: (212) 636-7076
E-mail: admission@bschool.fordham.edu
http://www.bnet.fordham.edu
Student Body: Full-time enrollment: 186.
Men: 61%. Women: 39%. International:
25%. Average Age: 28. Part-time enrollment: 1,291. Men: 61%. Women: 39%.
African American: 1%. Asian American:
5%. Latino: 3%.
Academics: Full-time faculty: 93. Part-time
faculty: 95. Degrees awarded: M.B.A.,
M.S., M.S. Tax, Transnational M.B.A.,
Global Professional M.B.A., M.B.A.
Professional Accounting, M.B.A. in Taxation
and Accounting. Joint Degree programs:
J.D./M.B.A., Evening program is offered.
Finances: Tuition (1998–99): $560/credit.
Admission Requirements: GMAT is required.
Application deadline for fall: June 1.
Selectivity: Applications received (full-time):
445. Admitted: 273. Enrolled: 95.
Applications received (part-time): 489.
Admitted: 347. Enrolled: 219. Average
GMAT: 580. Average undergraduate GPA:
3.3. GMAT section weighed most heavily:
weighed equally.
Placement: School has placement office.
Average starting salary: $59,670.

HOFSTRA UNIVERSITY

Frank G. Zarb School of Business
134 Hofstra University
Hempstead, NY 11550
Phone: (516) 463-5683
Fax: (516) 463-5268
E-mail: humba@hofstra.edu
http://www.hofstra.edu
Student Body: Full-time enrollment: 178.
Men: 68%. Women: 32%. African
American: 6%. Asian American: 8%. Latino:
1%. International: 29%. Average age: 25.
Students living on campus: 40%. Part-time
enrollment: 512. Men: 61%. Women: 39%.

Academics: Full-time faculty: 75. Part-time
faculty: 3. Degrees awarded: M.B.A., M.S.
Joint degree programs: J.D./M.B.A. Evening
program is offered. For fall 1996 entering
class: 81% completed program within 2
years. 15% continued towards degree.
Finances: Tuition (1998–99): $15,000.
Estimated tuition (1999–2000): $15,600.
75% of students receive some type of aid
(including loans). Average student debt
incurred by graduation: $12,000.
Admission Requirements: GMAT is required.
Application deadline for fall: June 1.
Selectivity: Applications received (full-time):
500. Admitted: 295. Enrolled: 95.
Applications received (part-time): 375.
Admitted: 218. Enrolled: 110. Average
GMAT: 570. Average undergraduate GPA:
3.2. GMAT section weighed most heavily:
fairly equally.
Placement: School has placement office.
Placement at time of graduation: 91%.
Placement rate 6 months after graduation:
96%. Average starting salary: $59,310.

MOUNT SAINT MARY COLLEGE

Division of Business
330 Powell Avenue
Newburgh, NY 12550
Phone: (914) 569-3582
Fax: (914) 562-6762
Student Body: Full-time enrollment: 3. Part-time enrollment: 79. Men: 48%. Women:
52%.
Academics: Full-time faculty: 7. Part-time
faculty: 6. Degrees awarded: M.B.A.
Evening program is offered.
Finances: Tuition (1998–99): $8,838.
Admission Requirements: GMAT is required.

NEW YORK UNIVERSITY

Leonard N. Stern School of Business
44 West 4th Street, Suite 10-160
New York, NY 10012-1126
Phone: (212) 998-0600
Fax: (212) 995-4231

E-mail: sternmba@stern.nyu.edu
http://www.stern.nyu.edu
Student Body: Full-time enrollment: 812.
Men: 62%. Women: 38%. African
American: 8%. Asian American: 46%.
Latino: 12%. International: 32%. Average
age: 27.5. Part-time enrollment: 2,090.
Men: 67%. Women: 33%.
Academics: Full-time faculty: 210. Part-time
faculty: 150. Degrees awarded: M.B.A.,
E.M.B.A., M.S., Ph.D. Joint degree pro-
grams: J.D./M.B.A., M.B.A./M.A. (French
Studies), M.B.A./M.A. (Journalism),
M.B.A./M.A. (Politics), M.B.A./M.S.
(Statistics & Operations Research). Evening
program is offered. For fall 1996 entering
class: 95% completed program within 2
years. 3% continued towards degree.
Finances: Tuition (1998–99): $27,448.
Estimated tuition (1999–2000): $27,448
80% of students receive need-based aid.
20% of students receive non-need-based aid.
Admission Requirements: GMAT is
required. Application deadline for fall: Jan
15 (early), March 15.
Selectivity: Applications received (full-time):
4,716. Enrolled: 419. Applications
received (part-time): 941. Enrolled: 401.
Average GMAT: 6/5. Average undergraduate GPA: 3.4. GMAT section weighed most
heavily: weighed equally.
Placement: School has placement office.
Placement rate at time of graduation: 95%.
Placement rate 6 months after graduation:
98%. Average starting salary: $92,503.

RENSSELAER POLYTECHNIC INSTITUTE

Lally School of Management and
Technology
Pittsburgh Building, Rm. 3218
Troy, NY 12180-3590
Phone: (518) 276-6586
Fax: (518) 276-2665
E-mail: management@rpi.edu
http://lallyschool.rpi.edu
Student Body: Full-time enrollment: 152.
Men: 77%. Women: 23%. African
American: 3%. Asian American: 7%. Latino:

3%. International: 45%. Average age: 26.
Part-time enrollment: 144. Men: 74%.
Women: 26%.
Academics: Full-time faculty: 36. Part-time
faculty: 16. Degrees awarded: M.B.A.,
M.S., Ph.D., E.M.B.A. Joint degree pro-
grams: M.B.A./M.S. or M.E. (engineer-
ing/science), M.B.A./Ph.D., Accelerated
B.S./M.B.A., M.B.A./J.D. Evening pro-
gram is offered.
Finances: Tuition (1998–99): $18,900 +
$1,100 in fees. 80% of students receive
some type of aid.
Admission Requirements: GMAT is required.
Application deadline for fall: February 1.
Selectivity: Applications received (full-time):
180. Admitted: 101. Enrolled: 46.
Applications received (part-time): 37.
Admitted: 30. Enrolled: 27. Average
GMAT: 604. Average undergraduate GPA:
3.2. GMAT section weighed most heavily:
Quantitative.
Placement: School has placement office.
Placement rate at time of graduation:
75.4%. Placement rate 6 months after grad-
uation: 95.4%. Average starting salary:
$58,477.

ROCHESTER INSTITUTE OF TECHNOLOGY

College of Business
Bausch & Lomb Center
60 Lomb Memorial Drive
Rochester, NY 14623-5604
Phone: (716) 475-6631
Fax: (716) 475-7424
E-mail: admission@rit.edu
http://www.rit.edu
Student Body: Full-time enrollment: 158.
Men: 63%. Women: 37%. African
American: 1%. Asian American: 1%. Latino:
2%. International: 68%. Average age: 26.
Students living on campus: 80%. Part-time
enrollment: 174. Men: 52%. Women: 48%.
Academics: Full-time faculty: 31. Part-time
faculty: 35. Degrees awarded: M.B.A.,
M.S. Finance, M.S. International Business,
E.M.B.A., M.S. Manufacturing
Management and Leadership, M.S.

Program Development. Evening program is
offered. For fall 1996 entering class: 57%
completed program within 2 years. 43%
continued towards degree.
Finances: Tuition (1998–99): $18,765.
Estimated tuition (1999–2000): $19,515.
60% of students receive some type of aid.
Average student debt incurred by gradua-
tion: $18,614.
Admission Requirements: GMAT is required.
Application deadline for fall: August 7.
Selectivity: Applications received (full-time):
350. Admitted: 189. Enrolled: 74.
Applications received (part-time): 42.
Admitted: 29. Enrolled: 22. Average
GMAT: 555. Average undergraduate GPA:
3.0. GMAT section weighed most heavily:
weighed equally.
Placement: School has placement office.
Placement rate at time of graduation: 47%.
Average starting salary: $48,000.

ST. JOHN'S UNIVERSITY

College of Business Administration
8000 Utopia Parkway
Bent Hall Room 111C, Grad Division
Jamaica, NY 11439
Phone: (718) 990-6114,
(718) 990-6132
Fax: (718) 990-1677
http://www.stjohns.edu/academics/
cba
Student Body: Full-time enrollment: 130.
Men: 56%. Women: 44%. African
American: 2%. Asian American: 7%. Latino:
5%. International: 39%. Average age: 25.
Part-time enrollment: 806. Men: 61%.
Women: 39%.
Academics: Full-time faculty: 41. Degrees
awarded: M.B.A. Joint degree programs:
B.S./M.S. in Accounting, M.B.A./J.D.
Evening program is offered.
Finances: Tuition (1998–99): $600/credit.
Estimated tuition (1999–2000):
$600/credit.
Admission Requirements: GMAT is required.
Application deadline for fall: rolling.
Selectivity: Enrolled (full-time): 33. Enrolled
(part-time): 170. Average GMAT: 492.
Average undergraduate GPA: 3.1. GMAT

section weighed most heavily: weighed equally.

Placement: School has placement office. Average starting salary: $37,500.

STATE UNIVERSITY OF NEW YORK—ALBANY

School of Business
Office of Student Services, BA 361
Albany, NY 12222
Phone: (518) 442-4961
Fax: (518) 442-3944
E-mail: busapps@cnsunix.
albany.edu
http://www.albany.edu/business
Student Body: Full-time enrollment: 186. Men: 58%. Women: 42%. African American: 4%. Asian American: 30%. Latino: 2%. Native American: 1%. International: 22%. Average age: 27. Students living on campus: 10%. Part-time enrollment: 300. Men: 55%. Women: 45%.
Academics: Full-time faculty: 25. Part-time faculty: 5. Degrees awarded: M.B.A., M.S. Acc. (1- and 2- year program). Evening program is offered. For fall 1996 entering class: 97% completed program within 2 years. 3% continued towards degree.
Finances: Tuition (1998–99): In-State: $5,100. Out-of-State: $8,416. Estimated tuition (1999–2000): In-state: $5,100. Out-of-state: $8,416. 31% of students receive some type of aid.
Admission Requirements: GMAT is required. Application deadline for fall: August 1.
Selectivity: Applications received (full-time): 317. Admitted: 125. Enrolled: 72. Applications received (part-time): 66. Admitted: 55. Enrolled: 49. Average GMAT: 540. Average undergraduate GPA: 3.3. GMAT section weighed most heavily: weighed equally.
Placement: School has placement office. Placement rate at time of graduation: 85%. Placement rate 6 months after graduation: 100%. Average starting salary: $55,000.

STATE UNIVERSITY OF NEW YORK—BINGHAMTON

School of Management
P.O. Box 6000
Binghamton, NY 13902-6000
Phone: (607) 777-2284
http://som.binghamton.edu
Student Body: Full-time enrollment: 210. Men: 56%. Women: 44%. Minorities: 8%. International: 26% Average age: 27. Part-time enrollment: 59. Men: 63%. Women: 37%.
Academics: Full-time faculty: 35. Part-time faculty: 16. Degrees awarded: M.B.A., M.S., Ph.D. Evening program is offered.
Finances: Tuition (1998–99): In-State: $5,590. Out-of-State: $8,906. Estimated tuition (1999–2000): In-State: $5,590. Out-of-State: $8,906.
Admission Requirements: GMAT is required. Application deadline for fall: April 15.
Selectivity: Applications received (full-time): 219. Admitted: 176. Enrolled: 79. Average GMAT: 562. Average undergraduate GPA: 3.1.
Placement: School has placement office.

STATE UNIVERSITY OF NEW YORK—BUFFALO

School of Management
Jacobs Management Center
Buffalo, NY 14260
Phone: (716) 645-3204
(877) BFLO-MBA
Fax: (716) 645-2341
E-mail: sommba@acsu.buffalo.edu
http://www.mgt.buffalo.edu
Student Body: Full-time enrollment: 413. Men: 68%. Women: 32%. African American: 2%. Asian American: 46%. Latino: 1%. International: 48%. Average age: 30. Students living on campus: 3%. Part-time enrollment: 280. Men: 66%. Women: 34%.
Academics: Full-time faculty: 59. Part-time faculty: 5. Degrees awarded: M.B.A., M.S. Acc. Joint degree programs: B.S./M.B.A., M.G.M.T. Pharmacy; Engin. B.A./M.B.A.

Sociology; Economics; Computer Science; Geography, M.Arch./M.B.A., M.D./M.B.A., M.A. Geography/M.B.A., J.D./M.B.A. Evening program is offered. For fall 1996 entering class: 82% completed program within 2 years. 16% continued towards degree.
Finances: Tuition (1998–99): In-State: $5,100. Out-of-State: $8,416. Estimated tuition (1999–2000): In-State: $5,100. Out-of-State: $8,416.
Admission Requirements: GMAT is required. Application deadline for fall: July 1.
Selectivity: Applications received (full-time): 727. Admitted: 356. Enrolled: 203. Applications received (part-time): 71. Admitted: 54. Enrolled: 45. Average GMAT: 595. Average undergraduate GPA: 3.1. GMAT section weighed most heavily: depends on applicant's overall record.
Placement: School has placement office. Placement rate at time of graduation: 80%. Placement rate 6 months after graduation: 90%. Average starting salary: $42,300.

SYRACUSE UNIVERSITY

School of Management
Suite 100
School of Management
Syracuse, NY 13244-2130
Phone: (315) 443-9214
Fax: (315) 443-9517
E-mail: MBAinfo@som.syr.edu
http://www.som.syr.edu
Student Body: Full-time enrollment: 198. Men: 63%. Women: 37%. African American: 4%. Asian American: 5%. Latino: 3%. International: 57%. Average age: 26. Part-time enrollment: 401. Men: 72%. Women: 28%.
Academics: Full-time faculty: 58. Part-time faculty: 10. Degrees awarded: M.B.A., M.S., M.P.S., Ph.D. Joint degree programs: J.D./M.B.A., J.D./M.S. Evening program is offered.
Finances: Tuition (1998–99): $17,584. Estimated tuition (1999–2000): $18,500. Average student debt incurred by graduation: $35,245. 50% of students receive non-need-based aid.

Admission Requirements: GMAT is required. Application deadline for fall: May 1.
Selectivity: Applications received (full-time): 559. Admitted: 172. Enrolled: 91. Applications received (part-time): 52. Admitted: 48. Enrolled: 42. Average GMAT: 585. Average undergraduate GPA: 3.2. GMAT section weighed most heavily: weighed equally.
Placement: School has placement office. Placement rate at time of graduation: 85%. Placement rate 6 months after graduation: 97%. Average starting salary: $69,000.

UNIVERSITY OF ROCHESTER

William E. Simon Graduate School of Business Administration
304 Schlegel Hall
P.O. Box 270107
Rochester, NY 14627-0107
Phone: (716) 275-3533
Fax: (716) 271-3907
E-mail: mbaadm@ssb.rochester.edu
http://www.ssb.rochester.edu
Student Body: Full-time enrollment: 413. Men: 75%. Women: 25%. African American: 2%. Asian American: 5%. Latino: 2%. International: 50%. Average age: 28. Part-time enrollment: 216. Men: 72%. Women: 28%.
Academics: Full-time faculty: 55. Part-time faculty: 9. Degrees awarded: M.B.A., M.S., Ph.D. in Business Administration. Joint degree programs: M.B.A./M.S. in Microbiology & Immunology, M.B.A./M.S. in Nursing, M.B.A./Master of Public Health, M.D./M.B.A. Evening program is offered. For fall 1996 entering class: 95% completed program within 2 years. 1% continued towards degree.
Finances: Tuition (1998–99): $23,970. Estimated tuition (1999–2000): $24,690. 75% of students receive some type of aid. Average student debt incurred by graduation: $25,316.
Admission Requirements: GMAT is required. Application deadline for fall: September 1.
Selectivity: Applications received (full-time): 1,661. Admitted: 459. Enrolled: 175.

Applications received (part-time): 60. Admitted: 45. Enrolled: 33. Average GMAT: 639. Average undergraduate GPA: 3.2. GMAT section weighed most heavily: weighed equally.
Placement: School has placement office. Placement rate at time of graduation: 89%. Placement rate 6 months after graduation: 99%. Average starting salary: $70,746.

North Carolina

APPALACHIAN STATE UNIVERSITY

John A. Walker College of Business
Graduate Studies & External Programs
P.O. Box 32037
Boone, NC 28608-2037
Phone: (704) 262-2922
Fax: (704) 262-2925
E-mail: mba@appstate.edu
http://www.business.appstate.edu
Student Body: Full-time enrollment: 46. Men: 67%. Women: 33%. Asian American: 4%. Latino: 2%. International: 7%. Average age: 28. Students living on campus: 1%. Part-time enrollment: 45. Men: 53%. Women: 47%.
Academics: Full-time faculty: 42. Degrees awarded: M.B.A. Evening program is offered. For fall 1996 entering class: 70% completed program within 2 years. 13% continued towards degree.
Finances: Tuition (1998–99): $1,781.
Admission Requirements: GMAT is required. Application deadline for fall: April 15.
Selectivity: Applications received (full-time): 46. Admitted: 34. Enrolled: 11. Enrolled (part-time): 1. Average GMAT: 509. Average undergraduate GPA: 3.02.
Placement: School has placement office. Placement rate at time of graduation: 60%. Placement rate 6 months after graduation: 95%. Average starting salary: $40,000.

DUKE UNIVERSITY

The Fuqua School of Business
Towerview Road, Room 134W
Durham, NC 27708
Phone: (919) 660-7705
Fax: (919) 681-8026
E-mail: fuqua-admissions@mail.duke.edu
http://www.fuqua.duke.edu
Student Body: Full-time enrollment: 671. Men: 67%. Women: 33%. African American: 7%. Asian American: 8%. International: 28%. Average age: 28.
Academics: Full-time faculty: 76. Part-time faculty: 28. Degrees awarded: M.B.A., Ph.D. Joint degree programs: M.B.A./J.D., M.B.A./M.F., M.B.A./M.P.P., M.B.A./M.S. Engineering, M.B.A./M.D., M.B.A./M.S. Nursing. Evening program is not offered. For fall 1996 entering class: 99% completed program within 2 years. 1% continued towards degree.
Finances: Tuition (1998–99): $25,250. 73% of students receive non-need-based aid. 76% of students receive need-based aid. Average student debt incurred by graduation: 42,500.
Admission Requirements: GMAT is required. Application deadline for fall: April 26, November 2, December 7, January 25, March 15.
Selectivity: Applications received (full-time): 3,399. Admitted: 540. Enrolled: 341. Average GMAT: 664. Average undergraduate GPA: 3.5. GMAT section weighed most heavily: quantitative (due to the curriculum).
Placement: School has placement office. Placement rate at time of graduation: 98%. Placement rate 6 months after graduation: 99%. Average starting salary: $79,300.

EAST CAROLINA UNIVERSITY

School of Business
3203 General Classroom Bldg.
Greenville, NC 27858-4353
Phone: (252) 328-6970
Fax: (252) 328-2106
E-mail: boldtd@mail.ecu.edu
http://www.business.ecu.edu/grad/

Student Body: Full-time enrollment: 235.
Men: 51%. Women: 49%. African
American: 7%. Minorities: 13%.
International: 12%. Average age: 28. Part-
time enrollment: 132. Men: 56%. Women:
44%.
Academics: Full-time faculty: 61. Degrees
awarded: M.B.A., M.S. Acc. Joint degree
programs: M.D./M.B.A. Evening program
is offered.
Finances: Tuition (1998–99): In-State:
$1,886. Out-of-State: $9,156. Estimated
tuition (1999–2000): In-State: $1,965.
Out-of-State: $9,600. 34% of students
receive need-based aid.
Admission Requirements: GMAT is required.
Application deadline for fall: June 1.
Selectivity: Applications received (full-time):
123. Admitted: 98. Enrolled: 64.
Applications received (part-time): 67.
Admitted: 39. Enrolled: 34. Average
GMAT: 513. Average undergraduate GPA:
3.1. GMAT section weighed most heavily:
weighed equally.
Placement: School has placement office.
Placement rate 3 months after graduation:
83%. Average starting salary: $40,100.

UNIVERSITY OF NORTH CAROLINA—CHAPEL HILL

Kenan-Flagler Business School
CB #3490, McColl Building
Chapel Hill, NC 27599-3490
Phone: (919) 962-3236
Fax: (919) 962-0898
E-mail: mba_info@unc.edu
http://www.bschool.unc.edu
Student Body: Full-time enrollment: 461.
Men: 73%. Women: 27%. Minorities: 9%.
International: 5%. Average age: 27.
Academics: Full-time faculty: 87. Part-time
faculty: 20. Degrees awarded: M.B.A.,
E.M.B.A., M. Acc., Ph.D. Joint degree pro-
grams: J.D./M.B.A., M.B.A./M. Regional
Planning, M.B.A./M. Public Health
Administration. Evening program is offered.
Finances: Tuition (1998–99): In-State:
$4,400. Out-of-State: $16,100. Estimated

tuition (1999–2000): In-State: $6,900.
Out-of-State: $19,100.
Admission Requirements: GMAT is required.
Application deadline for fall: March 5.
Selectivity: Applications received (full-time):
2,086. Admitted: 485. Enrolled: 245.
Average GMAT: 640. Average undergradu-
ate GPA: 3.2.
Placement: School has placement office.
Placement rate at time of graduation: 87%.
Placement rate 6 months after graduation:
98.5%. Average starting salary: $74,371.

UNIVERSITY OF NORTH CAROLINA—CHARLOTTE

The Belk College of Business Administration
Graduate Admissions
9201 University City Blvd.
Charlotte, NC 28223
Phone: (704) 547-3366
Fax: (704) 547-3279
E-mail: gradadm@email.uncc.edu
http://www.uncc.edu
Student Body: Full-time enrollment: 84.
Men: 61%. Women: 39%. African
American: 10%. Asian American: 2%.
Latino: 1%. International: 26%. Average
age: 29. Students living on campus: 1%.
Part-time enrollment: 358. Men: 67%.
Women: 33%.
Academics: Full-time faculty: 59. Degrees
awarded: M.B.A., M.S. Economics,
M. Acc. Evening program is offered.
Finances: Tuition (1998–99): In-State:
$1,838. Out-of-State: $9,108. Estimated
tuition (1999–2000): In-State: $2,200.
Out-of-State: $10,900. 15% of students
receive need-based aid. 4% receive non-
need-based aid. Average student debt
incurred by graduation: $6,100.
Admission Requirements: GMAT is required.
Application deadline for fall: rolling.
Selectivity: Applications received: 202.
Admitted: 144. Enrolled: 58. Average
GMAT: 541. Average undergraduate GPA:
3.2. GMAT section weighed most heavily:
weighed equally.
Placement: School has placement office.
Average starting salary: $50,000.

UNIVERSITY OF NORTH CAROLINA—GREENSBORO

Joseph M. Bryan School of Business and
Economics
1000 Spring Garden Street
220 Bryan Building
Greensboro, NC 27402-6165
Phone: (336) 334-5390
Fax: (336) 334-4209
E-mail: mbaoff@uncg.edu
http://www.uncg.edu/bae
Student Body: Full-time enrollment: 62.
Men: 58%. Women: 42%. African
American: 2%. Asian American: 16%.
Native American: 2%. International: 40%.
Average age: 30. Part-time enrollment:
170. Men: 69%. Women: 31%.
Academics: Full-time faculty: 57. Part-time
faculty: 1. Degrees awarded: M.B.A.
Evening program is offered.
Finances: Tuition (1998–99): In-State: $
2,031. Out-of-State: $10,319. Estimated
tuition (1999–2000): In-State: $2,132.
Out-of-State: $10,834.
Admission Requirements: GMAT is required.
Application deadline for fall: July 1.
Selectivity: Enrolled: 22. Enrolled: 38.
Average GMAT: 570. Average undergradu-
ate GPA: 3.2. GMAT section weighed most
heavily: weighed equally.
Placement: School has placement office.

WAKE FOREST UNIVERSITY

Babcock Graduate School of Management
P.O. Box 7659
Winston-Salem, NC 27109
Phone: (336) 758-5422
Fax: (336) 758-5830
E-mail: admissions@mba.wfu.edu
http://www.mba.wfu.edu
Student Body: Full-time enrollment: 250.
Men: 76%. Women: 24%. African
American: 5%. Asian American: 2%. Latino:
1%. International: 19%. Average age: 26.
Students living on campus: 1%. Part-time
enrollment: 417. Men: 76%. Women: 24%.
Academics: Full-time faculty: 36. Part-time
faculty: 3. Degrees awarded: M.B.A. Joint

degree programs: J.D./M.B.A.,
M.D./M.B.A., Ph.D./M.B.A. in sciences.
Evening program is offered.
Finances: Tuition (1998–99): $20,400.
Estimated tuition (1999–2000): $21,200.
4% of students receive non-need-based aid.
49% of students receive need-based aid.
Average student debt incurred by gradua-
tion: $45,872.
Admission Requirements: GMAT is required.
Application deadline for fall: April 1.
Selectivity: Applications received (full-time):
983. Admitted: 245. Enrolled: 111.
Applications received (part-time): 262.
Admitted: 197. Enrolled: 144. Average
GMAT: 633. Average undergraduate GPA:
3.2. GMAT section weighed most heavily:
weighed equally.
Placement: School has placement office.
Placement rate at time of graduation: 94%.
Placement rate 6 months after graduation:
100%. Average starting salary: $59,000.

WESTERN CAROLINA UNIVERSITY

Graduate Programs in Business
Forsyth Building
Cullowhee, NC 28723
Phone: (828) 227-7402
Fax: (828) 227-7414
E-mail: gwilliams@wcu.edu
http://www.wcu.edu
Student Body: Full-time enrollment: 60.
Men: 63%. Women: 37%. African
American: 3%. Asian American: 7%. Latino:
2%. Native American: 2%. International:
43%. Average age: 25. Students living on
campus: 50%. Part-time enrollment: 105.
Men: 52%. Women: 48%.
Academics: Full-time faculty: 39. Degrees
awarded: M.B.A., M.P.M., M.A.C.
Evening program is offered. For fall 1996
entering class: 100% completed program
within 2 years.
Finances: Tuition (1998–99): In-State:
$1,799. Out-of-State: $9,069. 40% of
students receive non-need-based aid. 20%
of students receive need-based aid.

Admission Requirements: GMAT is required.
Application deadline for fall: open.
Selectivity: Applications received (full-time):
60. Admitted: 55. Enrolled: 24.
Applications received (part-time): 38.
Admitted: 36. Enrolled: 25. Average
GMAT: 520. Average undergraduate GPA:
3.3. GMAT section weighed most heavily:
weighed equally.
Placement: School has placement office.
Placement rate at time of graduation: 80%.
Placement rate 6 months after graduation:
95%. Average starting salary: $35,000.

North Dakota

UNIVERSITY OF NORTH DAKOTA

College of Business & Public Administration
The Graduate School
P.O. Box 8178
Grand Forks, ND 58202-8179
Phone: (701) 777-2945
Fax: (701) 777-3619
E-mail: UNDGRAD@mail.und.nodak.edu
http://www.und.nodak.edu/dept/index.htm
Student Body: Full-time enrollment: 11.
Men: 55%. Women: 45%. Average age:
27. Part-time enrollment: 72. Men: 69%.
Women: 31%.
Academics: Full-time faculty: 39. Degrees
awarded: M.B.A. Evening program is
offered. For fall 1996 entering class: 90%
completed program within 2 years. 5% con-
tinued towards degree.
Finances: Tuition (1998–99): In-State:
$3,798. Out-of-State: $6,512. Estimated
tuition (1999–2000): In-State: $3,914.
Out-of-State: $6,628. 70% of students
receive some type of aid.
Admission Requirements: GMAT is required.
Application deadline for fall: August 15.
Selectivity: GMAT: 517. Average undergraduate GPA: 3.1. GMAT section
weighed most heavily: weighed equally.
Placement: School has placement office.
Placement rate at time of graduation: 75%.

Placement rate 6 months after graduation:
100%. Average starting salary: $43,500.

OHIO

BOWLING GREEN STATE UNIVERSITY*

College of Business Administration
Graduate Studies in Business
369 College of Business Administration Bldg.
Bowling Green, OH 43403
Phone: (419) 372-2488
Fax: (419) 372-2875
E-mail: mba-info@cba.bgsu.edu
http://www-cba.bgsu.edu/
Student Body: Full-time enrollment: 94.
International: 22%. Part-time enrollment: 141.
Academics: Full-time faculty: 71. Part-time fac-
ulty: 0. Degrees awarded: M.B.A., M. Acc.,
M.O.D., M.A. in Economics, M.S. in
Applied Statistics. Evening program is offered.
Finances: Tuition (1998–99): In-State:
$5,762. Out-of-State: $10,776. Estimated
tuition (1999–2000): In-State: $5,935.
Out-of-State: $11,100.
Admission Requirements: GMAT is required.
Application deadline for fall: June 1.
Selectivity: Applications received (full-time):
159. Admitted: 152. Enrolled: 61.
Average GMAT: 556. Average undergradu-
ate GPA: 3.1.
Placement: School has placement office.
Average starting salary: $38,400.

CASE WESTERN RESERVE UNIVERSITY

Weatherhead School of Management
10900 Euclid Avenue
Cleveland, OH 44106-7235
Phone: (216) 368-2030
Fax: (216) 368-5548
E-mail: wsommba@pyrite.cwru.edu
http://weatherhead.cwru.edu
Student Body: Full-time enrollment: 476.
Men: 64%. Women: 36%. African

American: 6%. Asian American: 4%. Latino: 2%. International: 42%. Average age: 28.5. Students living on campus: 10%. Part-time enrollment: 663. Men: 66%. Women: 34%.

Academics: Full-time faculty: 92. Part-time faculty: 18. Degrees awarded: M.B.A., M.S., E.M.B.A., M. Acc., M.S.M.S., M.N.O., E.D.M., M.S.M./I.S., Ph.D., M.S.M./O.R., M.S.M./S.C. Joint degree programs: J.D./M.B.A., M.D./M.B.A., M.S.M./I.S./M.B.A., M.S.M./O.R./M.B.A., M.S.M./S.C./M.B.A., M.S.N./M.B.A., M.I.M./M.B.A. (with Thunderbird). Evening program is offered. For fall 1996 entering class: 90% completed program within 2 years. 10% continued towards joint degree.

Finances: Tuition (1998–99): $21,000. Estimated tuition (1999–2000): $21,650. 35% of students receive non-need-based aid. 70% of students receive need-based aid.

Admission Requirements: GMAT is required. Application deadline for fall: April 15 (domestic), February 15 (international).

Selectivity: Applications received (full-time): 1,115. Admitted: 446. Enrolled: 194. Applications received (part-time): 189. Admitted: 159. Enrolled: 142. Average GMAT: 614. Average undergraduate GPA: 3.2. GMAT section weighed most heavily: weighed equally.

Placement: School has placement office. Placement rate at time of graduation: 95%. Placement rate 6 months after graduation: 99%. Average starting salary: $64,300.

CLEVELAND STATE UNIVERSITY

James J. Nance College of Business Administration
1860 E. 17th Street BU 219
Cleveland, OH 44114
Phone: (216) 687-3730
Fax: (216) 687-5311
E-mail: b.gottschalk@csu-e.csuohio.edu
http://csuohio.edu/mba
Student Body: Full-time enrollment: 129. Men: 56%. Women: 44%. Average age: 27.5. Part-time enrollment: 1,000. Men: 60%. Women: 40%.

Academics: Full-time faculty: 77. Degrees awarded: M.B.A., M.A.F.I.S., M.C.I.S., M.L.R.H.R. Joint degree programs: J.D./M.B.A. Evening program is offered.

Finances: Tuition (1998–99): In-State: $205/credit. Out-of-State: $407/credit. Estimated tuition (199-2000): In-state: $210/credit. Out of State: $418/credit.

Admission Requirements: GMAT is required. Application deadline for fall: rolling.

Selectivity: Applications received (full-time): 339. Admitted: 295. Enrolled: 93. Applications received: (part-time): 182. Admitted: 155. Enrolled: 93. Average GMAT: 512. Average undergraduate GPA: 3.13. GMAT section weighed most heavily: weighed equally.

Placement: School has placement office. Placement rate at time of graduation: 86%. Placement rate 6 months after graduation: 94%. Average starting salary: $51,120.

JOHN CARROLL UNIVERSITY*

Boler School of Business
20700 North Park Boulevard
University Heights, OH 44118
Phone: (216) 397-4204
E-mail: mmauk@jcvaxa.jcu.edu
Student Body: Part-time enrollment: 219. Men: 62%. Women: 38%.

Academics: Full-time faculty: 27. Part-time faculty: 3. Degrees awarded: M.B.A. Joint degree programs: M.A./Communications. Evening program is offered.

Finances: Tuition (1998–99): $1590 per course. Estimated tuition (1999–2000): $1590 per course.

Admission Requirements: GMAT is required. Application deadline for fall: August 15.

Selectivity: Applications received (full-time): 80. Admitted: 63. Enrolled: 44. Average GMAT: 513. Average undergraduate GPA: 3.1.

Placement: School has placement office. Average starting salary: $47,000.

KENT STATE UNIVERSITY

Graduate School of Management
P.O. Box 5190
Kent, OH 44242-0001
Phone: (330) 672-2282, ext. 235
Fax: (330) 672-7303
E-mail: gradbus@bsa3.kent.edu
http://business.kent.edu
Student Body: Full-time enrollment: 155. Men: 61%. Women: 39%. African American: 6%. Asian American: 3%. Latino: 1%. International: 26%. Average age: 25. Part-time enrollment: 249. Men: 63%. Women: 37%.

Academics: Full-time faculty: 56. Degrees awarded: M.B.A., E.M.B.A., M.S., M.A., Ph.D. Joint degree programs: M.B.A./Master of Science in Nursing, M.B.A./Master in Library Science. Evening program is offered. For fall 1996 entering class: 80% completed program within 2 years. 14% continued towards degree.

Finances: Tuition (1998–99): In-State: $5,076. Out-of-State: $9,736.

Admission Requirements: GMAT is required. Application deadline for fall: July 1.

Selectivity: Applications received (full-time): 186. Admitted: 108. Enrolled: 45. Applications received (part-time): 37. Admitted: 34. Enrolled: 25. Average GMAT: 536. Average undergraduate GPA: 3.1. GMAT section weighed most heavily: weighed equally.

Placement: School has placement office. Average starting salary: $44,477.

MIAMI UNIVERSITY

Richard T. Farmer School of Business
107 Laws Hall
Oxford, OH 45056
Phone: (513) 529-6643
Fax: (513) 529-2487
E-mail: miamiMBA@muohio.edu
http://www.sba.muohio.edu/mbaprogram
Student Body: Full-time enrollment: 63. Men: 62%. Women: 38%. African American: 11%. Latino: 2%. International: 33%. Average age: 25. Students living on

campus: 20%. Part-time enrollment: 46. Men: 70%. Women: 30%.

Academics: Full-time faculty: 118. Part-time faculty: 5. Degrees awarded: M.B.A., M. Acc., M.A. Economics. Joint degree programs: Master of Architecture. Evening program is offered. For fall 1996 entering class: 100% completed program within 2 years.

Finances: Tuition (1998–99): In-state: $5,947. Out-of-state: $12,407. Estimated tuition (1999–2000): In-state: $6,244. Out-of-State: $13,027.

Selectivity: Applications received (full-time): 86. Admitted: 64. Enrolled: 23. Applications received (part-time): 24. Admitted: 16. Enrolled: 12. Average GMAT: 550. Average undergraduate GPA: 3.2. GMAT section weighed most heavily: weighed equally.

Placement: School has placement office. Placement rate at time of graduation: 51%. Placement rate 6 months after graduation: 86%. Average starting salary: $43,650.

OHIO STATE UNIVERSITY

Max M. Fisher College of Business
2108 Neil Avenue
100 Gerlach Hall
Columbus, OH 43210-1144
Phone: (614) 292-8511
Fax: (614) 292-9006
E-mail: cobgrd@cob.ohio-state.edu
http://www.cob.ohio-state.edu/
Student Body: Full-time enrollment: 282. Men: 72%. Women: 28%. African American: 4%. Asian American: 4%. Latino: 2%. International: 22%. Average age: 28. Students living on campus: 12%. Part-time enrollment: 159. Men: 74%. Women: 26%.

Academics: Full-time faculty: 85. Part-time faculty: 1. Degrees awarded: M.B.A., M.L.H.R., Ph.D. Joint degree programs: M.B.A./J.D. Evening program is offered. For fall 1996 entering class: 88% completed program within 2 years. 2% continued towards degree.

Finances: Tuition (1998–99): In-State: $5,772. Out-of-State: $14,058. Estimated tuition (1999–2000): In-State: $6,061.

Out-of-State: $14,761. 5% of students receive need-based aid. 45% of students receive non-need-based aid. Average student debt incurred by graduation: $11,761 (for all grad students).

Admission Requirements: GMAT is required. Application deadline for fall: April 30.
Selectivity: Applications received (full-time): 1,244. Admitted: 330. Enrolled: 145. Applications received (part-time): 208. Admitted: 91. Enrolled: 80. Average GMAT: 642. Average undergraduate GPA: 3.2. GMAT section weighed most heavily: weighed equally.
Placement: School has placement office. Placement rate at time of graduation: 90%. Placement rate 6 months after graduation: 98%. Average starting salary: $68,720.

OHIO UNIVERSITY

College of Business
Copeland Hall 514
Athens, OH 45701
Phone: (740) 593-2007
Fax: (740) 593-0319
E-mail: rossj@ohiou.edu
http://www.cba.ohiou.edu
Student Body: Full-time enrollment: 50. Men: 64%. Women: 28%. African American: 10%. International: 42%. Average age: 26. Part-time enrollment: 113. Men: 70%. Women: 30%.

Academics: Full-time faculty: 55. Part-time faculty: 30. Degrees awarded: M.B.A., M.S. Acc. Evening program is offered through distance learning. For the 1996 entering class: 100% completed program within two years.

Finances: Estimated tuition (1999–2000): $7,240. 80% of students receive non-need-based aid.

Admission Requirements: GMAT is required. Application deadline for fall: March 1.
Selectivity: Applications received (full-time): 164. Admitted: 89. Enrolled: 50. Applications received (part-time): 106. Admitted: 69. Enrolled: 57. Average GMAT: 543. Average undergraduate GPA: 3.4. GMAT section weighed most heavily: weighed equally.

Placement: School has placement office. Placement rate at time of graduation: 70%. Placement rate 6 months after graduation: 98%.

UNIVERSITY OF AKRON

College of Business Administration
259 S. Broadway
Room 412
Akron, OH 44325-4805
Phone: (330) 972-7043
Fax: (330) 972-6588
E-mail: Gradcba@uakron.edu
http://www.uakron.edu/cba
Student Body: Full-time enrollment: 186. Men: 65%. Women: 35%. African American: 3%. Asian American: 2%. International: 52%. Average age: 28. Part-time enrollment: 304. Men: 65%. Women: 35%.

Academics: Full-time faculty: 48. Part-time faculty: 11. Degrees awarded: M.B.A., M.S.M., M.S.A., M. Tax. Joint degree programs: J.D./M.B.A., J.D./M Tax. Evening program is offered. For fall 1996 entering class: 81% completed program within 2 years. 11% continued towards degree.

Finances: Tuition (1998–99): In-State: $6,408. Out-of-State: $11,988. Estimated tuition (1999–2000): In-State: $6,728. Out-of-State: $12,707. 20% of students receive need-based aid.

Admission Requirements: GMAT is required. Application deadline for fall: July 1, Dec. 15, May 15.
Selectivity: Applications received (full-time): 128. Admitted: 95. Enrolled: 53. Applications received (part-time): 209. Admitted: 155. Enrolled: 87. Average GMAT: 569. Average undergraduate GPA: 3.1. GMAT section weighed most heavily: weighed equally.
Placement: School has placement office.

UNIVERSITY OF CINCINNATI

Graduate School of Business
103 Lindner Hall
Cincinnati, OH 45221-0020
Phone: (513) 556-7020
Fax: (513) 556-4891
E-mail: Graduate@uc.edu
http://www.cba.uc.edu
Student Body: Full-time enrollment: 70.
Men: 57%. Women: 43%. African
American: 11%. Asian American: 3%.
Latino: 3%. International: 21%. Average
age: 27. Students living on campus: 5%.
Part-time enrollment: 325. Men: 58%.
Women: 42%.
Academics: Full-time faculty: 30. Part-time
faculty: 2. Degrees awarded: M.B.A.,
M.S.B.A. in Quantitative Analysis,
M.S.B.A. in Taxation, M.S.B.A. in
Accounting. Joint degree programs:
M.B.A./J.D., M.B.A./Arts Administration,
M.B.A./Industrial Engineering,
M.B.A./M.D. Evening program is offered.
For fall 1996 entering class: 97% complet-
ed program within 2 years. 2% continued
towards degree.
Finances: Tuition (1998–99): In-State:
$7,500. Out-of-State: $14,000. Estimated
tuition (1999–2000): In-State: $12,500.
Out-of-State: $14,500. 60% of students
receive need-based aid. 5% of students
receive non-need-based aid. Average
student debt incurred by graduation:
$10,000.
Admission Requirements: GMAT is required.
Application deadline for fall: April 1.
Selectivity: Applications received (full-time):
215. Admitted: 106. Enrolled: 71.
Applications received (part-time): 184.
Admitted: 93. Enrolled: 85. Average
GMAT: 604. Average undergraduate GPA:
3.2. GMAT section weighed most heavily:
weighed equally.
Placement: School has placement office.
Placement rate at time of graduation: 75%.
Placement rate 6 months after graduation:
98%. Average starting salary: $51,500.

UNIVERSITY OF DAYTON

School of Business Administration
Miriam Hall 803
300 College Park
Dayton, OH 45469
Phone: (937) 229-3733
Fax: (937) 229-3301
E-mail: MBA@UDayton.edu
http://www.udayton.edu/~mba
Student Body: Full-time enrollment: 61.
Men: 52%. Women: 48%. International:
41%. Average age: 25. Students living on
campus: 1%. Part-time enrollment: 476.
Men: 61%. Women: 39%.
Academics: Full-time faculty: 53. Part-time
faculty: 4. Degrees awarded: M.B.A. Joint
degree programs: J.D./M.B.A. Evening pro-
gram is offered.
Finances: Tuition (1998–99): $409/credit
hour.
Admission Requirements: GMAT is
required. Application deadline for fall: Aug.
15, Dec. 15, May 1, June 1.
Selectivity: Applications received (full-time):
29. Admitted: 27. Enrolled: 27.
Applications received (part-time): 151.
Admitted: 135. Enrolled: 89. Average
GMAT: 532. Average undergraduate GPA:
3.2. GMAT section weighed most heavily:
weighed equally.
Placement: School has placement office.

UNIVERSITY OF TOLEDO

College of Business Administration
2801 West Bancroft
Toledo, OH 43606
Phone: (419) 530-4723
Fax: (419) 530-4724
E-mail: grdsch@utnet.utoledo.edu
http://www.utoledo.edu/gradschool
Student Body: Full-time enrollment: 79. Men:
56%. Women: 44%. Asian American: 1%.
International: 82%. Part-time enrollment:
257. Men: 69%. Women: 31%.
Academics: Full-time faculty: 67. Part-time
faculty: 3. Degrees awarded: M.B.A.,
M.S., M.S.A., E.M.B.A., Ph.D. Joint degree

programs: J.D./M.B.A. Evening program is
offered.
Finances: Tuition (1998–99): In-State:
$3,040. Out-of-State: $6,005.
Admission Requirements: GMAT is
required. Application deadline for fall:
August 1.
Selectivity: Applications received (part-time):
207. Admitted: 164. Enrolled: 76.
Average GMAT: 504. Average undergradu-
ate GPA: 2.9. GMAT section weighed most
heavily: weighed equally.
Placement: School has placement office.
Average starting salary: $41,000.

WRIGHT STATE UNIVERSITY*

College of Business and Administration
School of Graduate Studies
3640 Colonel Glenn Highway
Dayton, OH 45435
Phone: (937) 775-2975
Student Body: Full-time enrollment: 172.
Men: 57%. Women: 43%. International:
26%. Average age: 29.6. Part-time enrollment: 413. Men: 62%. Women: 38%.
Academics: Full-time faculty: 65. Degrees
awarded: M.B.A., B.S.B., M.S. in Social
and Applied Economics, M.S. in Logistics
Management, M. Acc. Joint degree pro-
grams: M.B.A./M.S. S.&A. Economics,
M.B.A./M.S. in Nursing. Evening program
is offered.
Finances: Tuition (1998–99): In-State:
$148 per credit hour. Out-of-State: $263
per credit hour. Estimated tuition
(1999–2000): In-State: $150 per credit
hour. Out-of-State: $265 per credit hour.
Admission Requirements: GMAT is required.
Application deadline for fall: rolling.
Selectivity: Applications received (full-time):
310. Admitted: 202. Enrolled: 108.
Average GMAT: 533. Average undergraduate GPA: 3.1.
Placement: School has placement office.

Oklahoma

OKLAHOMA STATE UNIVERSITY

College of Business Administration
M.B.A. Programs
102 Gundersen
Stillwater, OK 74078-0555
Phone: (405) 744-2951
Fax: (405) 744-7474
E-mail: mba-osu@okway.okstate.edu
http://www.okstate.edu
Student Body: Full-time enrollment: 118.
Men: 73%. Women: 27%. African
American: 2%. Latino: 1%. Native
American: 1%. International: 47%. Average
age: 24. Students living on campus: 25%.
Part-time enrollment: 235. Men: 69%.
Women: 31%.
Academics: Full-time faculty: 88. Degrees
awarded: M.B.A., M.S. Telecom Mgmt.,
M.S. Acc., M.S. Econ. Joint degree pro-
grams: M.B.A./M.P.H. Evening program is
offered. For fall 1996 entering class: 96%
completed program within 2 years. 2% continued towards degree.
Finances: Tuition (1998–99): In-State:
$80/credit + fees. Out-of-State:
$254/credit + fees. Estimated tuition
(1999–2000): In-State: $102/credit +
fees. Out-of-State: $270/credit + fees. 30%
of students receive need-based aid. 40% of
students receive non-need-based aid.
Admission Requirements: GMAT is
required. Application deadline for fall: July
1, November 1.
Selectivity: Applications received (full-time):
173. Admitted: 113. Enrolled: 59.
Applications received (part-time): 117.
Admitted: 71. Enrolled: 59. Average
GMAT: 580. Average undergraduate GPA:
3.4. GMAT section weighed most heavily:
weighed equally.
Placement: School has placement office.
Placement rate at time of graduation: 90%.
Placement rate 6 months after graduation:
95%. Average starting salary: $48,000.

UNIVERSITY OF OKLAHOMA

Michael F. Price College of Business
307 W. Brooks, Adams Hall
Room 105-K
Norman, OK 73019-4003
Phone: (405) 325-4107
Fax: (405) 325-1957
E-mail: awatkins@ou.edu
http://www.ou/business/mba
Student Body: Full-time enrollment: 130.
Men: 64%. Women: 36%. International:
29%. Average age: 24. Students living on
campus: 28%. Part-time enrollment: 131.
Men: 69%. Women: 31%.
Academics: Full-time faculty: 58. Part-time fac-
ulty: 4. Degrees awarded: M.B.A., M. Acc.,
Ph.D. Joint degree programs: J.D./M.B.A.,
M.B.A./C.S., M.B.A./M.P.H.,
M.B.A./Pharm., M.B.A./M.S. Math,
M.B.A./M.A. Language. Evening program is
offered. For fall 1996 entering class: 70%
completed program within 2 years. 30% con-
tinued towards degree.
Finances: Tuition (1998–99): In-State:
$3,134. Out-of-State: $8,718. 30% of stu-
dents receive non-need-based aid. Average
student debt incurred by graduation: $5,000.
Admission Requirements: GMAT is required.
Application deadline for fall: June 1.
Selectivity: Applications received (full-time):
235. Admitted: 130. Enrolled: 61.
Applications received (part-time): 44.
Admitted: 30. Enrolled: 27. Average
GMAT: 602. Average undergraduate GPA:
3.4. GMAT section weighed most heavily:
weighed equally.
Placement: School has placement office.
Placement rate at time of graduation: 92%.
Average starting salary: $45,000.

UNIVERSITY OF TULSA

College of Business Administration
600 South College, BAH 308
Tulsa, OK 74104
Phone: (918) 631-2242
Fax: (918) 631-3672
E-mail: millsbm@centum.utulsa.edu
http://www.cba.utulsa.edu

Student Body: Full-time enrollment: 45.
Men: 56%. Women: 44%. International:
24%. Average age: 25. Students living on
campus: 2%. Part-time enrollment: 206.
Men: 51%. Women: 49%.
Academics: Full-time faculty: 42. Part-time
faculty: 7. Degrees awarded: M.B.A.,
M.A.I.S., M. Tax. Joint degree programs:
J.D./M.B.A., M. Eng.Tech. Evening pro-
gram is offered.
Finances: Tuition (1998–99): $10,560.
Estimated tuition (1999–2000): $10,560.
Admission Requirements: GMAT is required.
Application deadline for fall: open.
Selectivity: Average GMAT: 538. Average
undergraduate GPA: 3.2. GMAT section
weighed most heavily: total score consid-
ered.
Placement: School has placement office.
80% of students are employed full time
while in the program.

Oregon

OREGON STATE UNIVERSITY

College of Business
Bexell Hall, Room 210
Corvallis, OR 97331
Phone: (541) 737-3150
E-mail: saveriano@bus.orst.edu
http://www.osu.orst.edu
Student Body: Full-time enrollment: 49.
Men: 63%. Women: 37%. International:
63%. Average age: 27. Part-time enroll-
ment: 37. Men: 57%. Women: 43%.
Academics: Full-time faculty: 37. Degrees
awarded: M.B.A. Evening program is
offered. For fall 1996 entering class: 86%
completed program within 2 years. 6% con-
tinued towards degree.
Finances: Tuition (1998–99): In-State:
$10,843. Out-of-State: $17,560.
Admission Requirements: GMAT is required.
Application deadline for fall: March 1.
Selectivity: Average GMAT: 565. Average
undergraduate GPA: 3.2. GMAT section
weighed most heavily: weighed equally.
Placement: School has placement office.

PORTLAND STATE UNIVERSITY

School of Business Administration
P.O. Box 751
Portland, OR 97207
Phone: (503) 725-3511
E-mail: adm@pdx.edu
http://www.pdx.edu
Student Body: Full-time enrollment: 77.
Men: 52%. Women: 48%. African
American: 10%. Asian American: 30%.
Latino: 4%. International: 64%. Average
age: 30. Part-time enrollment: 330. Men:
62%. Women: 38%.
Academics: Full-time faculty: 48. Part-time
faculty: 35. Degrees awarded: M.B.A.,
M.I.M., M.S.M. Financial Analysis. Evening
program is offered. For fall 1996 entering
class: 84% completed program within 2
years. 7% continued towards degree.
Finances: Tuition (1998–99): In-State:
$6,100. Out-of-State: $10,444.
Admission Requirements: GMAT is required.
Application deadline for fall: April 1.
Selectivity: Applications received (full-time):
136. Admitted: 37. Enrolled: 37.
Applications received (part-time): 146.
Admitted: 90. Enrolled: 90. Average GMAT:
592. Average undergraduate GPA: 3.3.
Placement: School has placement office.
Placement rate 6 months after graduation:
73%. Average starting salary: $51,000.

UNIVERSITY OF OREGON

Charles H. Lundquist College of Business
1208 University of Oregon
Eugene, OR 97403
Phone: (541) 346-3306
Fax: (541) 346-3347
E-mail: dposton@oregon.uoregon.edu
http://www.biz.uoregon.edu/
Student Body: Full-time enrollment: 188.
Men: 72%. Women: 28%. African
American: 2%. Asian American: 2%. Latino:
3%. Native American: 1%. International:
29%. Average age: 27.2. Students living
on campus: 10%.
Academics: Full-time faculty: 48. Part-time
faculty: 19. Degrees awarded: M.B.A.,

M.S., Ph.D. Joint degree programs:
J.D./M.B.A. Evening program is not
offered. For fall 1996: 98% completed program within 2 years.
Finances: Tuition (1998–99): In-State:
$7,389. Out-of-State: $11,562. Estimated
tuition (1999–2000): In-State: $7,389.
Out-of-State: $11,562. 60% of students
receive need-based aid. 3% receive non-
need-based aid. Average student debt
incurred by graduation: $24,720.
Admission Requirements: GMAT is
required. Application deadline for fall:
March 1.
Selectivity: Applications received (full-time):
294. Admitted: 189. Enrolled: 94.
Average GMAT: 571. Average undergraduate GPA: 3.2. GMAT section weighed most
heavily: weighed equally.
Placement: School has placement office.
Placement rate at time of graduation: 76%.
Placement rate 6 months after graduation:
94%. Average starting salary: $48,725.

UNIVERSITY OF PORTLAND

School of Business
Graduate School
5000 North Willamette Blvd.
Portland, OR 97203
Phone: (503) 943-7107
Fax: (503) 943-7178
E-mail: mba-up@up.edu
http://www.up.edu
Student Body: Full-time enrollment: 9. Men:
11%. Women: 89%. International: 11%.
Average age: 27. Students living on cam-
pus: 10%. Part-time enrollment: 92. Men:
68%. Women: 32%.
Academics: Part-time faculty: 25. Degrees
awarded: M.B.A. Evening program is
offered.
Finances: Tuition (1998–99): $540/credit.
Admission Requirements: GMAT is required.
Application deadline for fall: July 30.
Selectivity: Applications received (part-time):
79. Admitted: 31. Enrolled: 23. Average
GMAT: 525. Average undergraduate GPA:
3.2. GMAT section weighed most heavily:
weighed equally.
Placement: School has placement office.

WILLAMETTE UNIVERSITY

Atkinson Graduate School of Management
900 State Street
Salem, OR 97301
Phone: (503) 370-6167
Fax: (503) 370-3011
E-mail: agsm-admission@willamette.edu
http://www.willamette.edu/agsm
Student Body: Full-time enrollment: 125.
African American: 2%. Asian American:
2%. Latino: 1%. International: 27%.
Average age: 26. Students living on campus: 10%. Part-time enrollment: 33.
Academics: Full-time faculty: 12. Part-time
faculty: 6. Degrees awarded: M.M. Joint
degree programs: J.D./M.M. Evening program is not offered. For fall 1996 entering
class: 71% completed program within 2
years. 18% continued towards degree.
Finances: Tuition (1998–99): $15,500.
Estimated tuition (1999–2000): $15,950.
62% of students receive non-need-based
aid. 80% of students receive need-based
aid. Average student debt incurred by graduation: $32,367.
Admission Requirements: GMAT is
required. Application deadline for fall:
March 31.
Selectivity: Applications received (full-time):
146. Admitted: 110. Enrolled: 60.
Applications received (part-time): 9.
Admitted: 9. Enrolled: 6. Average GMAT:
550. Average undergraduate GPA: 3.2.
GMAT section weighed most heavily:
weighed equally.
Placement: School has placement office.
Placement rate at time of graduation: 84%.
Placement rate 6 months after graduation:
95%. Average starting salary: $42,217.

PENNSYLVANIA

CARNEGIE MELLON UNIVERSITY

Graduate School of Industrial Administration
Schenley Park
Pittsburgh, PA 15213
Phone: (412) 268-2272
Fax: (412) 268-4209
E-mail: gsia-admissionstoandrew@cmu.edu
http://www.gsia.cmu.edu/
Student Body: Full-time enrollment: 241.
Men: 75%. Women: 25%. International:
37%. Average age: 28.
Academics: Full-time faculty: 90. Part-time
faculty: 30. Degrees awarded: M.B.A.,
M.S., M.S. in Industrial Administration,
M.S. in Electronic Commerce, M.S. in
Computational Finance, M.S. in Civil
Engineering and Management. Evening
program is offered.
Finances: Tuition (1998–99): $24,680.
Estimated tuition (1999–2000): $24,680.
Admission Requirements: GMAT is required.
Application deadline for fall: November 13.
Selectivity: Average GMAT: 640. Average
undergraduate GPA: 3.85. GMAT section
weighed most heavily: weighed equally.
Placement: School has placement office.
Average starting salary: $77,461.

DREXEL UNIVERSITY

College of Business and Administration
32nd and Chestnut Streets
Philadelphia, PA 19104
Phone: (215) 895-6704
Fax: (215) 895-1012
E-mail: bighamdg@duvm.ocs.drexel.edu
http://www.coba.drexel.edu/
academics/grad/main.html
Student Body: Full-time enrollment: 300.
Men: 59%. Women: 41%. Average age:
25. Part-time enrollment: 516. Men: 65%.
Women: 35%.

Academics: Full-time faculty: 82. Part-time
faculty: 32. Degrees awarded: M.B.A.,
M.S. Evening program is offered.
Finances: Tuition (1998–99): $13,701.
Admission Requirements: GMAT is required.
Application deadline for fall: March 1.
Selectivity: Enrolled (full-time): 88. Enrolled
(part-time): 87. Average GMAT: 560.
Average undergraduate GPA: 3.2. GMAT
section weighed most heavily: weighed
equally.
Placement: School has placement office.
Average starting salary: $52,800.

DUQUESNE UNIVERSITY

Graduate School of Business
Room 704 Rockwell Hall
600 Forbes Avenue
Pittsburgh, PA 15282
Phone: (412) 396-6276
Fax: (412) 396-5304
E-mail: grad-bus@next.duq.edu
http://www.duq.edu
Student Body: Full-time enrollment: 139.
Men: 63%. Women: 37%. African
American: 10%. Asian American: 22%.
Latino: 3%. International: 45%. Average
age: 26. Students living on campus: 10%.
Part-time enrollment: 557. Men: 57%.
Women: 43%.
Academics: Full-time faculty: 45. Part-time fac-
ulty: 18. Degrees awarded: M.B.A., M.S.
Information Systems, M.S. Tax. Joint degree
programs: M.B.A./J.D., M.B.A./M.S.N.,
M.B.A./E.S.M., M.B.A./M.S.-Pharm,
M.B.A./M.L.S., M.B.A./M.S.-I.S.M.
Evening program is offered.
Finances: Tuition (1998–99): $481/credit
hour, $39 in fees. Estimated tuition
(1999–2000): $481/credit + $39 in
fees. 75% receive need-based aid.
Admission Requirements: GMAT is required.
Application deadline for fall: June 1.
Selectivity: Applications received (full-time):
66. Admitted: 54. Enrolled: 33.
Applications received (part-time): 263.
Admitted: 219. Enrolled: 141. Average
GMAT: 510. Average undergraduate GPA:
3.0. GMAT section weighed most heavily:
weighed equally.

Placement: School has placement office.
Placement rate at time of graduation: 70%.
Placement rate 6 months after graduation:
98%. Average starting salary: $45,000.

LEHIGH UNIVERSITY

College of Business and Economics
621 Taylor Street
Bethlehem, PA 18015
Phone: (610) 758-4450
Fax: (610) 758-5283
E-mail: incbe@lehigh.edu
http://www.lehigh.edu
Student Body: Full-time enrollment: 57.
Men: 72%. Women: 28%. International:
25%. Average age: 27. Students living on
campus: 12%. Part-time enrollment: 274.
Men: 68%. Women: 32%.
Academics: Full-time faculty: 55. Part-time
faculty: 7. Degrees awarded: M.B.A.,
M.S., Ph.D. Evening program is offered.
For fall 1996 entering class: 87% complet-
ed program within 2 years. 9% continued
towards degree.
Finances: Tuition (1998–99): $590/credit
hour. Merit-based aid only. Most students
are employed and reimbursed.
Admission Requirements: GMAT is required.
Application deadline for fall: July 15.
Selectivity: Applications received (full-time):
46. Admitted: 31. Enrolled: 24.
Applications received (part-time): 95.
Admitted: 71. Enrolled: 69. Average GMAT:
593. Average undergraduate GPA: 3.2.
GMAT section weighed most heavily: Math.
Placement: School has placement office. Most
students are employed throughout program.

PENNSYLVANIA STATE UNIVERSITY

Smeal College of Business Administration
106 Business Administration Building
University Park, PA 16802-3000
Phone: (814) 863-0474
Fax: (814) 863-8072
E-mail: smealmba@psu.edu
http://www.smeal.psu.edu/mba/main.html

Student Body: Full-time enrollment: 247. Men: 70%. Women: 30%. African American: 8%. Asian American: 6%. Latino: 3%. International: 21%. Average age: 27. Students living on campus: 12%.
Academics: Full-time faculty: 100. Degrees awarded: M.B.A., M.S., Ph.D. Joint degree programs: M.B.A./ M.H.A., J.D./M.B.A., B.S./M.B.A. Evening program is not offered. For fall 1996 entering class: 96% completed program within 2 years. 2% continued towards degree.
Finances: Tuition (1998–99): In-State: $7,216. Out-of-State: $14,140.
Admission Requirements: GMAT is required. Application deadline for fall: April 1.
Selectivity: Applications received (full-time): 1,208. Admitted: 326. Enrolled: 127. Average GMAT: 618. Average undergraduate GPA: 3.3. GMAT section weighed most heavily: weighed equally.
Placement: School has placement office. Placement rate at time of graduation: 82%. Placement rate 6 months after graduation: 96%. Average starting salary: $65,000.

TEMPLE UNIVERSITY

Fox School of Business and Management
Speakman Hall, Room 5
Philadelphia, PA 19122
Phone: (215) 204-7678
Fax: (215) 204-8300
E-mail: Linda@astro.ocis.temple.edu
http://www.sbm.temple.edu
Student Body: Full-time enrollment: 250. Men: 60%. Women: 40%. International students: 20%. Average age: 29. Students living on campus: 20%. Part-time enrollment: 1,000. Men: 60%. Women: 40%.
Academics: Full-time faculty: 140. Part-time faculty: 19. Degrees awarded: M.B.A., M.S.B.A., I.M.B.A., Ph.D./M.S. Joint degree programs: J.D./M.B.A., M.B.A./M.S., M.B.A./D.M.D. Evening program is offered. For fall 1996 entering class: 20% completed program within 2 years. 80% continued towards degree.
Finances: Tuition (1998–99): $450/credit + $300/fees.

Admission Requirements: GMAT is required. Application deadline for fall: June 1.
Selectivity: Applications received (full-time): 500. Admitted: 250. Enrolled: 200. Applications received (part-time): 1,000. Admitted: 500. Enrolled: 400. Average GMAT: 570. Average undergraduate GPA: 3.1. GMAT section weighed most heavily: weighed equally.
Placement: School has placement office. Average starting salary: $65,000.

UNIVERSITY OF PENNSYLVANIA

The Wharton School
102 Vance Hall
3733 Spruce Street
Philadelphia, PA 19104-6361
Phone: (215) 898-3430
Fax: (215) 898-0120
E-mail:
mba.admissions@wharton.upenn.edu
http://www.wharton.upenn.edu
Student Body: Full-time enrollment: 1557. Men: 71%. Women: 29%. Minorities: 18%. International: 31%. Average age: 27.
Academics: Full-time faculty: 279. Degrees awarded: M.B.A., E.M.B.A., M.S., Ph.D. Evening program is not offered.
Finances: Tuition (1998–99): $26,290. 85% of students receive some type of aid.
Admission Requirements: GMAT is required. Application deadline for fall: April 11.
Selectivity: Applications received (full-time): 8,313. Admitted: 1,087. Enrolled: 765. Average GMAT: 685. Average undergraduate GPA: 3.5. GMAT section weighed most heavily: weighed equally.
Placement: School has placement office. Placement rate within 3 months of graduation: 100%. Average starting salary: $90,000.

UNIVERSITY OF PITTSBURGH*

Joseph M. Katz Graduate School of Business
276 Mervis Hall
Roberto Clemente Drive
Pittsburgh, PA 15260
Phone: (412) 648-1700
Fax: (412) 648-1569
E-mail: MBA-Admissions@Katz.Business.Pitt.Edu
http://http://www.pitt.edu/~business/
Student Body: Full-time enrollment: 269. Men: 67%. Women: 33%. International: 13%. Average age: 27. Students living on campus: 0%. Part-time enrollment: 556. Men: 67%. Women: 33%.
Academics: Full-time faculty: 65. Part-time faculty: 20. Degrees awarded: M.B.A., E.M.B.A., Flex M.B.A. Joint degree programs: M.B.A./M.O.I.S., M.B.A./Master of International Business, M.B.A./Master of Arts in Area Studies, M.B.A./Master of Public & International Affairs. Evening program is offered.
Finances: Tuition (1998–99): In-State: $5,376. Out-of-State: $26,190. Estimated tuition (1999–2000): In-State: $446 per credit hour. Out-of-State: $836 per credit hour.
Admission Requirements: GMAT is required. Application deadline for fall: varies.
Selectivity: Applications received (full-time): 800. Admitted: 501. Enrolled: 242. Average undergraduate GPA: 3.2.
Placement: School has placement office. Placement rate at time of graduation: 90%. Placement rate 6 months after graduation: 99%. Average starting salary: $58,000.

VILLANOVA UNIVERSITY

College of Commerce and Finance
800 East Lancaster Avenue
Villanova, PA 19085
Phone: (610) 519-4336
Fax: (610) 519-6273
E-mail: mba@email.vill.edu
http://www.villanova-mba.edu

Student Body: Full-time enrollment: 41. Men: 76%. Women: 24%. Part-time enrollment: 578. Men: 65%. Women: 35%.
Academics: Full-time faculty: 88. Part-time faculty: 4. Degrees awarded: M.B.A., M.T. Joint degree programs: J.D./M.B.A. Evening program is offered.
Admission Requirements: GMAT is required. Application deadline for fall: June 30.
Selectivity: Applications received (part-time): 261. Admitted: 161. Enrolled: 120. Average GMAT: 589. Average undergraduate GPA: 3.2.
Placement: School has placement office.

Rhode Island

UNIVERSITY OF RHODE ISLAND

College of Business Administration
210 Ballentine Hall
7 Lippitt Road
Kingston, RI 02881-0802
Phone: (401) 874-5000
Fax: (401) 874-4312
E-mail: Hadz@uriacc.uri.edu
http://www.cba.uri.edu/graduate/mba.htm
Student Body: Full-time enrollment: 27. Men: 67%. Women: 33%. Asian American: 11%. International: 30%. Average age: 31. Students living on campus: 10%. Part-time enrollment: 179. Men: 66%. Women: 34%.
Academics: Full-time faculty: 52. Degrees awarded: M.B.A., M.S. Acc., Ph.D., E.M.B.A. Evening program is offered. For fall 1996 entering class: 100% completed program within 2 years.
Finances: Tuition (1998–99): In-State: $7,800. Out-of-State: $22,000.
Admission Requirements: GMAT is required. Application deadline for fall: July 15 (domestic), April 15 (international).
Selectivity: Applications received (full-time): 65. Admitted: 49. Enrolled: 21. Applications received (part-time): 47. Admitted: 43. Enrolled: 38. Average GMAT: 582. Average undergraduate GPA:

3.2. GMAT section weighed most heavily: weighed equally.
Placement: School has placement office.

South Carolina

CLEMSON UNIVERSITY*

College of Business and Public Affairs
124 Sirrine Hall
Clemson, SC 29634-1315
Phone: (864) 656-3196
Fax: (864) 656-0947
E-mail: MBA@Clemson.edu
http://http://business.clemson.edu/business.html
Student Body: Full-time enrollment: 116. Men: 73%. Women: 27%. International: 21%. Average age: 24. Part-time enrollment: 194. Men: 60%. Women: 40%.
Academics: Full-time faculty: 110. Part-time faculty: 0. Degrees awarded: M.B.A., M.A., M.S., M.P. Acc., Ph.D. Evening program is offered.
Finances: Tuition (1998–99): In-State: $3,600. Out-of-State: $7,200.
Admission Requirements: GMAT is required. Application deadline for fall: May 1.
Selectivity: Applications received (full-time): 589. Admitted: 298. Enrolled: 111. Average GMAT: 563. Average undergraduate GPA: 3.3.
Placement: School has placement office. Placement rate at time of graduation: 66%. Placement rate 6 months after graduation: 100%. Average starting salary: $33,500.

UNIVERSITY OF SOUTH CAROLINA

Darla Moore School of Business
H. William Close Building
Columbia, SC 29208
Phone: (803) 777-4346
Fax: (803) 777-0414
E-mail: gradadmit@darla.badm.sc.edu
http://www.business.sc.edu

Student Body: Full-time enrollment: 554. Men: 65%. Women: 35%. African American: 2%. Asian American: 2%. Latino: 2%. International: 26%. Average age: 26. Students living on campus: 33%. Part-time enrollment: 352. Men: 74%. Women: 26%.
Academics: Full-time faculty: 133. Part-time faculty: 28. Degrees awarded: M.B.A., M.S.B.A., M.A., M.I.B.S., M. Acc., M.T., M.H.R., Ph.D., I.M.B.A., M.A. Econ. Joint degree programs: J.D./M.B.A., J.D./M.I.B.S., J.D./M.H.R., J.D./M. Acc., J.D./M.S.B.A., J.D./M.A. Econ. Evening program is offered.
Finances: Tuition (1998–99): In-State: $3,844. Out-of-State: $8,114. 40% of students receive some type of aid. Average student debt incurred by graduation: $10,000.
Admission Requirements: GMAT is required. Application deadline for fall: February 1.
Selectivity: Applications received (full-time): 906. Admitted: 588. Enrolled: 293. Applications received (part-time): 195. Admitted: 158. Enrolled: 124. Average GMAT: 593. Average undergraduate GPA: 3.3. GMAT section weighed most heavily: weighed equally.
Placement: School has placement office. Placement rate at time of graduation: 83%. Placement rate 6 months after graduation: 92%. Average starting salary: $59,600.

WINTHROP UNIVERSITY

College of Business Administration
213 Thurmond
Rock Hill, SC 29733
Phone: (803) 323-2204
Fax: (803) 323-2539
E-mail: hagerp@mail.winthrop.edu
http://lurch.winthrop.edu
Student Body: Full-time enrollment: 82. African American: 83%. International: 13%. Average age: 28. Students living on campus: 7%. Part-time enrollment: 81.
Academics: Full-time faculty: 42. Part-time faculty: 8. Degrees awarded: M.B.A., E.M.B.A. Evening program is offered. For fall 1996 entering class: 91% completed

program within 2 years. 3% continued towards degree.

Finances: Tuition (1998–99): In-State: $164/credit. Out-of-State: $294/credit.

Admission Requirements: GMAT is required. Application deadline for fall: July 15.

Selectivity: Admitted: 28. Enrolled: 25. Admitted: 21. Enrolled: 18. Average GMAT: 500. Average undergraduate GPA: 2.9. GMAT section weighed most heavily: weighed equally.

Placement: School has placement office. Placement rate 6 months after graduation: 95%.

South Dakota

UNIVERSITY OF SOUTH DAKOTA*

School of Business
414 East Clark Street
Vermillion, SD 57069
Phone: (605) 677-5434

Student Body: Full-time enrollment: 128. Men: 61%. Women: 39%. International: 2%. Part-time enrollment: 339. Men: 57%. Women: 43%.

Academics: Full-time faculty: 45. Part-time faculty: 3. Degrees awarded: M.B.A. Evening program is offered.

Finances: Tuition (1998–99): In-State: $2,820. Out-of-State: $6,650.

Admission Requirements: GMAT is required. Application deadline for fall: July 15, November 1, March 15.

Selectivity: Applications received (full-time): 200. Admitted: 180. Enrolled: 100. Average GMAT: 508. Average undergraduate GPA: 3.1.

Placement: School has placement office.

Tennessee

EAST TENNESSEE STATE UNIVERSITY

College of Business
P.O. Box 70699
Johnson City, TN 37614
Phone: (423) 439-4213
Fax: (423) 929-5274

Student Body: Full-time enrollment: 39. Men: 64%. Women: 36%. Part-time enrollment: 90. Men: 57%. Women: 43%.

Academics: Full-time faculty: 52. Degrees awarded: M.B.A., M. Acc., M.P.M. Evening program is offered.

Finances: Tuition (1998–99): In-State: $2,700. Out-of-State: $7,300. Estimated tuition (1999–2000): In-State: $2,850. Out-of-State: $7,800.

Admission Requirements: GMAT is required. Application deadline for fall: July 1.

Selectivity: Applications received (full-time): 210. Admitted: 126. Enrolled: 84. Average GMAT: 540. Average undergraduate GPA: 3.1.

Placement: School has placement office. Average starting salary: $64,063.

MIDDLE TENNESSEE STATE UNIVERSITY

College of Business
P.O. Box 115
Murfreesboro, TN 37132
Phone: (615) 898-2964
Fax: (615) 898-4736
E-mail: fester@frank.mtsu.edu
http://www.mtsu.edu/

Student Body: Full-time enrollment: 102. Men: 55%. Women: 45%. Minority (part-time): 14%. International (part-time): 5%. Average age: 28. Students living on campus: 8%. Part-time enrollment: 446. Men: 62%. Women: 38%.

Academics: Full-time faculty: 111. Part-time faculty: 15. Degrees awarded: M.B.A.,

M.S. Acc., I.N.F.S. Evening program is offered.

Finances: Tuition (1998–99): In-State: $1,480. Out-of-State: $3,892.

Admission Requirements: GMAT is required. Application deadline for fall: July 1.

Selectivity: Average GMAT: 496. Average undergraduate GPA: 3.0.

Placement: School has placement office.

TENNESSEE TECHNOLOGICAL UNIVERSITY

College of Business Administration
Box 5023
Cookeville, TN 38505
Phone: (931) 372-3888
Fax: (931) 372-6250
E-mail: g-admissions@tntech.edu
http://www.tntech.edu

Student Body: Full-time enrollment: 63. Men: 63%. Women: 37%. African American: 13%. Asian American: 19%. Latino: 5%. International: 14%. Average age: 24. Part-time enrollment: 52. Men: 58%. Women: 42%.

Academics: Full-time faculty: 37. Degrees awarded: M.B.A. Evening program is offered. For fall 1996 entering class: 98% completed program within 2 years. 2% continued towards degree.

Finances: Tuition (1998–99): In-State: $2,476. Out-of-State: $6,812. Estimated tuition (1999–2000): In-State: $2,600. Out-of-State: $7,000. 20% of students receive non-need-based aid. 60% of students receive need-based aid.

Admission Requirements: GMAT is required. Application deadline for fall: 6 weeks prior to semester.

Selectivity: Applications received (full-time): 47. Admitted: 41. Enrolled: 25. Applications received (part-time): 25. Admitted: 22. Enrolled: 15. Average GMAT: 531. Average undergraduate GPA: 3.15. GMAT section weighed most heavily: weighed equally.

Placement: School has placement office. Placement rate at time of graduation: 94%. Placement rate 6 months after graduation: 100%. Average starting salary: $35,000.

UNIVERSITY OF MEMPHIS

Fogelman College of Business and
Economics
Graduate Admissions
AD 216
Memphis, TN 38152
Phone: (901) 678-2911
Fax: (901) 678-5023
E-mail: gradsch@memphis.edu
http://business.memphis.edu
Student Body: Full-time enrollment: 292.
Men: 66%. Women: 34%. African
American: 9%. Asian American: 29%.
Latino: 2%. International: 33%. Part-time
enrollment: 423. Men: 57%. Women: 43%.
Academics: Full-time faculty: 90. Part-time
faculty: 6. Degrees awarded: M.B.A.,
M.S., M.A., Ph.D. Joint degree programs:
M.B.A./J.D. Evening program is offered.
For fall 1996 entering class: 53% complet-
ed program within 2 years. 47% continued
towards degree.
Finances: Tuition (1998–99): In-State:
$3,182. Out-of-State: $8,054.
Admission Requirements: GMAT is required.
Application deadline for fall: August 1.
Selectivity: Applications received (full-time):
216. Admitted: 140. Enrolled: 94.
Applications received (part-time): 193.
Admitted: 124. Enrolled: 84. Average
GMAT: 550. Average undergraduate GPA:
3.2. GMAT section weighed most heavily:
weighed equally.
Placement: School has placement office.

UNIVERSITY OF TENNESSEE— CHATTANOOGA

School of Business Administration
615 McCallie Avenue
Chattanooga, TN 37403
Phone: (423) 755-4169
Fax: (423) 755-5255
Student Body: Full-time enrollment: 76.
Men: 42%. Women: 58%. International:
9%. Part-time enrollment: 634. Men: 56%.
Women: 44%.

Academics: Full-time faculty: 42. Degrees
awarded: M.B.A. Evening program is
offered.
Finances: Tuition (1998–99): In-State:
$2,282. Out-of-State: $6,062.
Admission Requirements: GMAT is required.
Application deadline for fall: June 1.
Selectivity: Applications received (full-time):
234. Admitted: 161. Enrolled: 136.
Average GMAT: 500. Average undergradu-
ate GPA: 3.1.
Placement: School has placement office.

UNIVERSITY OF TENNESSEE— KNOXVILLE

Graduate School of Business
527 Stokely Management Center
Knoxville, TN 37996-0552
Phone: (423) 974-5033
Fax: (423) 974-3826
E-mail: gchapmal@utk.edu
http://www.mba.bus.utk.edu
Student Body: Full-time enrollment: 180.
Men: 70%. Women: 30%. African
American: 6%. International: 12%. Average
age: 25.
Academics: Full-time faculty: 130. Part-time
faculty: 7. Degrees awarded: M.B.A. Joint
degree programs: J.D./M.B.A.,
B.A./M.B.A., M.B.A./M.S. in
Manufacturing Engineering. Evening pro-
gram is not offered. For fall 1996 entering
class: 82% completed program within 2
years. 3% continued towards degree.
Finances: Estimated tuition (1999–2000):
In-State: $3,154. Out-of-State: $8,210.
Admission Requirements: GMAT is
required. Application deadline for fall:
March 1.
Selectivity: Average GMAT: 615. Average
undergraduate GPA: 3.3. GMAT section
weighed most heavily: weighed equally.
Placement: School has placement office.
Placement rate at time of graduation: 98%.
Placement rate 6 months after graduation:
100%. Average starting salary: $61,755.

VANDERBILT UNIVERSITY

Owen Graduate School of Management
Director of Admissions
401 21st Avenue
Nashville, TN 37201
Phone: (615) 322-6469
Fax: (615) 343-1175
E-mail: Admissions@Owen.Vanderbilt.edu
http://http://www.vanderbilt/owen/
Student Body: Full-time enrollment: 426.
Men: 72%. Women: 28%. International:
5%. Average age: 27. Students living on
campus: 20%.
Academics: Full-time faculty: 47. Part-time
faculty: 8. Degrees awarded: M.B.A.,
E.M.B.A., Ph.D. Joint degree programs:
M.B.A./M.S.N., M.B.A./M.E.,
J.D./M.B.A., M.B.A./M.A., B.A./M.B.A.,
M.B.A./M.A. Latin American Studies.
Evening program is not offered.
Finances: Tuition (1998–99): $22,900.
Estimated tuition (1999–2000): $22,900.
Average student debt incurred by gradua-
tion: $45,466.
Admission Requirements: GMAT is required.
Application deadline for fall: April 15.
Selectivity: Applications received (full-time):
1,313. Admitted: 474. Enrolled: 201.
Average GMAT: 625. Average undergradu-
ate GPA: 3.2. GMAT section weighed most
heavily: total score.
Placement: School has placement office.
Placement rate at time of graduation: 85%.
Placement rate 6 months after graduation:
97%. Average starting salary: $65,083.

Texas

BAYLOR UNIVERSITY

The Hankamer School of Business
Graduate Programs
P.O. Box 98001
Waco, TX 76798
Phone: (254) 710-3718
Fax: (254) 710-1066
E-mail: MBA@hsb.baylor.edu
http://www.hsb.baylor.edu

Student Body: Full-time enrollment: 163. Men: 66%. Women: 34%. African American: 5%. Latino: 6%. International: 12%. Average age: 26.

Academics: Full-time faculty: 98. Part-time faculty: 10. Degrees awarded: M.B.A., M.S. Econ., M. Tax., M.B.A. International Management, M.S. Information Systems, M. Acc. Joint degree programs: J.D./M.B.A., J.D./M. Tax, M.B.A./M.S.I.S. Evening program is not offered.

Finances: Tuition (1998–99): $326 per credit hour. 70% of students receive some type of aid. Average student debt incurred by graduation: $10,000.

Admission Requirements: GMAT is required. Application deadline for fall: July 1.

Selectivity: Applications received (full-time): 163. Admitted: 110. Enrolled: 65. Average GMAT: 581. Average undergraduate GPA: 3.26. GMAT section weighed most heavily: all ranked equally.

Placement: School has placement office. Placement rate at time of graduation: 90%. Placement rate 6 months after graduation: 98%. Average starting salary: 43,000.

LAMAR UNIVERSITY

College of Business
P.O. Box 10059
Beaumont, TX 77710
Phone: (409) 880-8604
Fax: (409) 880-8088
E-mail: swerdlowra@hal.lamar.edu
http://www.lamar.edu

Student Body: Full-time enrollment: 33. Men: 61%. Women: 39%. Minority: 30%. International: 33%. Average age: 32. Students living on campus: 20%. Part-time enrollment: 65. Men: 62%. Women: 38%.

Academics: Full-time faculty: 18. Degrees awarded: M.B.A. Joint degree programs: M.B.A. Acc., M.B.A. Mgt. Evening program is offered.

Finances: Tuition (1998–99): In-State: $1,502. Out-of-State: $5,336. Estimated tuition (1999–2000): In-State: $1,600. Out-of-State: $5,500. 15% of students receive some type of aid.

Admission Requirements: GMAT is required. Application deadline for fall: October 15.

Selectivity: GMAT section weighed most heavily: weighed equally.

Placement: School has placement office. Placement rate at time of graduation: 80%. Placement rate 6 months after graduation: 90%. Average starting salary: $46,000.

RICE UNIVERSITY

Jesse H. Jones Graduate School of Management
Jones Graduate School—MS-531
P.O. Box 1892
Houston, TX 77251-1892
Phone: (713) 527-4918,
(888) 844-4773
Fax: (713) 737-6147
E-mail: enterjgs@rice.edu
http://www.rice.edu/jgs

Student Body: Full-time enrollment: 295. Men: 72%. Women: 28%. African American: 2%. Asian American: 8%. Latino: 3%. International: 15%. Average age: 28.

Academics: Full-time faculty: 29. Part-time faculty: 20. Degrees awarded: M.B.A. Joint degree programs: M.B.A./M.S. Engineering, M.B.A./M.D. Evening program is not offered.

Finances: Tuition (1998–99): $15,750. Estimated tuition (1999–2000): $17,000. 47% of students receive non-need-based aid. 39% of student receive need-based aid. Average student debt incurred by graduation: $36,000.

Admission Requirements: GMAT is required. Application deadline for fall: December 1, January 15, March 1, April 15.

Selectivity: Applications received (full-time): 511. Admitted: 249. Enrolled: 132. Average GMAT: 631. Average undergraduate GPA: 3.2. GMAT section weighed most heavily: weighed equally.

Placement: School has placement office. Placement rate at time of graduation: 98%. Placement rate 6 months after graduation: 100%. Average starting salary: $67,000.

SOUTHERN METHODIST UNIVERSITY

Edwin L. Cox School of Business
P.O. Box 750333
Dallas, TX 75275-0333
Phone: (214) 768-2630; (800) 472-3622
Fax: (214) 768-3956
E-mail: mbainfo@mail.cox.smu.edu
http://www.cox.smu.edu/

Student Body: Full-time enrollment: 272. Men: 68%. Women: 32%. African American: 1%. Asian American: 4%. Latino: 1%. International: 22%. Average age: 27.6. Students living on campus: 3%. Part-time enrollment: 583. Men: 76%. Women: 24%.

Academics: Full-time faculty: 77. Part-time faculty: 17. Degrees awarded: M.B.A. Joint degree programs: J.D./M.B.A., M.A./M.B.A. Evening program is offered. For fall 1996 entering class: 92% completed program within 2 years. 2% continued towards degree.

Finances: Tuition (1998–99): $22,598. Estimated tuition (1999–2000): $23,720.

Admission Requirements: GMAT is required. Application deadline for fall: November 30, February 15, April 15, rolling.

Selectivity: Applications received (full-time): 598. Admitted: 192. Enrolled: 119. Applications received (part-time): 623. Admitted: 272. Enrolled: 256. Average GMAT: 636. Average undergraduate GPA: 3.2.

Placement: School has placement office. Placement rate at time of graduation: 88%. Placement rate 6 months after graduation: 99%. Average starting salary: $63,408.

STEPHEN F. AUSTIN STATE UNIVERSITY

College of Business
Graduate Office
P.O. Box 13024, SFA
Nacogdoches, TX 75962
Phone: (409) 468-2807
Fax: (409) 468-1251
E-mail: gschool@titan.sfasu.edu
http://www.cob.sfasu.edu

Student Body: Full-time enrollment: 22. Men: 50%. Women: 50%. African American: 9%. Asian American: 5%. International: 5%. Average age: 25.7. Part-time enrollment: 50. Men: 66%. Women: 34%.
Academics: Full-time faculty: 48. Degrees awarded: M.B.A., M.P.A., M.S. Joint degree programs: B.B.A./M.P.A. Evening program is offered.
Finances: Tuition (1998–99): In-State: $1,898. Out-of-State: $7,010. Estimated tuition (1999–2000): In-State: $2,000. Out-of-State: $8,000.
Admission Requirements: GMAT is required. Application deadline for fall: July 15.
Selectivity: Applications received (part-time): 52. Admitted: 44. Enrolled: 28. Average GMAT: 509. Average undergraduate GPA: 2.9. GMAT section weighed most heavily: weighed equally.
Placement: School has placement office.

TEXAS A&M UNIVERSITY

Lowry Mays College & Graduate School of Business
212 Wehner Building
College Station, TX 77843-4117
Phone: (409) 845-4714
Fax: (409) 862-2393
E-mail: MaysMBA@tamu.edu
http://business.tamu.edu
Student Body: Full-time enrollment: 686. Men: 59%. Women: 41%. African American: 2%. Asian American: 4%. Latino: 4%. International: 27%. Part-time enrollment: 23. Men: 57%. Women: 43%.
Academics: Full-time faculty: 136. Part-time faculty: 14. Degrees awarded: M.B.A., E.M.B.A., M.S., M.A. Land Economics & Real Estate, Ph.D. Joint degree programs: M.S. in Life Cycle Engineering & Operations Management, Masters of Agribusiness. Evening program is not offered.
Finances: Tuition (1998–99): In-State: $3,500. Out-of-State: $9,200. Estimated tuition (1999–2000): In-State: $3,500. Out-of-State: $9,200. Average student debt incurred by graduation: $18,000.
Admission Requirements: GMAT is required. Application deadline for fall: May 1.

Selectivity: Applications received (full-time): 530. Admitted: 178. Enrolled: 90. Average GMAT: 619. Average undergraduate GPA: 3.4. GMAT section weighed most heavily: weighed equally.
Placement: School has placement office. Placement rate at time of graduation: 86%. Placement rate 6 months after graduation: 100%. Average starting salary: $63,100.

TEXAS A&M UNIVERSITY— COMMERCE

College of Business & Technology
Graduate School
Commerce, TX 75429
Phone: (903) 886-5167
Fax: (903) 886-5165
E-mail: MBA@tamu-commerce.edu
http://www.tamu-commerce.edu
Student Body: Total enrollment: 148. African American: 10%. Latino: 2%. International: 42%. Average age: 30.
Academics: Full-time faculty: 30. Degrees awarded: M.B.A., M.S. Econ., M.A. Econ. Evening program is offered.
Finances: Tuition (1998–99): $359/3 hours. Estimated tuition (1999–2000): $400/3 hours.
Admission Requirements: GMAT is required. Application deadline for fall: June 1.
Selectivity: Average GMAT: 510. Average undergraduate GPA: 3.3. GMAT section weighed most heavily: Verbal.
Placement: School has placement office.

TEXAS CHRISTIAN UNIVERSITY

M.J. Neeley School of Business
MBA Office
P.O. Box 298540
Fort Worth, TX 76129
Phone: (817) 257-7531
Fax: (817) 257-6431
E-mail: mbainfo@tcu.edu
http://www.neeley.tcu.edu
Student Body: Full-time enrollment: 184. Men: 66%. Women: 34%. African American: 2%. Asian American: 2%. Latino:

2%. International: 32%. Average age: 26. Part-time enrollment: 109. Men: 76%. Women: 24%.
Academics: Full-time faculty: 35. Part-time faculty: 1. Degrees awarded: M.B.A., M. Acc. Evening program is offered. For fall 1996 entering class: 91% completed program within 2 years. 1% continued towards degree.
Finances: Tuition (1998–99): In-State: $8,280 + $1,240 in fees. Out-of-State: $8,280 + $1,240 in fees. Estimated tuition (1999–2000): $8,695 + $1,300 in fees. 85% of students receive some type of aid.
Admission Requirements: GMAT is required. Application deadline for fall: April 30 (or as space remains available).
Selectivity: Applications received (full-time): 322. Admitted: 164. Enrolled: 92. Applications received (part-time): 75. Admitted: 55. Enrolled: 44. Average GMAT: 560. Average undergraduate GPA: 3.1. GMAT section weighed most heavily: weighed equally.
Placement: School has placement office. Placement rate at time of graduation: 30%. Placement rate 6 months after graduation: 93%. Average starting salary: $50,027.

TEXAS TECH UNIVERSITY

College of Business Administration
Box 42101
Lubbock, TX 79409-2101
Phone: (806) 742-3184
(800) 882-6220
Fax: (806) 742-3958
E-mail: bagrad@coba.ttu.edu
http://www.ba.ttu.edu/grad
Student Body: Full-time enrollment: 306. Men: 64%. Women: 36%. African American: 2%. Asian American: 2%. Latino: 5%. International: 26%. Average age: 24.7. Students living on campus: 3.3%. Part-time enrollment: 77. Men: 64%. Women: 36%.
Academics: Full-time faculty: 57. Degrees awarded: M.B.A., M.S., M.S.A., Ph.D. Joint degree programs: M.B.A./J.D., M.B.A./M.A. (Foreign Language),

M.S.A./J.D., M.B.A./M.S.N. (Nursing), M.B.A./M.A. (Architecture), M.B.A./M.S. (Chemical Engineering), M.B.A./M.D., B.B.A./M.B.A., B.B.A./M.S., B.B.A./M.S.A., B.A./M.B.A. (Foreign Language), B.A./M.B.A. (Architecture). Evening program is offered. For fall 1996 entering class: 64% completed program within 2 years. 16% continued towards degree. **Finances:** Tuition (1998–99): In-State: $3,224. Out-of-State: $8,336. Estimated tuition (1999–2000): In-State: $3,724. Out-of-State: $8,836. **Admission Requirements:** GMAT is required. Application deadline for fall: none. **Selectivity:** Applications received (full-time): 287. Admitted: 197. Enrolled: 108. Average GMAT: 570. Average undergraduate GPA: 3.5. GMAT section weighed most heavily: weighed equally. **Placement:** School has placement office. Placement rate at time of graduation: 63%. Placement rate 6 months after graduation: 80%. Average starting salary: $42,000.

UNIVERSITY OF HOUSTON

College of Business Administration
4800 Calhoun Boulevard
Houston, TX 77204-2161
Phone: (713) 743-1010
Fax: (713) 743-9633
E-mail: admissions@uh.edu, oss@cba.uh.edu
Student Body: Full-time enrollment: 433. Men: 61%. Women: 39%. African American: 4%. Asian American: 11%. Latino: 5%. International: 27%. Average age: 29.3. Part-time enrollment: 655. Men: 67%. Women: 33%.
Academics: Full-time faculty: 83. Part-time faculty: 14. Degrees awarded: M.S./Admin, M.S. Acc, M.S. Financial. Joint degree programs: M.B.A./J.D., M.B.A./M.S.W., M.B.A./M.S.I.E., M.B.A./M.A. Spanish, M.B.A./M.H.M. Dual degree M.B.A./M.I.M. with Thunderbird. Evening program is offered.
Finances: Tuition (1998–99): In-State: $1359/12 credit hours. Out-of-State: $3,579/12 credit hours. Estimated tuition

(1999–2000): In-State: $1359/12 credit hours. Out-of-State: $3,579/12 credit hours. **Admission Requirements:** GMAT is required. Application deadline for fall: May 1 (fall), October 1 (spring). **Selectivity:** Applications received (full-time): 294. Admitted: 208. Enrolled: 130. Applications received (part-time): 256. Admitted: 206. Enrolled: 159. Average GMAT: 577. Average undergraduate GPA: 3.2. GMAT section weighed most heavily: weighed equally. **Placement:** School has placement office. Placement rate at time of graduation: 91%. Placement rate 6 months after graduation: 99%. Average starting salary: $63,471.

UNIVERSITY OF HOUSTON— CLEAR LAKE

School of Business and Public Administration
Enrollment Services
2700 Bay Area Blvd, Suite 1510
Houston, TX 77058
Phone: (281) 283-2520
Fax: (281) 283-2530
E-mail: admissions@cl.uh.edu
http://www.cl.uh.edu/admissions
Student Body: Full-time enrollment: 2,635. African American: 20%. Asian American: 16%. Latino: 27%. International: 16%. Part-time enrollment: 4,184.
Academics: Full-time faculty: 52. Degrees awarded: M.B.A. Joint degree programs: M.H.A./M.B.A. Evening program is offered.
Finances: Tuition (1998–99): In-State: $216/3 credit hours. Out-of-State: $249/credit.
Admission Requirements: GMAT is required. Application deadline for fall: August 1.
Selectivity: Applications received (full-time): 441. Admitted: 333. Enrolled: 231. Average GMAT: 500. Average undergraduate GPA: 2.8.
Placement: School has placement office.

UNIVERSITY OF NORTH TEXAS*

College of Business Administration
Toulouse School of Graduate Studies
P.O. Box 5446
Denton, TX 76203
Phone: (940) 564-2636
Student Body: Full-time enrollment: 950. International: 1%.
Academics: Full-time faculty: 102. Part-time faculty: 2. Degrees awarded: M.B.A., M.S. Acc. Evening program is offered.
Admission Requirements: GMAT is required.
Selectivity: Applications received (full-time): 336. Admitted: 149. Enrolled: 98. Average GMAT: 530. Average undergraduate GPA: 2.9.
Placement: School has placement office.

UNIVERSITY OF TEXAS— ARLINGTON*

College of Business Administration
UTA Box 19376
Arlington, TX 76019
Phone: (817) 272-2681
Fax: (817) 272-2625
E-mail: graduate.school@uta.edu, admit@uta.edu
http://http://www.uta.edu/gradbiz/gradweb.htm
Student Body: Full-time enrollment: 191. Men: 63%. Women: 37%. International: 16%. Average age: 29. Part-time enrollment: 300. Men: 68%. Women: 32%.
Academics: Full-time faculty: 115. Part-time faculty: 0. Degrees awarded: M.B.A., M.S., M.A., Ph.D. Evening program is offered.
Finances: Tuition (1998–99): In-State: $3,691.50. Out-of-State: $10,411.50. Estimated tuition (1999–2000): In-State: $3,751.50. Out-of-State: $10,471.50.
Admission Requirements: GMAT is required. Application deadline for fall: June 30.
Selectivity: Applications received (full-time): 486. Admitted: 233. Enrolled: 119. Average GMAT: 550. Average undergraduate GPA: 3.2. GMAT section weighed most heavily: Verbal, Quantitative.

Placement: School has placement office. Average starting salary: $40,000.

UNIVERSITY OF TEXAS— AUSTIN

The Texas Graduate School of Business
P.O. Box 7999
Austin, TX 78713-7999
Phone: (512) 471-7612
Fax: (512) 471-4243
E-mail: Texasmba@bus.utexas.edu
http://texasinfo.bus.utexas.edu
Student Body: Full-time enrollment: 726. Men: 75%. Women: 25%. African American: 1%. Asian American: 6%. Latino: 5%. International: 20%. Average age: 29.
Academics: Full-time faculty: 127. Part-time faculty: 60. Degrees awarded: M.B.A., Ph.D. , M.P.A. Joint degree programs: M.B.A./M.P.A., M.B.A./M.A. Latin American Studies, M.B.A./M.A. Asian Studies, M.B.A./M.A. Communications, M.B.A./M.S. Nursing, M.B.A./J.D., others. Evening program is not offered. For fall 1996 entering class: 99% completed program within 2 years. 1% continued towards degree.
Finances: Tuition (1998–99): In-State: $6,294. Out-of-State: $15,504. Estimated tuition (1999–2000): In-State: $9,351. Out-of-State: $20,751. Average student debt incurred by graduation: $14,362.
Admission Requirements: GMAT is required. Application deadline for fall: April 15 (domestic), Feb. 15 (international).
Selectivity: Applications received (full-time): 2,684. Admitted: 622. Enrolled: 347. Average GMAT: 660. Average undergraduate GPA: 3.4. GMAT section weighed most heavily: equal.
Placement: School has placement office. Placement rate at time of graduation: 90%. Placement rate 6 months after graduation: 100%. Average starting salary: $70,890.

UNIVERSITY OF TEXAS— EL PASO

College of Business Administration
500 West University Drive
El Paso, TX 79968
Phone: (915) 747-5174
Fax: (915) 747-5147
http://www.utep.edu
Student Body: Full time enrollment: 75. African American: 3% Latino: 70% International: 15% Average age: 34. Part-time enrollment: 200.
Academics: Full-time faculty: 32. Part-time faculty: 6. Degrees awarded: M.B.A., M. Acc., Master of Science in Economics. Evening program is offered.
Finances: Tuition (1998–99): In-State: $2,063. Out-of-State: 5,753. Estimated tuition (1999–2000): In-State: $2,063. Out-of-State: 5,753.
Admission Requirements: GMAT is required. Application deadline for fall: July 1.
Selectivity: Average GMAT: 467. Average undergraduate GPA: 2.7. GMAT section weighed most heavily: weighed equally.
Placement: School has placement office.

UNIVERSITY OF TEXAS— PAN AMERICAN

College of Business Administration
Graduate Programs
1201 West University Dr.
Edinburg, TX 78539
Phone: (956) 381-2206
Student Body: Full-time enrollment: 111. Men: 68%. Women: 32%. International: 23%. Part-time enrollment: 87. Men: 69%. Women: 31%.
Academics: Full-time faculty: 17. Part-time faculty: 0. Degrees awarded: M.B.A., Ph.D. Evening program is offered.
Finances: Tuition (1998–99): In-State: $1,040. Out-of-State: $4,460.
Admission Requirements: GMAT is required. Application deadline for fall: July 18, December 20.
Selectivity: Applications received (full-time): 145. Admitted: 50. Enrolled: 43. Average

GMAT: 490. Average undergraduate GPA: 3.3.
Placement: School has placement office. Average starting salary: $30,000.

UNIVERSITY OF TEXAS— SAN ANTONIO

College of Business
6900 N Loop 1604 W
San Antonio, TX 78249-0631
Phone: (210) 458-4330
Fax: (210) 458-4332
E-mail: gradstudies@utsa.edu
http://www.utsa.edu
Student Body. Full time enrollment: 160. Men: 63%. Women: 38%. African American: 2%. Asian American: 5%. Latino: 14%. Native American: 1%. International: 11%. Students living on campus: 4%. Part-time enrollment: 358. Men: 63%. Women: 37%.
Academics: Full-time faculty: 100. Degrees awarded: M.B.A., E.M.B.A., M.S. Management of Technology, M.S. Tax., M.S. Acc., M.S. Finance, M.S. Information Technology. Joint degree programs: M.S. Management Technology is offered in conjunction with the College of Sciences and Engineering. Evening program is offered.
Finances: Tuition (1998–99): In-State: $1,230 (for 9 hours). Out-of-State: $3,147 (for 9 hours).
Admission Requirements: GMAT is required. Application deadline for fall: July 1.
Selectivity: Enrolled (full-time): 22. Enrolled (part-time): 58. Average GMAT: 536. Average undergraduate GPA: 3.0. GMAT section weighed most heavily: weighed equally.
Placement: School has placement office. Placement rate at time of graduation: 57%. Average starting salary: $50,000.

Utah

BRIGHAM YOUNG UNIVERSITY

Marriott School of Management
M.B.A. Program
640 Tanner Building (TNRB)
Provo, UT 84602-3013
Phone: (801) 378-7500
Fax: (801) 378-4808
E-mail: mba@byu.edu
http://msmonline.byu.edu
Student Body: Full-time enrollment: 271.
Men: 79%. Women: 21%. African
American: 2%. Asian American: 1%. Latino:
1%. International: 18%. Average age: 26.
Academics: Full-time faculty: 69. Degrees
awarded: M.B.A. Joint degree programs:
M.B.A./J.D., M.B.A./International
Relations, M.B.A./Mechanical Engineering.
Evening program is not offered. For fall
1996 entering class: 95% completed pro-
gram within 2 years. 2% continued towards
degree.
Finances: Tuition (1998–99): Latter-Day-
Saints: $5,120. Non-Latter-Day-Saints:
$7,680.
Admission Requirements: GMAT is required.
Application deadline for fall: March 1.
Selectivity: Applications received (full-time):
497. Admitted: 217. Enrolled: 131.
Average GMAT: 634. Average undergradu-
ate GPA: 3.52. GMAT section weighed
most heavily: Quantitative.
Placement: School has placement office.
Placement rate at time of graduation: 80%.
Placement rate 6 months after graduation:
91%. Average starting salary: $57,734.

UNIVERSITY OF UTAH

David Eccles School of Business
1645 E. Campus Center Drive
Room 101
Salt Lake City, UT 84112-9301
Phone: (801) 581-7785
Fax: (801) 581-3666
E-mail: masters@business.utah.edu
http://www.business.utah.edu

Student Body: Full-time enrollment: 113.
Men: 69%. Women: 31%. Asian
American: 10%. Latino: 5%. International:
26%. Average age: 28. Part-time enroll-
ment: 167. Men: 72%. Women: 28%.
Academics: Full-time faculty: 60. Part-time
faculty: 25. Degrees awarded: M.B.A.,
E.M.B.A., M.P.R.A. Joint degree programs:
J.D./M.B.A., M.B.A./Master of
Architecture. Evening program is offered.
For fall 1996 entering class: 81% complet-
ed program within 2 years. 5% continued
towards degree.
Finances: Tuition (1998–99): In-State:
$3,046. Out-of-State: $9,457. Estimated
tuition (1999–2000): In-State: $3,140.
Out-of-State: $9,740.
Admission Requirements: GMAT is required.
Application deadline for fall: March 1.
Selectivity: Applications received (full-time):
254. Admitted: 155. Enrolled: 102.
Applications received (part-time): 117.
Admitted: 73. Enrolled: 58. Average
GMAT: 591. Average undergraduate GPA:
3.4. GMAT section weighed most heavily:
weighed equally.
Placement: School has placement office.
Placement rate at time of graduation: 75%.
Placement rate 6 months after graduation:
97%. Average starting salary: $47,841.

UTAH STATE UNIVERSITY

College of Business
School of Graduate Studies
0900 Old Main Hill
Logan, UT 84322-0900
Phone: (435) 797-1189
Fax: (435) 797-1192
E-mail: gradsch@cc.usu.edu
http://www.usu.edu
Student Body: Full-time enrollment: 67. Men:
91%. Women: 9%. Average age: 27.
Students living on campus: 10%. Part-time
enrollment: 44. Men: 91%. Women: 9%.
Academics: Full-time faculty: 64. Degrees
awarded: M.B.A., M. Acc., M.S., Ph.D.
Evening program is offered.
Finances: Tuition (1998–99): In-State:
$1,869. Out-of-State: $5,503.

Admission Requirements: GMAT is required.
Application deadline for fall: June 15.
Selectivity: Applications received (full-time):
328. Admitted: 221. Enrolled: 97.
Applications received (part-time): 70.
Admitted: 44. Enrolled: 44. Average
GMAT: 560. Average undergraduate GPA:
3.4. GMAT section weighed most heavily:
weighed equally.
Placement: School has placement office.
Placement rate at time of graduation: 60%.
Placement rate 6 months after graduation:
98%. Average starting salary: $49,140.

Vermont

UNIVERSITY OF VERMONT

School of Business Administration
Kalkin Hall
University of Vermont
Burlington, VT 05405
Phone: (802) 656-0655
Fax: (822) 656-8279
E-mail: mba@bsadpo.emba.uvm.edu
http://www.bsad.emba.uvm.edu
Student Body: Full-time enrollment: 37.
Men: 54%. Women: 46%. International:
46%. Average age: 25. Part-time enroll-
ment: 100. Men: 65%. Women: 35%.
Academics: Full-time faculty: 26. Part-time
faculty: 3. Degrees awarded: M.B.A.
Evening program is offered.
Finances: Tuition (1998–99): In-State:
$302/credit. Out-of-State: $755/credit.
Admission Requirements: GMAT is
required. Application deadline for fall: July
15, Nov. 15.
Selectivity: Average GMAT: 575. Average
undergraduate GPA: 3.2.
Placement: School has placement office.

Virginia

COLLEGE OF WILLIAM AND MARY

Graduate School of Business
P.O. Box 8795
Williamsburg, VA 23187-8795
Phone: (757) 221-2900
Fax: (757) 221-2958
E-mail: sgrive@business.wm.edu
http://business.tyler.wm.edu
Student Body: Full-time enrollment: 228.
Men: 61%. Women: 39%. Minorities: 10%.
International: 30%. Average age: 28.
Students living on campus: 20%. Part-time
enrollment: 150. Men: 80%. Women: 20%.
Academics: Full-time faculty: 48. Part-time
faculty: 6. Degrees awarded: M.B.A. Joint
degree programs: M.B.A./M.P.P.,
M.B.A./J.D. Evening program is offered.
For fall 1996 entering class: 97% complet-
ed program within 2 years.
Finances: Tuition (1998–99): In-State:
$6,820. Out-of-State: $16,138. Estimated
tuition (1999–2000): In-State: $7,000.
Out-of-State: $16,500. 40% of students
receive non-need-based aid. 85% of stu-
dents receive need-based aid. Average stu-
dent debt incurred by graduation:
$38,000.
Admission Requirements: GMAT is required.
Application deadline for fall: May 1.
Selectivity: Applications received (full-time):
490. Admitted: 180. Enrolled: 116.
Applications received (part-time): 65.
Admitted: 45. Enrolled: 35. Average
GMAT: 630. Average undergraduate GPA:
3.3. GMAT section weighed most heavily:
Quantitative.
Placement: School has placement office.
Placement rate at time of graduation: 90%.
Placement rate 6 months after graduation:
100%. Average starting salary: $63,500.

GEORGE MASON UNIVERSITY

School of Management
Mailstop 5A2
Fairfax, VA 22030
Phone: (703) 993-2136
Fax: (703) 993-1886
E-mail: gradadms@som.gmu.edu
http://www.som.gmu.edu
Student Body: Part-time enrollment: 379.
Men: 69%. Women: 31%.
Academics: Full-time faculty: 73. Part-time
faculty: 23. Degrees awarded: M.B.A. Joint
degree programs: M.B.A./M.S.N. Evening
program is offered. For fall 1996 entering
class: 79% completed program within 2
years. 12% continued towards degree.
Finances: Tuition (1998–99): In-State:
$257 per credit hour. Out-of-State: $521
per credit hour. Average student debt
incurred by graduation: $15,000.
Admission Requirements: GMAT is required.
Application deadline for fall: April 1.
Selectivity: Applications received (part-time):
176. Admitted: 89. Enrolled: 58. Average
GMAT: 609. Average undergraduate GPA:
3.1.
Placement: School has placement office.
Placement rate at time of graduation: 56%.
Placement rate 6 months after graduation:
84%. Average starting salary: $58,502.

JAMES MADISON UNIVERSITY

College of Business
The Graduate School
MSC 1003
Harrisonburg, VA 22807
Phone: (540) 568-6131
E-mail: grad_school@jmu.edu
http://www.jmu.edu
Student Body: Full-time enrollment: 30.
Men: 60%. Women: 40%. International:
60%. Average age: 30. Part-time enroll-
ment: 150. Men: 60%. Women: 40%.
Academics: Full-time faculty: 50. Degrees
awarded: M.B.A. Evening program is
offered.

Finances: Tuition (1998–99): In-State:
$132 per credit hour. Out-of-State: $385
per credit hour.
Admission Requirements: GMAT is required.
Application deadline for fall: rolling.
Selectivity: Average GMAT: 530. Average
undergraduate GPA: 2.9. GMAT section
weighed most heavily: equal/total score.
Placement: School has placement office.

OLD DOMINION UNIVERSITY

Graduate School of Business & Public
Administration
Norfolk, VA 23529-0119
Phone: (757) 683-3638
E-mail: MBAInfo@wdu.edu
http://www.odu.edu/
Student Body: Full-time enrollment: 110.
Men: 58%. Women: 42%. African
American: 52%. International: 95%.
Average age: 30. Part-time enrollment:
368. Men: 58%. Women: 42%.
Academics: Full-time faculty: 85. Degrees
awarded: M.B.A., M.S. Acc., Ph.D., M.A.
Econ., Masters in Tax., M.P.A., Masters in
Urban Studies. Joint degree programs:
C.S./M.I.S. Evening program is offered.
Finances: Tuition (1998–99): In-State:
$180/credit hour. Out-of-State:
$477/credit hour.
Admission Requirements: GMAT is required.
Application deadline for fall: July 1.
Selectivity: Applications received (part-time):
310. Admitted: 265. Enrolled: 161.
Average GMAT: 530. Average undergradu-
ate GPA: 3.1. GMAT section weighed most
heavily: weighed equally.
Placement: School has placement office.

UNIVERSITY OF RICHMOND

Richard S. Reynolds Graduate School
The E. Claiborne Robins School of Business
University of Richmond, VA 23173
Phone: (804) 289-8553
Fax: (804) 287-6544
E-mail: mba@richmond.edu
http://www.richmond.edu/business/

Student Body: Full-time enrollment: 8. Men: 63%. Women: 38%. International: 38%. Average age: 26. Part-time enrollment: 227. Men: 64%. Women: 36%.
Academics: Full-time faculty: 47. Part-time faculty: 8. Degrees awarded: M.B.A. Joint degree programs: J.D./M.B.A. Evening program is offered. For fall 1996 entering class: 60% completed program within 2 years.
Finances: Tuition (1998–99): $18,695. 3.2% of students receive need-based aid. 5.8% receive non-need-based aid.
Admission Requirements: GMAT is required. Application deadline for fall: July 1.
Selectivity: Applications received (full-time): 12. Admitted: 7. Enrolled: 6. Applications received (part-time): 43. Admitted: 30. Enrolled: 29. Average GMAT: 612. Average undergraduate GPA: 3.0. GMAT section weighed most heavily: weighed equally.
Placement: School does not have placement office.

UNIVERSITY OF VIRGINIA

Darden Graduate School of Business Administration
P.O. Box 6550
Charlottesville, VA 22906-6550
Phone: (800) UVA-MBA1
Fax: (804) 243-5033
E-mail: darden@virginia.edu
http://www.darden.edu
Student Body: Full-time enrollment: 485. Men: 70%. Women: 30%. African American: 6%. Asian American: 7%. Latino: 3%. International: 20%. Average age: 28.
Academics: Full-time faculty: 56. Part-time faculty: 34. Degrees awarded: M.B.A., Ph.D. Joint degree programs: J.D./M.B.A., M.B.A./M.A., M.B.A./M.E., M.B.A./M.S.N., M.B.A./Ph.D. Evening program is not offered.
Finances: Tuition (1998–99): In-State: $16,057. Out-of-State: $21,479. 80% of students receive some type of aid.
Admission Requirements: GMAT is required. Application deadline for fall: January 15, February 15, March 15, November 2, December 1.

Selectivity: Applications received (full-time): 3,267. Admitted: 362. Enrolled: 237. Average GMAT: 685. Average undergraduate GPA: 3.4. GMAT section weighed most heavily: all factors.
Placement: School has placement office. Placement rate 6 months after graduation: 100%. Average starting salary: $78,000.

VIRGINIA COMMONWEALTH UNIVERSITY

School of Business
1015 Floyd Avenue
Box 844000
Richmond, VA 23298
Phone: (804) 828-6916
Fax: (804) 828-6949
http://www.vcu.edu/busweb/gsib
Student Body: Full-time enrollment: 190. Men: 53%. Women: 47%. African American: 14%. Asian American: 11%. Latino: 5%. International: 11%. Average age: 28. Students living on campus: 3%. Part-time enrollment: 294. Men: 61%. Women: 39%.
Academics: Full-time faculty: 93. Part-time faculty: 8. Degrees awarded: M.B.A., M.S., M.A., M. Tax., Ph.D. Evening program is offered. For fall 1996 entering class: 14% completed program within 2 years. 70% continued towards degree.
Finances: Tuition (1998–99): In-State: $4,960. Out-of-State: $12,652. Estimated tuition (1999–2000): In-State: $5,000. Out-of-State: $12,750.
Admission Requirements: GMAT is required. Application deadline for fall: July 1.
Selectivity: Applications received (full-time): 75. Admitted: 44. Enrolled: 29. Applications received (part-time): 73. Admitted: 55. Enrolled: 46. Average GMAT: 560. Average undergraduate GPA: 3.2.
Placement: School has placement office. Average starting salary: $50,000.

VIRGINIA POLYTECHNIC INSTITUTE AND STATE UNIVERSITY

Pamplin College of Business
1044 Pamplin Hall (0209)
Blacksburg, VA 24061
Phone: (540) 231-6152
Fax: (540) 231-4487
E-mail: vtmba@vt.edu
http://www.vt.edu:10021/business/mba/
Student Body: Full-time enrollment: 191. Men: 67%. Women: 33%. African American: 6%. Asian American: 2%. Latino: 2%. International: 31%. Average age: 24.5. Students living on campus: 1%. Part-time enrollment: 387. Men: 64%. Women: 36%.
Academics: Full-time faculty: 112. Part-time faculty: 6. Degrees awarded: M.B.A. Evening program is offered. For fall 1996 entering class: 79% completed program within 2 years. 6% continued towards degree.
Finances: Tuition (1998–99): In-State: $4,927. Out-of-State: $7,537. Estimated tuition (1999–2000): In-State: $5,100. Out-of-State: $7,800. 46% of students receive non-need-based aid.
Admission Requirements: GMAT is required. Application deadline for fall: July 12.
Selectivity: Applications received (full-time): 191. Admitted: 116. Enrolled: 89. Applications received (part-time): 149. Admitted: 107. Enrolled: 89. Average GMAT: 589. Average undergraduate GPA: 3.2. GMAT section weighed most heavily: weighed equally.
Placement: School has placement office. Placement rate at time of graduation: 72%. Placement rate 6 months after graduation: 93%. Average starting salary: $46,257.

Washington

EASTERN WASHINGTON UNIVERSITY*

College of Business and Public Administration
Riverpoint Phase I
668 N Riverpoint Suite A
Cheney, WA 99004
Phone: (509) 359-2397
Student Body: Full-time enrollment: 22. Men: 68%. Women: 32%. International: 68%. Part-time enrollment: 71. Men: 70%. Women: 30%.
Academics: Full-time faculty: 30. Part-time faculty: 0. Degrees awarded: M.B.A. Evening program is offered.
Finances: Tuition (1998–99): In State: $3,885. Out-of-State: $11,817.
Admission Requirements: GMAT is required. Application deadline for fall: August 1.
Selectivity: Applications received (full-time): 70. Admitted: 49. Enrolled: 25. Average GMAT: 529. Average undergraduate GPA: 3.4.
Placement: School has placement office.

GONZAGA UNIVERSITY

School of Business Administration
W. 502 Boone
Spokane, WA 99258-0001
Phone: (509) 323-3430
Fax: (509) 323-5811
E-mail: lewis@jepson.gonzaga.edu
http://www.gonzaga.edu/mba-macc/
Student Body: Full-time enrollment: 47. Men: 66%. Women: 34%. Asian American: 15%. Latino: 2%. Native American: 2%. International: 47%. Average age: 28. Part-time enrollment: 119. Men: 63%. Women: 37%.
Academics: Full-time faculty: 25. Part-time faculty: 5. Degrees awarded: M.B.A., M. Acc. Joint degree programs: M.B.A./J.D., M. Acc./J.D., M.B.A./B.S.

(Engineering), M.B.A./B.A. Evening program is offered.
Finances: Tuition (1998–99): $410/credit hour. 65% of students receive non-need-based aid. 65% of students receive need-based aid.
Admission Requirements: GMAT is required. Application deadline for fall: August.
Selectivity: Applications received: 75. Admitted: 60. Enrolled: 47. Average GMAT: 528. Average undergraduate GPA: 3.1. GMAT section weighed most heavily: weighed equally.
Placement: School has placement office.

PACIFIC LUTHERAN UNIVERSITY

School of Business
Tacoma, WA 98447
Phone: (253) 535-7250
Fax: (253) 535-8723
E-mail: business@plu.edu
http://www.plu.edu/~busa/mba.html
Student Body: Full-time enrollment: 53. Men: 64%. Women: 36%. Latino: 2%. International: 23%. Average age: 31. Part-time enrollment: 39. Men: 67%. Women: 33%.
Academics: Full-time faculty: 9. Part-time faculty: 5. Degrees awarded: M.B.A., M.B.A. Technology. Evening program is offered.
Finances: Tuition (1998–99): $11,760.
Admission Requirements: GMAT is required. Application deadline for fall: July 15.
Selectivity: Applications received: 75. Admitted: 62. Enrolled: 28. Average GMAT: 541. Average undergraduate GPA: 3.2. GMAT section weighed most heavily: weighed equally.
Placement: School has placement office.

SEATTLE UNIVERSITY

Albers School of Business & Economics
900 Broadway
Seattle, WA 98122
Phone: (206) 296-5900
Fax: (206) 296-5902
E-mail: grad-admissions@seattleu.edu

http://www.seattleu.edu/asbe
Student Body: Total enrollment: 702. Men: 60%. Women: 40%. African American: 1%. Asian American: 8%. Latino: 1%. Native American: 1%. International: 12%. Average age: 28.
Academics: Full-time faculty: 46. Part-time faculty: 9. Degrees awarded: M.B.A., M.S.F., M.A., M.I.B., M.A.E. Joint degree programs: J.D./M.B.A., J.D./M.I.B., J.D./M.S.F., J.D./M.A.E. Evening program is offered.
Finances: Tuition (1998–99): $11,950. Estimated tuition (1999–2000): $12,500.
Admission Requirements: GMAT is required. Application deadline for fall: August 20.
Selectivity: Applications received: 284. Admitted: 192. Enrolled: 142. Average GMAT: 573. Average undergraduate GPA: 3.1. GMAT section weighed most heavily: weighed equally.
Placement: School has placement office.

UNIVERSITY OF WASHINGTON

University of Washington Business School
Mackenzie Hall Box 353200
Seattle, WA 98195-3200
Phone: (206) 543-4661
Fax: (206) 616-7351
E-mail: mba@u.washington.edu
http://weber.u.washington/~bschool
Student Body: Full-time enrollment: 321. Men: 63%. Women: 37%. International: 20%. Average age: 29. Part-time enrollment: 137. Men: 73%. Women: 27%.
Academics: Full-time faculty: 98. Part-time faculty: 28. Degrees awarded: M.B.A. Joint degree programs: M.B.A./M.S. Engineering, J.D./M.B.A., M.B.A./M.A.I.S., M.B.A./M.H.A., M.B.A./M.P. Acc. (Taxation). Evening program is offered. For fall 1996 entering class: 95% completed program within 2 years. 5% continued towards degree.
Finances: Tuition (1998–99): In-State: $5,424. Out-of-State: $13,477. Average student debt incurred by graduation: $16,000.

Admission Requirements: GMAT is required. Application deadline for fall: Dec. 1, Jan. 8, Feb. 15, Mar. 15.
Selectivity: Applications received (full-time): 1,159. Admitted: 374. Enrolled: 157. Applications received (part-time): 216. Admitted: 51. Enrolled: 47. Average GMAT: 647. Average undergraduate GPA: 3.3. GMAT section weighed most heavily: weighed equally.
Placement: School has placement office. Average starting salary: $58,777.

WASHINGTON STATE UNIVERSITY

College of Business and Economics
Todd Hall #473
Pullman, WA 99164-4744
Phone: (509) 335-7617
Fax: (509) 335-4735
E-mail: MBA@wsu.edu
http://www.cbe.wsu.edu/graduate
Student Body: Full-time enrollment: 146. Men: 62%. Women: 38%. International: 34%. Average age: 27. Part-time enrollment: 200. Men: 60%. Women: 40%.
Academics: Full-time faculty: 80. Part-time faculty: 5. Degrees awarded: M.B.A., M. Acc., M.A. Economics, M.T.M., Ph.D. Evening program is not offered. For fall 1996 entering class: 82% completed program within 2 years. 6% continued towards degree.
Finances: Estimated tuition (1999–2000): In-State: $2,700/semester. Out-of-State: $6,700/semester. 30% of students receive non-need-based aid.
Admission Requirements: GMAT is required. Application deadline for fall: April 15.
Selectivity: Applications received (full-time): 203. Admitted: 75. Enrolled: 40. Average GMAT: 550. Average undergraduate GPA: 3.4. GMAT section weighed most heavily: weighed equally.
Placement: School has placement office. Placement rate at time of graduation: 78%. Placement rate 6 months after graduation: 90%. Average starting salary: $40,000.

WESTERN WASHINGTON UNIVERSITY

College of Business and Economics
Bellingham, WA 98225-9072
Phone: (360) 650-3898
Fax: (360) 650-4844
Student Body: Full-time enrollment: 16. Men: 38%. Women: 63%. Average age: 29. Part-time enrollment: 28. Men: 57%. Women: 43%.
Academics: Full-time faculty: 44. Degrees awarded: M.B.A. Evening program is not offered.
Finances: Tuition (1998–99): In-State: $140/credit. Out-of-State: $426/credit.
Admission Requirements: GMAT is required. Application deadline for fall: May 1.
Selectivity: Average GMAT: 581. Average undergraduate GPA: 3.3.
Placement: School has placement office. Average starting salary: $51,500.

West Virginia

WEST VIRGINIA UNIVERSITY

College of Business and Economics
P.O. Box 6025
Morgantown, WV 26506
Phone: (304) 293-5408
Fax: (304) 293-7061
E-mail: Thomas@wvubel.be.wvu.edu
Student Body: Full-time enrollment: 142. Men: 55%. Women: 45%. International: 10%. Average age: 28. Students living on campus: 1%. Part-time enrollment: 232. Men: 42%. Women: 58%.
Academics: Full-time faculty: 65. Part-time faculty: 2. Degrees awarded: M.B.A., M.A., Ph.D., M.S., M.P.A. Joint degree programs: J.D./M.B.A. Evening program is offered.
Finances: Tuition (1998–99): In-State: $4,200. Out-of-State: $12,800. Estimated tuition (1999–2000): In-State: $4,200. Out-of-State: $12,800.

Admission Requirements: GMAT is required. Application deadline for fall: February 1.
Selectivity: Applications received (full-time): 467. Admitted: 219. Enrolled: 188. Average GMAT: 590. Average undergraduate GPA: 3.3. GMAT section weighed most heavily: Verbal.
Placement: School has placement office. Placement rate at time of graduation: 84%. Placement rate 6 months after graduation: 98%. Average starting salary: $39,450.

Wisconsin

MARQUETTE UNIVERSITY

M.B.A. Program
P.O. Box 1881
Milwaukee, WI 53201-1881
Phone: (414) 288-7145
Fax: (414) 288-1660
E-mail: simmons@biz.mu.edu
http://www.busadm.mu.edu
Student Body: Full-time enrollment: 76. Men: 80%. Women: 20%. International: 53%. Average age: 28. Part-time enrollment: 574. Men: 66%. Women: 34%.
Academics: Full-time faculty: 60. Degrees awarded: M.B.A., M.S.H.R., M.S.A., M.S.A.E., M.S.E.M. Joint degree programs: M.B.A./J.D. Evening program is offered.
Finances: Tuition (1998–99): $510/credit. Estimated tuition (1999–2000): $520/credit.
Admission Requirements: GMAT is required. Application deadline for fall: rolling.
Selectivity: Applications received (part-time): 277. Admitted: 219. Enrolled: 170. Average GMAT: 565. Average undergraduate GPA: 3.2. GMAT section weighed most heavily: weighed equally.
Placement: School has placement office.

UNIVERSITY OF WISCONSIN— LA CROSSE

College of Business Administration
1725 State Street
La Crosse, WI 54601
Phone: (608) 785-8068
Fax: (608) 785-6700
E-mail: dittman@mail.uwlax.edu
http://www.uwlax.edu
Student Body: Total enrollment: 88. Men: 63%. Women: 38%. Average age: 27.
Academics: Full-time faculty: 15. Degrees awarded: M.B.A. Evening program is offered.
Finances: Tuition (1998–99): In-State: $235/credit. Out-of-State: $650/credit.
Admission Requirements: GMAT is required. Application deadline for fall: May 1.
Selectivity: Applications received (full-time): 37. Admitted: 32. Enrolled: 21. Average GMAT: 530. Average undergraduate GPA: 3.3. GMAT section weighed most heavily: weighed equally.
Placement: School has a placement office. Placement rate at graduation : 95%.

UNIVERSITY OF WISCONSIN— MADISON

School of Business
2266 Grainger Hall
975 University Avenue
Madison, WI 53706-1323
Phone: (608) 262-1555
Fax: (608) 265-4192
E-mail: uwmadmba@bus.wisc.edu
http://wiscinfo.doit.wisc.edu/bschool/
Student Body: Full-time enrollment: 439. Men: 68%. Women: 32%. African American: 5%. Asian American: 4%. Latino: 4%. International: 31%. Average age: 28. Part-time enrollment: 92. Men: 77%. Women: 23%.
Academics: Full-time faculty: 80. Part-time faculty: 5. Degrees awarded: M.B.A., M.S., M.A., M. Acc., E.M.B.A., X.M.B.A. Joint degree programs: J.D./M.B.A., Agribusiness/M.B.A. Evening program is offered.

Finances: Tuition (1998–99): In-State: $5,950. Out-of-State: $16,230. 50% of students receive some type of aid. Average student debt incurred by graduation: $22,000.
Admission Requirements: GMAT is required. Application deadline for fall: May 1.
Selectivity: Applications received (full-time): 834. Admitted: 383. Enrolled: 150. Applications received (part-time): 50. Admitted: 39. Enrolled: 31. Average GMAT: 613. Average undergraduate GPA: 3.3. GMAT section weighed most heavily: weighed equally.
Placement: School has placement office. Placement rate at time of graduation: 82%. Placement rate 6 months after graduation: 95%. Average starting salary: $57,047

UNIVERSITY OF WISCONSIN— MILWAUKEE

School of Business Administration
Sarah Sandin
P.O. Box 742
Milwaukee, WI 53201
Phone: (414) 229-5403
Fax: (414) 229-2372
E-mail: ssandin@uwm.edu.
http://www.uwm.edu
Student Body: Full-time enrollment: 156. African American: 12%. Asian American: 21%. Latino: 2%. Native American: 3%. International: 50%. Average age: 31. Part-time enrollment: 645.
Academics: Full-time faculty: 65. Degrees awarded: M.B.A., M.S., E.M.B.A., Ph.D. Evening program is offered.
Finances: Tuition (1998–99): In-State: $347/credit. Out-of-State: $987/credit.
Admission Requirements: GMAT is required. Application deadline for fall: January 1.
Selectivity: Applications received (full-time): 235. Admitted: 178. Enrolled: 106. Average GMAT: 541. Average undergraduate GPA: 3.1.
Placement: School has placement office. Placement rate at time of graduation: 85%. Placement rate 6 months after graduation: 95%. Average starting Salary: $40,000.

UNIVERSITY OF WISCONSIN— OSHKOSH

College of Business Administration
M.B.A. Program
Oshkosh, WI 54901
Phone: (902) 424-1436
Fax: (920) 424-7413
E-mail: mba@pobox.uwosh.edu
http://www.uwosh.edu
Student Body: Full-time enrollment: 25. Men: 60%. Women: 40%. International: 60%. Average age: 25. Students living on campus: 50%. Part-time enrollment: 500. Men: 65%. Women: 35%.
Academics: Full-time faculty: 40. Degrees awarded: M.B.A., M.S.I.S. Evening program is offered. For fall 1996 entering class: 100% completed the program within 2 years.
Finances: Tuition (1998–99): In-State: $225/credit. Out-of-State: $650/credit. Estimated tuition (1999–2000): In-State: $240/credit. Out-of-State: $690/credit. 1% of students receive some type of aid.
Admission Requirements: GMAT is required. Application deadline for fall: July 1.
Selectivity: Applications received (full-time): 40. Admitted: 20. Enrolled: 15. Applications received (part-time): 210. Admitted: 190. Enrolled: 150. Average GMAT: 540. Average undergraduate GPA: 3.2. GMAT section weighed most heavily: weighed equally.
Placement: School has placement office.

UNIVERSITY OF WISCONSIN— WHITEWATER*

College of Business and Economics
800 West Main Street
Whitewater, WI 53190-1797
Phone: (414) 472-1945
Fax: (414) 472-4863
E-mail: zahnd@uwwuax.uww.edu
Student Body: Full-time enrollment: 105. Men: 58%. Women: 42%. International: 16%. Part-time enrollment: 200. Men: 59%. Women: 41%.

Academics: Full-time faculty: 40. Part-time faculty: 5. Degrees awarded: M.B.A., M.P. Acc., M.S. Management Computer Systems. Evening program is offered.
Finances: Tuition (1998–99): In-State: $3,628. Out-of-State: $10,210.
Admission Requirements: GMAT is required. Application deadline for fall: August 15.
Selectivity: Applications received (full-time): 121. Admitted: 105. Enrolled: 50. Average GMAT: 510. Average undergraduate GPA: 3.2.
Placement: School has placement office. Average starting salary: $35,000.

Wyoming

UNIVERSITY OF WYOMING

College of Business
P.O. Box 3275
Laramie, WY 82071
Phone: (307) 766-2287
Fax: (307) 766-4028
E-mail: MBA@uwyo.edu
http://www.uwyo.edu/bu/mba/mba.htm
Student Body: Full-time enrollment: 37. Men: 43%. Women: 57%. Asian American: 8%. International: 3%. Average age: 30. Part-time enrollment: 47. Men: 57%. Women: 43%.

Academics: Full-time faculty: 43. Part-time faculty: 16. Degrees awarded: M.B.A. Evening program is offered. For fall 1996 entering class: 38% completed program within 2 years. 62% continued towards degree.
Finances: Tuition (1998–99): In-State: $2,816. Out-of-State: $7,906. Estimated tuition (1999–2000): In-State: $2,816. Out-of-State: $7,906.
Admission Requirements: GMAT is required. Application deadline for fall: March 30.
Selectivity: Applications received (full-time): 55. Admitted: 28. Enrolled: 22. Applications received (part-time): 22. Admitted: 12. Enrolled: 12. Average GMAT: 553. Average undergraduate GPA: 3.4.
Placement: School has placement office.

Alphabetical Index of Business Schools

University	Business School	State
American University	Kogod College of Business Administration	DC
Anderson School of Management: see University of California—Los Angeles		
Appalachian State University	John A. Walker College of Business	NC
Arizona State University	College of Business	AZ
Arkansas State University	College of Business	AR
Auburn University	College of Business	AL
Auburn University—Montgomery	School of Business	AL
Babson College	F.W. Olin Graduate School	MA
Ball State University	College of Business	IN
Baylor University	The Hankamer School of Business	TX
Bentley College	Bentley College Graduate School of Business	MA
Boise State University	College of Business & Economics	ID
Boston College	Wallace E. Carroll School of Management	MA
Boston University	Boston University School of Management	MA

University	*Business School*	*State*
Bowling Green State University	College of Business Administration	OH
Bradley University	Foster College of Business Administration	IL
Brigham Young University	Marriott School of Management	UT
California Polytechnic State University—San Luis Obispo	College of Business	CA
California State University—Bakersfield	School of Business & Public Administration	CA
California State University—Chico	College of Business	CA
California State University—Fresno	The Craig School of Business	CA
California State University—Fullerton	School of Business Administration & Economics	CA
California State University—Hayward	School of Business and Economics	CA
California State University—Long Beach	College of Business Administration	CA
California State University—Los Angeles	School of Business & Economics	CA
California State University—Northridge	College of Business Administration & Economics	CA
California State University—Sacramento	College of Business Administration	CA
Canisius College	Richard J. Wehle School of Business	NY
Carnegie Mellon University	Graduate School of Industrial Administration	PA
Case Western Reserve University	Weatherhead School of Management	OH
Central Michigan University	College of Business Administration	MI

University	*Business School*	*State*
City University of New York—Baruch College	Zicklin School of Business	NY
Claremont Graduate University	Peter F. Drucker Graduate School of Management	CA
Clark Atlanta University	School of Business Administration	GA
Clark University	Graduate School of Management	MA
Clarkson University	Clarkson University School of Business	NY
Clemson University	College of Business and Public Affairs	SC
Cleveland State University	James J. Nance College of Business Administration	OH
College of William and Mary	Graduate School of Business	VA
Colorado State University	College of Business	CO
Columbia University	Columbia Business School	NY
Cornell University	Johnson Graduate School of Management	NY
Creighton University	College of Business Administration	NE
Darden Graduate School of Business Administration: see University of Virginia		
Dartmouth College	Amos Tuck School of Business Administration	NH
DePaul University	Kellstadt Graduate School of Business	IL
Drake University	College of Business & Public Admin.	IA
Drexel University	College of Business and Administration	PA
Duke University	The Fuqua School of Business	NC
Duquesne University	Graduate School of Business	PA
East Carolina University	School of Business	NC
East Tennessee State University	College of Business	TN
Eastern Michigan University	College of Business	MI
Eastern Washington University	College of Business and Public Administration	WA

University	Business School	State
Emory University	Goizueta Business School	GA
Fairfield University	School of Business	CT
Florida Atlantic University	College of Business	FL
Florida International University	College of Business Administration	FL
Florida State University	College of Business	FL
Fordham University	Graduate School of Business Administration	NY
Fuqua School of Business: see Duke University		
George Mason University	School of Management	VA
George Washington University	School of Business & Public Management	DC
Georgetown University	The McDonough School of Business	DC
Georgia Institute of Technology	DuPree College of Management	GA
Georgia Southern University	College of Business Administration	GA
Georgia State University	J. Mack Robinson College of Business	GA
Gonzaga University	School of Business Administration	WA
Haas School of Business: see University of California at Berkeley		
Harvard University	Graduate School of Business Administration	MA
Hofstra University	Frank G. Zarb School of Business	NY
Howard University	School of Business	DC
Idaho State University	College of Business	ID
Illinois State University	College of Business	IL
Indiana State University	School of Business	IN
Indiana University—Bloomington	Kelley School of Business	IN
Indiana University—Northwest	Division of Business and Economics	IN

University	Business School	State
Indiana University—Purdue University at Indianapolis	Kelley School of Business	IN
Indiana University—Purdue University at Fort Wayne	School of Business & Management Sciences	IN
Indiana University—South Bend	Division of Business and Economics	IN
Iowa State University	College of Business	IA
James Madison University	College of Business	VA
John Carroll University	Boler School of Business	OH
Kansas State University	College of Business Administration	KS
Kellogg Graduate School of Management: see Northwestern University		
Kent State University	Graduate School of Management	OH
Lamar University	College of Business	TX
Lehigh University	College of Business and Economics	PA
Louisiana State University and A&M College	College of Business Administration	LA
Louisiana State University in Shreveport	College of Business Administration	LA
Louisiana Tech University	College of Administration and Business	LA
Loyola College in Maryland	Joseph A. Sellinger School of Business & Management	MD
Loyola Marymount University	College of Business Administration	CA
Loyola University Chicago	Graduate School of Business	IL
Loyola University New Orleans	Joseph A. Butt S.J. College of Business Administration	LA
Marquette University	Business School	WI
Marymount University	School of Business Administration	VA

University	Business School	State
Massachusetts Institute of Technology	Sloan School of Management	MA
McNeese State University	College of Business	LA
Miami University	Richard T. Farmer School of Business	OH
Michigan State University	The Eli Broad Graduate School of Management	MI
Middle Tennessee State University	College of Business	TN
Millsaps College	Else School of Management	MS
Mississippi State University	College of Business & Industry	MS
Mount Saint Mary College	College of Business	NY
Murray State University	College of Business & Public Affairs	KY
New Mexico State University	College of Business Administration and Economics	NM
New York University	Leonard N. Stern School of Business	NY
Nicholls State University	College of Business Administration	LA
Northeast Louisiana University	College of Business Administration	LA
Northeastern University	College of Business	MA
Northern Arizona University	College of Business Administration	AZ
Northern Illinois University	College of Business	IL
Northwestern University	Kellogg Graduate School of Management	IL
Oakland University	School of Business Administration	MI
Ohio State University	Max M. Fisher College of Business	OH
Ohio University	College of Business	OH
Oklahoma State University	College of Business Administration	OK
Old Dominion University	Graduate School of Business & Public Administration	VA

University	Business School	State
Oregon State University	College of Business	OR
Pacific Lutheran University	School of Business	WA
Pennsylvania State University	The Smeal College of Business Administration	PA
Portland State University	School of Business Administration	OR
Purdue University	Krannert Graduate School of Management	IN
Rensselaer Polytechnic Institute	Lally School of Management and Technology	NY
Rice University	Jesse H. Jones Graduate School of Management	TX
Rochester Institute of Technology	College of Business	NY
Rollins College	Crummer Graduate School of Business	FL
Rutgers University	Graduate School of Management	NJ
Sage Colleges	Sage Graduate School	NY
Saint Cloud State University	College of Business	MN
Saint John's University	College of Business Administration	NY
Saint Louis University	School of Business and Administration	MO
San Diego State University	Graduate School of Business	CA
San Francisco State University	Graduate School of Business	CA
San Jose State University	College of Business	CA
Santa Clara University	Leavey School of Business & Administration	CA
Seattle University	Albers School of Business & Economics	WA
Seton Hall University	W. Paul Stillman School of Business	NJ
Sloan School of Management: see Massachusetts Institute of Technology		
Southeastern Louisiana University	College of Business	LA

University	Business School	State
Southern Illinois University—Edwardsville	School of Business	IL
Southern Illinois University—Carbondale	College of Business & Administration	IL
Southern Methodist University	Edwin L. Cox School of Business	TX
Stanford University	Graduate School of Business	CA
State University of New York—University at Albany	School of Business	NY
State University of New York—Binghamton	School of Management	NY
State University of New York—Buffalo	School of Management	NY
State University of West Georgia	Richards College of Business	GA
Stephen F. Austin State University	College of Business	TX
Suffolk University	Sawyer School of Management	MA
Syracuse University	School of Management	NY
Temple University	Fox School of Business and Management	PA
Tennessee Technological University	College of Business Administration	TN
Texas A&M University	Lowry Mays College & Graduate School of Business	TX
Texas A&M University—Commerce	College of Business & Technology	TX
Texas Christian University	M.J. Neeley School of Business	TX
Texas Tech University	College of Business Administration	TX
Thunderbird, The American Graduate School of International Management		AZ
Tuck School of Business Administration: see Dartmouth College		

University	*Business School*	*State*
Tulane University	A.B. Freeman School of Business	LA
University of Akron	College of Business Administration	OH
University of Alabama	Manderson Graduate School of Business	AL
University of Alabama—Birmingham	Graduate School of Management	AL
University of Alaska—Fairbanks	School of Management	AK
University of Arizona	Eller Graduate School of Management	AZ
University of Arkansas—Fayetteville	Sam M. Walton College of Business Administration	AR
University of Arkansas—Little Rock	College of Business Administration	AR
University of Baltimore	Robert G. Merrick School of Business	MD
University of Bridgeport	College of Business	CT
University of California—Berkeley	Haas School of Business	CA
University of California—Davis	Graduate School of Management	CA
University of California—Irvine	Graduate School of Management	CA
University of California—Los Angeles	John E. Anderson Graduate School of Management	CA
University of Central Arkansas	College of Business Administration	AR
University of Central Florida	College of Business Administration	FL
University of Chicago	Graduate School of Business	IL
University of Cincinnati	Graduate School of Business	OH
University of Colorado—Boulder	Graduate School of Business Administration	CO
University of Colorado—Colorado Springs	College of Business and Administration	CO

University	Business School	State
University of Colorado—Denver	Graduate School of Business Administration	CO
University of Connecticut	School of Business Administration	CT
University of Dayton	School of Business Administration	OH
University of Delaware	College of Business and Economics	DE
University of Denver	Daniels College of Business	CO
University of Detroit Mercy	College of Business Administration	MI
University of Florida	Warrington College of Business Florida MBA Programs	FL
University of Georgia	Terry College of Business	GA
University of Hawaii—Manoa	College of Business Administration	HI
University of Houston	College of Business Administration	TX
University of Houston—Clear Lake	School of Business and Public Administration	TX
University of Illinois—Chicago	College of Business Administration	IL
University of Illinois—Urbana Champaign	College of Commerce & Business Administration	IL
University of Iowa	College of Business Administration School of Management	IA
University of Kansas	School of Business	KS
University of Kentucky	Carol Martin Gatton College of Business and Economics	KY
University of Louisville	College of Business & Public Administration	KY
University of Maine	Maine Business School	ME
University of Maryland—College Park	The Robert H. Smith School of Business	MD
University of Massachusetts—Amherst	Isenberg School of Management	MA

University	Business School	State
University of Massachusetts—Lowell	College of Management	MA
University of Memphis	Fogelman College of Business and Economics	TN
University of Miami	School of Business Administration	FL
University of Michigan	University of Michigan Business School	MI
University of Michigan—Dearborn	School of Management	MI
University of Michigan—Flint	School of Management	MI
University of Minnesota	Carlson School of Management	MN
University of Mississippi	School of Business Administration	MS
University of Missouri—St. Louis	School of Business Administration	MO
University of Missouri—Columbia	College of Business & Public Administration	MO
University of Missouri—Kansas City	H.W. Bloch School of Business & Public Admin	MO
University of Montana	School of Business Administration	MT
University of Nebraska—Lincoln	College of Business Administration	NE
University of Nebraska—Omaha	College of Business Administration	NE
University of Nevada—Las Vegas	College of Business	NV
University of Nevada—Reno	College of Business Administration	NV
University of New Mexico	Robert O. Anderson Graduate School of Management	NM
University of New Orleans	College of Business Administration	LA
University of North Carolina—Chapel Hill	Kenan-Flagler Business School	NC

University	*Business School*	*State*
University of North Carolina—Charlotte	The Belk College of Business Administration	NC
University of North Carolina—Greensboro	Joseph M. Bryan School of Business and Economics	NC
University of North Dakota	College of Business & Public Administration	ND
University of North Florida	College of Business Administration	FL
University of North Texas	College of Business Administration	TX
University of Notre Dame	College of Business Administration	IN
University of Oklahoma	Michael F. Price College of Business	OK
University of Oregon	Charles H. Lundquist College of Business	OR
University of Pennsylvania	The Wharton School	PA
University of Pittsburgh	Joseph M. Katz Graduate School of Business	PA
University of Portland	School of Business	OR
University of Rhode Island	College of Business Administration	RI
University of Richmond	Richard S. Reynolds Graduate School	VA
University of Rochester	William E. Simon Grad School of Business Administration	NY
University of San Diego	School of Business	CA
University of San Francisco	McLaren Graduate School of Management	CA
University of South Alabama	College of Business and Management Studies	AL
University of South Carolina	Darla Moore School of Business	SC
University of South Dakota	School of Business	SD
University of South Florida	College of Business Administration	FL
University of Southern California	Marshall School of Business	CA

University	Business School	State
University of Southern Mississippi	College of Business Administration	MS
University of Tennessee—Chattanooga	School of Business Administration	TN
University of Tennessee—Knoxville	Graduate School of Business	TN
University of Texas—Arlington	College of Business Administration	TX
University of Texas—Austin	The Texas Graduate School of Business	TX
University of Texas—El Paso	College of Business Administration	TX
University of Texas—Pan American	College of Business Administration	TX
University of Texas—San Antonio	College of Business	TX
University of Toledo	College of Business Administration	OH
University of Tulsa	College of Business Administration	OK
University of Utah	David Eccles School of Business	UT
University of Vermont	School of Business Administration	VT
University of Virginia	Darden Graduate School of Business Administration	VA
University of Washington	Business School	WA
University of Wisconsin—Milwaukee	School of Business Administration	WI
University of Wisconsin—Oshkosh	College of Business Administration	WI
University of Wisconsin—La Crosse	College of Business Administration	WI
University of Wisconsin—Madison	School of Business	WI

University	Business School	State
University of Wisconsin—Whitewater	College of Business and Economics	WI
University of Wyoming	College of Business	WY
Utah State University	College of Business	UT
Vanderbilt University	Owen Graduate School of Management	TN
Villanova University	College of Commerce and Finance	PA
Virginia Commonwealth University	School of Business	VA
Virginia Polytechnic Institute and State University	Pamplin College of Business	VA
Wake Forest University	Babcock Graduate School of Management	NC
Washington State University	College of Business and Economics	WA
Washington University	John M. Olin School of Business	MO
Wayne State University	School of Business Administration	MI
West Virginia University	College of Business and Economics	WV
Western Carolina University	Graduate Programs in Business	NC
Western Illinois University	College of Business & Technology	IL
Western Michigan University	Haworth College of Business	MI
Western Washington University	College of Business and Economics	WA
Wharton School: see University of Pennsylvania		
Wichita State University	W. Frank Barton School of Business	KS
Willamette University	Atkinson Graduate School of Management	OR
Winthrop University	College of Business Administration	SC
Wright State University	College of Business and Administration	OH
Yale University	Yale School of Management	CT

How Did We Do? Grade Us.

Thank you for choosing a Kaplan book. Your comments and suggestions are very useful to us. Please answer the following questions to assist us in our continued development of high-quality resources to meet your needs.

The Kaplan book I read was: _____

My name is: _____

My address is: _____

_____

My e-mail address is: _____

What overall grade would you give this book?   Ⓐ Ⓑ Ⓒ Ⓓ Ⓕ

How relevant was the information to your goals?   Ⓐ Ⓑ Ⓒ Ⓓ Ⓕ

How comprehensive was the information in this book?   Ⓐ Ⓑ Ⓒ Ⓓ Ⓕ

How accurate was the information in this book?   Ⓐ Ⓑ Ⓒ Ⓓ Ⓕ

How easy was the book to use?   Ⓐ Ⓑ Ⓒ Ⓓ Ⓕ

How appealing was the book's design?   Ⓐ Ⓑ Ⓒ Ⓓ Ⓕ

What were the book's strong points? _____

How could this book be improved? _____

Is there anything that we left out that you wanted to know more about?

Would you recommend this book to others?   ☐ YES   ☐ NO

Other comments: _____

_____

_____

Do we have permission to quote you?   ☐ YES   ☐ NO

Thank you for your help. Please tear out this page and mail it to:

Dave Chipps, Managing Editor
Kaplan Educational Centers
888 Seventh Avenue
New York, NY 10106

Or, you can answer these questions online at www.kaplan.com/talkback.

Thanks!

KAPLAN 60 · SIXTY · YEARS · OF · BUILDING · FUTURES ·

Want more information about our services, products, or the nearest Kaplan center?

 Call our nationwide toll-free numbers:

1-800-KAP-TEST for information on our live courses, private tutoring and admissions consulting
1-800-KAP-ITEM for information on our products
1-888-KAP-LOAN* for information on student loans

(outside the U.S.A., call **1-212-262-4980**)

 Connect with us in cyberspace:

On AOL, keyword:"Kaplan"
On the World Wide Web, go to: **http://www.kaplan.com**
Via e-mail: info@kaplan.com

 Write to:

Kaplan Educational Centers
888 Seventh Avenue
New York, NY 10106